GETTING STARTED ON THE PC-2

H C Pennington
Gary Camp
Ralph Burris

2

GETTING STARTED ON THE PC-2

First Edition
First Printing
May 1983
Printed in the United States of America

Copyright©1983 by IJG Inc.

ISBN 0-936200-11-1

Published by
IJG Inc
1953 West
11th Street
Upland, CA
91786 (714)
946-5805

Preface

The Authors . . .

There are three of us. Harvard Pennington, Gary Camp and Ralph Burris. We have been around since the early days of Radio Shack's entry into the computer field. All three of us got our first TRS-8Ø computer in early 1978; a TRS-8Ø Model I. We met as a result of our TRS-8Øs. At the time, the power of the Model I computer was beyond our wildest dreams. A complete computer that would fit into our pocket was just too incredible to think about, let alone dream about.

In those 'early' days there was a total lack of information about our computers. If we needed to know anything, it was up to us to figure it out for ourselves. It wasn't anybody's fault that there wasn't any information, it was just the way things were at the time — there was no 'computer industry' as there is today.

As time passed, we all grew-up, so to speak, on our TRS-80s. Each of us became, as they say, computer literate — and in time became fairly well known in the 'TRS-8Ø world.' When Radio Shack announced the first PC, the PC-1 Pocket Computer, there was a whole family of TRS-8Øs. The Model I, Model II and Model III — and now a complete computer that would fit in your pocket.

The incredible power of this first pocket computer was almost too much to comprehend. Then along came the next generation, the PC-2, an even more powerful pocket computer, with possibly the niftiest printer we have ever seen.

Each of us already had one or more Radio Shack computers — and we had all written a book, articles, software or documentation for software packages that ran on the TRS-8Ø family of computers. When we were asked to write "Getting Started on the PC-2" . . . we jumped at the chance.

Here was an opportunity to be paid while we learned about the latest and greatest addition to the TRS-8Ø family. And were we amazed! With the exception of disk files and a TV type video display, it was almost like having a TRS-8Ø Model III computer that would fit in our pocket.

"Getting Started on the PC-2" is the result of our latest love affair with a Radio Shack computer. We hope you enjoy reading this, and having your own love affair, as much as we enjoyed writing it.

Harvard, Gary, Ralph
Upland, California

Contents

8

IMPORTANT
Read This First

To set-up your TRS-8Ø PC-2 pocket computer, refer to your *"PC-2 Owner's Manual"* (Catalog Number 26-36Ø1).

This book is not a replacement for the manual that came with your computer. The purpose of this book is to guide you through a learning process with the help of expanded explanations and examples. It is especially important to read your *"PC-2 Owner's Manual."* Unlike a manual, you will learn the keyboard and programming language on an 'as you go' basis. This means that you will be able to make the computer 'do things' as we go along, rather than try to soak-up all the information in the manual, then try to figure out how to fit things together.

Let me explain a little about the way we have presented things in the book. At times, we must tell you to press a particular key on the PC-2. We have represented this by placing special symbols around the name of the key like this:

<ENTER>

Look at the PC-2's keyboard and you will see a key that has the identical word printed on it.

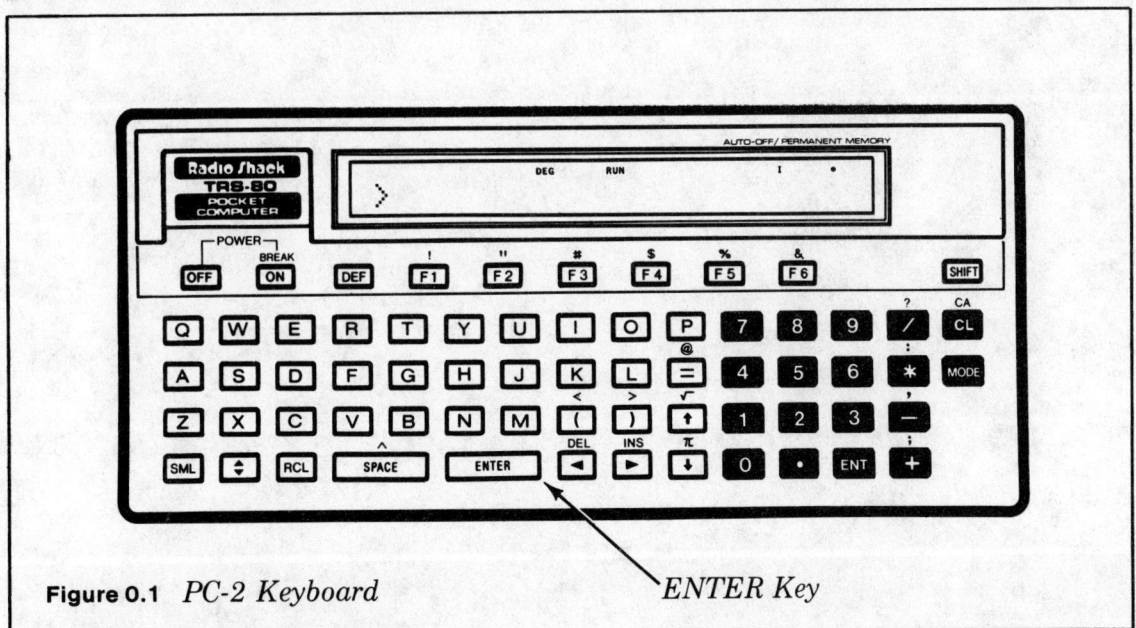

Figure 0.1 *PC-2 Keyboard*   *ENTER Key*

If we wanted you to type in the word 'enter,' we would say, "Type enter." If we wanted you to press the enter key, we would say — "Press the <ENTER> key" or "Press <ENTER>." If we want you to do something that the word would normally mean when used in conversation, it will not be capitalized. For instance, "Now, enter the numbers in order" would mean to type in (or enter) the numbers in their numerical sequence beginning with the smallest and ending with the largest.

Another situation that needs mentioning occurs when we describe the 'instructions' used by the computer, which are sometimes abbreviations or acronyms. For example, the instruction, CLS is used to '*CL*ear *S*creen.' Notice how we capitalized the part of a word that is also contained in the instruction. 'CLear Screen' is the way we will describe the computer instruction CLS.

We will also use whole commands or instructions as a part of speech, but only the command portion is capitalized, such as "PRINTed". When you see a word used in this way it means that the computer will carry out the instruction.

Another area of misunderstanding that needs to be cleared up is the difference between the letter O (oh), and the number Ø (zero). These two symbols, although they usually look alike, are not interchangeable. We will ALWAYS use a symbol that looks like this when referring to the number zero:

Ø *Slash Thru Zero*

You will also notice that there is a definite format to this book. Each time a new BASIC statement is introduced we will show you its **'Primary Form'** — the way it is presented in the manual, then we'll show you other ways it can be used. After every programming example there is a short paragraph called: **"Oops! What went wrong?"** If you entered an example and it didn't work for you, this paragraph may be of some help in making it function properly. Following that, you will find a list of commands that are related, or similar in function. You do not need to look these up right away, but you may if you wish. You'll find the manual is especially useful for this. Keep it near at hand as you read, *"Getting Started on the PC-2."*

1

Display: CHAPTER 1

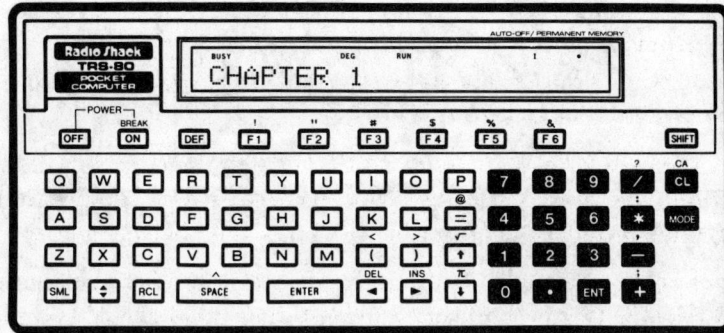

How to Talk to a Computer

A computer is a machine without eyes and ears. It cannot talk to us or see us as another person can. But we can talk to the computer by typing messages on its keyboard and the computer can talk to us by printing messages on its display. When we type the right kind of messages, the computer will respond by 'doing something.'

When we type a series of messages or instructions on the computer's keyboard to make it do something, we are 'programming' it. A program consists of a series of statements (like sentences) which detail the events we wish to make happen. Programming is something that we do every day of our lives, and is nothing more than a plan of action — carried out in a specific order.

For example, if you were a computer, your wake-up routine might be a program that looks like this:

1. Wake-up when alarm rings
2. Turn off alarm
3. Get out of bed
4. Brush your teeth
5. Get dressed

. . . and so on.

Each action you perform must be done in a certain order. If we take the above list and mix up the order of events, it would be impossible to carry out. Here is a list that's not in the proper order. Could you carry out these instructions?

1. Brush your teeth
2. Turn off alarm
3. Alarm rings
4. Get dressed
5. Get out of bed.

I don't think you would get very far with this list before deciding there was an error in the order of the instructions.

FIGURE 1.1 *Rise 'n Shine . . .*

BASIC – A Language for Our Computer

The PC-2 has a built-in 'language' which is called "BASIC." The BASIC computer language looks a little like English. Just like any other language, BASIC has rules (called syntax), and certain 'words' which the computer can understand. It's called "BASIC" for a couple of good reasons — it is a simple, basic type of language, consisting of only a few words and phrases. BASIC also stands for *"Beginners All-purpose Symbolic Instruction Code."*

FIGURE 1.2 *". . . Mplphgx . . ."*

FIGURE 1.3 *"Hello, Who are You?"*

These BASIC words and phrases are called 'statements,' 'commands' or 'instructions,' because they tell the computer what to do. The words in the PC-2's vocabulary are referred to as the 'instruction set.' An example of an instruction the computer understands is "CLS," which means *CL*ear the *S*creen. In the following chapters, we will discuss all of the words used in BASIC, and how they can be used to write a computer program.

Syntax is a term that used to describe how we put words together to form a sentence. Syntax is important because the computer can only recognize exact and precise forms of its vocabulary. In a language like English we can say the same thing in a number of ways. For example, "please erase the blackboard," can also be "erase the blackboard," or "clean the board." Everyone will know what we mean because we are dealing with concepts.

Computers, on the other hand, do not deal in concepts — only facts. The facts they deal with must be stated in specific ways. As we will see, the words chosen for the BASIC computer language were chosen to resemble English words (or at least shorthand versions of English words) to make it easy to communicate with the computer. In BASIC, the letters of the command CLS suggest the operation that it performs, CLear Screen, which clears the display screen. Other statements, such as PRINT, do exactly what they suggest and are very specific in their meaning. PRINT actually causes something to be PRINTed on the display, but it does not print on paper in red ink (it takes another command to do this).

In a BASIC program, each statement begins with a line number, just like our list of actions in the 'wake-up program,' above. Each line is 'read' by the computer just as you or I would read a book in English — beginning at the left side of the sentence and moving to the right until the end of the line is reached. Just as we 'digest' the contents of a line we are reading, the computer analyzes the program line as it 'reads' through it and causes the instructions we've entered to be carried out. This process is sometimes referred to as *parsing* the program line. If you've entered a list of instructions in the wrong order, the computer will print an error message on the display. This is the computer's way of telling you that it can't figure out how to carry out your program.

FIGURE 1.4 *". . . Once Upon a Time . . ."*

When a program line is entered in BASIC, it is preceded by a **line number**. A BASIC program instruction, using the CLS (CLear Screen) statement we mentioned above, would look like this:

1Ø: CLS

When this one-line program is RUN, it will clear the display of anything that is currently on it. We will discuss CLS again.

As we have previously stated, the computer's vocabulary is very limited. You don't have to worry about saying "please" and "thank you" when you want the computer to do something. The PC-2 neither knows nor cares about etiquette, unlike some of the computers in "sci-fi movies." All you have to do is tell it to do something. If you give it the correct instructions, it will carry them out. It is your servant. "CLear Screen, James!"

FIGURE 1.5 *"CLear Screen, James!"*

In our example of 'human' programming, the series of events described may change from time to time. But the human brain is a 'self-programming' device. Things may take place in a new order, or other things never considered may be done, such as: the alarm rings — smash the clock! A computer will do just what it is told, no more and no less. It will not deviate from the programmed instructions.

Errors

There are circumstances in which the program can be changed by the computer, but these are usually accidents, resulting from equipment or power failure. In rare cases, the program could be changed by some really tricky programming that 'went wrong.' This will usually cause the program to 'bomb' or 'crash' (programmer slang). A 'program crash' can happen when there is some type of hardware failure — but we won't concern ourselves with that now, because it is a rare event.

FIGURE 1.6 *"Anybody Get the Number of That Byte?"*

Another type of 'crash' is encountered when you have incorrectly entered a statement, or some of the computer's rules are not followed. The PC-2 is usually smart enough to know about most of these problems and will display an error message that relates to the mistake. As you are learning to program, this type of problem is to be expected, and can be corrected in a number of ways which we will explore later on. In fact, one of the rewarding features of writing a computer program is the discovery of errors and the instant correction of these mistakes. (No kidding, it really is!)

Of course, not all errors are easily corrected, but the most common types, such as a mistyped word, are simple to change. And, when a program works right, it's a good feeling.

Other Computers

Learning BASIC on the PC-2 is easy. Once you have the hang of it, you'll find that you can write programs on almost any other computer that uses the BASIC language.

There will be some differences between machines, but the PC-2's BASIC is quite universal. The main differences you will find are in the various ways in which input and output are handled. **Input** and **Output**, or **I/O**, refer to the moving of data and information from tapes, displays and the like. Each computer will have its own unique characteristics when it comes to input and output. The PC-2 for example, has a small display, whereas the TRS-8Ø Model III has a much larger display. Printing a message on the Model III is handled differently than on the PC-2, and although the details are different, the concepts are the same.

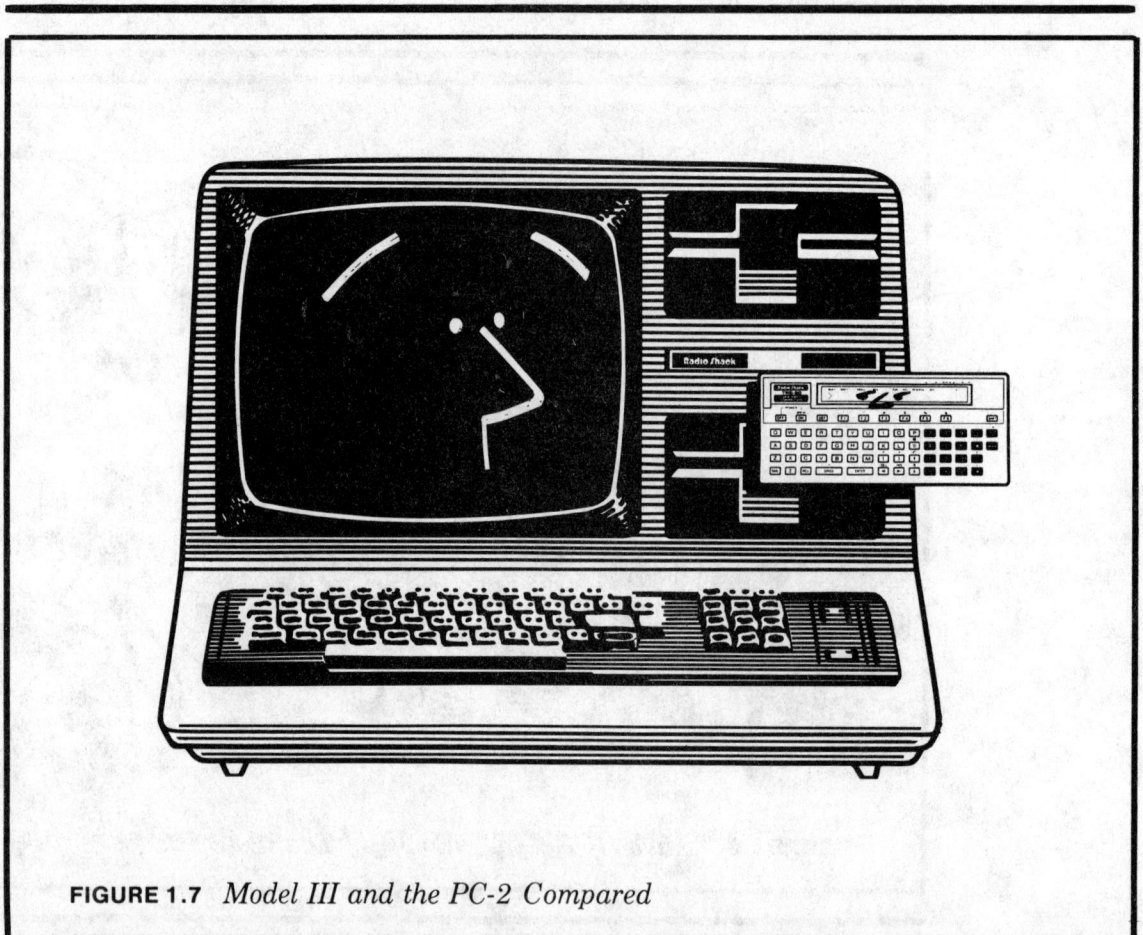

FIGURE 1.7 *Model III and the PC-2 Compared*

But enough of that — let's get on with the task at hand . . . .

Ready to Start Your First Program
Instant Gratification

Here is a program you can type into your PC-2 that will give you an idea of what the future holds in store.

Turn on the PC-2 by pressing the <ON> button. Press the <MODE> key until the word PRO appears on the upper portion of the display.

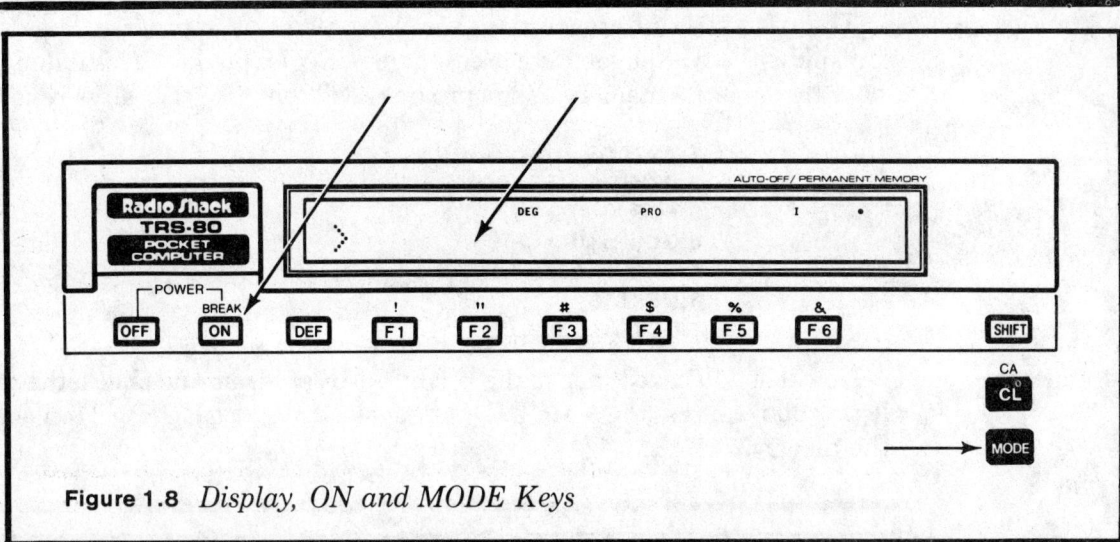

Figure 1.8 *Display, ON and MODE Keys*

You are now in the PROgramming mode. Type in the following lines exactly as shown below, and press the <ENTER> key at the end of each line. Don't worry about what the statements mean just now. We will discuss that after you have seen the program work. Be sure to include all the punctuation marks in each line. Notice that a colon (:) will appear after the line number, each time you press the <ENTER> key at the end of that line. This is how the PC-2 tells you that it has processed the line and added it to the rest of the program in memory.

```
1 WAITØ <ENTER>
2 PRINT "** WELCOME **" <ENTER>
3 FOR X = Ø TO 76 <ENTER>
4 GCURSOR X <ENTER>
5 GPRINT 255 – POINT X <ENTER>
6 NEXT X <ENTER>
7 GOTO 3 <ENTER>
```

When you have entered the lines, compare them with those shown below by using the [↑] and [↓] keys to move from one line to the next.

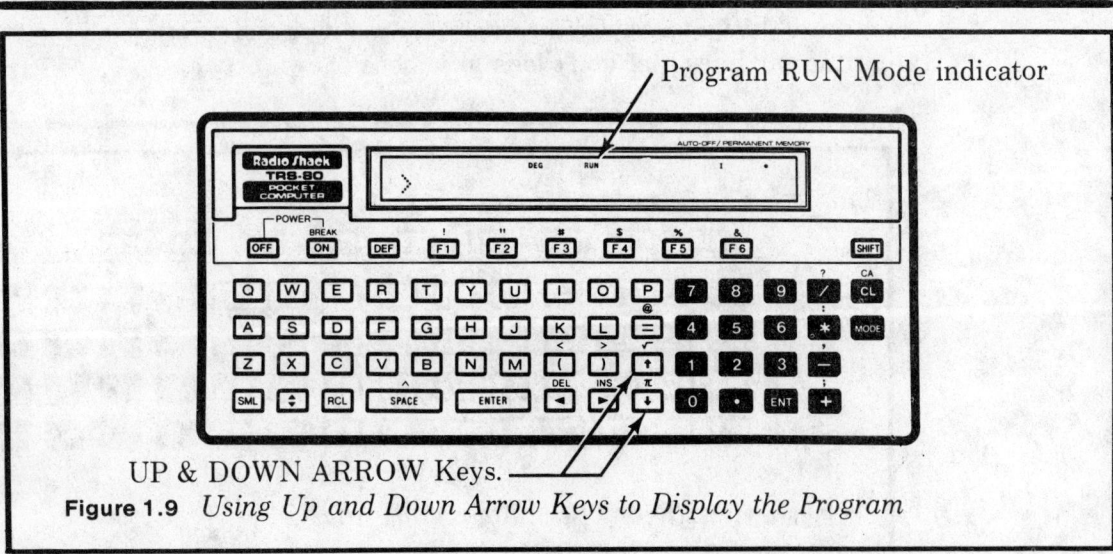

Figure 1.9 *Using Up and Down Arrow Keys to Display the Program*

There is a little difference in the way you typed in your program lines and the way the PC-2 displays them after you have pressed the <ENTER> key. This is due to the way the PC-2 puts things in its memory. Your program will look like this after it has been entered:

```
1:WAIT Ø
2:PRINT "** WELCOME **"
3:FOR X=ØTO 76
4:GCURSOR X
5:GPRINT 255–POINT X
6:NEXT X
7:GOTO 3
```

Now that you have typed in the WELCOME program and checked it against the program listing above, press the <MODE> key again. The word RUN will replace the word PRO on the display.

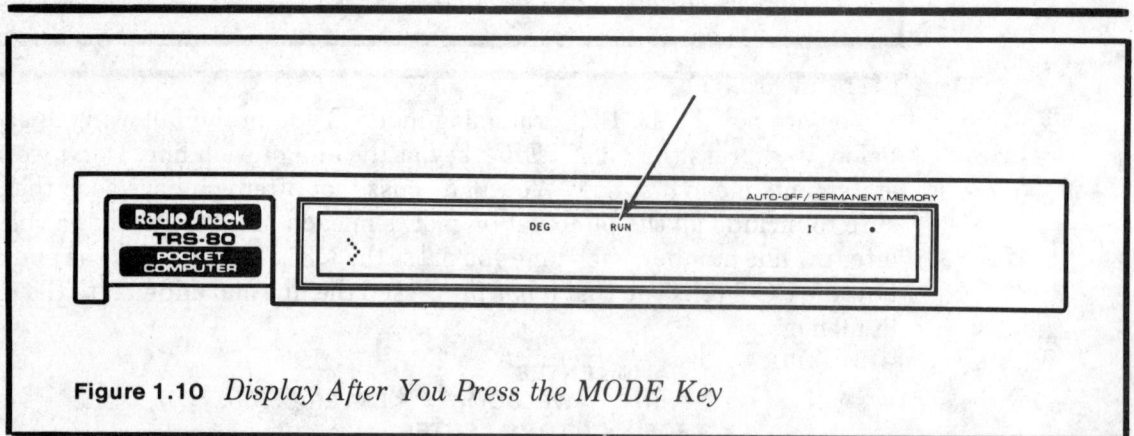

Figure 1.10 *Display After You Press the MODE Key*

You are ready to see the results of your labor! Type RUN and press <ENTER>.

If everything worked ok, you can skip the next couple of paragraphs and go to the heading, "See How Easy."

If you got an error message of some sort, press <BREAK> to clear the display, press <MODE> to return to the PROgram mode, and just re-type the error line for now. You may also use the up and down arrow keys to examine and compare all the other lines again; re-typing any lines that don't look like those shown above.

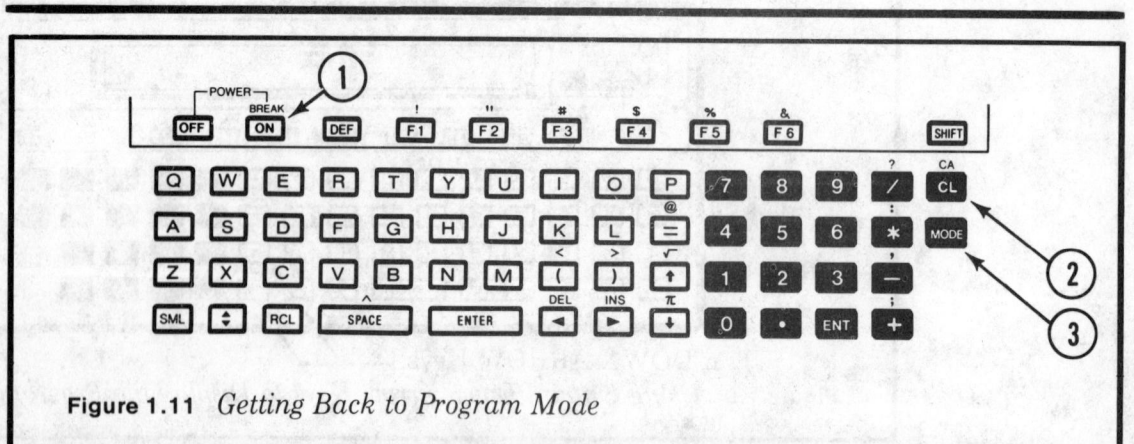

Figure 1.11 *Getting Back to Program Mode*

Later, you will have the opportunity to learn a little about the editing capability of the PC-2. Then you won't have to re-type program lines with errors in them. Now go back to the RUN mode, and try to run the program again.

Even if you have a lot of errors, don't get frustrated! You can go on with the next section, and worry about fixing the errors later on. It's important to your mental well-being not to let these things get to you!

See How Easy?

See how easy it was? When you get tired of watching the "WELCOME" message, press <BREAK> to stop the program.

Let's understand what we did. The welcome program you just typed in will serve as an example for the primary steps you go through to create a BASIC computer program:

1. Defining a Task

The first thing you have to do, is decide what you want to do! You wanted to use the PC-2, so you decided to get one and learn to use it. Writing a computer program is the same sort of process. First you decide what to do, and then act on it. In the welcome program, we wanted to show you some of the things the PC-2 can do, as well as giving you a feel for typing things in. We also wanted to entertain you a bit, so we decided to flash a message welcoming you to the PC-2 on the display.

2. Making a Plan to Accomplish the Task

The next step in creating a program is to figure out what order of events will be used to achieve the desired effect. The plan can be laid out on paper first, or you can dive in and go for it. The choice is yours. In the welcome program, each line represents a step in the progress of the programming plan, as we shall see.

3. Checking the Plan

After you have thought out the program, go over your plan. Make sure it makes sense and is in the right order. If you are winging it, this will consist of going to the RUN mode to make a 'trial RUN' of the program. You'll then need to add lines here and there in the program, as you see the results of what you have done so far, compared to what you wanted to do. This is also known as 'debugging.'

4. Determining the Instructions to Use

As you look over your plan, you will get a feel for the types of instructions necessary for the task. In the WELCOME program for example, we first want to have a clean display, so our first instruction is to CLear the Screen, and so on. You can study each process in the comments to the program listing, below.

5. Order of Instructions

Determining the order of instructions is as simple as following the logical progress of the program you are creating. You determine what events are to take place, and use the necessary statements to do the job.

6. A Logical Process

As we have seen, the construction of a program is a logical process consisting of figuring out what to do and, most important, when to do it.

7. Entering the Instructions

When you type in the program lines, start with the lowest line number then type in the statement, and press the <ENTER> key when you have finished the line. Select the next highest line number and enter the next program instruction and so on.

8. Verifying the Entries

You can verify that you have typed in each line correctly before pressing <ENTER>, or you can go over the line after entering it. If you wait until after you have pressed <ENTER>, you may have a slightly more difficult time correcting errors due to the compression ("tokenizing") which has taken place, but either way will work. (More on tokenizing later).

9. RUNning the Program

Now that you have checked out all the lines, press the <MODE> key and RUN will appear at the top of the display. Now type RUN (or R.), press <ENTER>, and let'er rip!

What the WELCOME Program Does

Here is a list of comments that explain each line of the WELCOME program. This is just a brief description, so refer to the sections that cover each statement for more information:

1 Set up for no WAITs after each PRINT statement.
2 PRINT the welcome message
3 Set-up a loop for the graphics cursor positions
4 Move graphics cursor to the next position to be LPRINTed
5 Turn on display points that are off – turn off points that are on
6 'Loop' to end of characters on the display
7 Repeat the program until the <BREAK> key is pressed

You are not expected to know what these "comments" mean just yet. As we progress through the book, you may come back to these comments. They will become clearer as you become more knowledgeable.

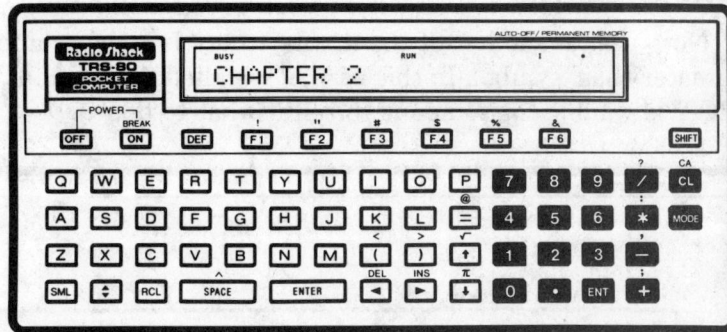

Getting Started — Ease Into It

Now that you have typed in and RUN the "WELCOME" demonstration program (you did try it, didn't you?), you can begin to learn how to do your own programming. Let's describe a few of the keys needed to get going. Refer to Figure 2.1 below.

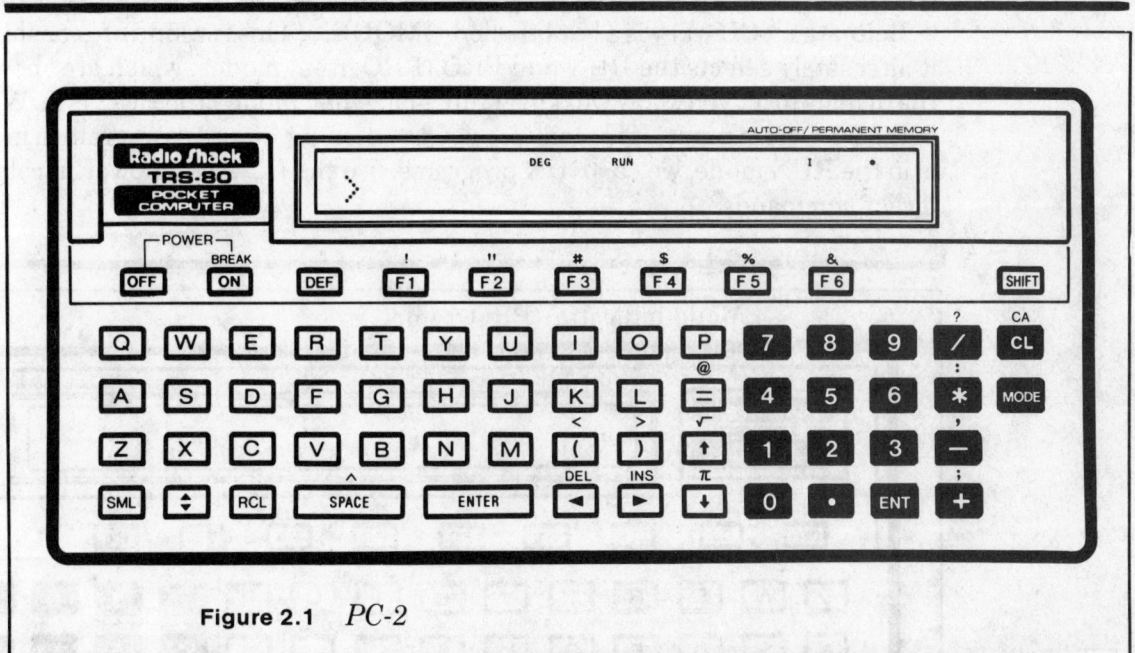

Figure 2.1 *PC-2*

There is a key to turn the PC-2 on, and a different one to turn it off. This is the push button age for sure. Pressing <ON> turns the PC-2 on, ready for use, provided there are good batteries installed (see Owner's Manual). Pressing <OFF> turns most of the computer off so that it uses the least amount of power from the batteries, yet still remembers programs until the next time it is turned on. Your PC-2 computer never forgets (sort of a hand-held elephant) unless it is told to or the batteries are dead.

On the right side of the PC-2 is a handy red key, <CL>, that clears the display of 'junk' or left over messages. You must also press the <CL> after certain types of errors in order to continue programming or using the computer. Press the <CL> key so we can start with a clean display.

Note that at the left of the display there is a '>' symbol, which is sometimes called a 'greater-than' symbol. In this case, it is called the 'prompt,' and it lets everyone know the PC-2 is waiting for someone to tell it what to do.

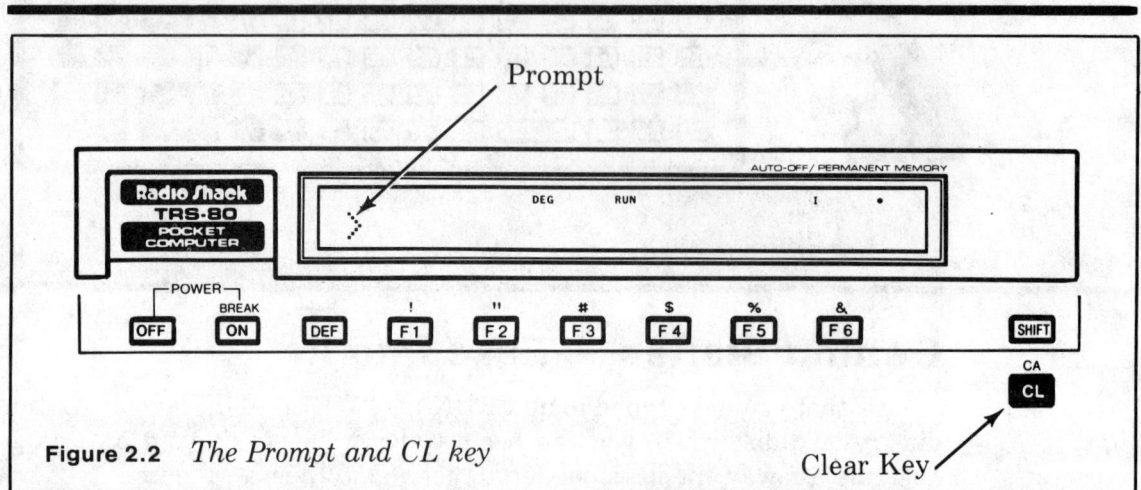

Figure 2.2 *The Prompt and CL key*

Below the <CL> key is a key labelled <MODE>. This is a kind of gear shift key. Pressing it alternately selects the RUN and PRO (PROgram) modes, which are shown at the top of the display to let you know what gear (uh, make that 'mode') the PC-2 is in. When the PC-2 is in the PROgram mode, it is ready for you to enter, modify and program in memory. When it is in the RUN mode, we can RUN programs, use the PC-2 as a powerful calculator or enter direct commands.

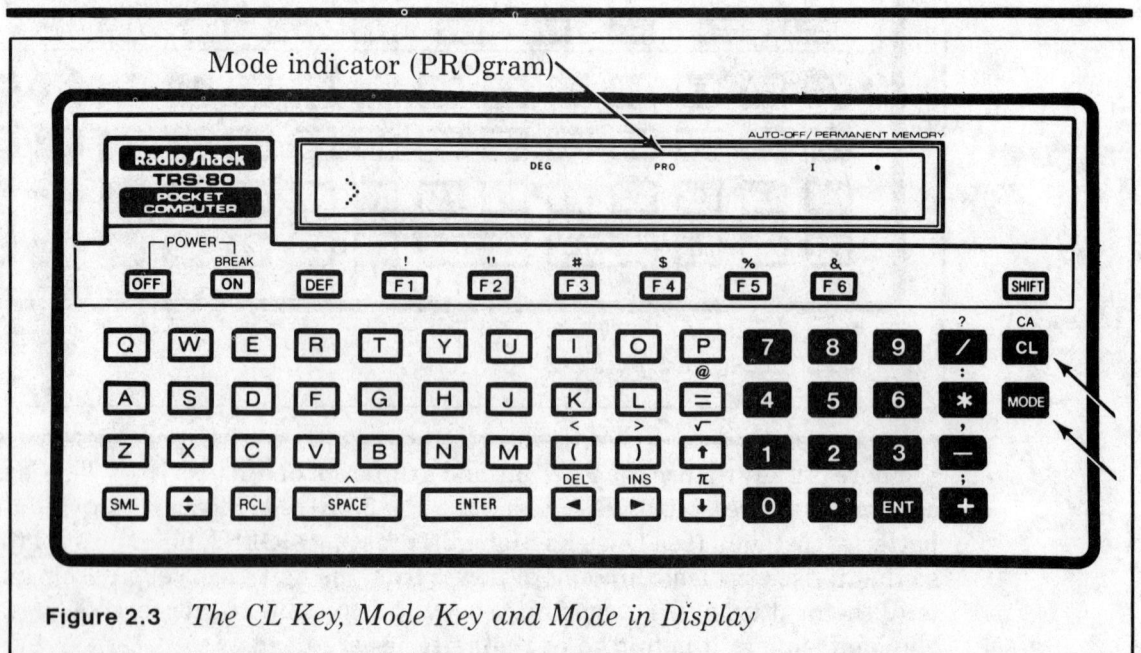

Figure 2.3 *The CL Key, Mode Key and Mode in Display*

NEW

Just as the <CL> key clears the screen (a BASIC language command), NEW clears out old programs from the computer's memory to make room for new programs. NEW is our first BASIC command, and we have to type it in since there is no NEW key.

Place the PC-2 in the PROgram mode by pressing the <MODE> key until PRO appears in the display. Type NEW and press the <ENTER> key. Try it, type NEW (that is, spell out NEW). Note that the cursor (the little bar on the display) moves one place to the right each time you type in a letter.

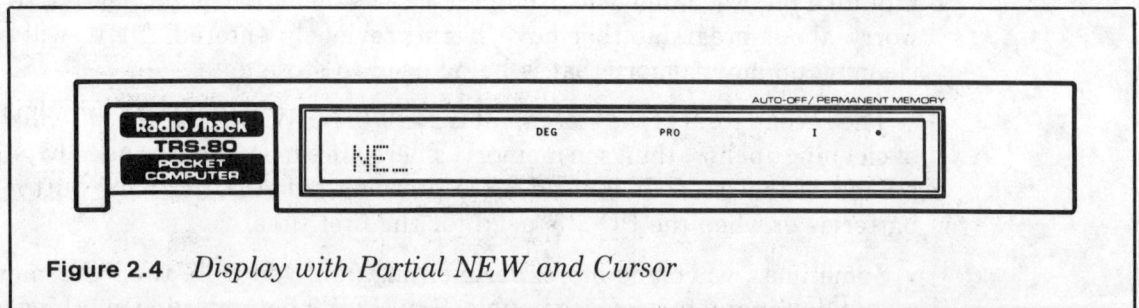

Figure 2.4 *Display with Partial NEW and Cursor*

By the way, have you noticed that there are two <ENTER> keys? One is <ENTER>, and the other is <ENT> over in the numbers section to make numerical entry easy. Either can be used at any time. After you have typed in the NEW command, press the <ENTER> key, – and the NEW instruction will be carried out by the computer. As a computer type, you should know that when an instruction is carried out by the computer, we say that it has been "executed."

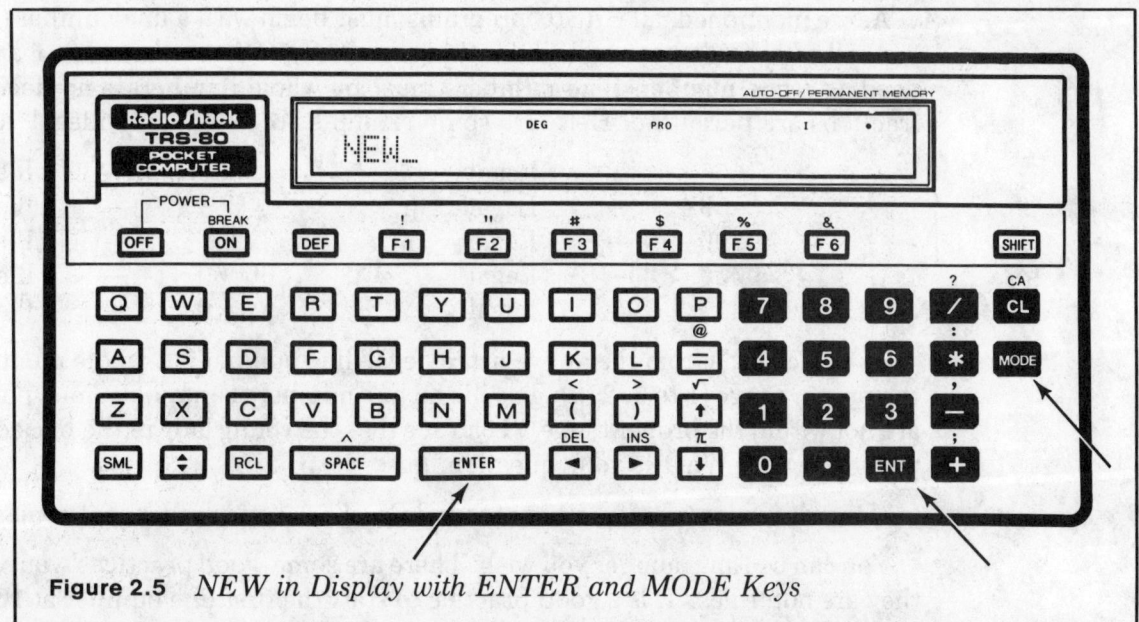

Figure 2.5 *NEW in Display with ENTER and MODE Keys*

NEW is like cleaning out all the shiny rocks, string, frogs and collected 'junk' from a boy's pockets, and washing the pants to make them ready for a NEW day.

The Primary Statement/Command
NEW <ENTER>

NEW is used in PROgram MODE only as a direct command to clear memory of all previously entered programs, variables and any text or numbers displayed on the display. NEW may not be used as a program statement.

Other Forms of the Statement/Command
NEWØ <ENTER>

We won't actually demonstrate NEW at this time. However, as we progress, we'll be using it quite a bit. Each time you use it, the PC-2's memory will be cleared, so we won't have to worry about programs that have been previously entered. NEW will also take care of cleaning up any memory that is being used to store data.

The second form of the statement is NEWØ. NEW, without the 'Ø', will do a very good job of cleaning up most things in memory. There are times when we need to go one step further. NEWØ is that step. It is used after pressing the ALL RESET button, after replacing batteries or when the PC-2 is used for the first time.

Sometimes, when you are experimenting (and you will), the PC-2 may hang-up or not respond properly to anything you do. Try NEWØ before trying anything else. It has saved my bacon a number of times. If NEWØ doesn't fix it, then the ALL RESET button is the only way out.

Oops! What went wrong? Mis-typed it. Retype the NEW or NEWØ statement and press the <ENTER> key. Wrong mode – make sure you are in the PROgramming mode.

Also see: NEWØ – CLEAR

Line Numbers

As we mentioned, all BASIC programs must begin with a line number (so the computer can tell what to do next and where things are). Any number between 1 and 65279 can be used as a line number. Line numbers must be whole numbers – no decimal numbers or fractions are permitted. Here are some examples of 'legal' and 'illegal' line numbers.

1	—	Legal	1.5	—	Illegal
9	—	Legal	3 ½	—	Illegal
2ØØ	—	Legal	.9Ø	—	Illegal
9ØØØ	—	Legal	66ØØØ	—	Illegal
421	—	Legal	Ø	—	Illegal

As you can see from the above list, a 'legal' line number is a whole number that is within the proper range (1 to 65279). The illegal line numbers contain decimal points, fractions or are not within the proper range. "I can see that the young lady in the back of the room has a question. Yes? What is your question, miss?"

"How do I know what numbers to use? Can I use any number that comes into my head?"

You can use any number you wish. There are some 'good practices' you should follow but they are not 'rules.' It is a good practice to start the first line number at 1Ø and make each succeeding number 1Ø greater, such as: 1Ø, 2Ø, 3Ø, etc., to leave room between line numbers. This way you can insert more lines later, without having to renumber an entire program. Each time you type in an instruction or statement that is preceeded by a line number, the computer will put it into its proper place in the program. For instance, suppose you were to enter a simple two line program that looks like this:

1Ø: REM DEMONSTRATION OF THE PRINT COMMAND
2Ø: PRINT"PC-2 READY...."

Then you decide that you would like to clear the display before you execute the PRINT statement. To do this you will have to insert a program line between line 1Ø and line 2Ø. All you have to do is simply enter a program line with any line number between 1Ø and 2Ø at any time, and the computer will take care of putting it in the proper place. For the purpose of this demonstration, we'll write a program line with the line number 15. This is what it looks like when we type it in:

15 CLS <ENTER>

and this is what the program will look like after we have typed it in and pressed the <ENTER> key:

1Ø: REM DEMONSTRATION OF THE PRINT COMMAND
15: CLS
2Ø: PRINT"PC-2 READY...."

So you see, we can use any 'legal' line number we want, and can enter the lines in any order. Remember that you should leave enough room between line numbers to add additional lines. "I see that the gentleman in the front row has a question."

"Can I use numbers like 1ØØ, 2ØØ, 3ØØ and so on?"

Yes, any legal number is OK. Those are legal numbers. If we had used those numbers in our program, it would look like this:

1ØØ: REM DEMONSTRATION OF THE PRINT COMMAND
2ØØ: CLS
3ØØ: PRINT"PC-2 READY...."

All right, now we know how to use line numbers, but I can see that you want to know why we need them in the first place. The computer executes a program in line number order. It starts with the lowest line number, executes that line, goes to the next highest line number, executes that line and so on. The order of the line numbers is the order in which the program lines will be executed.

From time to time, we (you or I, not the computer) 'don't' want the program lines executed in order. If we want the program lines to be executed out of order, we will instruct the computer to 'skip' that line, whatever it may be. Program lines will then be executed in order again, starting with the new line number.

Variables

There are lots of variables in this world. The weather varies; one day it's a nice sun-shiny day, the next is wet and cold. The river varies. One month it's full to overflowing, and the next, it's almost dry. The stock market varies. One minute stocks are are up, and the next minute, they're down. My bank account varies too. One day it has ten dollars in it, the next day it's empty – zero. Like I said, there are lots of variables in this world.

I'd like to introduce you to another type of variable: the 'computer variable.' This type of variable is used for storing data – numbers and keyboard characters. There are two main types of variables. The first type of variable is called a 'numeric variable.' The second type is called a 'string variable.'

We can store numbers in numeric variables, and words or characters in string variables. What makes variables unique is that they have 'names.' The reason they have names is so that we don't have to remember where we put them. Anytime we want one of them, all we have to do is use its name. Let me illustrate what I mean. We'll use 'numeric variables' for our examples.

Suppose your name is Bill, and I say, "Bill, remember this number for me. 12345." (You see, I'm very forgetful and this number is my secret Swiss bank account number.) You say, "Sure, I'll remember that." A couple of days pass, and I need to use the number but cannot remember it, so I call you and say, "Bill, what was that number I asked you to remember for me?" Of course, you remembered it instantly and said, "12345."

From the RUN mode, type this on the PC-2:

BILL=12345 <ENTER>

As soon as you pressed the <ENTER> key, 12345 appeared on the right hand side of the display, and what you originally typed had disappeared. Now press the <CL> key and type:

BILL <ENTER>

Amazing isn't it? Instead of pestering you to remember numbers for me, I can now use the PC-2 to remember them. Now type:

BILL=6789 <ENTER>

Then type BILL and <ENTER> again. You see, the value we stored with the 'name' BILL 'varied' from 12345 to 6789. Because we can vary the number we store under the name, we call it a 'named variable,' or just a 'variable,' for short.

Don't type NEW or put another value into BILL just yet, because we are going to use that name some more.

Here are the rules concerning the names we can use for our numeric and string variables. There are a couple of additional rules for string variables, and we'll discuss those a little later on.

1. They *must* always start with a letter of the alphabet.

● Type: B=12345 <ENTER>. Now type: 1B=12345 <ENTER>. This second example will cause an "ERROR 1" message to be displayed.

2. They may have a number as a second character.

● Type: B1=456. This demonstrates that the second character of the name may be a number, as long as the first character is a letter of the alphabet.

3. They may have any length.

● Let's go back to our first variable, BILL, and add a few characters to the name. Type: BILLWALTBURGER=12345 <ENTER>.

4. Regardless of the length of the variable name, only the first two characters of the name are actually used.

● Type: BI <ENTER>. You see, BI is the only part of the variable name that the PC-2 remembers. Type this: BIXYZ <ENTER>. You still got the same answer, right? Right! A variable name may be any length, but only the first two characters are used by the PC-2.

5. Any part of the name, after the first letter, may be a letter or a number.

● Type: B1 <ENTER>. In our second example of the rules, we used this variable name, and it still contains the original value we stored in it. Now try this: B∅=111 <ENTER>. Zero is a number. It can be used just like any other number. Type: BB=1∅∅∅ <ENTER>. The second character may be a letter of the alphabet also.

6. They may *not* contain spaces or symbols (?, @, &, etc.) as part of the variable name.

● This rule says that you may not use spaces in the variable name. Actually, you *can* use them between the first character and the second character but the PC-2 throws them away. You can prove this by entering: B   B=4567 <ENTER>. Now type: BB <ENTER>. Got the right answer, didn't you? Type: B   B <ENTER> (use a bunch of spaces) and you'll still get the right answer because the PC-2 throws them away. This rule also states that the second character may *not* be a character such as a comma, pound sign or any other *symbol*. Prove it to yourself by typing: B#=12345 <ENTER>. "ERROR 1" again – just remember, I told you so.

7. Variables may be used at *any* place that requires the use of a value or number.

● This is the real reason that variables are so handy. We can use them wherever we need to use a number or a value. I'm sure you have seen text books that use math formulas that look like this: A + B = C. That formula is telling us that whatever the value of A is, it is to be added to whatever the value of B is, and the result is represented by C. Ok, sounds simple enough, let's try it. First, we'll just use numbers and see what happens. Enter this:

1∅+5∅ <ENTER>

You will instantly see the answer (6∅) on the right side of the display. Let's prove the point, type these few lines (in the RUN mode):

A=1∅ <ENTER>
B=5∅ <ENTER>
C=A+B <ENTER>
C <ENTER>

First, we loaded the variable A with a value of 1∅. Then we loaded variable B with a value of 5∅. The third step was to enter the formula, but with a twist. Instead of putting =C at the *end* of the formula, we placed it at the *beginning.* Finally, we entered C and got the answer. We could have simply typed: A+B <ENTER> and received the same answer, but we wouldn't be able to use the answer in a calculation that we might want to do later.

8. A variable that has not been loaded or *initialized* (made equal to some number) will *always* be equal to zero.

● If you use a variable without first making it equal to a value, it will always contain a zero. Type: Z <ENTER> then: Q <ENTER> and finally: Y <ENTER>. Each time you pressed the <ENTER> key, a zero was displayed on the right side of the display. Why? Because we haven't loaded those variables with anything, so they can only be equal to zero.

When we make a variable equal to a number, we say that we have *assigned* a value to it. Because we can assign numbers to variables, we call this an *assignment statement*: A=1∅. Even though it uses none of the BASIC language keywords or statements, such as PRINT or NEW, we can still call it a *statement*.

9. A variable may not be, or contain, a BASIC keyword or statement as part of its name.

●There are certain words that make up the BASIC language. These words are called *keywords*. You may not use these words as variables or as part of a variable name. "TO" is a BASIC keyword (it is used as a part of the FOR/NEXT loop – a subject we'll discuss at a later time). Suppose you wanted to use the variable TOTAL like this:

TOTAL=A+B

Ordinarily, this would be an acceptable variable, except that it contains "TO" as part of its name. There are a number of these *keywords*, and you will learn them all as you read on. This would also cause an error:

LATOT=A+B

because it also contains the keyword, "TO", even though it is not one of the first two letters of the variable name. When you have "ERROR 1" displayed and cannot see any logical reason for the error, if it is an assignment statement, you may have used a keyword as part of the variable name.

There is one exception to this rule, however. There are certain keywords that are not stored in the PC-2 itself. They are stored in the peripherals that attach to the PC-2, the most common of which is the printer/plotter. The keywords I am referring to are used with the printer/plotter. Since these keywords are not used when the printer/plotter is not attached, they are not checked when you enter them into a program or use them in the RUN mode as variables.

If you attach the printer/plotter or any other peripheral device while you have a program stored in memory, they will be unaffected. However, you may not edit them as long as the peripheral device is attached. Like the man says, "You pays 'yer money and you takes 'yer chances." Use them if you must, but it's not a good programming practice, as there could be some undesireable consequences later on.

At the beginning of this explanation of variables, I said there were two main types: numeric and strings. A string variable is radically different from a numeric variable. A string variable can contain (or be assigned) letters, numbers and symbols; whereas a numeric can contain *only* numbers.

In a later chapter, we cover strings in great detail. For now, we'll cover just their names. Of course we'll have to create a few *strings*, in order to use them. You will have to take it on faith for a little while that they work. We will reward your faith with a detailed explanation later on.

The main difference between a numeric name and a string name is that a string name *always* has a *dollar sign* ($) as part of its name. A string variable looks like this: **Z$.**

The name of this varaiable is "Z string." Here is how we assign a string its contents:

Z$="THIS IS A STRING" <ENTER>

Notice that there are quote marks on either side of the message, THIS IS A STRING. Everything between the quote marks is assigned to the variable Z$.

String names, such as AA$, A1$, DF$, Q$, A∅$ and ZX$ follow the same rules as the numeric variables but have the dollar sign as the last character in the variable name.

Here is a little more information about strings before we move on. When we have assigned some characters to a string, we sometimes say we have given it a *value*, even though we didn't put any numbers into it. If a string is empty, we refer to it as a *null* string. We also refer to anything *between the quotes* as a *literal* because what is between the quotes is to be treated *as it is – literally.*

Any character you can type from the keyboard (and some you can't), including numbers, can be part of a string. A string can be as short as one character or as long as 8∅ characters (if certain steps have been taken). For now, our strings can only be 16 characters long.

Roll up your sleeves and pull down your hat. We are about to write our first program line…

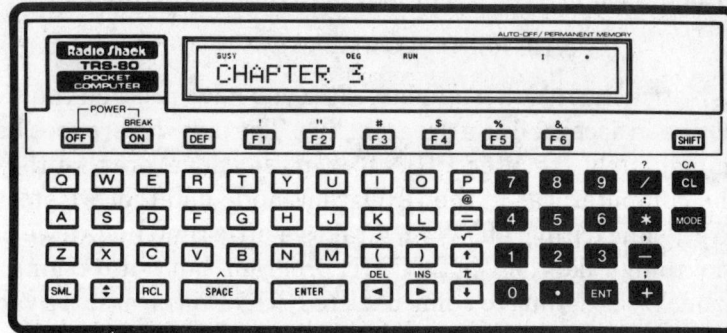

PRINT

Possibly the most used statement is PRINT. Surely it is among the top 5 because it is used in nearly every program, sometimes many times. PRINT does just what it says; it PRINTs (on the display) whatever is put between quotes after the word PRINT, or the contents of a variable if no quotes are used.

Let's use the PRINT statement to see what it does. First we'll use it as a direct statement; then we'll use it as a program statement. A 'direct statement' is one that is simply typed into the computer without a line number and executed right then and there — no delay; no RUN — you get the results immediately. Come to think of it, it is also called an 'immediate statement.'

Make sure the computer is on, in RUN mode and is showing the prompt (>). If not, press the <CL> key; make sure the PC-2 is in the RUN mode; then type the following line exactly as it is below:

PRINT "PC-2 READY. . ." <ENTER>

Immediately after pressing the <ENTER> key the display will show:

PC-2 READY. . .

with no quotes or anything else. If not, you may have typed PRINT incorrectly or missed the quotes. Press <CL> and try it again.

The quote symbols are typed by first pressing the <SHIFT> key then the quote key. The quote key is in the top row of keys and has 'F1' on it. Above the <F1> key are the quote marks. Do not hold the <SHIFT> key down. Simply press it once; then press the <F1> key with the quotes above it. (If the <F1> function key has not been programmed, as we will be looking into a little later, you don't have to use the <SHIFT> key first; just press <F1> and the quote mark is entered).

This is not a program line as such; it is an 'immediate' or 'direct' command or statement. PRINT, as well as some of the other commands can be executed as 'direct commands,' even in the PROgram mode.

To make a program line out of this line, press the <MODE> key for PROgram; type NEW, and press the <ENTER> key to clear out anything that may be left over in memory.

Now, type it in again using a line number, like this:

10 PRINT "PC-2 READY..." <ENTER>

If you have it right it will look like this on the display:

10: PRINT "PC-2 READY..."

Notice that a colon appears after you have pressed the <ENTER> key and that the line has been accepted as a program line. The only differences between our program line and the immediately executed PRINT example above, are that the program line was entered while the computer was in the PROgram mode and that we started the line with a line number. Pretty unexciting, eh? Well, it takes a little time before we can make programs that actually 'do' things like the WELCOME program, but not too long. It will get ver-r-r-ry interesting soon. We are going to come back to PRINT often as it is a very versatile command with many more features. For now, we'll keep it simple.

If it doesn't look exactly like the text above, press the <CL> key and try again, you may have mis-typed it, forgot the quotes, or accidentally gotten into the RUN mode when you typed in the program line (check the top of display). It's easy to make small mistakes while typing, and computers are notoriously unforgiving about mistakes. This is why we are mentioning mistakes so often, as it is a good idea to learn early that computers are exacting beasts with sharp tongues that jump to complain at the slightest mistake (have you seen "ERROR 1" yet? You will !!!).

The Primary Statement/Command

PRINT "literal string of characters"

Other Forms of the Statement/Command

PRINT number
PRINT variable
PRINT string variable
10: PRINT variable
10: PRINT string variable
10: PRINT number
10: PRINT (calculation)

This is one of the most used statements that you will find in the BASIC language. Not only that, but as you'll see, it is versatile. This statement works in any mode, RUN, PROgram and RESERVE. We will learn more about PRINT, its modifiers, its various forms and the ways in which it can be used throught out this book.

Here is a program that will demonstrate the various ways it can be used in the PROgram mode. Press the <MODE> key until PRO appears in the display. Then type: NEW <ENTER>. Enter everything that follows, just as you see it:

```
10: WAIT 100
20: A$="ANOTHER TEST"
30: PRINT"THIS IS A TEST"
40: PRINT 250
50: PRINT A$
60: PRINT 10+50 * (22)
70: PRINT A$+A$
80: A=66
90: PRINT A
```

When you have completed tying in this program, go back to RUN mode by pressing the <MODE> key once. Type: RUN <ENTER> and you will see the various forms of PRINT at work. We will become very familiar with it as we go.

Some suggested uses — PRINT is so versatile, that to suggest all the things that you can use it for would fill a book in itself. However, PRINT can be used to issue instructions from a program, PRINT the results of a program calculation, prompt the person who is using your program and to PRINT error messages. Here are some more examples using the PRINT statement.

10: PRINT"MY NAME IS"	PRINTing a message.
20: A=10	initialize variable
30: A$=" PC-2"	initialize string variable
40: PRINT A	PRINTing a numeric result.
50: PRINT A$	PRINTing a string.
60: PRINT A*50+20	PRINTing a calculation result.

Oops! What went wrong? Mis-typed it. Forgot to use the quote marks at the beginning and end of your message.

Also see: LPRINT - PAUSE - WAIT

Let's move on and see how to RUN our program.

RUN

RUN is a "direct command" which is entered from the RUN mode. Note that there are two RUNs here — the RUN *mode* and the RUN *command*. RUN (the command), causes a BASIC program in computer memory to be executed. To RUN our 'program' we must first get the computer into the RUN mode. Press the mode key, and check the top of the display to make sure that the computer is in RUN mode. You may remember the RUN command from our WELCOME program. Like PRINT, it does what it says. It RUNs a program that you have stored in the computer's memory. Now that we have a program in memory, our "PRINT" program above, let's RUN it.

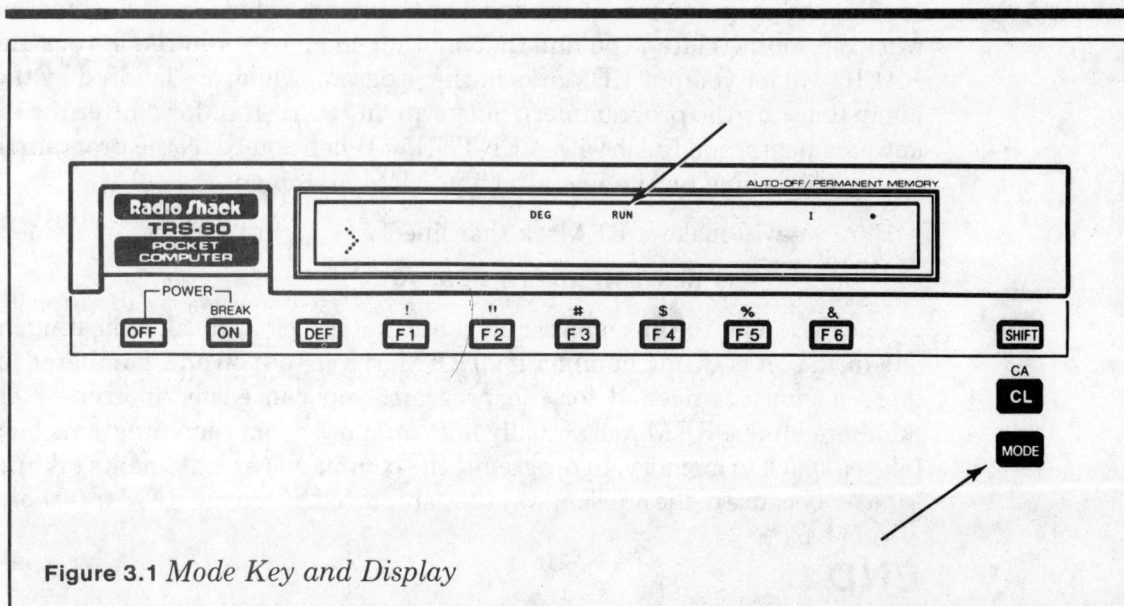

Figure 3.1 *Mode Key and Display*

First make sure the PC-2 is in RUN mode; type RUN, and press the <ENTER> key. The program will instruct the computer to PRINT the message between the quote marks on the display. Your display will look like this:

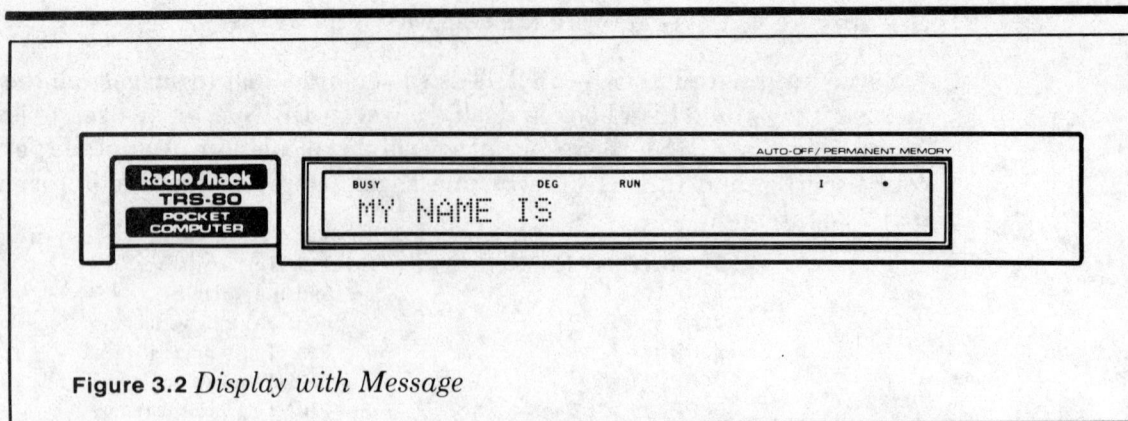

Figure 3.2 *Display with Message*

NOTE: After each message is PRINTed, press the <ENTER> key.

RUN cannot be used in a program, that is, with a line number in front of it. It only works in RUN mode and only when you type it in and press the <ENTER> key. If it is used in a program, the computer will halt and PRINT an error message (ERROR 1).

That's it, you just ran your first program (not counting WELCOME), and though your fingers didn't shoot sparks, they did not throb with pain either. Press <CL> and we'll press on.

Also see: ARUN — GOTO — <DEF> Key

REM

Let's add another line, now that your lightning-quick, bear-trap mind is running hot. This is also a good place to mention some good programming practices. When writing programs that are long (you may not believe this yet, but all programs get longer and longer, even after you think you have finished them!), it is a good idea to add remarks to tell you(or anyone else reading the program) what, how and why things were done. This becomes especially helpful when, six months later, you find that another change is required in your 'finished' program. BASIC will let you put REMarks in the program, which are ignored by the computer (and many times by the programmer). Just type in REM (REMark) after the line number, then any comments, and finish with <ENTER>. When you RUN the program the computer will ignore everything on the line after the REM statement.

Here we will make a REMark that line 1Ø is an introductory statement like this:

11 REM LINE 1Ø IS A MESSAGE

The reason for the line number eleven is that it is close to 1Ø, indicating that it goes with it, and further, it is an odd number. If all REMarks are put on odd-numbered lines, then later, if more memory is needed for the program, you can easily shorten or eliminate all odd numbered lines. REMarks actually take up more room than programs because each letter takes a space in memory. In programs, the commands or statements take up only one or two 'spaces' because of the efficient way they are stored. Keep the REMarks short and to the point.

END

Every program needs an end, even if it is going to be made bigger later. In BASIC, the END statement is used. Lets put a big line number on it so we can easily insert more lines ahead of it later. Type this in:

1ØØØ END

The END is not actually necessary in all forms of BASIC, and the PC-2 does not need it if there is only one program in memory, such as now. If we were to have two or more programs in memory that we wanted separated, we would need to use the END statement to tell the computer this is the END of a particular program. The PC-2 can have as many programs as there is room for. That's an advantage not many other computers have (just a little bragging here).

When the computer gets to the END statement, it stops RUNning the program and returns control of the computer to you.

Also see: STOP — <BREAK> Key

LIST

When you are writing a program, there are times when you would like to review what has been entered into the computer — you would like to LIST the program on the display. Fortunately, there is just such a command and it is called (of all things) LIST.

LIST is a command that will list out the program one line at a time so that you can examine each line. From the PROgram mode (LIST only works in the PROgram mode), press the <MODE> key until PRO is displayed) type in LIST, and press <ENTER>.

The first line of the program will be displayed. It should be line 1Ø (unless you mis-typed it or forgot to change to the PROgram mode).

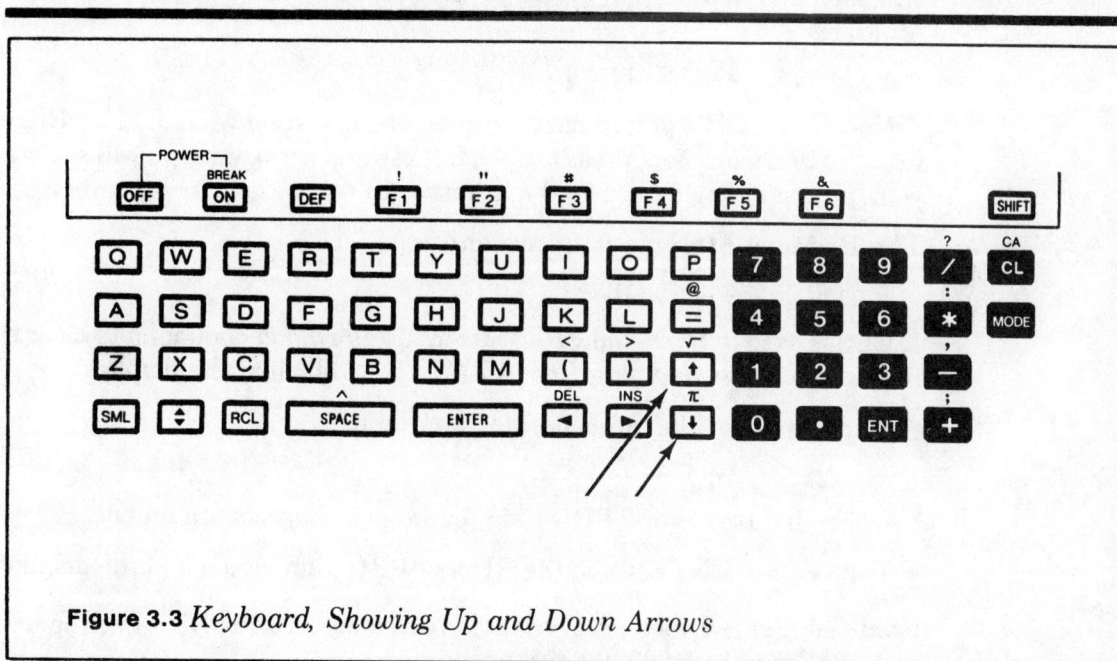

Figure 3.3 *Keyboard, Showing Up and Down Arrows*

Press the [↓] key, and note that the display now shows line 11 in all its radiant beauty. Press it again. Line 1ØØØ is displayed. It is the next higher numbered line and also the last line of the program. If you press [↓] again nothing will happen because there are no more lines of code ('code' is a computer programmers' term for program statements). Press the [↑] key and you'll see that the next lower numbered line is displayed, line 11 again. Press it again, and line 1Ø appears. Isn't that better than having to write it down on a napkin?

The LIST command will display a 'listing' of each program line for your review whenever the PC-2 is in the PROgram mode. It won't work while a program is RUNning, and it won't work in a program line – it is a *direct* command only. However, if you want to list out a specific line number (in PROgram mode, of course) just put a number after the LIST command like this:

LIST 1000 <ENTER>

Did you try it, or did you take my word for it? (If you'll take my word, I have a nice bridge in Brooklyn I'd like to sell you!)

Oops! What went wrong? Mis-typed it – retype the command and enter it. Wrong mode — make sure the computer is in the PROgram mode.

Also see: ↑ — ↓ — LLIST

CLS

There are times when we would like to have a blank display, or clear it temporarily (to make it flash off and on, say). CLS CLears the display of anything that was on it. It's an eraser in three letters.

CLS is used to prepare the display for the output of the program. Under some circumstances, something that was on the display, before your program uses it, may be left over and would clutter your program's output. CLS just tidies up things a bit.

CLS is a way of clearing the display screen from a program. CLS simply clears the display and leaves not a trace (not even a prompt, like the <CL> key leaves). Add this line to your program:

30 CLS <ENTER>

Now RUN it. Did you remember to enter the correct MODE? No? ERROR 26, eh? If at first you don't succeed, press the <CL> key and try again. You will see many errors during your programming career so don't bother to count them or be embarrassed by them.

The Primary Statement/Command

CLS <ENTER>

CLS is used in RUN and PROgram mode as a *direct* command to clear the display. As in the example above, typing CLS <ENTER> will clear the display.

Other Forms of the Statement/Command

10: CLS

It may be used in the PROgram mode as a program statement.

Type CLS <ENTER> in the RUN or PROgram mode, and the display will be cleared.

Some suggested uses — To clear the screen before PRINTing at a special location. Also see PRINT and PRINT modifiers).

Oops! What went wrong? Mis-typed it. LIST the program and check your last entry. If it's incorrect, re-enter it. You may have forgotten to press the <ENTER> key. Wrong mode — check the MODE before typing RUN.

Also see: Keys <CL>/<CA> — PRINT — CLEAR — <ALL RESET>

4

CHAPTER 4

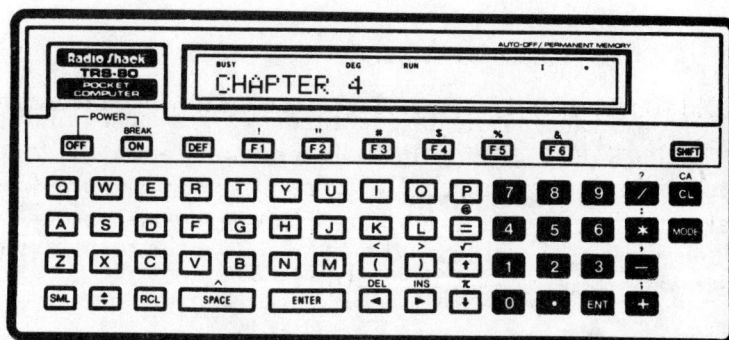

Arithmetic Operators: $+ - / * =$

'Arithmetic operators' is a high-falutin' term for some things we have called the plus, minus, multiply, divide and equal signs most of our lives. If you have ever used a small calculator, then you already know how to use 'arithmetic operators.' There are five of these 'arithmetic operators.' They are:

+ **Plus Sign**
– **Minus Sign**
* **Multiplication Sign**
/ **Division Sign**
= **Equal Sign**

The plus, minus and equal ($+ - =$) signs are familiar enough, but the other two look a little strange, don't they? We are used to seeing the multiplication sign as an '$\times$' like this: $2 \times 2 = 4$, and the division sign like this: $4 \div 2 = 2$. Another way of presenting a division problem is like this:

$$\frac{4}{2} = 2$$

It's not convenient to use the usual divide and multiply signs, because the computer could confuse the multiply's '$\times$' with a variable, and the divide sign just doesn't fit on the keyboard without adding an extra key. The easy way out is to use a couple of keys that already exist. The computer uses an asterisk ($*$) symbol for the multiplication sign, and a slash (/) symbol for the division sign.

A multiplication looks like this . . .

$2 * 2 = 4$

. . . and a division problem looks like this . . .

$4 / 2 = 2$

It is easy to visualize the multiplication sign, because all we did was substitute an '*' for an '$\times$.' The division is a little harder to visualize, but try this. Imagine that everything to the left of the slash is what we would normally place above the division line and that everything on the right is what we would place below the division line.

$$\frac{4}{2} = 2$$

. . . . is the same as

4 / 2 = 2

Now, let's use what we have learned. We'll do a little multiplication and a division on the PC-2. Place the computer in RUN mode and enter the following:

2 * 2 <ENTER>

The answer (4) will be in the right side of the display. Here is a simple division:

4 / 2 <ENTER>

Notice that we did not need to enter the equal sign in order to have the computer display the answer. Just to prove a point, enter this:

2 * 2 = <ENTER>

When you use the equal sign without a variable, an ERROR 1 message will be displayed. Now try to do the same thing from PROgram mode. The computer will think that the first '2' is a BASIC program line number, and after you have pressed the <ENTER> key, your entry will look like this:

2: *2=

You won't get an error message until you try to RUN a program, and the program will 'crash' when it gets to line number 2. Let's move along to other matters and find some new ways to use the computer . . . .

Besides being able to write programs, we can use the PC-2 in the RUN mode, just like a super calculator. We can use the arithmetic operators like a calculator or use them like a computer program does, that is, we can set a variable equal to a combination of arithmetic operations. Enter the following example in RUN mode with a CLeared screen:

2 + 3 − 1 <ENTER>

which will PRINT a 4 on the right side of the display.

There are ways to 'label' the results of equations and operations before they are done. This gives the computer a place to put the results after it completes a calculation. "And," you ask, "what is this 'label' we can use?" Very simple. Remember those variables we talked about? Well, our 'labels' will be variable names. By setting the variable equal to our operation, the computer knows that we want a place reserved for the result and also that we will want to retrieve it later on.

Now type in:

A = 2 + 3 − 1 <ENTER>

The answer (4) will be displayed again, but this time, the variable A also contains the answer (4). To prove that, type PRINT A <ENTER>.

Note that the variable name 'A' must be on the left side of the equal sign and that there can only be one variable name on the left side of the equal sign. The PC-2 will take the answer from whatever operations it finds to do on the right (including just making the left side equal to the right side, such as A = B or A = 23).

Like a west Texas whirlwind, we've covered a lot of ground, and we're not through yet. Some of the things we've investigated are a number of the PC-2's features, some BASIC language commands and statements, we've discovered variables, reviewed the arithmetic operators and found that our PC-2 is a super calculator as well as a full-fledged computer. Take a few minutes and experiment with a few of these things. Programming a computer is somewhat like playing a piano, the more you do it, the better you get. Don't forget to make a few mistakes — you'll learn from them. After you're finished with that, we'll continue.

More on PRINT

The old saying is, "There is more than meets the eye." Nothing could fit that adage more than the PRINT statement. There are so many things we can do with PRINT that it's tough just trying to figure out where to start. But, start we will, and we'll start with the . . .

Print Modifiers (; and ,)

Stay with me while we hark back to ye olde days of manual (ugh!) typing machines. If you have ever seen a typewriter (and I suspect that you have), you are familiar with how they work. First you feed paper into the rollers and then, after aligning the paper, you start typing by pressing the keys.

So far, our description of a typewriter and a computer printout is not all that different. Instead of paper, we use the computer display. The keyboard part is about the same. When we press the computer's keys, the typing appears on the display instead of typewriter paper.

When we want to start a new line on a manual typewriter, we simply throw the carriage return lever to the left, causing the carriage to bang into its stops, and we continue typing. If we were using an electric typewriter, we would use the carriage return key to accomplish the same thing.

Figure 4.1 *Manual Typewriter with Carriage Return*

A computer has a similar key that does a similar job. On the PC-2, it is called the <ENTER> key. Like the carriage return, when we press the <ENTER> key, the line we are typing is entered into the computer in much the same way a line of typing is put onto paper. With a typewriter, we can see the whole sheet of paper all at once — well, almost all of it. On the PC-2, we see only one line at a time. Just imagine that the PC-2's display is a window and that we can see just one line of our 'electronic' paper through the window. Imagine that it looks like this:

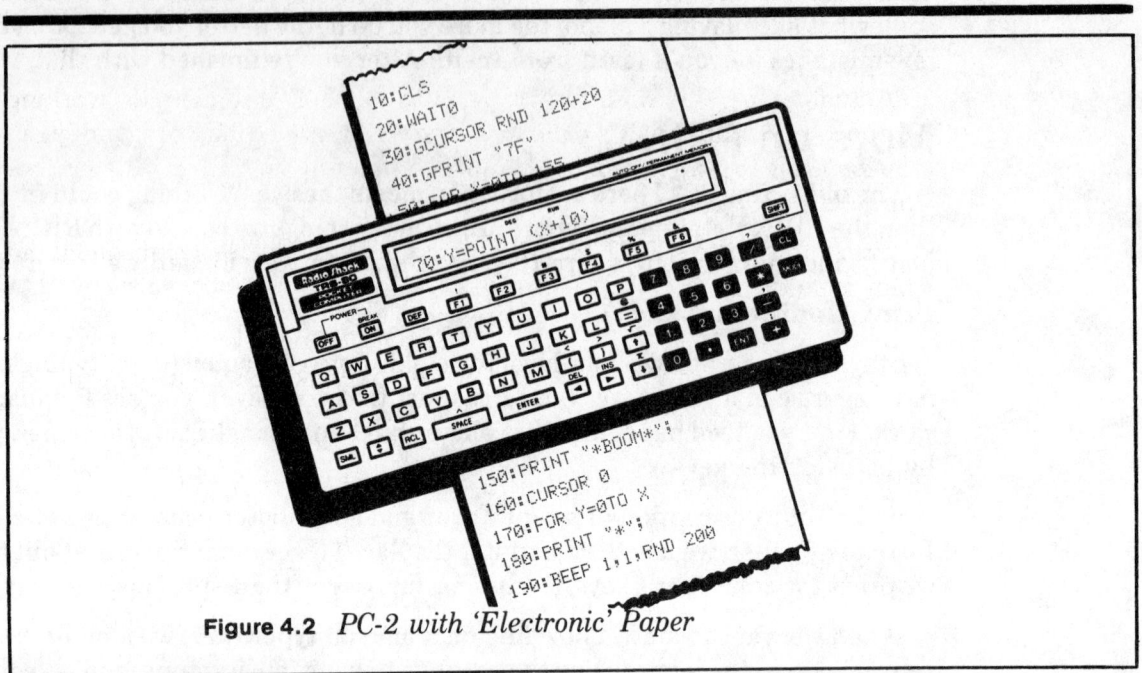

Figure 4.2 *PC-2 with 'Electronic' Paper*

Of course, this is not the way it really is, it's just a way of thinking of it so that it makes sense as a concept. Moving on — pressing the <ENTER> key causes the line we are working on to be completed and entered; it causes the place we are working at to be moved down one line and to the left side of our electronic paper.

Now we have the concept of typing on paper and typing on 'electronic' paper down fairly well. On a manual typewriter, we can control where we type by simply moving the paper and the carriage to the exact spot we want and then typing there. Since the PC-2 doesn't have a carriage or paper (in the usual sense), we need other ways of controlling the way messages and data are PRINTed on the display. (Finally — we're getting to the point!)

The two most common and easiest ways of controlling the PRINT statement are by using the comma (,) and the semicolon (;). Before you try them out, put the PC-2 in the proper mode (haven't forgotten, have you?) and enter this program:

```
10 PRINT "THIS "
20 PRINT "IS A "
30 PRINT "TEST "
40 PRINT "OF THE "
50 PRINT "PC-2"
```

Before you type in and RUN this program, we need to consider what we expect this program to do. Personally, I would expect it to PRINT the four lines of PRINT statements so fast that I would barely have time to read them. Zip-zip-zip-zip, and they would be gone without much of a chance to read them.

The easiest way to find out something is to do it, so let's RUN it and see what really happens. No, I'm not going to walk you through the typing-in of this program, but I want you to take special note of the blank space at the end of each line . . . we're going to need that blank later on. By now you should be able to do it all by yourself, and soon you'll be able to type a program into your PC-2 with the skill of a surgeon and the speed of a mongoose.

Now that you have typed it in, RUN it. What is it doing? Well, for one thing, not much — it's sitting there displaying the very first PRINT line (THIS). Let's wait a few seconds to see if it does anything else. Nope, it isn't doing anything. Do you suppose there is something wrong?

Actually, there is nothing wrong. The PRINT statement is working exactly as it is supposed to. It is displaying the message you wanted PRINTed, and (just to make sure that you had time to read it) it is waiting for you to press the <ENTER> key before it will display the next line.

Try it. Press the <ENTER> key, and the PC-2 will display the next line. The display will then look like this:

IS A

Another press of the <ENTER> key will make the display read:

TEST

then:

OF THE

and finally:

PC-2

Now that we know what to expect, let's use the semicolon to change (or modify) the PRINT statements' output to the display. This is a simple change, so we'll edit the program lines we have already typed-in.

Begin by going to the PROgram mode.

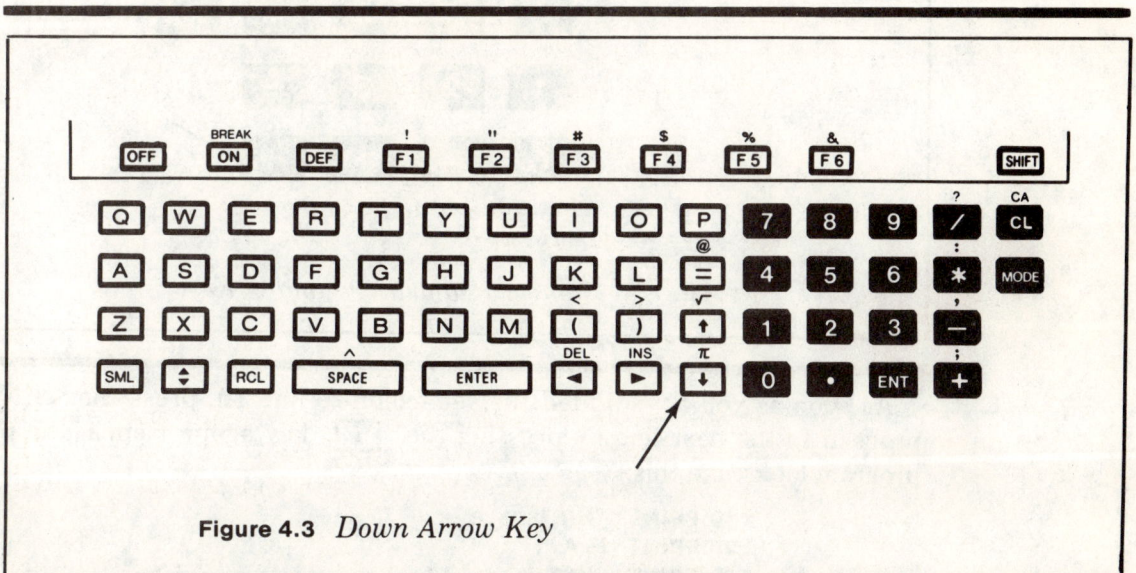

Figure 4.3 *Down Arrow Key*

Press the ⬇ key, and this will be on the display:

1Ø:PRINT "THIS "

To 'edit' this line without having to re-type it, press the ▶ key.

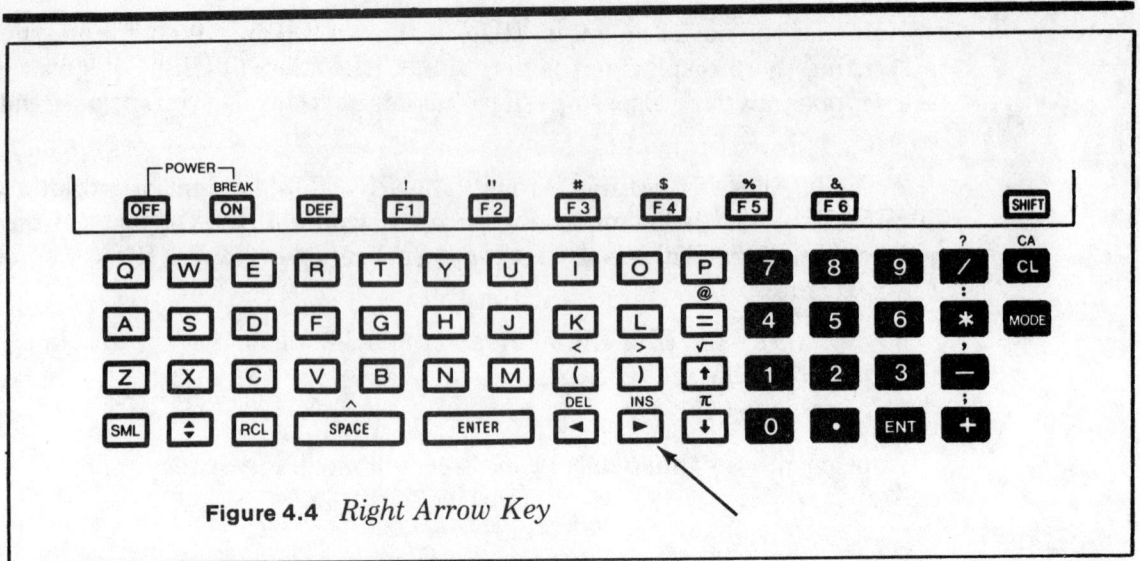

Figure 4.4 *Right Arrow Key*

As soon as you press the ▶ key, a black square will appear over the first character of the line to the right of the line number, and the colon between the line number and the program statement will disappear. Hold down the ▶ key until it is at the end of the program line. Then type a semicolon by first pressing the <SHIFT> key and then the <+> key in the lower right hand corner of the number pad.

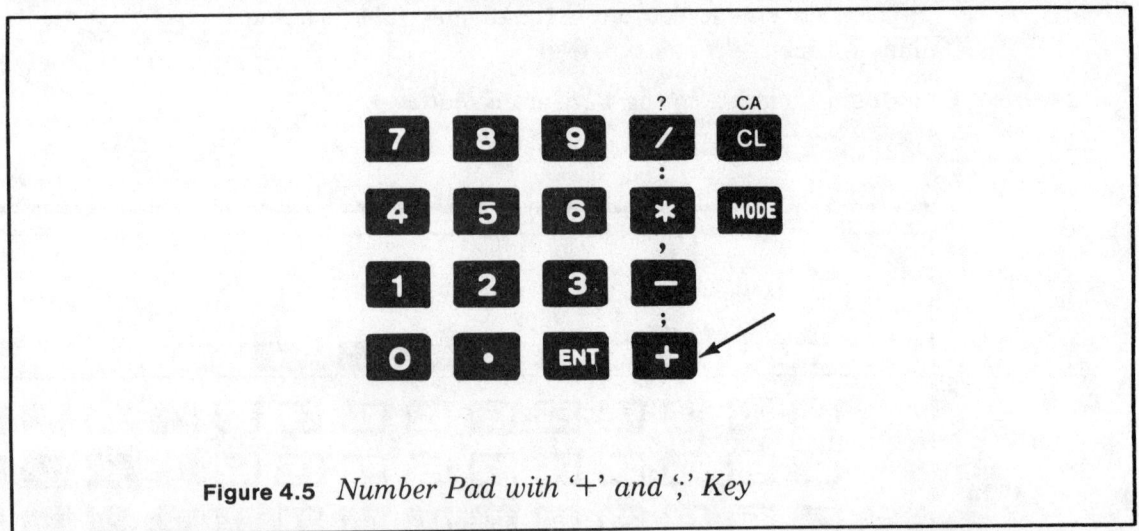

Figure 4.5 *Number Pad with '+' and ';' Key*

As soon as you have added the semicolon to line 1Ø, press the <ENTER> key and proceed to the next line by pressing the ↓ key again. Repeat the process until the program looks like this:

```
1Ø:PRINT "THIS ";
2Ø:PRINT "IS A ";
3Ø:PRINT "TEST ";
5Ø:PRINT "OF THE ";
6Ø:PRINT "PC-2"
```

Notice that there is no semicolon at the end of line 6Ø. Go to the RUN mode and RUN the program. Press the <ENTER> key (just as you did before) to make each line display.

Amazing! This time the display didn't clear the previous message; it simply PRINTed each message at the end of the previous one until the display looked like this:

THIS IS A TEST OF THE PC-2

Using the semicolon is like controlling the carriage on a manual typewriter. If you want to PRINT a message and PRINT another message at the end, then place a semicolon at the end of the first PRINT statement — it will keep our imaginary typewriter carriage from rolling the imaginary paper up and beginning a fresh line.

Next is the comma (,). Place a comma at the end of the first line of our test program like this:

```
10 PRINT "THIS ",
20 PRINT "IS A ";
30 PRINT "TEST ";
40 PRINT "OF THE ";
50 PRINT "PC-2"
```

. . . and RUN it.

The first display (after you press the <ENTER> key) will look like this:

THIS   IS A

Notice that there is a big gap between THIS and IS. That's because the comma acts like a tab key on the typewriter. I know that you are dying to try a few things out on you own, so why don't you take a break to experiment with some of the things we've just learned, and I'll fix myself a tuna malt and some liver cookies (I told you programmer types are a little crazy).

Using the Comma and Semicolon (, ;)

Now we know that we can modify the PRINT statement, but you want to know why we would want to. Ok, here are some reasons.

PRINT can PRINT more than one thing at a time. It can also PRINT either variables as previously defined, or immediate numbers (constants) and characters. Here is an example:

```
10 PRINT "TEST"
20 PRINT "TEST",2
30 PRINT "TEST";3
```

Line 10 PRINTs TEST as we have seen before, but line 20 will PRINT TEST on the left and 2 on the right. Line 30 PRINTs TEST 3 almost together (note that we did not put the space in between the TEST and the 3, as we did in the example above). Here the computer took care of it so that it would have room if the number were negative (like –3), and it needed the extra room for the minus sign. With a comma, the number always goes to the right. With a semicolon, the number always goes immediately after the string or previous number. Remember, a space is always placed in front of a number to allow for a positive (+) or a negative (–) sign.

From the discussion above, you'll remember that the comma in BASIC is a kind of tab, like a typewriter tab. A tab moves over a certain number of spaces on a typewriter for writing things in even columns. The comma is used for the two columns that our small display screen is set up for.

Enter these lines and RUN them. You'll have to press <ENTER> after each PRINTing to tell the PC-2 when you are finished looking at that printout. OK, let's try these:

```
130 PRINT 1,2
140 PRINT 1,"TEST"
150 PRINT 1,2,3
```

Line 13Ø is a little odd, yes? It puts the numbers in the middle and to the right. Yet the 1 is next to TEST in 14Ø. It so happens that the PC-2 puts text on the left (if it can) and numbers on the right. When it gets a number first, it compromises and puts it to the right of the first half of the display. When it gets text second, it puts the text to the left side of the second half. Well, try 13Ø to 14Ø again to see what I mean. Its easier with pictures.

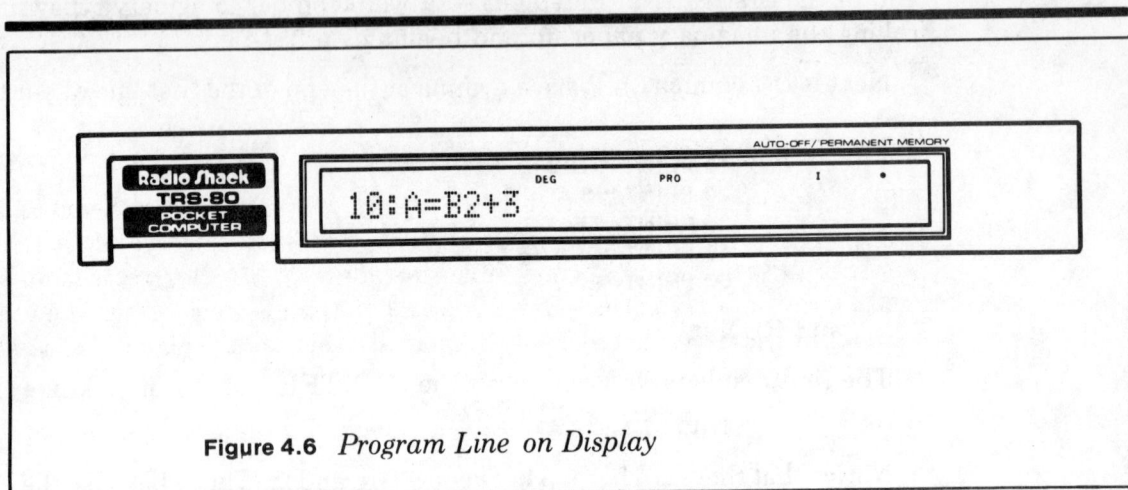

Figure 4.6 *Program Line on Display*

It all has to do with the two tab-like 'columns' the PC-2 has.

You got an error at line 15Ø, right? That's because the PC-2 can only show two items when PRINTing with commas. Try the semicolon. You can get as many things on the screen as there is room for (26 characters). The semicolon puts things 'back to back,' with no spaces in between. Don't forget that numbers take a character location for the sign which looks like a space if the number is positive because the PC-2 doesn't PRINT the + sign.

More on MODEs

Speaking of modes, how would you like some keyboard a la mode? It's very crunchy. Ok, then how would you like to press one key and have the PC-2 printout a line up to 77 characters long? The RESERVE mode will let you define the function keys to do just that. To get to the RESERVE mode, press <SHIFT> and then <MODE>. To program a function key, say F1, press the <F1> key (just below the display).

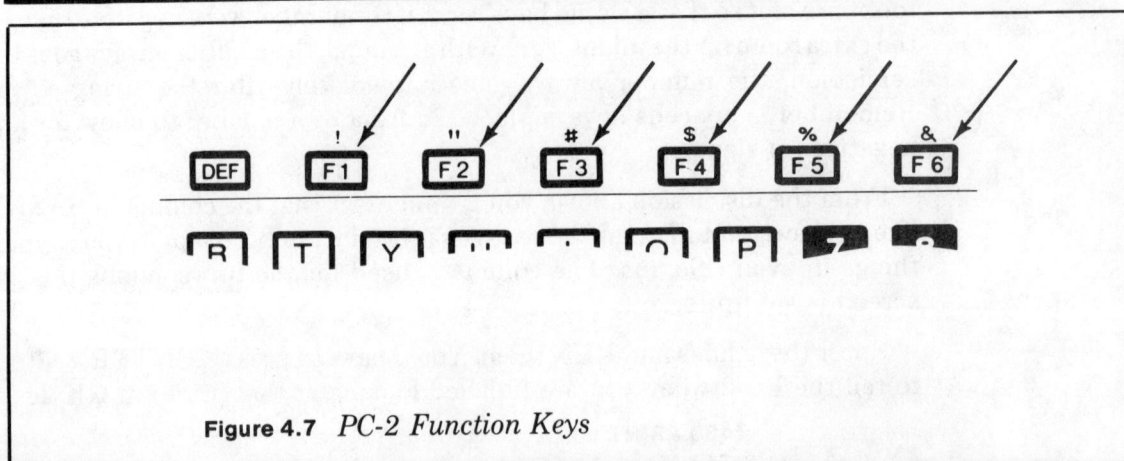

Figure 4.7 *PC-2 Function Keys*

Now type in whatever you want (PRINT "TIME =";TIME@ for instance). The @ symbol tells the PC-2 to execute the line as if you had pressed <ENTER>. After typing this in, press <ENTER>, then <MODE>. This will return you to the RUN mode. Now press the <F1> key, and the TIME is PRINTed out. Give it a whack. You'll have to see the TIME section for a decoding of the compact way the PC-2 displays time.

The 77 characters mentioned earlier is the maximum possible for all the function keys together, not just each key, so be a little conservative. The 77 characters go a lot further with commands because they are stored more compactly, as we shall see.

Some Computer Concepts

It's time to set aside the PC-2 for a few minutes while we expose you to some more ideas and concepts about computers. A computer is an idiot. It is not smart . . . your program is 'smart.' But the computer is fast. It is a fast idiot, so don't expect it to do anything 'smart.' Let's clarify something that has become a popular misconception. Many things have been done with computers that make them seem like they are intelligent, and the fact is, that's not exactly the case. But it is not exactly wrong either!

Let's get it straight, or at least take out some of the kinks. The computer is only a tool, a machine that follows instructions (quickly). The fact that it is fast and follows instructions makes it seem smart when programmers put in programs that make it do smart things. It's you, the programmer, that is smart! You are like an artist that leaves a part of himself in the work he does. As a rule, you can consider that a computer can only be as smart as the programmer that programs it. It can seem smarter than it is because it is fast, but it cannot do anything the programmer couldn't do, given the time. So it is up to you to make the computer 'smart' — the computer is just a tool to express your ability and talent (remember, it takes good tools to do good work; the PC-2 is one of them).

You could start writing some programs now with what you have already learned. Further, you could expand some of the short programs we have used as you pick-up more capabilities. This could also lead to a good programming technique called modular design, which means each program segment can be used as a module or segment of others. In this way, a library of program segments of common routines can be accumulated and used in other programs.

Enough of this palaver. Time to move on to the next BASIC language statement.

LET

Getting back to commands and programming, let's examine LET. LET is an optional statement except in a couple of cases. When it comes to LET, why is it that our PC-2 (which is usually more finicky than that famous cat on television) has such a 'take it or leave it' attitude (or should we say, "Live and LET live.")?

The word LET conveys to the computer about the same thing that the words 'make' or 'set' mean to us. When we tell the computer to "LET X=5", it's as if we were saying, "Make X equal to five," or, "Set X equal to five." No matter what the value of X was before, X will be equal to five after the computer executes this command.

A statement such as "LET X=5" is called an 'assignment' statement because a value (5) is assigned to the variable (X). In the Bad Old Days (BOD), LET was required in all BASIC assignment statements because computers were even more finicky than they are these days. But your PC-2, like most modern computers, will understand "X=5" without the LET, under most circumstances.

This explains some seemingly paradoxical computer statements such as "X=X+1". Consider the following sequence of statements:

```
1Ø:X=5
2Ø:X=X+1
```

Line 2Ø isn't telling the computer that 5=6. It's telling the computer to LET (or make) X equal to X plus 1. In other words, make the value of X be one unit bigger than whatever it was before. After the computer executes lines 1Ø and 2Ø, the value of X will be equal to six.

The Primary Statement/Command
```
LET variable = value
```

Other Forms of the Statement/Command
```
1Ø:LET A = 25
1Ø:LET A = B
1Ø:LET A$="YOUR NAME"
1Ø:LET B$=A$
1Ø:A=25    (LET is optional, and implied in this program line).
```

```
1Ø:IF B = 1 THEN LET A = 5
```

In IF/THEN statements, which we'll get to down the road, LET is not optional following the THEN statement (although THEN is actually optional in this example, as we will see). It is never wrong to use LET when assigning values to variables, but it is not always needed.

The LET statement provides one method of assigning a value to a variable. For example, LET IT = 25 means to let the variable IT be equal to the number 25. It is usually optional, except under certain circumstances. Thus, IT = 25 is basically the same thing, with no LET required.

Using the LET statement allows your programs to be consistent with other BASICs that require it, and it is required under certain cases like the one just mentioned.

Some suggested uses – you may wish to use the LET statement when writing programs that are to be published in a magazine article or that may be used on other computers.

Oops! What went wrong? Mis-typed it.

Also see: Variables

WAIT

WAIT works with the PRINT statement, another one of those 'modifiers' like the semicolon and the comma. WAIT is different though. It is not used after the PRINT statement, it's used before the PRINT statement. In fact, WAIT is a statement all by itself, and it modifies the way the PRINT statement works.

WAIT is used to establish a delay length following the PRINTing of a message on the display and will cause the computer to go on to the next statement without your having to press the <ENTER> key after each message is PRINTed.

IF no WAIT has been specified in the program, BASIC will halt after each PRINT to the display, and you must press the <ENTER> key to continue to the next program statement. WAIT Ø will cause BASIC to keep going after PRINTing on the display. Put a WAIT Ø as the first line of one of our example PRINT programs and ... zip, zip, zip! Those messages will go so fast, you probably won't even be able to read them. Then try WAIT 1Ø or WAIT 2Ø and see what happens. The delay value can be in the range of Ø to 65535, which will WAIT about 18 minutes!

Simply precede a PRINT statement with a WAIT statement. Every PRINT used after that will WAIT for whatever time you have specified or until you change it later in your program.

The Primary Statement/Command
WAIT delay

The delay value specified will be used for the length of time to WAIT after a PRINT statement. WAIT may be used in the RUN, PROgram and RESERVE mode.

Other Forms of the Statement/Command
10: WAIT
10: WAIT value
10: WAIT variable
10: WAIT (calculation)

When the WAIT statement is used without a value, it cancels any value that was previously specified, and it causes BASIC to wait for the <ENTER> key to be pressed after PRINTing something on the display.

10: WAIT 0

Using 0 as a delay value means that BASIC does not WAIT after PRINTing, but goes on to the next statement.

WAIT can be used in the RUN mode, as well as in a program line.

10: WAIT delay

10: A = 25
20: WAIT A

Some suggested uses – before prompts and displays, to allow time to read the display. Here is an example of WAIT:

10: WAIT 1000
20: PRINT"Waiting . . ."
30: WAIT 5
40: PRINT "THIS "
50: PRINT "IS A "
60: PRINT "TEST "
70: PRINT "OF THE "
80: PRINT "PC-2"

Oops! What went wrong? Mis-typed it. Delay value out of range. Forgot to put a number after WAIT or used the wrong number.

Also see: PRINT – PAUSE

CURSOR

A cursor is a symbol that is displayed to show you your present PRINT position. On the PC-2, the cursor is an underline character.

When a program is RUNning, the cursor is not visible in the display. The current PRINT position is referred to as the cursor position even though you cannot see it. The CURSOR statement sets the PRINTing position for the next character to be PRINTed on the display to one of 26 possible locations numbered 0 through 25.

If we wanted to start PRINTing in the sixth character position on the display, we would write a statement like this:

10:CURSOR 6

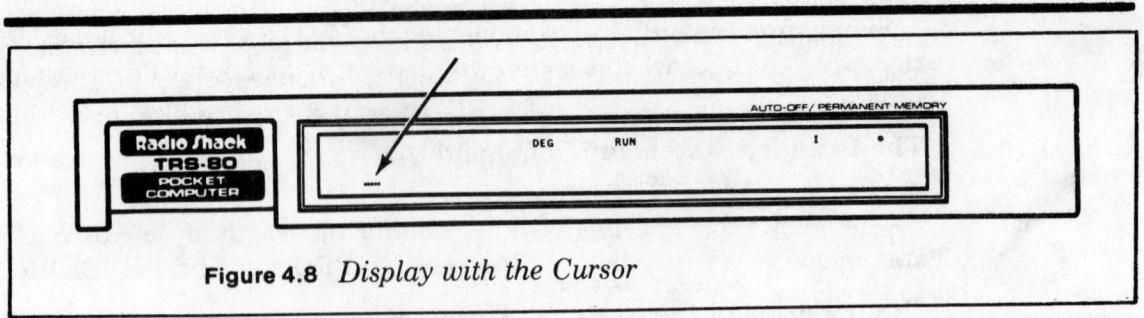

Figure 4.8 *Display with the Cursor*

It is a lot like spacing a typewriter carriage six spaces over before we start typing. This allows us to begin PRINTing anyplace that we want to. We're not tied to PRINTing on the left side of the display.

The Primary Statement/Command
CURSOR position

The CURSOR statement sets the position specified for the next character to be PRINTed (position can be any value from Ø to 25). The cursor position may be a constant or a variable.

Other Forms of the Statement/Command

```
1Ø: CURSOR
1Ø: CURSOR value
1Ø: CURSOR variable
1Ø: CURSOR (calculation)
```

Use of the CURSOR statement without specifying a value will set the cursor position to the beginning of the line on the next PRINT statement.

1Ø: CURSOR X
or
1Ø: CURSOR 6

The position at which to place the cursor can be specified as a numeric variable, as well as a constant value. The CURSOR statement works in the RUN mode as well as in PROgram mode.

Use CURSOR to put the next displayed (PRINTed) message at a special location.

Some suggested uses – Data entry, formatting, prompts, special displays. Use the CURSOR statement to position the output values or messages on the display. Here is an example in which each time the variable X is PRINTed, it is PRINTed in a different position on the display:

```
1Ø: WAIT Ø
2Ø: FOR X = Ø TO 9
3Ø: CURSOR X *2
4Ø: PRINT X
5Ø: NEXT X
```

Oops! What went wrong? Mis-typed it. Wrong mode. Number too large (greater than 25) or negative (less than zero).

Also see: GCURSOR – GLCURSOR – PRINT

BEEP

My word! Talking computers! The PC-2 has a built-in speaker that can be used for a number of things. BASIC provides us with a way to use the speaker to generate sounds by using the BEEP command. . . Have you ever said, "When that TV special comes on, call me"? The BEEP statement can serve the same purpose. You can use the BEEP statement to signal you (or whoever is RUNning your program) when the PC-2 has reached a certain result or needs a special input. BEEP can also be used to play music! In the RUN mode, type:

BEEP 25,45,14 <ENTER>

Then type:

BEEP 25,1Ø0,5Ø <ENTER>

With the BEEP statement, you can add sound effects or warning sounds to your program for special effects in games, or prompts for input and output. You can even make your PC-2 an alarm clock.

The Primary Form of the Statement/Command
BEEP ON
BEEP OFF

BEEP repeats, frequency, duration
    Repeats = Ø to 65535
    Frequency = Ø to 255
    Duration = Ø to 6527ፀ

Other Forms of the Statement/Command
    1Ø: BEEP repeats,frequency,duration

BEEP 1

If you type this in, the PC-2 will emit one short beep sound, using the default values of approximately 1,8,2ØØ.

1Ø: BEEP OFF

When this line executes, no further sounds will be heard until a BEEP ON command is issued, either in a program line or in the RUN mode. When the computer is turned off, the BEEP is not reset to the ON condition. You must specifically execute a BEEP ON command to restore the BEEP. Also, once BEEP OFF has been executed, the computer ignores all BEEP statements except a BEEP ON.

1Ø: BEEP ON

This statement turns the BEEP function ON. Normally it is on, but if a BEEP OFF has been executed, no sounds will be made if a BEEP statement is encountered. Issuing the BEEP ON command makes the PC-2 ready for beeping.

1Ø: BEEP 25,45

When BASIC executes this line, 25 beeps of the frequency set by the second parameter (45) will be issued from the speaker.

1Ø: BEEP 25,45,1Ø

This line will produce 25 beeps of frequency 45, each of which is 1Ø units long.

BEEP 2Ø

This does 2Ø beeps immediately, using the default frequency and duration.

BEEP OFF will also turn off sound during cassette I/O. With BEEP ON, you can signal an end to an operation or a calculation, or signal a certain result. Use it for sound effects in games or (if you are musically inclined) to play a tune that you have written.

Some suggested uses – alarms, tunes and simple music and as a reminder. Here is an example of using BEEP to signal an input:

```
10: CLS
20: BEEP 10
30: INPUT"ENTER YOUR NAME";NA$
```

Oops! What went wrong? Mis-typed it. Values out of range. Used BEEP but forgot to turn BEEP on.

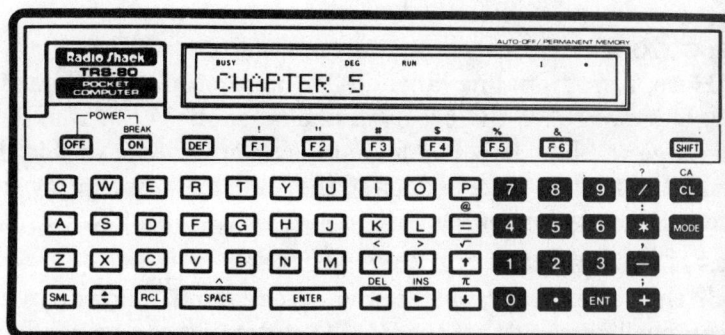

GOTO

This BASIC statement is easy to understand — we use it in our everyday lives. I'll bet you have said something like this many times, "When you finish what you are doing, go to the garage and bring me the hammer." GOTO works just like "go to" works in everyday life, except that we can't send the program to another part of the house; we have to send it to a program line number. GOTO can also be considered as a 'jump' from one place in a program to another.

In our everyday lives, we use the words 'go to' as two separate words. The computer uses them as one word: GOTO. In our everyday lives, we always 'go to' a place — like, "Go to the store and get me a loaf of bread," or "go to the kitchen and turn out the lights." The computer doesn't have a *place* it can go to, it has line numbers or labels (labels are explained below.) so it is reasonable to say to the computer: GOTO 1ØØ. This will cause program execution to 'jump' from wherever it is currently executing to line number 1ØØ. Here is a demonstration of GOTO:

```
10: WAIT 100
20: GOTO 50
30: PRINT"LINE 30"
40: END
50: PRINT"LINE 50"
60: PRINT"LINE 60"
70: GOTO 30
```

GOTO directs BASIC to go to the line number or label you have specified. In this example, line number 2Ø causes program execution to 'jump' to line number 5Ø — in this case, line 5Ø PRINTs a message. Then line 6Ø PRINTs a message. Next line 7Ø is executed, which causes program execution to 'jump' to line 3Ø, where another message is PRINTed. Then line 4Ø, which is the END statement, is executed. At this point, the program stops, and control of the computer is returned to you.

The Primary Statement/Command
GOTO line number

When BASIC executes this line, program control will pass to the line number specified.

Other Forms of the Statement/Command
```
10: GOTO line number
10: GOTO variable
10: GOTO (calculation)
10: GOTO "label"
```

10: GOTO"A"

Here, a program line labelled "A" is referenced. When BASIC executes this line, it will transfer control to the program line labelled "A," if it exists. (If it does not exist, an error message will be PRINTed.) There is an advantage to this that is not readily apparent and won't be, until we have explained the <DEF> key. Simply stated, the advantage is that with the <DEF> key, you can RUN a program with 2 keystrokes. More on that later.

10:PRINT"WORKING HERE BOSS":GOTO500

In this line, a program statement is executed, followed by a transfer to a line number. This example illustrates that the GOTO statement can be used in a multiple statement line (two BASIC statements with a colon between them). Each statement is treated as if it were on a separate line number. Of course, any statements which occur after the GOTO statement, on the same program line, would not be executed, as program control is transferred to another part of the program before they would be reached.

10: A=100
20: GOTO A

Using a variable to point to a line number is allowed in conjunction with the GOTO statement, as long as the line number exists. In this case the variable A is equal to 100 and the GOTO statement will 'jump' to line number 100.

10: GOTO "SECTIONA"

Here, we are using a program segment called "SECTIONA" as the target for the GOTO statement. You can use several letters to give a descriptive name to a program segment. Although this does seem to waste memory, it makes the program easier to understand when you are reading the program listings. Another example is: 10: GOTO "LABEL 1".

GOTO line number

GOTO may be executed as a direct statement from the RUN mode, as well as in a program line. When used in the RUN mode, current variable values are preserved, as opposed to the RUN statement, which clears the temporary variables.

10: GOTO (10+(100/2))

Using a calculated line number is a 'legal' operation, with the GOTO statement. In this case, the calculation will send program execution to line number 60 (10+(100/2)=60). A variable may also be used in the calculation.

Use GOTO to *jump* from one place in a program to another. A word of caution: too many GOTOs in a program can make it confusing to read the listing or follow the program logic — the computer won't have any trouble following the code, but you might. It is hard to follow the logic of programs that jump all over the place. On the other hand, using labels will help some programs when the labels themselves contain a meaning, as in this example:

190: GOTO "FINISH".

Oops! What went wrong? Mis-typed it. Trying to GOTO a line number or label that does not exist. Trying to GOTO a line number in a MERGEd program (GOTO "A" ok).

Also see: ON – ON ERROR – DEF – MERGE – RUN – ON GOTO

Program "Labels"

One of the nice features of the PC-2 is that it lets you use *program labels* – a feature not found on most larger computers.

What's a label good for? Well, you can use it instead of a line number in a GOTO or GOSUB statement. If you create *meaningful* labels, they are a lot more mnemonic (easy to remember) than line numbers and make the listings more readable. For instance,

```
650 GOTO "CALCULATE INDEX"
```

is easier to remember than

```
650 GOTO 10260
```

A label is also easier to understand when reading the program listing. To label a line, simply start the line with the desired label enclosed in quotes. Here's a sample line label:

```
10260 "CALCULATE INDEX"
```

If there is no other statement, on the program line except a label, the second quote may be omitted like this:

```
780 "RESTART
```

A label may be as simple as a single letter:

```
780 "R"
```

Here's an example of how to use labels to make the purpose of your program sections easy to remember and to keep the program code readable. The program is trivial but the idea can be applied to almost any programming task.

```
10: REM PROGRAM TO CALCULATE YOUR AGE
20: GOSUB "INITIALIZE"
30: GOSUB "INPUT"
40: GOSUB "CALCULATE"
50: GOSUB "OUTPUT"
60: GOSUB "REPEAT?"
70: END
100: "INITIALIZE"
110: WAIT 100
120: CLS
130: RETURN
200: "INPUT
210: INPUT "WHAT IS YOUR NAME? ";NM$
220: INPUT "YEAR OF BIRTH? ";BY
230: INPUT "THE CURRENT YEAR IS? "; CY
240: "GET YET" PRINT "HAVE YOU HAD A BIRTHDAY?"
250: INPUT "YET THIS YEAR (Y/N)? "; YN$
260: IF YN$<>"Y"AND YN$<>"N"THEN GOTO "GET YET"
270: RETURN
300: "CALCULATE"
310: AG=CY-BY
320: IF YN$="N"THEN GOSUB "ADJUST
330: RETURN
400: "OUTPUT
410: PRINT NM$;":"
420: PRINT "YOU ARE ";AG;" YEARS OLD.
500: "REPEAT?"
510: INPUT "REPEAT (Y/N)? "; RE$
520: IF RE$="Y"THEN GOTO "RUN"
530: IF RE$="N"THEN GOTO "RETURN"
540: GOTO "REPEAT" REM BAD USER INPUT
600: "ADJUST" AG=AG-1
610: "RETURN" RETURN
700: "RUN" CLEAR : GOTO 10
```

This is also an example of *modular* programming. Notice how lines 1Ø through 7Ø provide the 'control-structure' of the program. If you come back to this program months later and want to figure out what's going on, this program will be a lot easier to comprehend than a program written without this sort of technique.

Here are a few other special uses for labels. If you use the <DEF> key feature, the <DEF> key sequence *must* start with a label.

If you are going to merge programs, each merged program (when both programs use the same line numbers) must start with a label, or you will not be able to access *all* the program lines of all the merged programs (see MERGE).

Loops – Conditional and Unconditional

We've all seen loops. There are hula-hoop loops, crochet loops, noose loops and loop-de-loops. There are also (in case you're wondering how the subject came up) computer program loops.

Program loops are pretty similar to some of the more familiar kinds. From a programmer's perspective, there are two kinds of loops, endless loops and uh, well, the other kind. A good way to refer to that other kind (for reasons that will become clear in a moment) is 'conditional loops.'

The planet Earth revolves around the Sun. (Or does it rotate. . .uh, just a minute, let me see. . .er, yes, it revolves.) In so doing, the Earth describes a loop.

Or you might jump onto a merry-go-round, whirl about a few times, and jump off. In this case, you would be looping around the center of the merry-go-round as long as you stayed on it.

Your merry-go-round ride is a conditional loop. You remain in the loop under one condition, namely that you don't get tired of it and decide to jump off. The Earth, on the other hand, can't decide to jump out of its orbit, so its loop is of the endless variety.

You've probably seen those little whirlwinds that form for a few minutes and pick up dry leaves and the like? Picture an old sheet of newspaper that gets caught by such a whirlwind. It might circle around in the air a few times and then get dropped. This is another conditional loop. The paper stays in the loop under certain conditions — in this case, aerodynamic conditions.

Remember: conditional loops always have an escape clause, or, if you will, a loop-hole, which, under specified conditions, lets you out of the loop. Now let's consider the following program:

```
1Ø: WAIT 5Ø
2Ø: X=1
3Ø: PRINT X;
4Ø: X=X+1
5Ø: GOTO 2Ø
```

What happens when we RUN this program? First line 1Ø tells the computer how long to pause whenever a PRINT statement displays new data. Next, line 2Ø is executed, and X is assigned a value of one. Then, line 3Ø is executed, and 1 is PRINTed on the display. Next comes line 4Ø, in which X is assigned a value one greater than whatever it was before. Line 5Ø sends the computer back to line 2Ø. 2 is PRINTed on the display. Then line 4Ø changes X from 2 to 3, and line 5Ø sends us back to line 2Ø.

As you can see, this program contains an endless loop. The computer will loop through lines 2Ø through 5Ø indefinitely. If we just let it run, the program will count till the cows come home or the computer gets to a number that's too large for it to handle — a very long time, in this case.

Endless loops have their uses in programming, but often they are there by accident; they can be 'bugs.' If you write a program which suddenly stops doing anything, or does too much of the same thing over and over again, it may be caught in an accidental endless loop.

Conditional loops are one of the most frequently used programming structures. Here's an example of a conditional loop:

```
1Ø: WAIT 5Ø
2Ø: PRINT "COUNTING TO 5"
3Ø: X=Ø
4Ø: X=X+1
5Ø: PRINT X;
6Ø: IF X<>5 GOTO 4Ø
7Ø: PRINT "DONE"
```

In this case, line 1Ø sets the display pause just as it did in the previous example. Line 2Ø causes the message COUNTING TO 5 to be PRINTed on the display. Line 3Ø sets X equal to zero. Line 4Ø bumps the value of X up by 1, in the first case making it equal to 1. Line 5Ø PRINTS the value of X on the display. It PRINTs a 1 this time through the loop.

Line 6Ø contains the condition of this conditional loop. The computer is sent back to line 4Ø on the condition that X is not equal ($<>$) to 5. Since X is equal to 1 at this stage, it isn't equal to 5 (tricky logic, huh?). Therefore, the program loops back to line 4Ø where X is bumped up to 2.

The program continues looping through lines 4Ø, 5Ø and 6Ø until X is equal to 5. When line 6Ø is executed while X has a value of 5, the condition for staying in the loop is not met. (Or, you could say the condition for exiting from the loop has been met. It's all how you look at it!) Instead of looping back to line 4Ø, the program will 'fall through' to line 7Ø, which will display the word "DONE." Then the program will end.

The loop, as the word suggests, is a set of events which repeat themselves.

A *conditional loop*, such as the FOR/NEXT loop we are about to discuss, is one in which the repetition continues until a certain condition is met.

FOR/NEXT–The Conditional Loop

The FOR/NEXT loop is a conditional loop. We can think of it as a digital clock. Every time the clock comes to the next hour it adds one to the hours digit (from 3 to 4 o'clock, say). With this idea in mind we can allocate many tasks for the computer to do during the 'hour' and then let the computer repeat everything each hour until the number of hours we have set has passed.

There are three BASIC language statements that make-up the loop structure. They are FOR, TO and NEXT. The FOR/NEXT loop sets up a 'counter.' This is the FOR part of the loop. It looks like this:

```
1Ø: FOR X=1 TO 1ØØ
3Ø: NEXT X
```

The variable X is the counter. The "1" is where the counter is to start counting *from* and the "1ØØ" is where it is to count *to*. During the execution of the FOR/NEXT loop, other things may be done. Each time the NEXT statement is reached, the value of the variable used to keep track has 1 added to it, until it reaches the last value in the variable — in this case, 1ØØ. We can insert any program operations between the FOR and the NEXT part of the loop that we want. We'll insert a line 2Ø, between lines 1Ø and 3Ø, and PRINT the value of the counter:

```
5: WAIT 5
10: FOR X=1 TO 100
20: PRINT X
30: NEXT X
```

Just PRINTing the value of a counter is not a very valuable task for a sophisticated piece of equipment like the PC-2. We could insert one hundred program lines between the FOR and the NEXT statements to do any task that needs to be repeated. A good example would be the calculation of how much money we would make over a period of five years at a yearly interest rate of 9%, compounded monthly, if we started with 1ØØ dollars. Here is an example of such a program:

10: CLS	Clear the display.
20: WAIT 50	Set the WAIT value to 5Ø.
30: D=100	Set the beginning dollar amount to 1ØØ dollars.
40: FOR X=1 TO 5*12	Set the loop size to 12 months times 5 years.
50: D=D+(D*.09)/12	Calculate each month's interest and add it to the principal.
60: PRINT "MONTH";X;" =";D	PRINT the monthly results.
70: NEXT X	Loop until finished.

You can do all kinds of things with loops. Any type of a program operation that requires repetitive calculations is ideal loop material. Loops are fast, simple and effective. Use them whenever possible.

In the loop examples we have used so far, we have always added to our loop counter. Later, we shall see that the FOR/NEXT loop can be an automatic subtracting process as well. Be sure to use the same variable in the FOR and the NEXT statements; that is, use NEXTA if you used FORA.

The Primary Statement/Command

```
FOR variable = start value TO end value
NEXT variable
```

Other Forms of the Statement/Command

```
10: FOR A = 1 TO 10
20: NEXT A
```

```
10: FOR A = variable TO variable
20: NEXT A
```

```
10: FOR A = number TO number
20: NEXT A
```

```
10: FOR A = (calculation) TO (calculation)
20: NEXT A
```

```
10: FOR A = B TO 10
20: NEXT A
```

This uses a *named* variable (B, in this case) that must be previously set to the required number for the starting value and a constant (number) for the ending value. You may use any legal variable, constant or calculation for the starting and ending values.

```
10: FOR A = B TO C
20: NEXT A
```

Here we have used variables for the starting values and the ending values. Each variable must have been previously initialized with a value.

```
10: FOR X = (A/2) TO (A*10)
20: NEXT X
```

A calculation may be used for the starting and ending values. In this case the starting value is contained in the A variable and is divided by 2. The ending value is the same variable, but multiplied by 10. If A were equal to 10, the starting value would be 5 and the ending value would be 100. Using those values would cause the program to perform 95 loops.

Nested Loops

No doubt you have seen a stack of Dixie cups. They are *nested* one inside the other. We can nest loops one inside another too. Here is an example of a 'nested loop':

```
10: CLS                          Clear the display.
20: WAIT 50                      Set the WAIT value to 50.
30: D=100                        Set the beginning dollar amount
                                     to 100 dollars.
35: FOR Y=1 TO 5                 Set the outer loop to 5 years.
40: FOR M=1 TO 12                Set the inner loop to 12 months.
50: D=D+(D*.09)/12               Calculate each month's interest
                                     and add it to the principal.
60: PRINT "MONTH";X;" =";D       PRINT the monthly results.
70: NEXT M                       Loop through the number of months.
80: NEXT Y                       Loop through the number of years.
```

You will notice that two FOR counters are set up (Y and M) each with its own variable, and the loops are *closed* with a NEXT statement for each of the variables. The inner loop is the 'nested' loop. You can have loops within loops within loops within loops if you find it necessary. Be careful though, too many nested loops can spell trouble if the logic becomes too complicated.

In a nested loop, the NEXT statement is related to the closest FOR statement. If you switched the order of the NEXT statements (if line 70 was changed to NEXT Y, and line 80 to NEXT M), the inner loop, which is counted by the M variable, will never execute, because after the Y outer loop finishes, the program will crash with a NEXT without FOR error. This is because it has used up the Y counter before it got to the M counter.

The FOR/NEXT loop cannot be used in the RUN mode, and the range of numbers available to the FOR counter is limited to values from −32768 to +32767. If you wish to use the value of the FOR counter variable for processes requiring higher (or lower) values, you will have to add the difference to the counter. For instance, if you wanted to count from 33000 to 34000, your loop variable could count from 0 to 1000, and another variable can be used to represent the desired value by adding 33000 to the result of the FOR counter variable, like this:

```
5: WAIT 5
10: FOR X= 0 to 1000
20: Y= X+33000
30: PRINT Y
40: NEXT X
```

The FOR/NEXT loop is handy for a number of things such as repeating messages, counting through a list of INPUT or DATA statements, timing events, and so on. You will find that the FOR/NEXT loop will be one of the most commonly used elements in your programs.

Some suggested uses – Counting loops, timing loops or repeating procedures.

Oops! What went wrong? Mis-typed it. Wrong mode. Forgot NEXT variable – a variable is necessary. Parameters too large. Counter allowed to go one too many. FOR counter variable changed by some other operation in the loop.

Also see: STEP

STEP

You may take five giant steps and one tiny step. Remember that game called, "Mother, may I?" The STEP statement is a modifier for the FOR/NEXT loop which we talked about earlier. By adding a STEP value, you can tell the FOR/NEXT counter what amount (or size STEP) to use during the execution of the loop. If STEP is not used, the loop counter automatically adds by 1 until the counter exceeds the limit specified. Thus you could think of the FOR/NEXT command as stepping by 1 each time it goes through the loop if you do not specify a STEP size. In the following example, the value of 2 is added each time the loop is counted.

```
20: FOR X = 1 TO 100 STEP 2
30: PRINT X
40: NEXT X
```

STEP can also be used to set up a loop that counts in reverse, by using a minus value. You can see this in action by changing line 20 in the example to read:

```
20: FOR X = 100 TO 1 STEP –1
30: PRINT X
40: NEXT X
```

This will cause the numbers to PRINT in reverse order. As you can see, in order to go in reverse, even in increments of one, you must use the minus (–) sign with the step value. If you use the minus on the 1 in the original example, it will stop after one 'loop,' like this:

```
10: FOR X= 1 TO 10 STEP –1
20: PRINT X
30: NEXT X
```

This is because after –1 is added to the start (1), it is outside the given range of 1 to 10 (The counter X is zero because 1 and the –1 step add up to 0). If you try to put a minus on the 10, it will work, but there will be 11 steps (including 0). If you are obstinate enough, put –1 to –10, with a STEP of –1. You will be rewarded with a correct count down action and a free "GOTTA DO IT MY WAY" bumper sticker.

The Primary Statement/Command
```
FOR variable = start value TO finish value STEP value
```

Other Forms of the Statement/Command
```
10: FOR X = number TO number STEP number
10: FOR X = number TO number STEP negative number
10: FOR X = variable TO variable STEP variable
10: FOR X =(calculation)TO(calculation)STEP(calculation)
```

Here is an example of the STEP statement:
```
5: WAIT 10
10: FOR X = 1 TO 100 STEP 2
20: PRINT X
30: NEXT X
```

This particular example uses a STEP of 2. Since counting will start with 1, an odd number, this loop would be useful for counting in odd-numbered STEPs. A slight change (1 to 0, or 2) would cause the loop to count in even-numbered STEPs.

```
10: FOR A = 1 TO 10 STEP 2
20: NEXT A
```

This loops through 5 times changing the counter, (A), by two each time.

```
10: FOR A = 10 TO 1 STEP -1
20: NEXT A
```

counts backwards from 1Ø to 1 or . . .

```
10: FOR A = -1 TO -10 STEP -1
```

counts from –1 down to –1Ø. Then again . . .

```
10: FOR A = -1 TO 10 STEP -1
```

counts –1 and stops because the next number is outside the permitted range.

In a positive FOR/NEXT loop (without a STEP statement, or with a STEP statement that has a positive value), the starting value of the FOR counter must be less than the end value. When using a minus STEP value in the loop, the starting value must be larger than the final value.

The use of the STEP statement in a FOR/NEXT loop saves time and memory and is easier to use than setting up the counters and the tests required to do it the 'hard way,'

Some suggested uses – Repeating procedures with multiple counts. Processing a series of values that are all odd or all even. Processing data that is in some fixed format which requires a series of fixed values. Setting up indexes into an array.

Oops! What went wrong? Mis-typed it. Wrong mode. Values too large or too small. The starting number is larger than the ending number on a positive step. The starting number is smaller than the ending number on a negative step.

Also see: FOR/NEXT

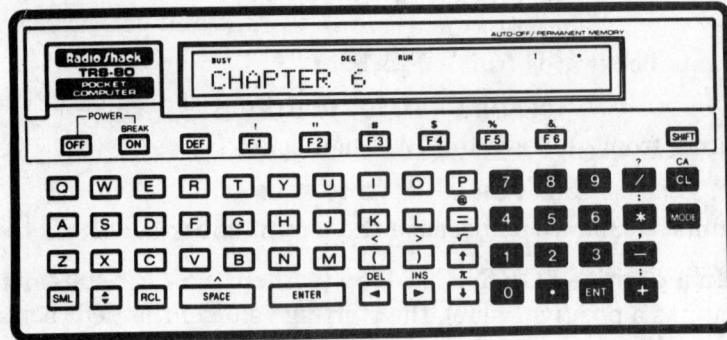

MEM

How much wood could a woodchuck chuck, if a woodchuck could chuck wood? That's a tough question. I guess it would depend on your average woodchuck or, perhaps, your average tree. Anyway, it seems that we always want to know how much, or what's left, or how big or small something is. With our PC-2, we have a need to know, from time to time, how much memory we have available. Sometimes we need to know how much memory we have available only when we are going to RUN a certain program. Other times we just want to know without any good reason. The MEM statement fills our need to know very nicely.

Using the MEM statement is like looking in a drawer or on a shelf to see how much room is left so we may put something there. In our case, the something is program lines and variables. We can look into memory with the MEM command like this:

MEM <ENTER>

As soon as this statement is executed, the amount of free memory will be PRINTed on the right side of the display. If your PC-2 does not have a 4K or 8K RAM expansion module, your display should look like this after using the MEM statement:

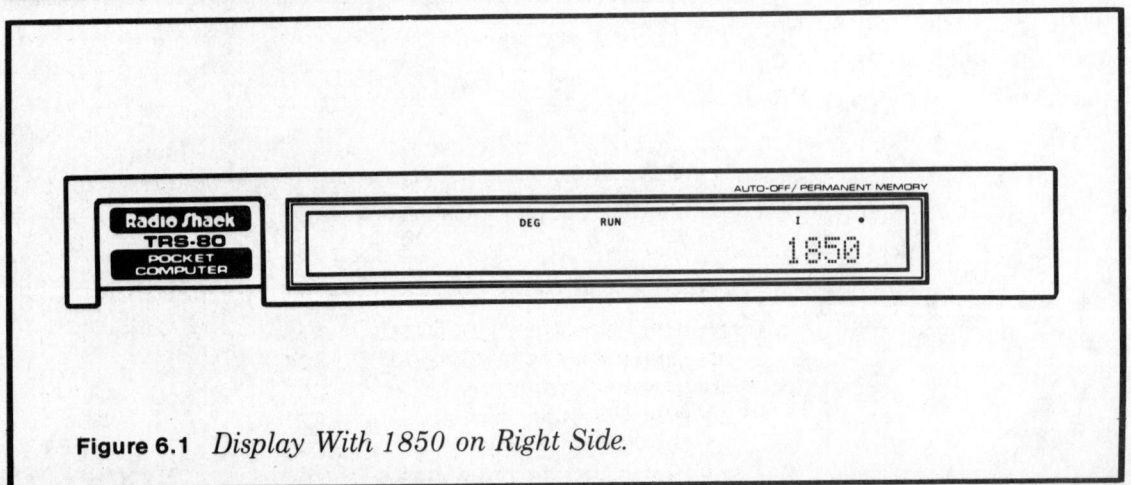

Figure 6.1 *Display With 1850 on Right Side.*

Did you notice that we didn't have to use the PRINT statement? The MEM statement can be used in PROgram as well as RUN mode.

The Primary Statement/Command
MEM

Other Forms of the Statement/Command
10: A = MEM

In the RUN or PROgram mode, type: MEM <ENTER>

MEM tells you how much memory you have left for programs.

10: PRINT MEM

When this line executes, the amount of free memory available is displayed.

10: A = MEM

Here we are using a variable to store the available memory in a program line.

MEM works in PROgram as well as RUN mode.

Some suggested uses – test to see if nearly out of memory. Keep track of how much memory is used in a program to prevent an 'out of memory' error.

Oops! What went wrong? Mis-typed it.

Also see: STATUS

INPUT

Computer output, as we have already seen, is fairly easy with the PRINT statement and its variations. So far, we have *input* data by programming it into our program with statements such as A=25. However, it is inconvenient to have to re-program the computer every time we need to change the data.

With the INPUT statement, we can change the data every time the program is RUN. Actually, the concept of data INPUT is not as strange as it would seem. In our everyday experiences we are constantly 'inputting' data. We just don't think of it as *inputting* anything — we think of it as filling out a form.

There is almost no difference between filling out a form and INPUTing data to the computer. Here is a typical "INPUT" using a form:

Name _____

Address _____

City _____ State _____ Zip _____

Age _____

We don't think anything about filling out a form. We whip out our pencil and immediately start filling in the blanks. Nothing to it. Form input even has *prompting* — a prompt is the title of each blank, like "Name," "Address," "City," "State" and "Zip." Computer INPUT is not much different. Here is the same 'form,' as we would INPUT it, on the PC-2:

```
20: INPUT"ENTER YOUR NAME  "; NA$
30: INPUT"ENTER ADDRESS     "; AD$
40: INPUT"ENTER CITY        "; CI$
50: INPUT"ENTER STATE       "; ST$
60: INPUT"ENTER ZIP         "; ZP$
70: INPUT"ENTER YOUR AGE    "; AG
```

The INPUT statement does four things. First, it PRINTs the prompt message (if there is one). Second, it halts program operation and waits for you to type the data and press the <ENTER> key. Third it causes your INPUT to be displayed, and fourth, it places the INPUT you have entered in the variable you have designated.

In this example, we have used strings for our INPUTs for everything but the 'AGE' (line 7∅), and it is a numeric variable. We could have used a numeric variable for the 'ZIP' INPUT, but numeric INPUT strips off the leading zeros, and some zip codes have zeros as beginning digits. (We have also used two letter variables that use letters from the main prompt, in this example. This makes the variable names easier to remember — NA$ is easier to remember as the string that contains the name than A$ string is.)

Our prompt message, in the INPUT statement, is the message contained between the two quote marks. In this respect, the INPUT statement behaves like the PRINT statement, except that it is unaffected by WAIT (since it always 'waits' for your INPUT).

It is not necessary to use the INPUT statement with the prompt. It can be used like this:

```
2∅: INPUT NA$
```

Of course, without prompts it would be a little difficult to know what information you wanted INPUT, but it does work. There is a slight difference between an INPUT statement with or without prompts. When using INPUT with prompting, you must always use a semicolon (;) between the last quote mark and the variable. When using INPUT *without* prompting, **never** use the semicolon. Another caution: a string INPUT cannot be longer than 16 characters — unless it has been defined by a DIM statement, which we'll get to later. For now, just remember that only 16 characters are allowed in string variables.

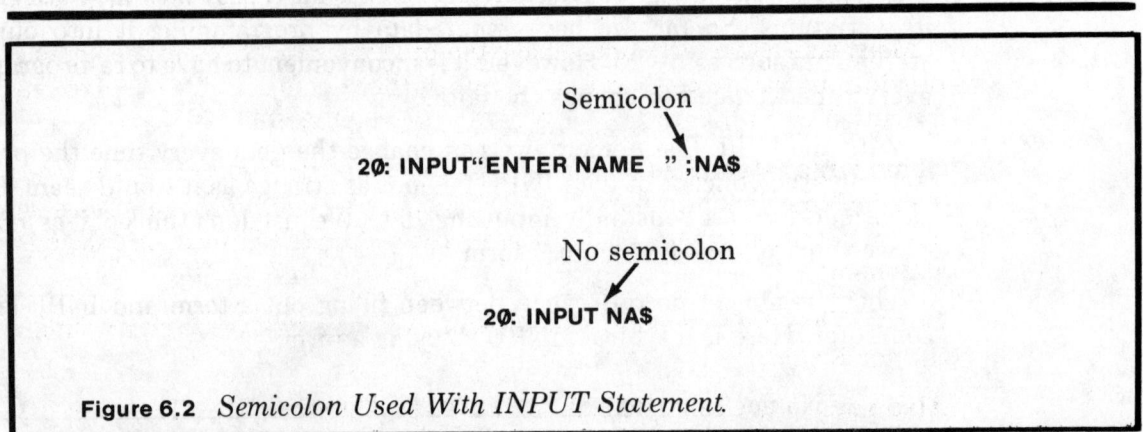

Semicolon

```
2∅: INPUT"ENTER NAME    ";NA$
```

No semicolon

```
2∅: INPUT NA$
```

Figure 6.2 *Semicolon Used With INPUT Statement.*

Here is a simple example of the INPUT statement that you can enter as a program:

```
1∅: INPUT "ENTER YOUR NAME    ";NA$
2∅: PRINT "HI, ";NA$
```

You are now prepared to write the world's greatest income tax program. Simply INPUT the data, calculate the results and PRINT the results of your calculations. It sounds so easy, doesn't it?

The Primary Statement/Command
```
INPUT variable
INPUT string variable
```

Other Forms of the Statement/Command
```
1∅: INPUT "Message";varariable
1∅: INPUT "Message";string variable
```

10: INPUT A

When this line executes, a question mark (?) will appear on the screen. The program is now waiting for a numeric value to be typed in, followed by <ENTER>. The variable A will now contain the value which was typed in.

10: INPUT"Message";A

The INPUT statement PRINTs a message, contained betwen quotes as a prompt, to indicate that you want data typed into the program. When a message is included with the INPUT statement, the question mark is not PRINTed, just the message. For a neater appearing INPUT prompt, leave a space between the last letter of the message and the final quote. Notice that a semicolon (;) is required between the final quote and the variable.

10: INPUT A$

Here we are using a string variable as the *receiver* for the INPUT statement. Up to sixteen characters may be INPUT into this named string.

10 INPUT A$(X)

This illustrates that a dimensioned array variable may be used as the receiver as well. Although we haven't discussed arrays yet, this is an important bit of information. Make a mental note of the use of arrays, and later we will examine the dimensioned array variables in more detail.

A unique feature of the INPUT statement, as used by the PC-2, is that a numeric variable (other than the receiver) may be entered to supply the required value. Let's say that the variable B has a value of 100. When the INPUT line is executed, you can type in the letter B as an answer, and A will now contain 100, the value of B. This works only with numeric variables, not with strings.

INPUT will not work in RUN mode. It can only be used in a program line.

Many times you will want to have the program get data from the keyboard, and INPUT provides us with a method to accomplish this task. It can also be used to cause program execution to stop until the <ENTER> key is pressed.

Some suggested uses – to get parameters and data from the person using your program. This includes numeric, as well as string data such as names, addresses, and the like. Any information that is likely to be different from RUN to RUN can be entered with the INPUT statement.

Oops! What went wrong? Mis-typed it. Wrong mode. Variable missing. Incorrect use of the semicolon.

Also see: INKEY$ – PRINT – INPUT # – PAUSE – WAIT

Relational Operators

For some unknown reason, explanations about computer operations are more complicated than the operation they are trying to explain. Take *relational operators,* for instance. Have you used a relational operater today? Yesterday? Well then, did you use any last month? You probably answered, "No!" but, actually, you use a form of *relational operators* every day — at least in principle. They are so commonplace that you don't even notice that you are using them. Here is a story that will illustrate what I mean:

Mr. and Mrs. Marlow and their young daughter, Tobey, walked up to the movie cashier's booth at the Kludge Street Cinema. "What's playing?" asked Mr. Marlow. "Tobey likes cowboy films. In fact, we don't want to go in unless you're showing *Home on the Buffalo.*"

"You're in luck sir," said the cashier. "*Home on the Buffalo* is just about to begin."

"Three tickets, please." said Tobey's mother. The movie cashier glanced at Tobey.

"How old are you?" she asked. "Eleven," answered Tobey, "Why?"

"Well," said the cashier, "if you're under twelve, you can get in for half price."

"Lucky us," said Mr. and Mrs. Marlow.

On her way through the lobby, Tobey noticed the refreshment stand. "May I have some candy?" she asked.

"Ok," said her father. "But if it costs more than 75 cents, you'll have to pay for it out of your own allowance."

Tobey picked out a box of Fruity-Junks. Since it cost $1.00, Tobey paid for it out of her own pocket. Candy in hand and mouth, she followed her parents into the theater.

Though the Marlows may not have realized it, they made use of three *relational operators* before they got to their seats.

The first use of a *relational operator* occurred when Mr. Marlow explained that they weren't interested in seeing the movie unless it was *Home on the Buffalo*. The relationship in question is one between the movie shown at the Kludge Street Cinema and the movie, *Home on the Buffalo*. Mr. Marlow wants the relationship to be such that the two movies are one and the same. In other words, he wants the movie being shown to *equal Home on the Buffalo*. If such is the case, the Marlows will buy tickets and watch the movie. Otherwise, they won't.

The equal sign (=) is used on the PC-2 to indicate this relationship. "A=B" is read, "A equals B" and means that A and B must be the same.

The second use of a relational operator occurred when the cashier said that Tobey could get in for half price if she were under 12. The relationship being discussed here is that between Tobey's age and the number 12. If Tobey's age is less than 12, Tobey can get in for less money.

The PC-2 uses the left-pointing caret (<) to indicate the less-than relationship. "A<B" is read, "A is less than B." It is easy to remember this because the left side of the caret is smaller than the right side.

The final use of a relational operator occurred when Tobey picked out her candy. This time the relationship was between the price of the candy and the number 75. The relationship was a *greater than* relationship. If the price of the candy is *greater than* 75 cents, she would have to pay it out of her allowence.

On the PC-2, the greater-than relationship is represented with a right-pointing caret (>). "A>B" is read, "A is greater than B." This is easy to remember because the left side of the caret is larger than the right.

Symbols such as =, < and > describe relationships and control the flow of operations. They are called *relational operators* and are used to compare one thing to another. The symbols used to perform these types of operations suggest the function they represent:

= (equal)	Tests two items for equality
> (greater than)	Tests two items to see if the first is greater than the second.
< (less than)	Tests two items to see if the first is smaller than the second.

The symbols may be used in combinations to perform two tests in one operation:

>= greater than *or* equal to.
<= less than *or* equal to.
<> not equal to — either greater than *or* less than but *not* equal.

The result of a relational operation is a condition of either true or false. To express the true/false condition, the PC-2 uses Ø as false and 1 as true, so the comparison 1Ø < 5 (ten is less than five) would equal Ø (false) and 1Ø > 5 (ten is greater than 5) would equal 1 (true). In the RUN mode, try these tests:

5>1Ø	<ENTER>	(Answer: Ø false)
5<1Ø	<ENTER>	(Answer: 1 true)
5=5	<ENTER>	(Answer: 1 true)

The numbers (1 true or Ø false) are provided for convenience, in case you want to test the conditions now and use the result later on, but usually you would do something *based* on the true or false *condition* right away, rather than use the result of 1 or Ø, as we shall see.

IF/THEN

Here is another example of something that we do every day. The PC-2 (all computers, for that matter) is capable of 'testing' conditions, and then, based on the result of the test, taking one of several possible actions. Here is another story that will relate the concept of the computer statement to something that we do every day:

We are visiting at the home of the Marlows — remember them? Mrs. Marlow is busy talking on the phone; Tobey is in the living room watching the afternoon movie on Channel 13 and Mr. Marlow and I, also in the living room, are talking about our PC-2 computers. Mr. Marlow says he is thirsty. He turns to his daughter and says, "Tobey, honey. Would you go to the kitchen, and if there are any sodas in the refrigerator, would you then bring them to us?"

Let's review Mr. Marlow's request and see if we can find the IF/THEN elements. He said, "Would you go to the kitchen, and IF there are any soda pops in the refrigerator, would you THEN bring them to us?" The IF and THEN are clearly part of the sentence structure, and there is a valid test. We could simpify Mr. Marlow's request so that it looked like this:

IF soda pops are in the refrigerator –
    THEN bring them to us.

The IF part of the sentence makes a test — IF the number of sodas in the refrigerator are greater than (>) zero. If, indeed, there were one or more sodas in the refrigerator then the result of the test would be TRUE (1), and the IF part of the test would have passed. If there were no sodas in the refrigerator, then the test would be FALSE (Ø), and the test would have failed.

In the case of a *true* answer, *then* Toby would have brought us the sodas. If the result were FALSE, she wouldn't have done anything — she would have skipped or ignored the THEN part of the sentence.

A further simplification would be:

IF soda pops >Ø
    THEN bring them

This is very close to the way you would actually write the IF/THEN statements in a computer program. We have actually simplified this to the point where we can write a simulation program. We'll use the variable SP for the number of soda pops in the refrigerator. Enter this program:

```
10: CLS
20: WAIT 100
30: INPUT "# OF SODAS IN FRIGE? "; SP
40: IF SP>0 THEN GOTO 70
50: PRINT "NO SODA"
60: GOTO 30
70: PRINT "ENJOY THE REAL THING"
80: GOTO 30
```

Line number 40 represents Mr. Marlow's request and is almost identical (at least in concept to our super-simplified version); "IF soda pops >0" is the same as "IF SP>0", and "THEN bring them" is translated to "THEN GOTO 70", which represents bringing the soda pops.

Here is a commented version of the program:

```
10: CLear the Screen
20: Set the WAITS to 100 for the PRINT statement
30: (INPUT) the number of sodas in the refrigerator
      The INPUT will be in variable SP
40: (IF) the number of sodas (SP) is greater than (>) 0. . .
      . . .(THEN) go to line number 70.
   (IF) the number of sodas (SP) is NOT greater than 0, don't
      do anything; 'fall through' this test and execute
      line number 50
50: (PRINT) the message, "NO SODA" and WAIT 100 time units
60: (GOTO) line number 30
70: (PRINT) the mesage, "ENJOY", and WAIT 100 time units
80: (GOTO) line number 30
```

You will find that almost every computer statement and concept parallels some everyday activity that we do and IF/THEN is just one more example of how easy computer concepts really are.

The Primary Statement/Command
```
10: IF variable = value THEN (execute) statement
```

Other Forms of the Statement/Command
```
10: IF statement is true THEN (execute) statement
10: IF statement is false THEN (execute) statement
```

Note: in the following forms, variable and value are interchangable and can be:

variable – variable
value – value
variable – value
value – variable

A value may be a *constant* such as the number 5, or a variable or a calculated result, such as 5*10+A, or any combination of constants, variables and calculations.

```
10: IF variable > value THEN (execute) statement
10: IF variable < value THEN (execute) statement
10: IF variable <> value THEN (execute) statement
10: IF variable >= value THEN (execute) statement
10: IF variable =< value THEN (execute) statement
```

Here is another example that will demonstrate the IF/THEN statement:

```
1Ø: INPUT A
2Ø: IF A = 1 THEN PRINT "ONE" : END
3Ø: PRINT "NOT ONE" : END
```

The IF/THEN tests for a condition, and based on the result of the test, performs some other action, like adding two values together, going to another line, and so on.

1Ø: IF X = 1 THEN LET X = 3

In this instance, we are checking the value of X against a fixed value. When this line executes, X is tested for the value of 1. If X is equal to 1, then the rest of the line is executed, and X will be equal to 3. If the value of X was not equal to 1, then the rest of the line is skipped. The logic is the same as that in the sentences we are using to describe it!

1Ø: IF X = 1 THEN "X"

Here, BASIC will look for a program called "X" and will go to the line number that has that label. This is similiar to using the <DEF> key to RUN a program, which will be covered later.

1Ø: IF X = 1 THEN Y

In this case, the numeric variable Y is used to contain the line number to GOTO. Again, GOTO is implied in this line.

1Ø: IF X = 1 CLS

This is an example of using an executable statement (other than LET) with the IF/THEN test. When this line executes, IF X equals 1 THEN the screen is cleared (CLS). As you can see, THEN is optional if an executable statement (like CLS, PRINT, STOP, etc.) follows the test.

You must use THEN after the IF test in some cases, so for now use it all the time. Unlike some BASICs you will encounter, the PC-2 does not have an ELSE statement to bypass the IF/THEN test if it fails. IF/THEN can only be used in program lines, not in the immediate mode.

Special note concerning the LET statement

1Ø: IF X = 1 THEN LET X = 3

Say, this looks familiar! Actually, the point we want to make is that if you are going to assign a value to a new variable after the IF test passes, you **must** use the word LET to assign the value. If LET is omitted, BASIC will assume that the next thing it will encounter is either a statement that can be executed or a line number (or program name) to GOTO.

Oops! What went wrong? Mis-typed it. Wrong mode. Forgot THEN or LET in your program line.

Also see: NOT – AND – OR

CLEAR

CLEAR is to the variables in memory what CLS is to the display. It will not get rid of the program — only the variables and their associated values. Simply stated, CLEAR erases all variables. In the example below, the CLEAR statement in line 3Ø erases the value of A, so that line 4Ø will PRINT Ø, because A no longer has a value assigned to it. If any other variables were stored, it would have erased them too. CLEAR also works in the PROgram and RUN mode as a direct statement.

```
 5: WAIT 50
10: A = 10
20: PRINT A
30: CLEAR
40: PRINT A
```

The first time A is PRINTed, it is equal to 50. After the CLEAR statement is executed, it is reset to 0, and PRINT A displays the result of using tthe CLEAR statement.

The Primary Statement/Command
CLEAR

Other Forms of the Statement/Command
10: CLEAR

CLEAR <ENTER>

This statement can be used in either PROgram or RUN mode.

10: CLEAR

This example uses the statement in a program line. There are no additional parameters attached to this statement. All variables are CLEARed to zero or null values.

The PC-2's main memory variables are erased when you RUN a program, but the fixed area variables are cleared only with CLEAR or NEW. It is necessary to use the CLEAR statement when you are going to use any of the 'primary' variables, that is to say, *single* letter variable names.

Two letter variables and dimensioned array variables are automatically CLEARed when you enter the RUN statement. Single letter variables are not affected by the RUN statement — only the CLEAR statement.

No variables are cleared if GOTO or a <DEF> key is used to RUN a program.

Some suggested uses – use the CLEAR statement at the beginning of any program, that needs no previous variables, to be sure all are cleared before use (a safety precaution). CLEAR also resets the variables to zero with one command.

Oops! What went wrong? Mis-typed it.

Also see: RUN – GOTO – NEW – NEW0

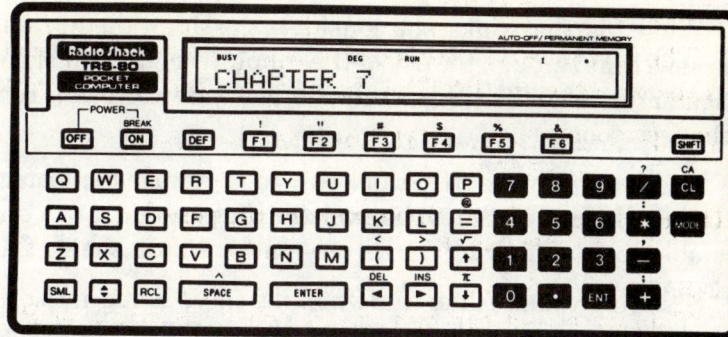

Subroutines

Are you ready for another story? Too bad, I'm going to tell one anyway . . . .

I'd like you to meet Martha Fringorbler. Martha is a busy woman. She's a professional writer. She works at home in an office she converted from an unused guest-bedroom. She also refinishes furniture in the garage; she does all this on top of her normal day-to-day housekeeping.

All this work makes Martha thirsty. She frequently goes to the kitchen, gets a glass of ice water, and brings it back to wherever she's working at the moment, so she can sip while she labors.

Being the busy person that she is, Martha decides she doesn't have time to waste running to and from the kitchen all day. So she purchases a domestic robot named Ydnat Rewot. (Oh, did I forget to tell you? This story is taking place in the not too distant future – say, in Octember of 1984.)

Martha has never dealt with a robot before. After spending a little while with it, she concludes that Ydnat is an obedient idiot with a perfect memory. Once she describes a routine, Ydnat never forgets how to do it. But she has to describe the routine in minute detail.

For instance, when Martha is refinishing an old rocking chair, she decides to have Ydnat bring her a drink. In the process of describing how to bring water to the garage, she has to tell Ydnat to walk to the kitchen, open the china cabinet, remove a glass, bring it to the refrigerator, open the freezer, remove some ice and put it in the glass, walk over to the sink, turn on the cold water, let it run a minute, fill the glass almost to the brim, and then bring the glass of ice-water to the garage and hand it to her.

An hour later, when Martha is working in her office, she wants another glass of water. She askes Ydnat to bring her the water as he had before. Ydnat seems to have it all together until the task is nearly finished. He finds the kitchen and fills a glass with ice and water. However, instead of bringing it to Martha in the office, he carries it to the garage, as he had been instructed to do.

By the time Martha finds Ydnat, the ice has melted and the water is warm. Martha leads

68

Ydnat to her office and once again describes the process of getting water. She has to explain about the cabinet, the refrigerator, the sink and everything all over again. But this time, she tells him to bring it to the *office*.

While Martha drinks, she considers the situation. At first, she despairs of ever being able to save time through the use of the robot. It seems as if she will have to go through the whole rigamarole of telling Ydnat how to get water to every room in the house every time she changes rooms.

Suddenly, Martha thinks of a way to re-phrase her instructions so that she will only have to state them once. After she explains the procedure to Ydnat using the new instructions, he is able to fetch a drink for her no matter where she is. Can you guess what Martha says?

She simply tells Ydnat that when she says "Bring me a drink!" he is to go to the kitchen, do the glass, ice and water stuff, and then RETURN *to wherever he started from*.

By separating the description of how to prepare the ice-water from the description of where to bring it, Martha has created a *subroutine*. Martha can cause Ydnat to execute the subroutine (send the robot for water) from any room in the house. Because of the RETURN instruction at the end of the Ydnat's 'fetch water routine,' he will always be able to find the right place to deliver the results.

When writing a program, we will often want to perform some function over and over again, just like Martha. Rather than writing the same program code each time we need to use it, we can employ a *subroutine* to do the job.

Let's say that you wish to clear the screen and PRINT a particular phrase, such as 'PRESS ENTER,' at several places in your program. Instead of repeating the same program lines over and over, you can write a subroutine to take care of these chores and 'jump' to it whenever you need it.

Once the subroutine has completed its task, program execution is RETURNed to the original place from which it was called. Now we'll look at the statements used to create and 'call' subroutines.

GOSUB

GOSUB is a BASIC language statement that means 'GO to the SUBroutine.' It is pure simplicity to use. All that is necessary to use it is to give GOSUB some sort of address or pointer to 'jump' to, which is usually a line number like this:

10: GOSUB 500

GOSUB operates with another statement: RETURN. The RETURN statement is used at the end of the subroutine and causes control to return to the statement *following* the GOSUB statement. Here is an example that will illustrate the point: (Don't forget to type NEW before entering this program.)

```
 10: WAIT 100
 20: GOSUB 200
 30: PRINT "I'M AT LINE 30"
 40: GOSUB 200
 50: PRINT "I'M AT LINE 50"
 60: GOSUB 200
 70: PRINT "I'M AT LINE 70"
 80: GOSUB 200
 90: PRINT "I'M AT LINE 90"
100: GOSUB 200
110: PRINT "I'M AT LINE 110"
```

```
120: GOSUB 200
130: PRINT "I'M AT LINE 130"
140: END
190: REM – LINE 200 SUBROUTINE –
200: PRINT "I'M AT LINE 200"
210: RETURN
```

By RUNning this program, you will demonstrate to yourself how the GOSUB works. Wait! there is more. GOSUB is more versatile than just being able to use line numbers. Here is the same program with a couple of modifications. It uses "labels" and "calculated" addresses.

```
10: WAIT 100
12: A = 100
14: SR$ = "LINE 200 ROUTINE"
20: GOSUB SR$
30: PRINT "I'M AT LINE 30"
40: GOSUB "LINE 200 ROUTINE"
50: PRINT "I'M AT LINE 50"
60: GOSUB A * 2
70: PRINT "I'M AT LINE 70"
80: GOSUB (A * 10)/5
90: PRINT "I'M AT LINE 90"
100: GOSUB "LINE 200 ROUTINE"
110: PRINT "I'M AT LINE 110"
120: GOSUB A + A
130: PRINT "I'M AT LINE 130"
140: END
190: REM – LINE 200 SUBROUTINE –
200: "LINE 200 ROUTINE"
210: PRINT "I'M AT LINE 210"
220: RETURN
```

This example uses the GOSUB statement in every way possible. At line 12, we have set the value of A to 100. Line 20 uses a string variable for GOSUB's 'label' address. Line 40 however, uses the 'label' method of identifying the subroutine we want to use. Lines 60, 80 and 120 use a 'calculated address' to locate the desired subroutine.

The Primary Statement/Command
GOSUB line number

Other Forms of the Statement/Command
10: GOSUB 100

The GOSUB statement sends program execution to the specified subroutine.

10: GOSUB 100
When BASIC executes this line, the subroutine beginning at line 100 will be executed.

10: GOSUB "A"
10: GOSUB "SEGMENT1"
This form illustrates that you can GOSUB to a named program segment, as well as a line number.

10: GOSUB A
10: GOSUB A$
Here, the line number or label (program segment name) is contained in a variable, which is permitted in the PC-2.

GOSUB statements are useful to save memory, and to save typing in the same routines over and over.

Some suggested uses – in INPUT and prompt routines that are used extensively in a program, the GOSUB can make an enormous difference in program size (smaller) and ease of use. Sometimes it is easier to jump to a subroutine to do a complex operation than it would be to use the same program code over and over.

Oops! What went wrong? Mis-typed it. Wrong mode. Wrong variable values. Line does not exist. No RETURN statement.

Also see: ON – RETURN – GOTO

RETURN

As we have seen in GOSUB above, the RETURN statement cannot be used alone. It must be used with the GOSUB statement in the actual subroutine itself. RETURN is the last statement of a subroutine. RETURN tells BASIC to go back to the next statement *after* the GOSUB was executed, to execute the next statement in the program.

```
 5: WAIT 100
10: GOSUB 40
20: PRINT"I'M AT LINE 20"
30: END
40: PRINT"I'M AT LINE 40"
50: RETURN
```

The Primary Statement/Command
```
100: RETURN
```
200: RETURN

When this line is encountered, control returns to the next statement following the GOSUB that called the subroutine.

All subroutines must end with a RETURN statement.

Oops! What went wrong? Mis-typed it. Used RETURN without GOSUB. Wrong mode. Forgot to end subroutine with a RETURN.

Also see: GOSUB

ARUN

Another way to RUN a program . . . here is another short story that will give you the concept of one of the PC-2's unique BASIC language statements. I'd like you to meet a fellow with a very unusual name: Mr. Nomel Supp.

Mr. Nomel Supp has remarkable night vision. In fact, to all intents and purposes, he can see in the dark as well as he can in the daylight.

Mr. Supp's cat-like vision is matched only by his parsimoniousness. He is very concerned about his monthly electric bill. To reduce his utility costs, he installed a special switch on the outside of his refrigerator. He calls it his 'auto' switch because it controls the circuit that makes the inside light come on automatically when the door is opened.

Mr. Supp normally keeps the switch in the down position. This prevents the light from turning on at any time. Since he can see anyway, this is a good way to save electricity.

When Mr. Supp's friends come to visit, they can reactivate the refrigerator light by throwing the auto-switch to the up position. This causes the light to turn on automatically whenever the door is opened.

The ARUN command is similar to Mr. Supp's switch. If there is no ARUN statement in the PC-2, the computer won't do anything special when you turn it on. That is like Mr. Supp's refrigerator when he has the switch in the off position.

If, on the other hand, the first statement in a program is ARUN, the PC-2 will automatically run the program as soon as the computer is turned on. That is like Mr. Supp's refrigerator when a guest has moved the switch to the up position to make the light come on whenever the door is opened. Try this very short program to see how it works. First enter the program; then go to RUN mode and turn the computer off. Now, turn it on . . . .

```
10: ARUN
20: PRINT"HI THERE"
```

The Primary Statement/Command
```
10: ARUN
```

ARUN (or Automatic RUN), causes the first program in memory to RUN when the PC-2 is turned on. Of course, the second program line can be a GOTO, and you can jump to any program you wish.

10: ARUN

The ARUN statement must appear as the first line of the first program in memory in order for it to execute, as you can see in this example.

There may be times when you would like the PC-2 to instantly start a program as soon as it is turned on. With ARUN you can cause this to happen.

Some suggested uses – games or reminder programs such as time and date or an 'alarm clock' program. Use ARUN as the first line of a program that you use all the time. Example: suppose you were an engineer and constantly used a particular calculation. ARUN could run a menu program that would let you select one of several programs you had in memory all the time.

Oops! What went wrong? Mis-typed it. Wrong mode. ARUN is not the first statement in memory. The PC-2 was not turned off with the <OFF> key, but turned itself off.

Also see: RUN – <DEF> key – FUNCTION key

More on PRINT

The PRINT statement is the most usual method of outputting data used by BASIC. Usually, PRINT causes some information to be displayed on the screen, but when used in combination with other statements, PRINT can be a very powerful tool, which can do everything from supply a pattern, or 'format' for the data displayed to directing the data to other devices, such as the printer/plotter and cassette recorder. PRINT can even be used to create 'graphics' on the screen or printer, as we shall see in a later section.

PAUSE — PRINT Again!

I told you that PRINT was a versatile statement. The PAUSE statement is a special type of PRINT statement. So far, when we have wanted to PRINT something without having to press the <ENTER> key after every PRINT statement, we have used the WAIT command to set how long the PRINTed message will stay on the display. There is an easier way — the PAUSE statement.

PAUSE is a PRINT with an automatic one second WAIT built into it *if* it is followed by another PAUSE or PRINT statement. If there is no other PRINT or PAUSE statement, then the message will remain on the screen until a CLS statement is executed; however, the computer still stops execution of the next statement until the one-second delay has passed.

Here is a brief example using PAUSE:

```
10: FOR X=1 TO 10
20: PAUSE "WARNING"
30: CLS
40: BEEP 5
50: NEXT X
```

The Primary Statement/Command
```
10: PAUSE
```

Other Forms of the Statement/Command
```
10: PAUSE "message"
```

The PAUSE statement causes program execution to stop for about one second before continuing. This statement also allows a message to be PRINTed on the display while the program is in this 'holding pattern.' It's a red light on the 'program road' that lets the program automatically continue after PAUSEing and PRINTing a message. PAUSE may also be used without a message. With this technique, you may introduce one second delays into the program — the reason for the delay is left to your own creative genius.

10: PAUSE

When this program line executes, the program will pause for about 1 second, then continue on.

10: PAUSE"message"

In this example, the word "message" (that is, whatever is between the quotes), will be PRINTed on the display while the program pauses.

10: PAUSE A$

Here the message is contained in a string variable. The message will be PRINTed as though it were between the quotes as in the previous example.

10: PAUSE A

Here, the PAUSE statement will PRINT the value of the numeric variable A, while program execution is suspended for one second.

The PAUSE statement can be used to slow the computer down once in a while, so we mere humans can see what's happening. This is different from an INPUT prompt in that it does not wait for any input, and differs from WAIT because it executes directly, while WAIT modifies the length of time a PRINT statement is delayed. PAUSE has no effect on the PRINT statement.

The PAUSE statement can use the same *modifiers* (comma, semicolon, etc.) as the PRINT statement.

Some suggested uses – this could be used to display messages to the operator about what's happening in a program, but does not require him to pay attention if he doesn't want to, as the program will continue without his attention. Without the message feature, it will leave whatever is displayed on the screen long enough to be read if desired.

Oops! What went wrong? Mis-typed it. Wrong mode. Forgot the quotes on a string literal.

Also see: PRINT – WAIT

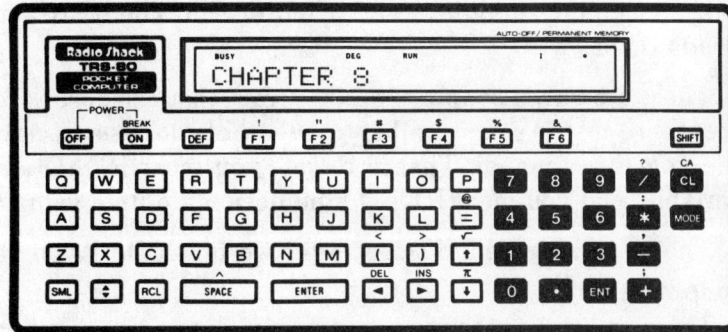

DATA

You have probably heard the word 'data' being used to refer to any body, or group, of information which is available about a certain subject or group of subjects. Scientists are always running about gathering data, as are census takers, pollsters and the like. In fact, we are all gathering data all the time, – when we read a news story, study our school books or even when we watch television. Sometimes, the data is not too important (or doesn't seem to be at the time), but we are always taking it in, anyway. As this constant data input flows through our brains, it is pretty much sorted out for future reference or discarded as unnecessary, without our taking particular notice of the process.

The computer has to deal with data in particular ways, and as we have seen, it can be INPUT from the keyboard, directly from constant information in a program line (such as A$="HI THERE"), or (as we shall see) it can be read from within a program line by using the DATA statement. DATA statements are a compact way to store moderate amounts of data for program use.

The DATA statement is used with another statement: READ. However, before we can READ anything, we first have to store the data by using the DATA statement.

The Primary Statement/Command
>   10: DATA item 1, item 2, item 3, . . .

Other Forms of the Statement/Command
>   10: DATA number,number,number
>   10: DATA "string","string","string"
>   10: DATA "string", number,"string"
>   10: DATA variable,variable,variable

The DATA statement informs the program that the information on that line is to be used by the READ statement. When BASIC encounters a DATA line, it ignores it (like it would a REMark line) and goes on to the next program line that can be executed. As you can see, each DATA item is separated from the previous one by a comma, which is used to tell BASIC where the next DATA item starts.

When using variables in the DATA statements, make sure that the variable has been initialized to your desired value before trying to read it; otherwise, it will contain a zero.

The DATA statements in our computer are somewhat like a notebook page that the PC-2 references when the need arises.

DATA statements are very easy to use. You can put them anywhere you like. They can be at the beginning, middle or end of a program. The READ statement will find them when it needs them.

There are only a couple of minor errors that can occur. To avoid those errors, make sure that there are the same number (or more) of *data items* as there are READs and be sure that the *data types* match. That is to say, you must READ a string data item using a string variable, and you must READ a numeric data item using a numeric variable.

The next thing we'll discuss, after we finish DATA, is the READ statement.

10: DATA 1,2

This is a line containing two items of data – the numbers 1, and 2.

10: DATA "dog","cat"

In this form, the data is in the form of strings: the words "dog" and "cat", which are contained between quotes. The two forms may be intermixed in a line, so long as the correct variable types are used to read them.

10: DATA X,Y

When you use this form, you must remember to have previously initialized the variables with a value; otherwise, they will contain zeros when read by the READ statement.

The DATA statement can be used to store data that your program will need to use over and over again, or which will appear in array storage.

Some suggested uses – to fill arrays with special information, storing graphics data, storing data in one place that may need editing or additions, such as in a name, address list or a phone list. To store machine-language routines or data.

Oops! What went wrong? Mis-typed it. Wrong mode. Forgot commas. Wrong data type (strings or numeric).

Also see: RESTORE – READ

READ

We have figured out how to store data within a program. Now we need to know how to use it.

The READ statement actually READs the data that is contained in the DATA statements starting with the first DATA line (or the next item of available data, if some has already been read). After READing the DATA, the data pointer (a secret counter that BASIC maintains) automatically points to the next available item of data, if there is one. Later, we shall see how we can manipulate RESTORE's hidden pointer, to suit our needs.

Below is an easy demonstration of the READ and DATA statements. You will notice that we made the variable A equal to zero. This is to 'prove' that the value contained in A was actually read by the READ statement.

```
10: DATA 1,2,"DATA ","TEST"
20: WAIT 100
30: A = 0
40: READ A,B
50: READ A$,B$
40: PRINT A,B
50: PRINT A$;B$
```

The Primary Statement/Command
10: READ variable

Other Forms of the Statement/Command
10: READ A,B,C,D$

10: READ A

In this form, the READ statement is looking for a numeric variable. When it finds a DATA line (or the next item of data), it will assign the number to the variable A.

10: READ A$

In this example, the READ statement expects to find a string constant (between quotes) or a string variable (such as B$) with another string as the next data item. When the line has executed, A$ will contain the data.

10: READ A$,A,B$

Here we are READing three types of data in the same line. First, A$ is read, then the numeric variable A, and finally, B$ is read. An appropriate DATA line for this READ statement would look like this: 20: DATA "DOG",2,"CAT"

If this were the DATA line encountered by the READ statement in the example, the variables would be read as A$ = "DOG", A = 2 and B$ = "CAT".

The use of DATA in a program can make your program more compact. It also provides the ability to manipulate the contents of variables to suit your needs and allows you to set up values that can be easily altered. Use the READ statement to access the DATA in your program.

DATA can also be read from one numeric variable to another, as in the case of:

10: X = 5
20: READ Y
30: DATA X

After Y is read, it will contain the value contained in the variable X.

Oops! What went wrong? Mis-typed it. Wrong mode. Wrong type of variable (string or numeric value).

Also see: RESTORE – DATA – INPUT #

RESTORE

RESTORE resets BASIC's DATA pointer. Each time a READ statement is executed, the DATA pointer is increased by 1. When all the data items have been read, the pointer must be RESTOREd if you wish to reREAD the data, or an 'Out of Data' error will occur. In the PC-2's BASIC, the DATA pointer may be RESTOREd to any DATA line in the program, or to a given program area (by using the name of the program, such as "A") if more than one program is in memory.

This will illustrate the point: When you read a book, you begin reading at the first page. If you have already read some of it, you may want to review an earlier page, so you go back (RESTORE your place, so to speak) to a previously read page and begin reading again. This command tells the PC-2 to go back to the beginning or to an earlier 'page' of its data notebook.

RESTORE is quite versatile. You can RESTORE all of the data or you can RESTORE data beginning at a specific line number.

10: RESTORE
20: WAIT 100

```
30: READ A,B,A$,B$
40: PRINT A$;B$
50: RESTORE 80
60: READ A
70: PRINT A
80: DATA 10,20
90: DATA "ONE","TWO"
```

The Primary Statement/Command
```
RESTORE
```

Other Forms of the Statement/Command
```
10: RESTORE
10: RESTORE 10
10: RESTORE "A"
10: RESTORE variable
```

10: RESTORE
In this case, the DATA pointer is reset to point to the first program line with a DATA statement.

10: RESTORE 1000
Here, the DATA pointer is reset to line number 1000 instead of the beginning of the program. The line number referenced in the RESTORE statement does not have to be a DATA line. If it is not a DATA line, the READ statement will go find the first data line after the one to which the pointer was RESTOREd. If a line number is used, however, it must exist as a valid line in the program.

10: RESTORE "A"
In this example, the DATA pointer is RESTOREd to the beginning of a program called "A" and labeled with that letter. A label can be a short phrase which will make the program easier to understand, such as:

100: "INFO LIST" DATA 10,157,99,37,64

Using this label will require a label exactly like the one used in line one-hundred: RESTORE"INFO LIST". Don't forget to include any spaces that may be in the label.

10: RESTORE A
This example uses a variable to restore the DATA pointer. You can also use a calculated line number, such as A*5, or any combination of arithmetic operators.

Whenever you wish to reuse data contained by a DATA statement, RESTORE provides you with a method to start at any given DATA line.

Let's use a program, like a mailing list for example, to see how the RESTORE statement can be useful. In our program, we are going to PRINT a list with labels for each line:

```
Name
Address
City
State
Zip code
```

Note, this example uses *array variables*, which are explained in a later chapter.

Now, we want to use these labels in conjunction with the correct data for each person, so that data would be stored in an array. To make it easy, let's use a double-dimensioned array (we'll get to arrays soon, and we wouldn't have used them yet except that this is too good to pass up).

The program could read like this:

```
10: WAIT 100
19: REM   NUMBER OF PEOPLE ON LIST = 10
20: FOR X = 1 to 10
30: PRINT"NAME ";A$(X,1)
40: PRINT"ADDRESS ";A$(X,2)
50: PRINT"CITY ";A$(X,3)
60: PRINT"STATE ";A$(X,4)
70: PRINT"ZIP CODE ";A$(X,5)
80: NEXT X
```

A better way to do it would be to READ the DATA for each label, something like this:

```
10: WAIT 100
20: FOR X = 1 TO 10
30: RESTORE
40: FOR Y = 1 TO 5
50: READ A$
60: PRINT A$;"-";A$(X,Y)
70: NEXT Y
80: NEXT X
90: DATA "NAME", "ADDRESS", "CITY", "STATE", "ZIP CODE"
```

This approach works the same, but shows how you can re-use the DATA each time through the program with the RESTORE statement in line 2Ø. If you have other DATA statements in the program, you can RESTORE to the line which contains them, or you could READ the DATA into another array and use it as much as you like:

```
10: WAIT 100
20: RESTORE
30: FOR X = 1 TO 5
40: READ N$(X)
50: NEXT X
60: FOR X = 1 TO 10
70: FOR Y = 1 TO 5
80: PRINT N$(Y);" ";A$(X,Y)
90: NEXT Y
100: NEXT X
110: DATA "NAME", "ADDRESS", "CITY", "STATE", "ZIP CODE"
```

Note – array A$(X,Y) would contain the data whereas N$(Y) would contain the data names such as ADDRESS, CITY, etc.

Some suggested uses – manipulation of tables such as tax tables. Any place in which data must be reused.

Oops! What went wrong? Mis-typed it. Wrong mode. Line number or label does not exist.

Also see: READ – DATA

my 10, 43

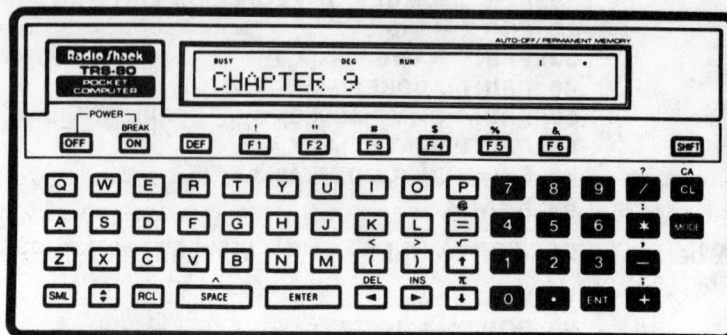

Parentheses

Parentheses are those two little curved brackets that are used in all kinds of ways. They are usually used to make a parenthetical expression (like this). There are two of these little devils. This one is called a 'left parenthesis' or an 'open parenthesis': (and this one is called (HA!) a 'right parenthesis' or a 'close parenthesis':).

On a computer, they have another use — they tell the computer the order in which an arithmetic, logical or mathmetical calculation is to be made.

When performing complex math or logical operations on the PC-2, it is often necessary to separate parts of a calculation so that the correct results will be obtained. For instance, enter the following program and RUN it — the results are striking!

```
5: WAIT Ø
1Ø: PRINT 1Ø*15+5/5;
2Ø: PRINT (1Ø*15)+5/5;
3Ø: PRINT (1Ø*15+5)/5;
4Ø: PRINT 1Ø*(15+5/5);
5Ø: PRINT 1Ø*(15+5)/5
6Ø: GOTO 6Ø
```

Your display will look like this:

151 151 31 16Ø 4Ø

You'll notice that the first two numbers of our printout are the same, while the rest are different. The only difference in each line is the placement of the parentheses. The reason is because the PC-2 (in fact, most computers) do multiplication and division before they do addition and subtraction. In the first two lines, the math expressions were evaluated like this:

$$1Ø * 15 = 15Ø \qquad 5 / 5 = 1 \qquad 15Ø + 1 = 151$$

Notice that the parentheses in line number 2Ø made no difference at all. That's because the parentheses enclosed the numbers and their arithmetic operators in the same order in which they would have been evaluated had the parentheses not been there at all.

In line number 3Ø, the result was 31. Here is how that answer was arrived at:

$$(1Ø * 15 = 15Ø \quad 15Ø + 5 = 155) \qquad 155 / 5 = 31$$

Line number 4Ø obtained the following results — note that the order in which the calculations are presented is the same order as the computer does them — not the order in which they are programmed:

$$(5 / 5 = 1 \quad 15 + 1 = 16) \qquad 16 * 1\emptyset = 16\emptyset$$

Finally we arrive at line 5Ø:

$$(5 + 5 = 2\emptyset) \quad 2\emptyset * 1\emptyset = 2\emptyset\emptyset \quad 2\emptyset\emptyset / 5 = 4\emptyset$$

You can see that parentheses can be very important to your calculations. Their use can make all the difference in the world. If you are unsure of a particular calculation's order, especially a very complex one, use parentheses to control your results. Parentheses can also be 'nested' like this:

```
1Ø: PRINT 5.33+((1Ø*15)/(5*22+9)+12*12)
```

The innermost calculations will be completed first — then those in the outermost, and finally, those outside the parentheses.

RND

RND is short for 'RaNDom number.' A random number is one that is picked out of thin air, so to speak — it can be any number — like when someone says, 'pick any number,' so you pick one out of your head. Or, you could say it was just like picking a number out of a hat.

Random numbers are the perfect answer for 'computer simulations,' that is, programming a make-believe situation that is supposed to represent a real-life situation so that it may be studied. Many games can be 'computer simulations.'

One of the easiest games to simulate is a dice game. For an example, we'll use just one die. A single die has six sides, and they are numbered one to six. With the RND statement, we'll simulate rolling a die 1Ø times:

```
5: WAIT Ø
1Ø: FOR X = 1 TO 1Ø
2Ø: PRINT RND 6;
3Ø: NEXT X
4Ø: GOTO 4Ø
```

When you RUN this program, you'll see a series of numbers PRINTed across the display. Each number represents a different 'roll' of the die. Each time you RUN it, there will be a different series of numbers — a series of *random* numbers. The value immediately after the RND statement (6) determines the maximum value of the random number generated. The smallest number RND will generate is 1 when the specified number is a number greater than 1.

The Primary Statement/Command
RND number

Other Forms of the Statement/Command
1Ø: variable = RND variable
1Ø: variable = RND (calculation)

1Ø: A = RND 1ØØ
When this line executes, the numeric variable A will contain some value from 1 through 1ØØ.

10: A = RND 0

In this form, using 0 as the random number parameter, a decimal value in the range of 0 to 1 will be returned, but the result will never be 0 or 1. Actually, any number less than 1 will do the same thing — not just 0. However, 0 is much simpler. If you do use RND1, you will *always* get a 1 as your random number.

10: A = RND (10*2+10)

The PC-2 will look at the results of operations inside parentheses, if they are used, for its final value. If, for example, you want the value used by RND to be the result of 10*2+10, you would use the form RND (10*2+10). On the other hand, RND 10*2+10 will use 10 as the random value, then multiply the result by 2 and add 10, which will return a somewhat different answer than you may expect.

Remember, if the result of the calculation is 1, you will get a random value of 1. However, if it is *less than* 1, but *greater than* or *equal* to 0, then a value between 0 and 1 will be returned. A negative number (less than 0) will cause an error.

One of the big limitations of any computer is that it has no 'imagination.' It can only do EXACTLY what it is told to do in program form. Many times, we want the computer to show some imagination, especially in artificial intelligence research.

The RND function gives you the ability to put some form of 'unpredictability' into the computer, which is (you may have noticed) disgustingly predictable in many situations. Another use is in games, where we need to be unpredictable also, or it would be too easy to win (and boring besides!). RND can be used in RUN and PROgram mode.

Some suggested uses – games, artificial intelligence, statistical research. Computer simulations or anything that needs some form of unpredictability.

Oops! What went wrong? Mis-typed it. Forgot value.

Also see: RANDOM

RANDOM

We just told you that the RND statement returns some value from 1 through the value specified. But, there is a fly in the ointment. This is not a *true* random value, as the name of the RND statement suggests. Rather, it is a number based on a given starting value, somewhere in the dark memories of the PC-2.

For most applications, the value returned will be random enough, but you can get a more random value by using the RANDOM statement. To test this out, you can type in the sample die-rolling program we used for the RND function. Now RUN it several times but between each RUN turn the PC-2 off, — then on.

Got the same values each time, right?! Thats not very 'random.' Now do it again, but type RANDOM before you RUN (just after turning it ON). Now it is more nearly random.

It will almost never come up with the same string of numbers after a RANDOM is executed. This has a good use. We can develop programs that use random numbers and have a way of being sure they work correctly and with repeatbility by *not* including the RANDOM. Once we know our program works correctly, then we include the RANDOM statement.

The Primary Statement/Command
    RANDOM
Other Forms of the Statement/Command
    10: RANDOM

10: RANDOM
20: PRINT RND 10

RANDOM *re-seeds* the PC-2'S pseudo-random number generator, so that a new beginning for the RND statement is set up. Using RANDOM is like shaking a hat that we are drawing the RANDOM number out of.

10: RANDOM

This is the only form you can use for the RANDOM statement. It has no parameters and may be used in the RUN, PROgram and RESERVE modes.

We mentioned earlier that the series of 'random numbers' generated by the PC-2 is always the same right after start-up (see RND), and the RANDOM statement 'shakes the hat,' so to speak, so that you are not likely to get the same series of numbers thereafter.

Some suggested uses – after testing any program that needs a random number, insert this command at the beginning to insure that it is indeed a random number.

Oops! What went wrong? Mistyped it.

Also see: RND

ON/GOTO and ON/GOSUB

Remember how handy GOSUB and GOTO were? They are about to become even handier. Here is one of our stories to illustrate the nature of this new statement.

Let's assume that you are a student going to school. Each hour of the school day, you have a different class. Here is your class schedule for Monday:

```
Hour  1    8 A.M. — English  10
Hour  2    9 A.M. — History  20
Hour  3   10 A.M. — Computer Science 30
Hour  4   11 A.M. — Engineering Principles 40
Hour  5   12 A.M. — Lunch 50
Hour  6    1 P.M. — Computer Programming PC-2 60
Hour  7    2 P.M. — Tandy Leather Working 70
Hour  8    3 P.M. — Ancient History (FORTRAN) 80
Hour  9    4 P.M. — Study Hall 90
```

That is a pretty heavy schedule — nine hours! Notice that each class (including lunch) is conveniently numbered from 10 to 90. For our example below, we'll use the variable H to represent HOUR. Here is how ON/GOTO works:

ON the value of each hour GOTO the appropriate class.

200: ON H GOTO 10,20,30,40,50,60,70,80,90

If the value of H is 1, we'll go to the first class in the list, which is 10. If the value of H is 5, we'll go to the fifth class in the list, which is 50 and so on. We can use GOSUB in exactly the same way as we use GOTO.

Here is an actual program which illustrates the use of ON/GOTO and ON/GOSUB. We'll use GOSUB for the first demonstration.

```
2: CLS
4: WAIT 100
6: GOTO 100
10: PRINT "ENGLISH 10" : RETURN
20: PRINT "HISTORY 20" : RETURN
30: PRINT "COMP. SCI. 30" : RETURN
40: PRINT "ENG. PRINCIPLES 40" : RETURN
50: PRINT "LUNCH 50" : RETURN
60: PRINT "COMP. PROG. 60" : RETURN
70: PRINT "LEATHER 70" : RETURN
80: PRINT "ANCIENT HISTORY 80" : RETURN
90: PRINT "STUDY HALL 90" : RETURN
100: INPUT "ENTER A NUMBER";H
110: ON H GOSUB 10,20,30,40,50,60,70,80,90
120: GOTO 100
```

Here is how the same program would work using GOTO, instead of GOSUB:

```
2: CLS
4: WAIT 100
6: GOTO 100
10: PRINT "ENGLISH 10" : GOTO 100
20: PRINT "HISTORY 20" : GOTO 100
30: PRINT "COMP. SCI. 30" : GOTO 100
40: PRINT "ENG. PRINCIPLES 40" : GOTO 100
50: PRINT "LUNCH 50" : GOTO 100
60: PRINT "COMP. PROG. 60" : GOTO 100
70: PRINT "LEATHER 70" : GOTO 100
80: PRINT "ANCIENT HISTORY 80" : GOTO 100
90: PRINT "STUDY HALL 90" : GOTO 100
100: INPUT "ENTER A NUMBER";H
110: ON H GOTO 10,20,30,40,50,60,70,80,90
120: GOTO 100
```

See, there isn't any difference in the way either ON/GOTO or ON/GOSUB works. And you thought it was going to be tough! It was so easy that I almost let you figure it out for yourself.

Oh, I almost forgot, — the variable list can also use variables and labels. Change line 130 to look like this:

```
130: ON H GOTO A,B,C,"FORTY",50,60,70,80,90
```

and add a line 5 and a line 45 that look like this:

```
5: A = 10 : B = 20 : C = 30
45: "FORTY"
```

Amaze yourself and RUN the program again. We can say, without equivocation or weasel-wording, that the PC-2 is an amazing machine. It may be small, but it packs more wallop and power than a lot of machines one-hundred times its size!

The primary statement/command

```
ON variable GOTO line number, line number, line number
                    or
ON variable GOSUB line number, line number, line number
```

Other Forms of the Statement/Command

```
10: ON variable GOTO line number, line number, line number
10: ON variable GOTO variable, variable
10: ON variable GOTO "label", "label", "label"
10: ON variable GOTO line number, variable, "label"
```

ON/GOTO uses the value of the variable as an index to a list of line numbers or program label names. The first item in the list is used if the variable value is 1. The second item is used if the variable value is 2, and so on. If the variable value is zero, or higher than the number of items in the list, the GOTO part of the line is skipped, and the next line following the ON/GOTO line, is executed.

10: ON X GOTO 100,200,300

Here we have a list of 3 lines to choose from. As we have seen, if X is 0 or greater than 3, the program will fall through to the next line, which could be an error recovery routine, or simply could continue the mainline program.

10: ON X GOSUB 100,200,300

This form uses the GOSUB statement, rather than the GOTO statement, to illustrate that the ON function works equally as well with each form. Of course the subroutine will be terminated with a RETURN, which means the program will come back to the next line after the ON...GOSUB line, so the next line after line 10 had better be a logical continuation of the program, — not an 'error trap,' such as would be used for falling through the GOTO list of line numbers.

This could be done if the program is in a subroutine when you use the ON . . . GOSUB statement, and want to RETURN to the main program when the subroutine is completed, or if the nested subroutine falls through, like this:

```
10: X = 3
20: GOSUB "CHECK"
    •
    •
    •
100: "CHECK"
110: ON X GOSUB 150,160
120: RETURN
```

In this case, the subroutine call in line 110 is not made because there are only two choices, and X is equal to 3, so the return in line 120 is reached. If X had been 2, the subroutine in line 160 would have executed and returned to line 120, where the RETURN brings us back to the main program.

10: ON X GOTO "A", B, 100, 200

In this instance, we are mixing program names with line numbers and a variable to illustrate how you can use a program label, as well as a line number or a variable containing a value equivalent to a line number, in your index list. If X=1, then program "A" is executed; if X=2, then the line number referenced in the numeric variable B is executed, and so on.

Many times while executing a program, there is a series of choices to be made by the program and something to do for each choice, that is, a routine to execute based on a decision. This is the perfect statement to accomplish that.

Some suggested uses – common uses for this technique are menus, decoding schemes, and other branching points in a program. It allows easy selection of alternatives by the program, based on input or other conditions.

Oops! What went wrong? Mis-typed it. Wrong mode. Line does not exist. Numbers out of range. Label does not exist.

Special Note

Later on, we will examine a special case for the ON. . .GOTO statement, which is the ON ERROR GOTO statement. The ON ERROR GOTO statement is not the same as the normal ON. . .GOTO situation. It is used for 'trapping' certain kinds of errors in a program.

Also see: GOTO – GOSUB – ERROR

Really Big and Small Numbers

Exponents

You probably know that 'squaring' a number means multiplying the number by itself. For instance, 3 squared equals 3 * 3 equals 9; 6 squared equals 6 * 6 equals 36; n squared equals n * n, etc.

Another way to write 6 squared would be like this 6^2. This can be read as 6 to the *second power*, or just 6 to *the second*. The 2 indicates that there are two sixes being multiplied. Count them: 6 * 6, two.

This notation is called exponential notation. In the expression 6^2, the 6 is called the *base* and the 2 is called the *exponent*.

'Cubing' a number is similar to squaring it, except that you multiply it by itself an additional time. 3 cubed equals 3 * 3 * 3 equals 27; 6 cubed equals 6 * 6 * 6 equals 216; n cubed equals n * n * n.

Using exponential notation, we could write 6 cubed like this: 6^3. Here, 6 is still the base and 3 is the exponent. Of course, you can use any base and any exponent you want. For example, You can make 5 the base and 4 the exponent. This would give us 5^4 equals 5 * 5 * 5 * 5 equals 625. In general, X^n is read X to the power of n and means X multiplied by itself n times.

Your PC-2 understands exponential notation. However, there's no way to type superscripts into the computer, nor can it display superscripts. A superscript is the little number following and above the big number: 2^4. The 4 is the superscript.

This means that you have to use a slightly different form of notation to indicate exponents. An upward pointing caret ($\wedge$) is used for this purpose. You type it in by pressing the <SHIFT> key and then the <SPACE> bar. Instead of typing 3^2 (which can't be done) for 3 squared, you would type $3 \wedge 2$. In general, to tell the PC-2 that you mean X to power of n, you type in $X \wedge n$ (where 'n' is the power you wish to raise X to). You can try this by typing some expressions (an *expression* is a math formula like 2+5*4) into the PC-2 and pressing <ENTER>. For instance, put the PC-2 in the RUN mode, type in $3 \wedge 2$ and press <ENTER>. You will see 9 appear in the display.

Roots

A square root is the opposite of a square. If 3 squared is 9 (which it is), then the square root of 9 is 3. Another way of putting it would be to say that the square root of X is that number, which when multiplied by itself, yields X.

There happens to be a square root function on the PC-2 keyboard. This is fine, as far as it goes, but what about other roots? For instance, there is something called a cube root, which 'undoes' a cube in the same way that a square root undoes a square. How can we get the PC-2 to figure out cube roots, fourth roots, etc?

Well, as you have seen, a square root 'undoes' a square. For instance, 6 squared is 36, so the square root of 36 is 6. Well ½ usually 'undoes' anything done by a two, right? 1ØØ times two is 2ØØ and half of 2ØØ is 1ØØ.

Now 6 squared is the same as six to the power of two. Wouldn't it be nice if a power of ½ undid a power of 2? Well it does! 6 to the power of two is 36; and 36 to the power of ½ is 6. So raising a number to the power of ½ (or .5, which, of course, is the same thing) is the same as taking its square root.

You can try this out on the PC-2 by going into the RUN mode and typing 36 $\wedge$ .5 <ENTER>. 6 will appear in the display. To find a cube root, you want to undo a three instead of a two, so you have to use a power (or exponent) of one third.

There are two ways you might enter an exponent of ⅓. One would be like this: 27 $\wedge$ (1/3) <ENTER>. Notice the use of parentheses to control the order in which the expression is evaluated. Another way to enter this expression would require no parentheses, but could be slightly less precise: 27 $\wedge$ .3333333333 <ENTER>.

Scientific Notation

How many atoms are there in the universe? If memory serves me correctly, there are about 3×10^{74} atoms in the entire universe. This is an easy way to write very large and very small numbers. That number, 3×10^{74}, would be inconvenient to write out each time we wanted to use it, because it would look like this:

$$300,000,000,000,000,000,000,000,000,000,000,000,000,—$$
$$000,000,000,000,000,000,000,000,000,000,000,000$$

Besides being a large number, it's longer than the PC-2 display. Most inconvenient. Scientific notation solves our problem by telling us how many decimal places to add to the number. A number like this: 1367×10^{5}, would actually be 136700000. Actually, we moved the decimal place five places to the right and filled in the empty spaces with zeros.

That takes care of big numbers; what about small numbers. No difference. A really small number would look like this: 1367×10^{-5} and would translate to Ø.Ø1367. Notice that all we did was move the decimal point 5 places to the left and fill in the blank spaces with zeros.

The PC-2 uses scientific notation to display large and small numbers. Try this; type: .ØØØØØ123456789 <ENTER>. Your answer will be 1.23456789E–Ø6. The E–Ø6 is short for *Engineering* or scientific notation. The –Ø6 means that the decimal place is to be moved six places to the left in order for the answer to look like the original. Here is an example of a big number.

Type: 123456789 * 123456789 <ENTER>.

The answer will be 1.524157875E 16, meaning move the decimal place sixteen places to the right.

Each time we move the decimal point one place to the right, it is the same as multiplying by 1Ø. Each time we move the decimal point one place to the left, it is the same as dividing by 1Ø. In our small number example above, we divided by 1Ø, 6 times, and in the big number example, we multiplied by 1Ø, 16 times.

You can see that by just moving the decimal point and adding zeros, we lose some accuracy, but when numbers are big enough, or small enough, it is usually of little consequence.

A short review and we'll move on. When the notation is a negative number, move the decimal to the left. When it is a positive number, move it to the right.

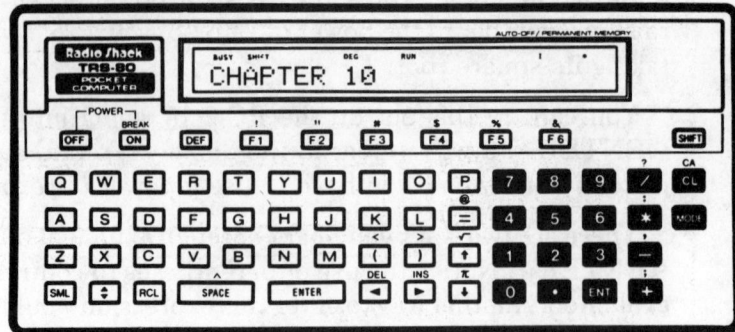

Debugging

If a program fails to perform as expected, after you've typed it in and RUN it, it probably has an error in it — somewhere. These ubiquitous (a fancy word meaning 'all over the place') little devils are known as 'bugs,' and correcting them is what is known as *debugging*.

There are several types of 'bugs' that can crop up, but the most common type are those producing an "ERROR 1" (syntax error) while RUNning a program. These are the easiest to fix as well. It usually means you only need to fix a spelling error. The more exotic types of bugs, such as incorrect results from numerical operations, may require a little more work to fix, as some of your logic is probably not organized correctly.

The PC-2 can pin-point quite a few errors for you, and you can usually figure out what went wrong, from the error number that is displayed. After getting an error, press the <CL> key, then go to the PROgram mode and press the ⬆ key. The offending program line (the one with the error in it) will be displayed, and lo 'n behold, the editing cursor will be over the exact spot that caused the error!

That's enough on debugging for now — we have a lot of ground to cover. There is more information on debugging in the appendix section.

Editing

Fixing errors in a program, or changing a previously typed program line, is done by editing or retyping the program line in which the error occurred. When an error occurs in the RUN mode, go into the PROgram mode and press the ⬆ key.

This will put the cursor on the exact spot where program execution was halted by an error. You can then fix the mistake.

By using the ◀ and ▶ keys, you can move the cursor to the spot on the line that you want to change. You can then type in the correct character or statement, and insert or delete letters by pressing <SHIFT>, followed by the key marked <INS> or <DEL>.

When INSerting, a blank space (indicated by a graphics character) is displayed. You can guess how many characters you will have to insert and put that many blanks in the line before you type in the additions. If any are left over when you have finished, they will disappear (as will all other spaces that are not mandatory) when the <ENTER> key is pressed.

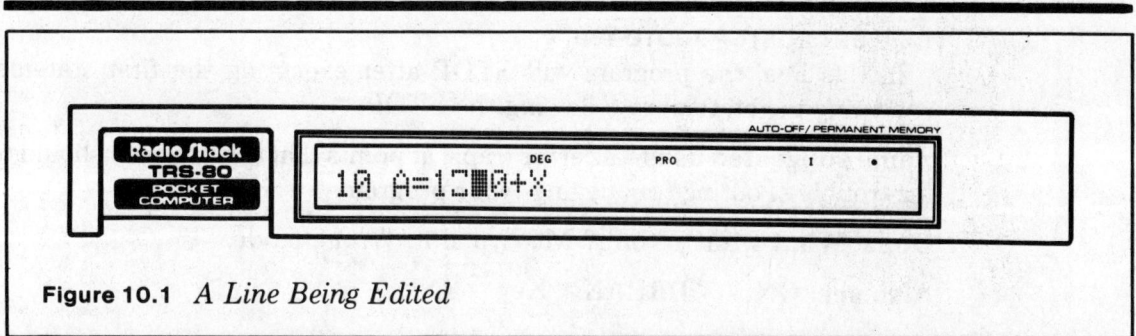

Figure 10.1 *A Line Being Edited*

When you have fixed-up the problem, go back to the RUN mode and RUN the program again to see what new errors, if any, may crop up.

Another form of 'editing' is used when initially entering the program. This form of 'editing' can be as simple as typing in each line, character by character, but there are some tricks you can use to speed things up. For instance, when you are entering lines that are very similar to each other, type in the first one and press <ENTER>. Then, press the ◄ key until the blinking cursor is over the line number. Now you can change the line number to any number you desire by typing over the old numbers. Then move the cursor to the right to make any changes required for the new line. The old line remains, and you get the new one when you press <ENTER>. Do this for all similar lines — it saves gobs of time and typing!

If you define the function keys as much-used entries, then a single key stroke can type in a line of code. See the section on function keys for more information on this technique.

In the same vein, the built-in abbreviations for command words are a big help. Typing "P.", instead of PRINT each time, sure helps me.

Using STOP, CONTinue and the BREAK Key

When the PC-2 is on, pressing the <BREAK> key causes a program that is RUNning, to BREAK (stop), wherever it is during RUN, or it terminates the input you are currently making, in any mode. It is also used to clear the display of an error message so you may continue. You can also cause a program to halt at a pre-determined point for debugging purposes by using the STOP statement, which we shall now investigate . . . .

STOP

Using the STOP statement will cause the program to halt its execution at a pre-determined place. It is used primarily for debugging and gives you an opportunity to see if everything is going the way you expect it to. You can restart the program's execution at the point it was STOPped by simply typing CONT and pressing <ENTER>.

Later, after you have determined that the program is functioning properly, you can remove the lines containing the STOP statement. Also see the section on debugging in the appendix.

The Primary Statement/Command
      1Ø: STOP

88

STOP can only be used in a program line.

10: STOP

When BASIC reaches this line, program execution is halted, and the message "BREAK IN 10" will appear on the display, indicating that the program STOPped in line 10.

10: PRINT X : STOP : GOTO 150

In this line, the program will STOP after executing the first statement, and before executing the statement following the STOP.

Some suggested uses – as error traps; at points that the program should never get to, and for trouble-shooting (debugging) your program.

Oops! What went wrong? Mis-typed it. Wrong mode.

Also see: ON — <BREAK> Key – END

CONT

Here is another statement that has an everyday life parallel. CONTinue, like so many other BASIC statements, means what you think it does — to CONTinue something after you have stopped. Something like this: you are reading the newspaper. The phone rings. You STOP reading the paper and answer the phone. After you hang-up, you go back to your chair and CONTinue reading the newspaper. You see, it is utter simplicity.

The CONT statement causes program execution to CONTinue after a STOP statement is encountered or the <BREAK> key is pressed during a program's RUN. After checking some part of the program you are concerned with, CONT restarts program execution from the exact place it had STOPped as though nothing had happened.

You cannot CONTinue after the END of the program is reached, after editing a line of the program, after the program aborted due to a syntax error or after most other types of error conditions.

However, you *can* use GOTO to get back to the program if you remember the line number or know a good place to go back into the program. Don't try to GOTO the middle of a FOR/NEXT loop that has not executed the FOR statement after <BREAK> or STOP. The loop will not have been initialized; the NEXT statement will not be able to figure out where it is, and you'll get an error message.

Try this on for size. Enter this simple program and RUN it. You will get a "BREAK" message when line 20 is executed. Then type: CONT <ENTER>, and the program will pick-up where it left off.

```
5: WAIT 100
10: PRINT "LINE 10"
20: STOP
30: PRINT "LINE 30"
```

The Primary Statement/Command
CONT

CONT has no other forms. It is used only in the RUN mode.

CONT <ENTER>

The CONT statement may only be used from the RUN mode, and cannot be used in a program line. There are no parameters to this statement. It will pick up program execution with the next statement in the list.

It is most useful to CONTinue execution of a program you may have just stopped by pressing the <BREAK> key or executing the STOP statement, without having to start all over and lose all the data stored in the variables up that point.

Some suggested uses – trouble–shooting, examining variables as a program RUNs, breaking a RUNning program to do a quick calculation, to check variables or a program's execution sequence, and then continuing.

Oops! What went wrong? Mis-typed it. Wrong mode. Changed variables or lines by editing the program.

Also see: STOP – <ON> / <OFF> (<BREAK> key) – GOTO

TRON/TROFF

It's Sunday afternoon and you're watching the L.A. Rams play the Dallas Cowboys. There has just been an exciting play on the Dallas 4-yard line. The sportscaster is going wild describing the *instant replay*.

On television, the instant replay lets us examine each crucial play in minute detail. The PC-2 has some *instant replay* features that make it very easy to examine a program's operation. A couple of these instant replay features are the TRON and TROFF statements.

TRON and TROFF act as 'switches' for a built-in debugging aid known as the TRace function. TRace ON (TRON) and TRace OFF (TROFF) are used to turn this function on and off, as the statements suggest.

When the TRace is enabled (TRON), the line number currently being executed is shown on the display, prior to executing the instructions on that line. Pressing the ↓ key causes the line to execute. The line to be executed next can be examined by pressing the ↑ key. The TRace function can be turned off with the TROFF command, and you can CONTinue the program from that point, if you wish.

So you see, the TRON and TROFF statements are an *instant replay*, a step-by-step and slow-motion analysis of a program's operation. Here is a demonstration of them used within a program. Later, after you have completed your debugging, simply remove the lines with the TRON and TROFF statements.

```
10: WAIT 50
20: PRINT "Line 20
30: TRON
40: PRINT "Line 40
50: TROFF
60: PRINT "Line 60
```

It is also useful to know that you can use these statements in the RUN mode. That way you can press the <BREAK> key, type the TRON command, and check the program's operation. Then, when you are satisfied, press the <BREAK> key again and type TROFF and everything is back to normal.

The Primary Statement/Command
```
TRON
TROFF
```

Other Forms of the Statement/Command
```
10: TRON
10: TROFF
```

TRON <ENTER>
Turns the TRace ON.

TROFF <ENTER>
Turns the TRace OFF.

```
1Ø: TRON
1Ø: TROFF
```

This illustrates that TRON and TROFF can be imbedded in the program to automatically turn the TRace ON and OFF at pre-determined places in a program. Both statements may be used in RUN, PROgram and RESERVE modes.

The TRace ON and OFF statements are useful for debugging programs and segments of programs. With it, you can see if your program is performing as expected.

Some suggested uses – debugging – decoding someone else's program to figure out how it works.

Oops! What went wrong? Mis-typed it.

Also see: Single-Stepping – debugging section of appendix.

Single-stepping

There is another way to view the progress of a program without using the TRace function. (This is not to be confused with the STEP statement.)

In the RUN mode, you can stop the program by pressing the <BREAK> key, and then cause the program to execute one statement at a time by pressing the ⬇ key.

The line numbers will not be displayed, as in TRON, but you will be able to see the results of each program step, each time you press the ⬇ . You can also test the variables as each line is executed, since control returns to you after each instruction is completed.

You can also *view* the line being executed by pressing the ⬆ key when in the command mode. As long as you hold this key down, the line will be displayed on the screen, with the cursor at the position in the line at which execution was halted.

How's that for sophistication? Not even PC-2's big brothers have that feature as a built-in bonus!

STATUS

"Status report, Mr. Spock," said the captain. Spock studied the console-readouts while he listened to various ship's officers on the intercom. After a moment he said, "Engineering reports power level at 7Ø%. Damage control shows all repairs complete. Sickbay is treating five crew members for minor injuries. Sensor Station One reports two Klingon cruisers at twenty parsecs and closing. Weapons Control reports all photon torpedo tubes loaded and ready."

A state-of-the-art starship has all the communications systems necessary to bring a complete report of the ship's status to the captain on request. Likewise, a state-of-the-art computer, such as the PC-2, has the ability to report various aspects of its memory usage and program-flow.

STATUS is a command with which you can determine certain conditions in the PC-2. There are 5 possible things you can check the STATUS of:

Ø — Program steps used (memory locations) — actual bytes used By the program (each byte of program material is considered as a 'step,' in the PC-2).
1 — Program steps available.
2 — The address of the end of your program.
3 — The address of the end of variable storage.
4 — The last line number executed.

Although STATUS allows a parameter value of up to 255, only Ø thru 4 are significant; all values greater than 3 will return the last line number executed.

"Quick, Mr. Spock! Type this in and give me a status report!"

```
 5: WAIT 1Ø
1Ø: FOR X = Ø TO 4
2Ø: PRINT STATUS X;
3Ø: NEXT X
4Ø: GOTO 4Ø
```

The Primary Statement/Command
STATUS number

Other Forms of the Statement/Command
1Ø: STATUS number
1Ø: STATUS variable
1Ø: variable = STATUS number

STATUS number
Here, the STATUS command is issued from the RUN mode. The value (number) following the STATUS statement, will determine which STATUS is reported on the display. STATUS may be used in RUN, PROgram and RESERVE modes.

1Ø: PRINT STATUS number
This example is the same as the primary form, but used in a program line to PRINT the STATUS requested, on the display.

1Ø: A = STATUS number
In this case, the variable A will contain the result of the status statement after execution.

When writing programs, it's often necessary to have some of the computer's internal information, such as memory size and program location.

Some suggested uses – writing programs that protect themselves from getting too large or renumbering the program (that's not one for beginners!). Planning memory usage.

Oops! What went wrong? Mis-typed it. No STATUS value.

Also see: MEM

ERROR (ON ERROR GOTO)

ON ERROR GOTO is the roach motel of the programming process. It is used to 'trap errors' and send program execution to a special routine that you may write to analyze and correct the error without halting program execution.

"How could such an error occur?" you ask. Easy. Here is an example of just such an error. You are selling electronic components — resistors, transistors, capacitors and the like. You have written a program that determines your profit margin. The INPUT statement asks for the selling and cost price. The program will divide the selling price into the cost price to determine the percentage of margin. The formula looks like this:

Cost Price / Selling Price = Percent Margin.

Now if someone accidentally enters a selling price of zero, an error will occur because you cannot divide a number by zero. By using the ON ERROR GOTO statements you can send program execution to your 'error trap,' determine the cause of the error and then return to the INPUT line to ask for the selling price again.

When you use techniques like this, you'll find that non-programmers who use your program think that the computer is 'smart' — really it's only you and your programming ability that make it seem smart.

You can set error traps at various places in the program, depending on the types of errors you anticipate and how you have decided to handle them.

The following is a demonstration of how ON ERROR works. In this short example, we have created an error by having a READ statement without any DATA statements.

```
10: ON ERROR GOTO 80
20: PAUSE"ERROR DEMO"
30: READ A
40: PAUSE A
50: IF A=100 THEN END
60: GOTO 20
70: WAIT 100
80: PRINT"THIS PROGRAM HAS AN ERROR"
90: PRINT"ADD DATA STATEMENTS & RETRY"
100: GOTO 10
```

RUN this and then add the following DATA statements and RUN it again.

```
110: DATA 10,50,11.2,99,101,100
```

After you add line 110, the ON ERROR statement will no longer affect the program's operation unless a new error crops up.

The Primary Statement/Command
```
10: ON ERROR GOTO line number
```

Other Forms of the Statement/Command
```
10: ON ERROR GOTO 100
10: ON ERROR GOTO "E"
10: ON ERROR GOTO A
```

10: ON ERROR GOTO line number

In this form, program errors will cause execution to GOTO the line number specified.

10: ON ERROR GOTO "A"

You can use program labels, as well as line numbers, to send program execution to the desired place in your program.

10: ON ERROR GOTO 0

This is a special case of the ON ERROR GOTO statement. Using zero as the line number to GOTO actually *cancels* the ON ERROR statement, and causes BASIC to enter the normal error handling routines (like stopping the program with an error message).

ON ERROR GOTO is used to trap errors that might be expected due to the way the program works (such as trapping division by zero in a 'super calculator' program).

Some suggested uses – trapping any unexpected error and then jumping to a place in the program that can restart the program, like the menu page, without re-RUNning and losing the variables already entered.

Oops! What went wrong? Wrong mode. Mis-typed it. Line does not exist. Program label does not exist.

Also see: ON GOTO – TRON – TROFF

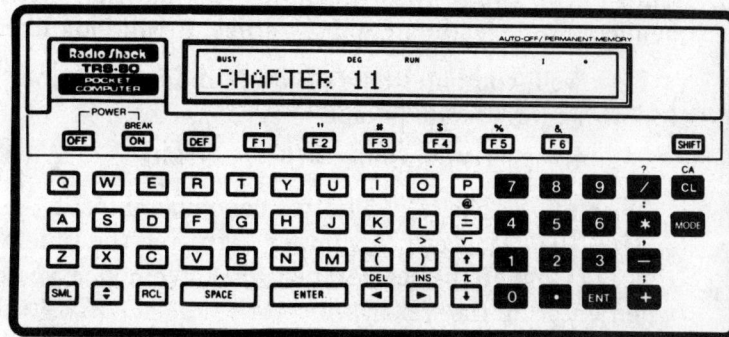

Time and Date

For some reason, we always want to know what time it is. Before electronic clocks, there were mechanical clocks. Before that were water clocks and sand clocks, and before that, sundials. Would you believe . . . the PC-2 has a *built-in clock*, and a way to read it?

Not only is this handy to tell time with, but you can also use it to *bench mark*, or 'time,' program execution. It can be used as a very accurate stopwatch, as well as a calendar. Hmmmm . . . that calls to mind a few program ideas right there! Let's take a look at this marvelous statement.

TIME

TIME tells you what time it is if you have set the clock in the PC-2. (If you haven't set the clock, then I suppose it tells you what time it **isn't**). TIME displays the month, day, hours, minutes and seconds as a decimal number. Not only does TIME **tell** you the time, it is also used to *set* TIME.

Before we try to read the time, we had better set it. Today is February 14th, and the time is 7:3Ø P.M. Lessee . . . the TIME function is very fussy about how you enter the months, days, hours and minutes, so we need to look at how the data is formatted (how do you like that fancy computer jargon ? — "How the data is formatted?").

MMddHH.mmSS is the TIME format, where MM represents the month, dd represents the day, HH is the hour, mm is the minutes and SS is seconds. Notice that TIME gives us a decimal number, with the minutes and seconds on the right of the decimal point. Also notice that each item is composed of two digits. This is important, so pay attention:

When an element of the TIME command consists of a single digit (such as the first day of the first month), you might write such a date as: 1/1/1983. This is ok for writing, but could be confusing for the computer, because it is expecting two digits for each item. If you wrote it, using two digits for each entry, it would look like this: Ø1/ Ø1/1983. Since the computer does not need the year and the slash marks, we can throw them out, so that the month and day now look like this: Ø1Ø1 . . . .

Next are the hours. And, wouldn't you know it, it is coincidentally, the first hour (1 A.M.), the first minute and the first second. So, the time (as we write it on paper) looks like this:

(1:1:1). If that isn't a pickle — everything is a one! Oh well, it's just perfect for our example.

To write the time for the computer, the same rule applies — two digits are needed. The time (using two digits) will now look like this: Ø1:Ø1:Ø1, and since we don't need the semicolons or leading/trailing zeroes, it will look like this when we type it in: (1.Ø1Ø1).

Now we'll combine the date and time information to set the TIME function. Enter the following: (any mode is ok.)

      TIME = 1Ø1Ø1.Ø1Ø1 <ENTER>

With this stroke of genius, we have just entered the date and time as January 1st, 1:1:1 A.M. If the date were November 14th, and the time were 9:45:1Ø A.M., it would look like this: (1114Ø9.451Ø). Remember: for convenience, you may drop any *leading* or *trailing* zeros when entering the TIME.

So far, so good. But how do we enter the P.M. hours? The PC-2 uses *military time* — a 24 hour system. Midnight is Ø Ø hours, and noon is 12 hours; whereas 1 P.M. is 13 hours, 2 P.M. is 14 hours and so on until we get to 24 hours, which is the same as ØØ hours. Using this system, 6 P.M. is 18 hours, and 9 P.M. is 21 hours. If the TIME is entered as 24 hours, the PC-2 will change it to ØØ hours.

When TIME PRINTs the date/time, it is a numeric value — not a string value. The result is that the leading **and** trailing zeros are stripped off. That means that you must interpret the TIME printout. From the decimal point to the right is minutes and seconds, and from the decimal point to the left is hour, day and month. For example, a TIME display that looks like this . . .

62213.Ø9

. . . would be interpreted (reading right to left from the decimal point) as the 13th hour (1 P.M.), 22nd day of the 6th month (June). Reading to the right from the decimal point, we have 9 minutes and Ø seconds. It is as if it were displayed as: Ø62213.Ø9ØØ . . . .

Now that we can read and set TIME, how can we make use of it? Suppose we just want to use the day in a program? Once again, very easy. In a few chapters we'll meet some new friends: RIGHT$, LEFT$, MID$ and STR$. With these string statements (and one or two others), we can *extract* any part of the TIME display that's needed.

The Primary Statement/Command
    TIME

Other Forms of the Statement/Command
    TIME = MMddHH.mmSS
    1Ø:TIME = A
    1Ø:PRINT TIME

TIME

    This form of TIME displays the month, day, hour, minute and seconds. It returns the time as a decimal number: the month, year and hours to the left of the decimal point, and the minutes and seconds on the right. I'm sure you realize that although the PC-2 will **always** display the time, it will only be the *right* time if you have told the PC-2 what time it is . . . .

1Ø: A = TIME

    After this line executes, the variable A will contain the date and time in decimal format.

1Ø: PRINT TIME

    Here, the date and time (in decimal format) will be PRINTed on the display after this line executes.

1Ø: TIME = A

This is one method of setting the time. If the numeric variable A has the correct date and time, in decimal format, prior to execution of this line, then, after this line executes, the TIME will be set to the value in A.

TIME = MMddHH.mmSS

In this example, the time is set from the RUN mode, by supplying a constant value as the time, in which MM is the month, dd is the day, HH is the hour, mm is the minutes and SS the seconds.

TIME, like the other statements we have discussed, may be used in any mode of operation.

Some suggested uses – to make a very expensive clock, calender, or reminder program. TIME is also very useful for business applications where time and dates need accurate tracking.

Oops! What went wrong? – Mis-typed it. TIME must be on the left side of the equation when setting (TIME = 11Ø1Ø9.5Ø3Ø) and on the right when putting the time into a variable (A = TIME).

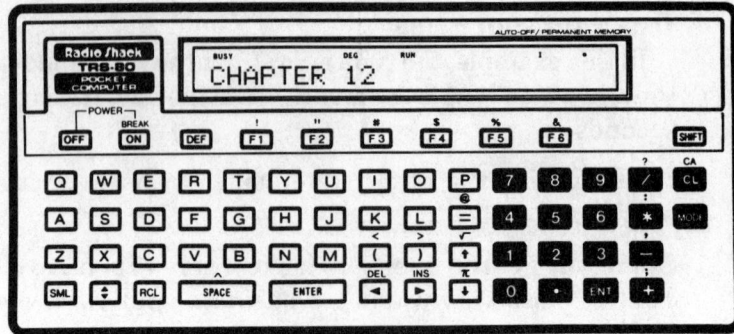

More on Strings

As was mentioned in an earlier chapter, there are two types of data the computer can recognize. One is called numeric data, which, of course, means numbers. The other type of data is string data. It can consist of letters, numbers and a variety of other characters. To us humans, a number may *look* like a string, but in fact, to the PC-2, strings may or may not be numbers.

To the computer, numbers look like they do to you and me, but strings are read in a different fashion, although they can still appear to be numbers to us mere mortals.

There is a standard value assigned to each letter of the alphabet (upper case and lower case have different values), numerals Ø thru 9, each punctuation mark and all the other symbols (some of which are on the keyboard, while others are not). The value for these characters is the ASCII code (short for "American Standard Code for Information Interchange" — a committee set up to make it easier to deal with computer communications).

Thus, the character '1' has a numeric ASCII value which differs from its arithmetic value of 1, because it is a string character, not a number. It is necessary to use this ASCII coding method to represent characters or symbols because the computer can only deal with numbers.

Unlike the computer, people can usually tell the difference between a numeric value and the ASCII number code, which represents that value. Thus, to tell a computer that you mean the character '1,' as opposed to the number 1, you either give it the ASCII value of the character intended . . . or enclose the number in quotes, and the computer will take care of it automatically.

Let's use a thread (or 'string') of 1Ø beads as an example. Each of the beads has a number on it from Ø thru 9, as shown in the figure below. Imagine reading the whole thread as a number.

Imagine that on the back of each bead is another number, which represents the ASCII value of the number on the front side. Flip the string of beads over, and you will find the ASCII value (in decimal) of each bead as shown below.

Figure 12.1 *A String Of Beads*

As you will see, there are quite a few ways to tell the computer that it is looking at a string rather than a number. The most straight-forward way is to include the string in quotes so the 'beads' look like this:

"Ø123456789"

Figure 12.2 *The Back of the Beads*

When you use the quotes, the computer looks at the ASCII number (on the back of the beads) to see what value it should use and how they should be treated.

There is a special symbol (the dollar sign '$') which is used with variables to tell the computer that it is dealing with a string variable rather than a numeric variable. It looks like this:

A$="Ø123456789"

The '$' is usually referred to as the word "string" when discussing strings, so the variable A$ is called 'A string.'

To treat our string of beads as a number, you would use the form:

A=Ø123456789

In this example, the value of the numeric variable A is equal to 123456789 since the leading Ø doesn't count. The computer will not bother to find out the ASCII value for this string — it will simply treat them as a number. In the string representation, the zero counts as one member of the string and always stays there.

Strings are very useful to the programmer for dealing with data that is not easily handled as numbers, such as names, addresses, and so on. There are several ways to put a string into the computer: as a literal initialization of a string variable in a program line, by an INPUT statement, the DATA statement, the cassette recorder or some other *input device*. A literal is any character or series of characters enclosed in quotes — "this is a literal".

String Limitations

Size limits: the PC-2 permits string variables to be up to 16 characters long. In other words, you can have 16 beads on any one "string of beads." If you need to use longer strings, you have to tell the computer you will be needing them by inserting a DIMension statement *before* you use them which will make them sub-scripted string variables. We will examine this in another section. For now, each string will be 16 characters or less in length. (Refer to DIMensioning arrays for more information).

Sub-strings

What is a *sub-string* anyway? Quite simply, a *sub-string* is a portion of another string which can vary in length from one character of the original string to the entire length of the original string.

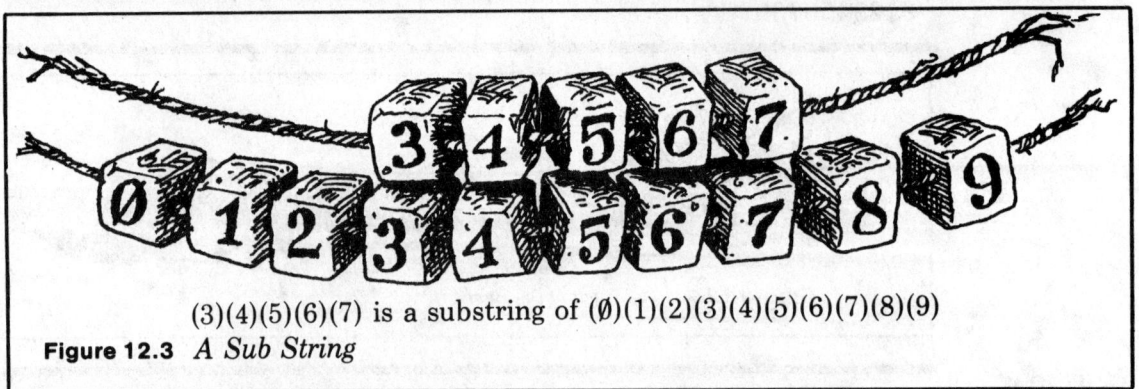

(3)(4)(5)(6)(7) is a substring of (Ø)(1)(2)(3)(4)(5)(6)(7)(8)(9)

Figure 12.3 *A Sub String*

By using the program statements in the following sections, you can manipulate and interchange the contents of string variables to your heart's content:

LEFT$

LEFT$ returns a sub-string that is the left side of a string, containing as many characters as specified. Suppose we have a string (A$) with the first and last name of a close friend in it, EDWARD P. FROMP. We want to write him a letter (using the computer, of course). And we don't want to be formal, so all we want is his nick-name, ED.

This means that we want just the first two letters of the left side of the string. We will use LEFT$ to put the first two letters of A$ into B$.

Now we can use B$ (which is ED), for our letter. It will look like this:

```
10: A$="EDWARD P. FROMP"
20: B$=LEFT$(A$,2)
30: PRINT B$
```

We'll reuse our first example of a string of beads for another demonstration. Suppose you want to give the two beads on the left, to your friend Harv, who collects antique beads. To accomplish this task, you take the two left-most characters with the LEFT$ statement, like this:

BEAD$ = "Ø123456789"
HARV$ = LEFT$(BEAD$,2)
Ø1 ◀— 23456789

and hand them over. Harv now has two beads ("Ø" and "1"). This is the same as the statement, A$ = LEFT$("Ø123456789",2). Now take 'em back, 'cause we'll need them later on!

Here's a sample program. Go to the PROgram MODE and type it in; then RUN it.

```
10: A$ = "EDWARD P. FROMP"
20: B$ = LEFT$(A$,2)
30: PRINT "DEAR ";B$
```

The Primary Statement/Command
LEFT$ (string, length)

Other Forms of the Statement/Command
```
20: B$ = LEFT$ ("string", number)
20: B$ = LEFT$ (A$, number)
20: B$ = LEFT$ (A$, variable)
20: B$ = LEFT$ ("literal", number)
20: B$ = LEFT$ ("literal", variable)
```

20: B$ = LEFT$ (A$, 6)

Using the string variable B$ as the receiver and the string variable A$ as the target string, this form will place the first 6 characters on the left side of A$ into B$. Note: A *target* is the variable, program or item we are working *on*.

20: B$ = LEFT$ ("EDWARD P. FROMP", 6)

This example uses a *string constant* or *string literal* (in parentheses which are required) as the target string. The first six characters on the left side ("Edward"), will be in the string variable B$ after execution of this operation.

20: PRINT LEFT$ (A$, 6)

In this example, the first 6 characters of the target string (A$) will be PRINTed on the display, rather than being assigned to a receiver string variable, demonstrating another way of using this statement.

20: B$ = LEFT$ (LEFT$ (A$, 6), 2)

This example illustrates how LEFT$ (and other string handlers) can be *nested*. B$ will be "Ed" after execution of this statement. While this example is redundant, in that the left side of the string is going to be the target anyway, it does illustrate the point. Later, we shall see how the nesting of these string functions is a useful feature which can create powerful combinations to separate parts of strings into smaller segments or *sub-strings*.

You will note that the LEFT$ statement (as well as the other string statements we will look at) can only be used on the right side of an equation. You cannot use a statement that looks like this: LEFT$(A$,5) = B$.

LEFT$ can be used in the RUN mode as well as in program lines.

Strings can be used for manipulation of names, addresses, data, graphics etc. Some numerical information can be handled as strings easier than as numbers — especially in reports.

Some suggested uses – searching a phone list by the first three digits in the number, searching a name list for all names beginning with some letter, looking for certain names in a list. Formatting string dates for output. Reorganize dates to be used in various ways. To look for occurances of certain letter combinations. To look for sub-strings in a given range of characters in a string starting at the left most position in the string.

Oops! What went wrong?: Mis-typed it. String is too short for the specified length of the left string sub-string. The target string does not exist or is a null (it has nothing in it). Used LEFT$ on the wrong side of the equation.

Also see: RIGHT$ — MID$

RIGHT$

RIGHT$ returns the right side of the target string, starting at the right side *for* the number of characters specified. Let's say we have a string with the name of a *not* so close friend in it, and we want to write him a letter using the computer. We don't want to be informal, as in the first example, so we want to use his last name, Fromp. This means that we want the last FIVE letters of the right side of the string, so we tell RIGHT$ to give us the last 5 letters of A$ in B$. Now we can use B$ (which is FROMP), for our letter. It will look like this: A$ = "EDWARD P. FROMP": B$ = RIGHT$(A$,5).

Again, using our example of a string of beads, you want to give the two beads on the right to your old pal Harv. So you take the right-most two characters with the RIGHT$ statement like this:

BEAD$ = "Ø123456789"
HARV$ = RIGHT$(BEAD$,2)
Ø1234567 ⟶ 89

and hand them over. Harv now has two beads ("8" and "9"). Now take 'em back again, 'cause we'll be needing them later.

The Primary Statement/Command

RIGHT$ (string, number)

Other Forms of the Statement/Command

```
20: B$ = RIGHT$ (A$, number)
20: B$ = RIGHT$ (A$, variable)
20: B$ = RIGHT$ ("literal", number)
20: B$ = RIGHT$ ("literal", variable)
```

Here's a sample program. Go to the PROgram MODE and type it in...

```
10: A$ = "EDWARD P. FROMP"
20: B$ = RIGHT$(A$,5)
30: PRINT "Dear Mr. ";B$
```

Now change MODEs and RUN this sample.

20: B$ = RIGHT$ (A$, 5)

Will put the last five characters found in A$ into B$. That is, the five characters on the RIGHT side of the string are returned in the string variable, B$.

20: B$ = RIGHT$ ("EDWARD P. FROMP",5)

As in the LEFT$ example, we use a string literal (enclosed in quotes) as the target. The five characters on the RIGHT side of the string, "FROMP", are returned in the string variable, B$

```
10: A$ = "EDWARD P. FROMP"
20: PRINT RIGHT$ (A$, 5)
```

This example uses the PRINT statement instead of putting the results in a string variable. On execution of this statement, the word "FROMP" is PRINTed on the display.

```
10: A$ = "EDWARD P. FROMP"
20: B$ = RIGHT$(LEFT$( A$, 9), 2)
```

Here is another example of *nesting* string handlers. You can use a modifier,such as LEFT$, to change the target area of a string before getting to the part you wish to use. In this illustration, we don't want to change the actual target string, but we want to limit its length so we can aim at a different RIGHT$ portion than we would get using the entire string. As this line executes, it will shorten the length of A$, as seen by the RIGHT$ statement, to 9 characters. It then looks at the right side of the result and returns it in B$, so that B$ will be "P." after execution of the line. RIGHT$ can be used in the immediate mode as well as in a program line.

Strings can be used for manipulation of names, addresses, and so on. Some numerical information can be handled as strings easier than as numbers — especially in reports and mailing lists.

Some suggested uses-input routines. Sorts. Text and data handling routines. Searching for names in a list. Looking for occurences of certain letter combinations. To look for substrings in a given range of characters in a string beginning at the right most position.

Oops! What went wrong?: Mis-typed it. String is too short for the specified length of the right string sub-string. The target string does not exist or is a null (it has nothing in it). Used RIGHT$ on the wrong side of the equation.

Also see: LEFT$ – MID$

MID$

MID$ returns the middle portion of the target string, beginning at a specified starting point from the left most character, for a specified length of characters. In this example, we again have a string (A$) with the name of a close friend, Julius Frack, in it, and we want to write him a letter. Now we want to be a bit jive, so all we want is the first letter of his last name. In order to get this result, we count over from the left to the first letter of his last name (8 counting the space). We tell MID$ to give us the 8th letter of A$ in B$. Now we can use B$ (which is "F"), for our letter, as in "DEAR Mr.";B$. It will look like this: A$="JULIUS FRACK":B$ = MID$(A$,8,9).

Once again, using our string of beads example, you want to give the two beads in the middle to your antique collector friend. So you take the MID$ like this:

BEAD$ = "Ø123456789"
HARV$ = MID$(BEAD$,6,2)

```
    56
Ø1234 ↑ 789
```

and hand them over. Harv again has two beads ("5" and "6"). These are yours Harv, you can keep them.

The Primary Statement/Command
    MID$ (String, start position, length)

Other Forms of the Statement/Command
    2Ø: B$ = MID$ (string, variable, variable)
    2Ø: B$ = MID$ (string, number, number)
    2Ø: B$ = MID$ (string, variable, number)
    2Ø: B$ = MID$ ("literal", number, variable)
    2Ø: B$ = MID$ ("literal", variable, number)

Here's a sample program. Go to the PROgram MODE and type it in. . .
    1Ø: A$ = "JULIUS FRACK"
    2Ø: B$ = MID$(A$,8,1)
    3Ø: PRINT "DEAR MR. ";B$;"."
Now change MODEs and RUN this sample.

2Ø: B$ = MID$ (A$, 7, 2)
After the execution of this line, B$ will contain the two characters starting at the seventh character (from the left) that are in the string variable, A$.

2Ø: B$ = MID$("HORTON P. HIJET", 8 , 2)
This example uses a string literal (in quotes) as the "target" string. The two characters in the middle ("P."), will be in the string variable B$ after execution.

20: PRINT MID$ (A$, 8, 2)

In this example, the middle 2 characters of the target string will be PRINTed on the display, rather than being assigned to a "receiver" string.

20: B$ = MID$ (LEFT$(A$, 11)6, 2)

This example illustrates how MID$ (and other string handlers) can be nested. Of course, it is only necessary to perform the truncating operation on the target string if some other calculation is necessary, since the result of this example would have been the same with or without the LEFT$ operation, but it does give you an idea of how to use the compound operation.

Strings can be used used for manipulation of names and addresses. Some numerical information can be handled as strings more easily than as numbers.

Some suggested uses – searching for names in a list. Looking for occurances of certain letter combinations. To look for sub-strings in a given range of characters in a string.

Oops! What went wrong? Mis-typed it. The string is too short for the specified length of the MID string sub-string. The target string does not exist or is a null (it has nothing in it). MID$ was used on the wrong side of the equation

Also see: LEFT$ – RIGHT$

Using Strings in a Compound Statement

A final note: In the string operations we have just discussed you will have to keep track of the length of the target strings, as BASIC does not note an error when the target string is too short for the parameters specified. For instance, if you wanted to make B$ be equal to the LEFT$ ("Harry", 8), B$ will wind up being "Harry", as the LEFT$ function will not recognize that "Harry" only has 5 letters in it!

LEN

We hate to tell you this, but you're going to have to get those beads back from Harv for a minute!, Putting our string of beads back together, we find that there are 10 of them (unless Harv resisted, in which case there are 8 left on the string). The number of beads in the string is the LENgth.

LEN tells you how many characters are in a string by returning its LENgth. The string can be in a variable or may appear as a literal enclosed in quotes.

The Primary Statement/Command
```
LEN string
```

Other Forms of the Statement/Command
```
10: B = LEN string variable
10: PRINT LEN string variable
10: B = LEN("literal"+string variable)
```

Here's a sample program. Go to the PROgram MODE and type it in. . .
```
10: A$ = "HARRY MOONER"
20: B = LEN A$
30: PRINT B
```
Now change MODEs and RUN this sample.

20: B = LEN A$

In this example, the numeric variable B will contain the LENgth of the string variable A$, after execution of the program line.

20: B = LEN (A$)

This format is essentially the same as the primary form, but illustrates that you can enclose the target string in parentheses, which are optional.

20: PRINT LEN A$

Here we are reporting the length of A$ directly to the display, rather than assigning it to a variable.

20: B = LEN "GOOSEHEAD WITHY"

As with other string operations, the LEN function may be performed on a string literal, as well as on string variables.

20: A$ = MID$(A$, 8, LEN C$)

Here we have an example of using the LENgth of one string variable to establish a parameter for another string operation. Let's assume that you are using C$ a standard length in a PRINTout. You want B$ to be the same length as C$, for whatever reason. This combination will measure the LENgth of C$, so that B$ will start at the eighth character of A$ and be the same length as C$.

LEN is used to find the length of strings, so you can compare them and look for given lengths of strings.

Some suggested uses – testing for legal input of strings that must be a set length. Defining a field in a group of strings in a list, such as zip codes. Check the length of strings after an INPUT statement for correct length of input. Verify that strings are of a length expected by your program.

Oops! What went wrong? Mis-typed it. String doesn't exist.

Also see: VAL – ASC

CHR$

Lets' say that you and your friend Harv each have a secret code ring. On each ring is a row of numbers and a row of characters next to the numbers. Since ASCII is no big secret, you have decided to use it as your code, figuring that nobody would expect your rings to be that simple. Well, anyway, you want to send a secret message to Harv, so you write down the ASCII numbers associated with the letters of the message you want to send. When compared to an ASCII chart (or dialed in on Harv's ring), this is the result:

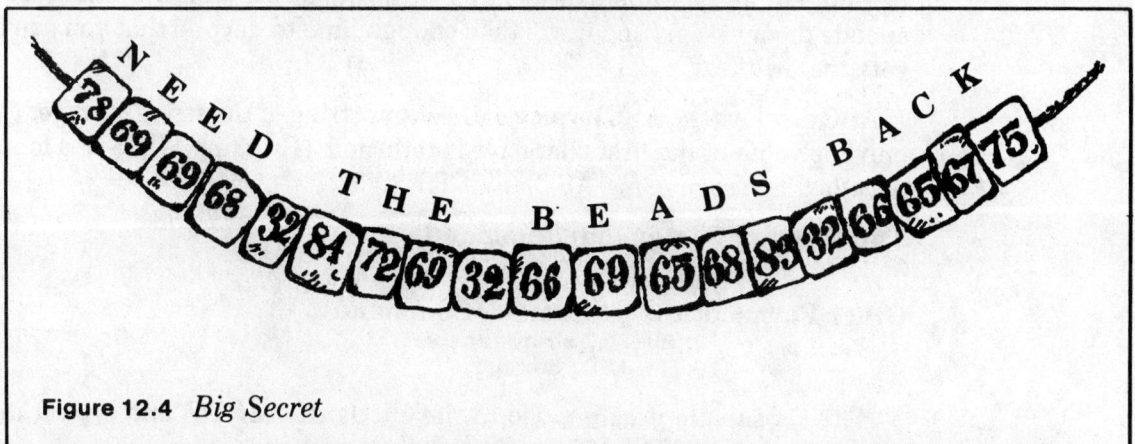

Figure 12.4 *Big Secret*

CHR$ returns the ASCII character represented by the specified number. CHR$ 78 is the "N" of "NEED". All values from 32 to 127 will PRINT a character. The ASCII codes Ø thru 31 and 128 thru 255 have no PRINTable characters associated with them on the PC-2, so nothing will show up on the display if you try to PRINT one of them. The remainder of the characters show up as numbers, letters, symbols and punctuation characters.

The Primary Statement/Command
> CHR$ value

Other Forms of the Statement/Command
> 20: B$ = CHR$ number
> 20: B$ = CHR$ variable
> 20: B$ = CHR$ (calculation)

Here's a sample program. Go to the PROgram MODE and type it in. . .
> 10: WAIT 100
> 20: FOR X = 32 TO 127
> 30: PRINT CHR$ X;
> 40: NEXT X

Now change MODEs and RUN it.

10: B$ = CHR$ 65

After execution of this program line, B$ will contain ASCII character number 65, which is the letter "A".

10: B$ = CHR$ (65)

This is a different format for the primary form, showing that you may use the optional parentheses.

10: PRINT CHR$ 65

This example PRINTs the letter "A" on the display, and does not use a variable.

Some suggested uses – testing for a character. Sending or PRINTing a character.

Oops! What went wrong? Mis-typed it. Not a number. VALUE OUT OF RANGE

Also see: ASC – VAL – STR$

ASC

Using the previous example of a code ring, ASC would be used to encode, rather than decode, your message. In other words, the message, "NEED THE BEADS BACK" would be entered, and numbers associated with the letters would be the result. Thus, you can encode the message, and it will take enough time to decode that you can leave before Harv gets the drift!

ASC displays the ASCII value of the input string. If the string is longer than one character, only the value of the first character is returned. (By using MID$ in a loop, you can code or decode a message using ASC and CHR$.)

The Primary Statement/Command
> ASC string

Other Forms of the Statement/Command
> 10: B = ASC string variable
> 10: B = ASC "literial"

Here's a sample program. Go to the PROgram MODE and type it in. . .
> 10: WAIT 100
> 20: INPUT A$

64
? }
78

```
30: PRINT ASC A$
40: GOTO 20
```

Now change MODEs and RUN this sample.

```
10: A = ASC B$
```

After the execution of this line, the numeric variable A will contain the ASCII value of the first character on the left side of the string variable, B$.

```
10: PRINT ASC B$
```

The execution of this line causes the ASCII value of the first character in the string variable, B$, to be PRINTed on the right side of the display.

```
10: A = ASC (B$)
```

After execution of this program line, the numeric variable A will contain the ASCII value of the first character in B$. This illustrates that parentheses may be used with this statement.

```
10: A = ASC "B"
```

Here we are using a string literal (between quotes) to assign a value to the numeric variable, A.

ASC can be used to search or test for characters, punctuation symbols, and so on, which may be contained in strings.

Some suggested uses – searching for punctuation marks in names on a list. Looking for key symbols on a list.

Oops! What went wrong? Mis-typed it.

Also see: VAL – CHR$ – STR$

STR$

The easiest way to visualize the STR$ function is to go back to our story of the string of beads. Earlier, we looked at the string of beads in two different ways: as a number and as a string. The STR$ function actually converts the numeric contents of the beads into a string, as though we had put quotes around it.

STR$ converts a number to a string. If the number is negative, a minus sign appears as the first character. A positive number has no leading space when STR$ converts it to a string, and does not put a plus (+) sign in front of it, because all numbers without a minus sign are considered to be positive (plus) numbers.

The Primary Statement/Command

```
STR$ number
```

Other Forms of the Statement/Command

```
10: B$ = STR$ variable
10: B$ = STR$ number
10: B$ = STR$ (calculation)
```

Here's a sample program. Go to the PROgram MODE and type it in. . .

```
10: WAIT 100
20: INPUT A
30: PRINT STR$ A
40: GOTO 20
```

Now change MODEs and RUN this sample.

```
10: A$ = STR$ B
```

After execution of this line, A$ will have the string representation of the numeric value of the variable B in it. If B equals –1Ø, say, then A$ is "–1Ø".

1Ø: A$ = STR$ 61

This example illustrates that the target value of the STR$ statement can be a variable or a constant (61 in this case).

1Ø: A$ = STR$ (61)

The target value of STR$ may be contained in parentheses, which are optional in this statement.

1Ø: PRINT STR$ 123

The result of this line will be to PRINT the string "123" on the display. Like other commands we have discussed, STR$ may be used in this fashion, and may be used in the RUN mode.

Note: The target value can contain a decimal point, but if the last digit in the fractional portion is zero (Ø), it will not be in the string. Also, most non-numeric characters will terminate the translation, from numeric representation to string representation, with an ERROR 1 (syntax error), although scientific notation is ok, such as, 8E 14.

STR$ is useful for converting totals or other values into strings that can be mixed easily with names and such, in a data file.

Some suggested uses – data entries can be made in the form of numbers and easily converted to strings for future use. String data can be more useful in preparation of reports and so on.

Oops! What went wrong? Mis-typed it. Wrong mode. Not a number. Target value contains an illegal character.

Also see: VAL – CHR$ – ASC

What You Can Do with Strings

Concatenation

Strings may be added together with the '+' symbol. When two strings (like A$ and B$) are concatenated, the second one is appended (added on) to the end of the first one. Thus, if A$ = "GOING" and B$ = "SOUTH", the operation "C$ = A$ + B$" would result in C$ = "GOINGSOUTH". To make C$ more readable we'll put a space between the words like this: C$ = A$ + " " + B$ which produces: C$ = "GOING SOUTH". You could also use the form: C$ = A$ + CHR$ 32 + B$, which would give the same result, since CHR$ 32 is the ASCII value for a space character.

Logical String Operations

Strings may be compared in a number of ways. If the length of the string is in question, it can be compared using the LEN statement. If the actual contents of the string are to be compared, the ASCII value of each character is considered. Thus, if A$ = "1" (49 ASCII) and B$ = "2" (5Ø ASCII), then A$ is less than B$, since their ASCII values are in the order you would expect. However, if you changed B$ to be "+2", it would now be of *lesser* ASCII value in a comparison, since the plus ("+") sign has an ASCII value of 43. It is important to remember that the ASCII values of the characters are being considered in logical operations, not the literal numeric values that appear in the string.

">" greater than
"<" less than
"=" equal
"<>" not equal

Strings can also be compared directly using the 'greater than', 'less than' or 'equals' 'not equal', 'greater than or equal' or 'less than or equal.' For instance:

1ø: IF A$ = B$ THEN PRINT "EQUAL"

This line tests A$ and if it is identical to B$ (spaces, punctuation and all), it will PRINT the word EQUAL. The way it does this is by comparing each character one-at-a-time until all are tested (it's equal), or the comparison fails and falls through to the next program line, if there is one. The same is true of the other tests:

1ø: IF A$ <> B$ THEN PRINT "NOT EQUAL"
1ø: IF A$ > B$ THEN PRINT "GREATER THAN"
1ø: IF A$ < B$ THEN PRINT "LESS THAN"
1ø: IF A$ >= B$ THEN PRINT "GREATER THAN OR EQUAL"
1ø: IF A$ <= B$ THEN PRINT "LESS THAN OR EQUAL"

Of course, you would probably do something more interesting with the result of one of these string comparison operations, but this gives you an idea of what result is achieved with each test.

\<SML\> — The Upper/lower Case Key

The \<SML\> key switches to *upper* or *lower* case letters, like a shift-lock key on a typewriter. When in *lower* case, 'SMALL' appears on the upper portion of the display, all letter keys pressed will PRINT lower-case letters. Number keys and function keys are unaffected. To type an upper-case letter when in 'small mode,' you have to press the \<SHIFT\> key, then the desired letter key. Commands may not be entered in lower-case, but you may wish to fancy-up the PRINTed message by mixing upper and lower-case letters, as you would when typing or writing by hand.

A message that looks like this:

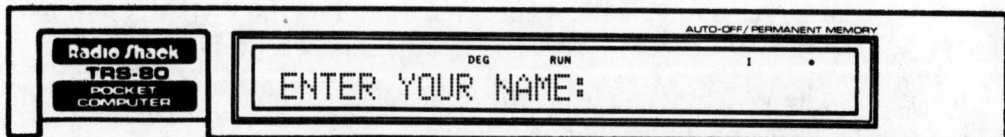

Can be spiffed-up to look like this:

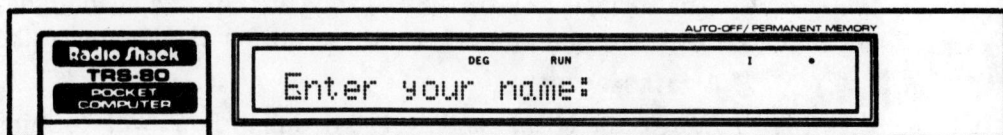

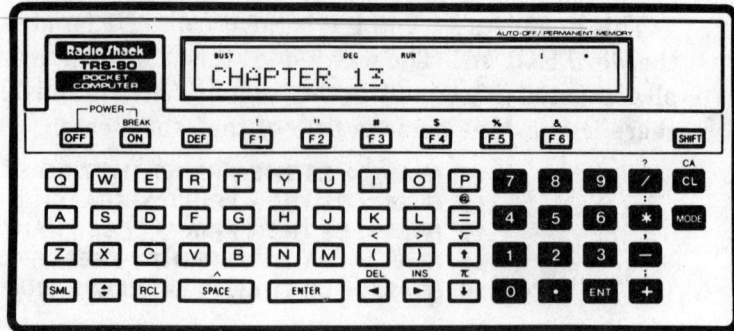

VAL

Here is another method of dealing with the contents of strings, which makes it easy to convert a string to a number.

VAL returns the numeric representation contained on the left side of a string. If the entire string contains numbers, VAL will return the actual value in the string (up to the PC-2's ability to do so).

If a character other than a number (or a decimal point or a scientific notation symbol) occurs in the string after the first number appears, the evaluation of the string is cut off. Thus, the string "12345" has a VALue of 12345, but "123A4" will show a VALue of 123. If the first character in the string is not a number, the VALue is zero, except that a "+" or "-" in the first position of a string of numbers is acceptable.

The VAL function bears the same relationship to STR$ as ASC does to CHR$, in that it performs the opposite operation.

I hate to bug Harv again, maybe I'll give him 5 beads, just as soon as I finish this! If you look at the string of beads again and consider them as a string (with quotes at each end), then the VALue of the string is 123,456,789. If you yanked out a bead in the middle, say the "5", and replaced it with a non-numeric character, other than a space like this:

> "Ø1234A6789"

then the VALue of the string is only 1234, since the A will terminate the conversion process as a non-number.

The Primary Statement/Command
>   VAL string

Other Forms of the Statement/Command
>   1Ø: B = VAL A$
>   1Ø: B = VAL "1234567890"

Here's a sample program. Go to the PROgram mode and type it in.
>   1Ø: WAIT 1ØØ
>   2Ø: INPUT A$
>   3Ø: PRINT VAL A$
>   4Ø: GOTO 2Ø

10: B = VAL A$

After the execution of this line, the numeric variable B will contain the value of the string variable A$

10: B = VAL "123 CENTS"

In this example, a string constant is used. After this line executes, the numeric variable B will contain the value 123, as the evaluation of the string stops at the character "C".

10: PRINT VAL B$

This line will PRINT the VALue of the string variable B$ on the right side of the display. VAL can also be used in the RUN mode.

VAL can be used to convert string data, into a file of numbers, so that they can be used in calculations.

Some suggested uses – storing numbers as strings in checkbook programs and the like is sometimes handy, especially when they are used to PRINT reports on a print device other than the display. VAL can convert the string data back to numbers so you can add 'em up.

Oops! What went wrong? Mis-typed it. The string must be convertible to a numeric value, or a zero is returned.

Also see: STR$ – ASC – CHRS$

INKEY$

Here is a special kind of string statement, that is in a class all to itself. . .

"Mr. Spock! Check the sector scanner! Report any activity to the bridge, immediately!"

Now what you would expect Spock to do? Report any activity on the scanner, right? Right! The PC-2 has a *scanner* all its own. It is called the INKEY$ function or statement. INKEY$ checks the keyboard for any activity. If there is some, it can report back to you. Notice that I said, "can." It doesn't have to report, but it will if you set your program up to accept the reports.

INKEY$ looks at the keyboard to see if a key is being pressed. If no key is pressed when the INKEY$ statement executes, a value of zero is returned. If a key is pressed, a one-character string, of the key being pressed, is returned. Here is a demonstration of our INKEY$ *scanner*:

```
10: WAIT 0
20: PRINT"Press any key"
30: A$=INKEY$
40: IF ASC A$ <32 THEN GOTO 20
50: PRINT "You have pressed the ";A$;" key."
60: GOTO 30
```

Now that you have RUN the program, did you try pressing the <ENTER> key? Did anything happen? No? Hmmm. . . I guess that I should tell you that the <ENTER> key generates an ASCII code of 13. Some of the other keys generate higher codes, but they don't generate a character that is PRINTable – only the ASCII code number. Change line 40 to:40 A$=STR$(ASCA$) and RUN it again. This time, press every key except <BREAK> and you will see the ASCII code on the display.

The Primary Statement/Command
      string variable = INKEY$

Other Forms of the Statement/Command

```
10: A$ = INKEY$
10: IF INKEY$ = condition THEN statement
```

```
10: A$ = INKEY$
```

After execution of this line, A$ will contain the character returned by a scan of the keyboard. If no key was pressed, A$ will be null (zero length, no contents).

```
10: IF INKEY$ = "" THEN 10
```

This line will cause the program to loop until a key is pressed.

```
10: IF INKEY$ <> "" then 10
```

This line will loop back to itself *only* if a key is pressed.

You may want to pause your program until a key is pressed, or (in a game) you can test for certain keys being pressed to tell which way the player wants to move. INKEY$ is the method of choice for these operations.

Some suggested uses – games: testing for arrow keys. PRINT a message and wait until a key (other than <ENTER>) is pressed before continuing. One key-press menu selections.

Oops! What went wrong? Mis-typed it. Wrong mode. More than one character is accepted (INKEY$ is fast).

Also see: INPUT

Putting it together

By using the string statements we have just discussed, we can create a program to test for the arrow keys, which may prove useful in writing a game:

Go to the PROgram mode and type in these lines. . .

```
10: WAIT 100
20: A$ = INKEY$: IF A$="" THEN 20
30: A = ASC A$
40: IF A =  8 PRINT "Left"
50: IF A = 10 PRINT "Down"
60: IF A = 11 PRINT "Up"
70: IF A = 12 PRINT "Right"
80: GOTO 20
```

Now go to the RUN mode and see the results.

This example only tests for arrow keys being pressed. Other keys may be tested in this way, and the results used in your program. Most keys return their normal ASCII value (that is, the <A> key returns a 65), but some return other values. Use this routine to test the various keys on the PC-2:

```
10: WAIT 100
20: A$ = INKEY$: IF A$ = "" THEN 20
30: PRINT ASC A$
40: GOTO 20
```

This program will PRINT the ASCII value of any key you press, except <BREAK>, which will stop the program execution

More on PRINTing...

Yes PRINT is still with us. Once again, we'll see how this versatile statement can be used in yet another way. The PC-2 provides you with a handy way to PRINT out numbers or numeric results of operations. This method is known as print formatting. It uses a modifier to PRINT called the USING statement.

USING (PRINT USING)

PRINT USING provides an easy way to convert raw numeric or string data to a pre-determined format for PRINTing. For instance, large numbers look like this on the display: 123456789Ø, and we would like them to look like this: 1,234,567,89Ø – with commas every so often.

PRINT USING will automatically insert the commas in the correct positions, as well as allow the use of some other special symbols, such as the asterisk ('*') and plus or minus signs. It will even format combinations of strings and numbers.

The PRINT USING statement is a somewhat unique feature designed to make the PRINTout of numbers and strings fit the desired format. The symbols used in this function are called *print formatters*, and consist of the following:

#	(pound sign)	— refers to a numeric value
.	(period)	— places a decimal point in the result
*	(asterisk)	— fills any empty spaces preceding a number
&	(ampersand)	— refers to string values
.∧	(caret)	— generates scientific notation in the result

Here's a sample program. Go to the PROgram MODE and type it in. . .
```
10: INPUT"4 Digits? ";A
20: PRINT USING"####,###";A
```
Now change MODEs and RUN this sample.

The Primary Statement/Command
PRINT USING format modifiers; variable or constant

Other Forms of the Statement/Command
```
10: PRINT USING "+**#,###.##∧ &&&"
```

```
10: PRINT USING "#####&";A;"string"
```
Upon execution, the value contained in the variable A will be formatted on the display. You can have more digits than pound signs to the right of the decimal point, but not to the left. The ampersand (&) will format the literal string following the variable 'A.'

```
10: PRINT USING "&&&";X$
```
Using the '&' character formats strings into the length indicated by the number of '&' symbols in the quotes. In this example, the first 3 letters of the string following the semicolon (X$) will be PRINTed. If 3 characters or less, are in the string, all will be printed.

```
10: PRINT USING "*#####";X
```
This form is used with numeric formats to fill in blank spaces which may occur before the number. In this example, FIVE numbers are specified for PRINTing. If less than 5 digits are entered, the blanks before it will be filled with asterisks.

```
10: PRINT USING "##,###";X
```
This format will insert a comma between the third and fourth digits. Remember that the target number must have fewer digits than the number of pound signs.

```
10: PRINT USING "+##";X
```
Using a plus sign in combination with the pound sign will either cause a '+' to be PRINTed in front of the target number, or a '–' sign if the number is a negative (minus) value.

```
10: PRINT USING "##.##";X
```
Placing a decimal point between two numeric specifiers (pound signs) will cause any fractional portion of the number to be PRINTed, up to the number of places indicated. If there is no fractional portion, zeros will appear after the decimal point. In this example, two decimal places will be shown in the result (even if more decimal numbers were in the target value) or two zeros, if there are no decimal markers.

10: PRINT USING "###. ^ ";X

This form of specifier (the up arrow), will force the number to be PRINTed using scientific notation.

10: F$ = "###.##"
20: PRINT USING F$;X

In this example, the PRINT format modifier is stored in a string (F$), which has been defined as the *print formatting list* before executing the PRINT USING statement.

PRINT USING is handy anyplace that needs an exact placement of words, text, especially numbers and in a particular format. The advantage is in placing things that are odd-sized in a fixed, neat format.

Some suggested uses – PRINTing columns of names, addresses or numbers is a classic example. Take numbers, – they are of all different lengths, and the decimals may be in different positions, but you would like them all to line up on the decimal point. Use PRINT USING with the numeric field specifiers, and only the portion of the number you wish to display will be shown, with the decimal point in the same place for each number displayed. This is probably more useful in conjunction with the printer/plotter, as we shall see in a later chapter.

Oops! What went wrong? Mis-typed it. Wrong mode. Wrong data types.

Also see: PRINT – LPRINT

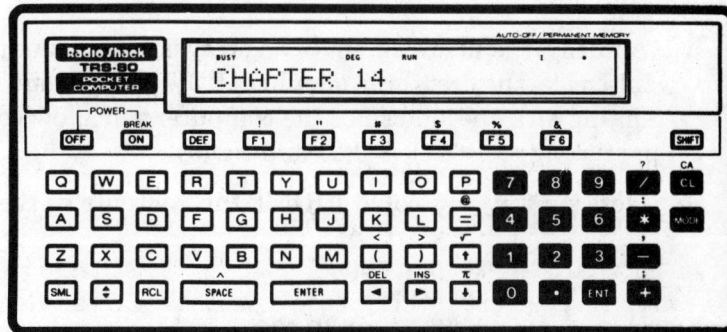

ARRAYS

Many of you have been in a post office and seen the walls with all the little postal boxes. (I'd be tempted to say *most* of you instead of *many*, but I know a lot of you city slickers get the mail delivered right up to your door and have never had to rent a Post Office box.) Each box has its own number and they're all arranged in order from left to right and up to down.

Figure 14.1 *An Array* of Post Office Boxes

Well, all those boxes on the wall comprise an *array* of boxes. They're similar to a computer array. In the post office, you can always find the P.O. box you want by looking under the right number (P.O.Box 1, P.O.Box 3, P.O.Box 1ØØ, etc). Computer arrays work the same way. For instance, you might define an array to correspond to the various post office boxes. We will use the variable PO for this array because it reminds us of the 'Post Office'.

Just as the post office's array of boxes had a number to identify each box, the computer's

PO array has a number for each box of its array. In the post office, the box number is simply written on each box. This wouldn't be convenient on the PC-2, so we use parentheses instead. For instance, the first three members (or boxes) of the PO array are PO(1), PO(2) and PO(3).

Actually, the first element of an array is usually numbered zero. Counting in this manner would make the first three members PO(∅), PO(1) and PO(2). But, it's more natural to start counting with one, and since the computer will allow you to do so if you like, in this example I'm sticking to PO(1), PO(2) and PO(3).

Here's a way you could PRINT the contents of the first five members of the array:

```
10: WAIT 100
20: DIM PO(5)
30: FOR I = 1 TO 5
40: PO(I) = RND 100
50: NEXT I
60: FOR I = 1 TO 5
70: PRINT PO(I)
80: NEXT I
```

This little program is a loop. The program cycles through two loops five times. The first loop loads the five elements (post office boxes) of the array with RaNDom numbers. In the second loop, they are PRINTed on the display.

The first time through the first loop, 'I' will be equal to 1 and line 3∅ will load a RANDom value in PO(1). The second time through the first loop, 'I' will be equal to 2, and line 3∅ will load another RANDom value in PO(2) and so on, until all five elements (P.O. Boxes) contain some RaNDom value.

In the second loop, the process is repeated, except that the values contained in the five array elements will be PRINTed. When 'I' is equal to 1, the value contained in PO(1) will be PRINTed. The second time through the loop, 'I' will be equal to 2, and line 6∅ will PRINT the value contained in PO(2). And so it goes.

The *array* variable is a different form of a variable, which is one of the most powerful in the PC-2. A *double dimensioned array* is one which has layers of post office boxes.

As we shall see, the arrays are set up to provide easily accessed variable storage, and, in some ways, are simpler to use than the other variables which we have examined.

As with the other variables, arrays can be numbers or strings. Arrays are often referred to as sub-scripted variables, with the number in parentheses being the sub-script.

The variable, referred to by the number or numbers in parentheses, is called an array *element*. Each sub-scripted element is distinct from every other element, and is independent of other variables using a similar name; thus, the variable A is different from the variable A(1), and the variable AA(1) is a different variable from either A(1) or A.

Using array variables with strings actually allows more versatility than the normal strings. As we have seen, a normal string (such as A$), can contain only 16 characters, where the string array A$(1) can hold up to 8∅ characters per element.

Before we can use arrays to their full potential we must learn how to use the DIMension statement.

DIM

Here is another story, to illustrate the concept of the DIM statement.

The Marlows were going on vacation. Much to Tobey's delight, her friend Patti was coming along – at least for the beginning of the trip. Patti lived about a mile down the road from the Marlows, who were planning to pick her up on their way out of town and drop her off at her summer camp, about 3ØØ miles later down the road.

The night before they departed, the Marlows spent a couple of hours packing their suitcases and bringing them out to the station wagon.

As they were throwing the luggage into the hatch back, Mrs. Marlow wondered out loud about how much luggage Patti planned to bring. Mr. and Mrs. Marlow were sure that there would be plenty of room for everything. But they wanted to be able to throw Patti's bags in quickly when they picked her up, and then be able to take them out quickly when they arrived at Camp Minikinnish.

The problem was, that if they put all their own stuff in back near the hatch, getting Patti's stuff in and out would be awkward. Obviously, they needed to push their stuff farther forward, so there would be room for Patti's luggage, right at the hatch. But they didn't want to push their stuff *too* far forward either. That would be a waste of effort, and it would make it harder to retrieve later.

Mr. Marlow asked Tobey to phone Patti to find out how much baggage she was planning to bring. Tobey did so and soon delivered the message that Patti was planning to bring two medium-sized valises.

The Marlows pushed their own bags just far enough forward to allow for Patti's luggage. The following morning at Patti's house, they were able to put Patti's bags right into the car and were on their way almost immediately.

Putting a DIM statement in your program is a lot like calling Patti's house to find out how much luggage she's going to bring.

Your PC-2 dynamically allocates memory for variables. This means that if you think of the computer's memory as being like the inside of the station wagon, the computer just keeps throwing stuff in, until everything is on board that's going aboard. This works fine with ordinary variables (in computer jargon they're called scalar variables), including number and string variables.

But sometimes, you use special variables that you want to be kept together so you can locate them in an especially convenient manner. In such a case, you would set up an *array*.

Since array variables are stored in a special way, you have to tell the computer the size and shape of the array so it can save some room near the door, so to speak.

The DIM statement is used to set up arrays for future use in your program. You can configure each array to suit your needs, by the depth and number of elements for each one. The array A(3), for example, can be thought of as one filing cabinet with 4 drawers in it. What's that? Why 4 drawers? Well, as you may have guessed, A(Ø) counts as the first one, so you always have one more than the number specified in the parentheses. Anyway, a double dimensioned array, like A(2,3), can be looked at as 3 filing cabinets with 4 drawers each.

The Primary Statement/Command
    DIM variable name (value (,value) . . .)

Other Forms of the Statement/Command
    1Ø: DIM A(5)
    1Ø: DIM A$(5)
    1Ø: DIM A(5,3)
    1Ø: DIM A$(5,3)
    1Ø: DIM A$(5,3)*2Ø

Figure 14.2 *File Cabinet – (double Dimension A(2,3))*

Here's a sample program. Go to the PROgram MODE and type it in. . . .

```
10: DIM A(3)
20: FOR X = 0 TO 3
30: INPUT A(X)
40: NEXT X
50: FOR X = 0 TO 3
60: PRINT"A(";X;") = ";X
70: NEXT X
```

Now change MODEs and RUN this sample.

10: DIM A(10)

This is the format for a singly – DIMensioned array. As we have seen, this example would produce 11 variables to work with; A(∅) through A(1∅)

10: DIM A(3,5)

This is an example of the double-DIMensioned array. In this case, you have 24 variables to work with: A(∅,∅) through A(3,5) (think of it as four drawers across by 6 down).

String arrays are set up in the same way as those for numeric variables, except that you can also specify a length for the strings in the array.

10: DIM A$(11,3)

This example illustrates a double-DIMensioned string array. Because no length for the strings is specified, they can be a maximum of 16 characters, which is the default length for strings in the PC-2.

10: DIM A$(1)*80

Here we are setting up a singly-dimensioned string array and setting the string length to 8∅ characters each, which is the maximum length for a string in the PC-2. You would use the same format to specify a length in a two-dimensional array.

Groups of things (words, names, addresses, phone numbers, etc.) are conveniently stored in arrays, and easily accessed. Things that are easily put into rows and columns are easily stored in multiple DIMensioned arrays. For example, a holiday gift list (named L(4,4)) for the family could look like this:

GET GIFT FOR –	Ø MOM	1 DAD	2 DAD JR.	3 JAMMIE	4 DOG
Ø MOM	——	BOOTS	SHIRT	PAMPERS	BONE
1 DAD	BROOM	——	SUITCASE	TRAINS	CHAIN
2 DAD JR.	BON-BON	VEST	——	BALL	KICK
3 JAMMIE	SMILE	WET HAND	WHINE	——	A YANK
4 DOG	PANT	LICK	GROWL	SNIF	——

L(1,2) = **"VEST"**

Figure 14.3

To put this list in the PC-2, or set it up for a similar array, the DIMension should be A$(4,4)*8 because there are 5 rows of 5 columns each, and the *8 allows only 8 characters in each element. Of course, you would make these things to be whatever would fit your needs.

Some suggested uses – using DIMensioned variables is an efficient way to store and access data in mailing lists, accounting applications, and many other such data-manipulation programs.

Oops! What went wrong? Mis-typed it. Wrong mode. Out of memory range, or too many levels – only two are allowed.

Also see: Variables – Arrays

An Array You Don't Need to DIM

@(1) to @(26) and @$(1) to @$(26) are built-in singly–DIMensioned arrays — 16 characters for each of the @$( ). They are set for 26 variables and are identical to variables A to Z and A$ to Z$ (load one and read the corresponding simple variable where you like). These arrays provide another way of addressing the primary variables, and are quite handy for testing or assigning values to the primary varibles in a loop. This means that you can treat the primary variables as though they were actually DIMensioned arrays.

Here is a sample program which illustrates the @(n) array being used in conjunction with the logical string operators we have seen earlier. The program sets up values for the @(n) array, and compares input for position in the list.

```
10 @$(1) = "A"
20 @$(2) = "B"
30 @$(3) = "C"
40 @$(4) = "D"
50 @$(5) = "E"
60 @$(6) = "F"
70 @$(7) = "G"
80 @$(8) = "H"
90 INPUT "TYPE A WORD";A1$
100 FOR I = 1 TO 8
110 IF A1$ > @(I) THEN PRINT A1$; " AFTER "; @(I)
120 NEXT I
```

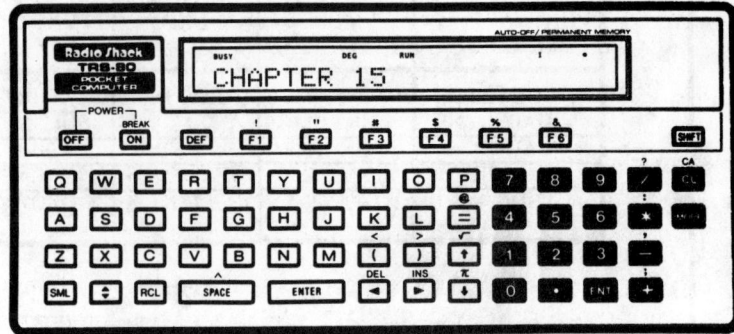

Logical Operations

LOGIC. Don't let that word make you nervous... it's not logical to let a mere word get to you. Especially one so clean and well-behaved. We have already looked at logical operations with strings, so the concept is nothing new. You do it (use logic, I mean) all the time. Your mind works that way naturally, every moment. The problems arise from the way people twist what goes in and comes out, of the logical process.

Time to Think in Binary

The binary number is used in the computer for LOGICAL operations. When binary logic is used, it is really doing something to each BIT in the number, rather than considering the number as a whole. A simple way to look at binary numbers is to consider that each byte in memory can contain a value of 255 decimal, which looks like this in binary:

1111 1111

This is a byte of memory in the PC-2, which has 8 bits (or BInary digiTs) in it. The space between the left side and right side is just to make it easier to look at it. The two sides are called nybbles. To translate the value of the byte into a decimal number, you consider each bit position as having these values:

128	64	32	16	8	4	2	1
1	1	1	1	1	1	1	1

Now, looking at the number 255, which has all the bits on (that means equal to 1), we decode it by the value of bit position that has a 1 in it until all 8 positions are considered:

128 + 64 + 32 + 16 + 8 + 4 + 2 + 1 = 255 (decimal)

Here is another binary number: 1Ø1Ø 1Ø1Ø. This number is decoded as follows:

1	Ø	1	Ø	1	Ø	1	Ø
128	Ø	32	Ø	8	Ø	2	Ø

128 + Ø +32 + Ø +8 +Ø +2 +Ø = 17Ø (decimal)

Now we'll consider some logical operations you can do with numbers and see how they relate to binary calculations.

AND, OR and NOT as Logical Operators

"Operator, please get me area code (714) 555-1212. This is a peripheral-to-peripheral call for Mr. Com P. Uters." Mr. Modem sat back and waited. In a moment, the connection was made and Mr. Modem began discussing plans for a new PC-2 book with his friend (known affectionately as 'CPU').

Just as a telephone operator connects two people in a particular manner for a particular purpose, so does a logical or arithmetic operator connect two program variables or expressions. Everyone's familiar with arithmetic operators such as '+' for add and '-' for subtract. They connect two values — say, for instance, '3+6.' The two values which the operators operate *on* are called *operands*.

For the most part, logical operators are pretty familiar. The ones your PC-2 recognizes are 'AND,' 'OR' and 'NOT.' They're treated the same way you would use them in normal conversation.

In everyday English, the word 'and' connects two or more statements or items. The statements are operands, and the 'and' is the operator. The 'and' indicates that the statements it connects are both true. Suppose I say, "I just drank some coffee, and I feel wide awake." If I haven't had any coffee recently, the sentence can't be true, no matter how awake I feel. If I feel sleepy, then I am a liar even if I just drank some coffee. I can only utter the sentence truthfully if *both* the statement about the coffee *and* the statement about feeling awake are true. The rule for 'and' is "Both are true, and nothing else will do."

When the PC-2 uses AND as a logical operator, it treats it just the way we normally do. Here's a sample program using the AND operator.

```
5:  WAIT 100
10: INPUT "ENTER YOUR FIRST NAME";FN$
20: INPUT "ENTER YOUR LAST NAME";LN$
30: IF FN$="JOHN" AND LN$="SMITH" THEN PRINT "MAY I SEE SOME I.D.?"
```

The program will PRINT the message in line 3Ø *only* if the the person using your program enters the name "JOHN SMITH." Remember, the rule for AND is, "Both are true, and nothing else will do."

'OR' is similar to 'AND' except that if *either* statement connected by the 'OR' is true, the whole sentence is true. If I told you that I left your towel in the chest-of-drawers OR in the linen closet, my statement is true if I left it in either place. The sentence can only be false if both sides of the 'OR' are wrong — in other words, I'm wrong if I didn't put the towel in one OR the other of the two places I referred to.

Here's an example of how you could use OR in your program:

```
5:  WAIT 100
10: INPUT "ENTER YOUR LAST NAME"; LN$
20: IF LN$="SMITH" OR LN$="JONES" THEN PRINT "YOU HAVE A COMMON LAST
    NAME": GOTO 40
30: END
40: PRINT "WHY DON'T YOU CHANGE IT"
50: PRINT "TO BEEBLEBROCKS?"
```

The message in line 2Ø will be PRINTed if you enter either SMITH *OR* JONES. If you enter any other name, the message will not be PRINTed. AND can be combined with OR in the same statement. Consider this variation of the AND program above:

```
10: INPUT "ENTER FIRST NAME";FN$
20: INPUT "ENTER YOUR LAST NAME";LN$
30: IF FN$="JOHN" AND (LN$="SMITH" OR LN$="JONES") THEN PRINT "MAY I
    SEE SOME I.D?"
```

In this case the message, will be PRINTed if, and only if, either of the names JOHN SMITH or JOHN JONES is entered. Notice how the parentheses in line 3Ø show the program what order to evaluate the operators in.

NOT is a little different from AND and OR, in that it operates on one value (operand) instead of two. In English, 'not' reverses the truth of a statement. For instance, if 'Tobey is under 12 years old,' is true, then 'Tobey is *not* under 12 years old,' is false. If 'Toledo is the capital of China,' is false, then 'Toledo is *not* the capital of China,' is true.

NOT works the same way in a PC-2 program, when used as a logical operator, except that it isn't embedded in the program expression the way it is in an English sentence. Instead, it precedes the expression. Here's an example:

```
1Ø: INPUT"ENTER A VALUE";N
2Ø: IF NOT N = –4 THEN PRINT "N = 3"
```

AND, OR and NOT may all be combined in a single statement. The following example combines AND and OR:

```
 5: WAIT 1ØØ
2Ø: G$="GROUCHO"
25: H$="HARPO"
3Ø: C$="CHICO"
35: Z$="ZEPPO"
4Ø: M$="MARX"
5Ø: INPUT "ENTER YOUR FIRST NAME"; F$
6Ø: INPUT "ENTER YOUR LAST NAME"; L$
7Ø: IF ((L$=M$) AND (F$<>G$ OR F$<>H$ OR F$<>C$ OR
     F$<>Z$) THEN PRINT "A MARX; NOT A MARX BROTHER"
```

The message in line 7Ø will be PRINTed only if you enter a last name of "MARX" and don't enter any of the following for a first name: GROUCHO, HARPO, CHICO, ZEPPO.

NOT cannot be used with strings. Here is a purely numeric example using AND, OR and NOT in a single statement:

```
1Ø: WAIT 1ØØ
2Ø: A=1Ø
3Ø: B=2Ø
4Ø: C=3Ø
5Ø: D=12Ø
6Ø: IF ((A<B) AND (C>B)) OR ((C=121) AND (C=NOT D))
     THEN PRINT"PASSED":END
7Ø: PRINT"FAILED"
```

In this example the left half of line 6Ø passes the test, ((A<B) AND (C>B)) which is 'true.' The right half is tested as an OR condition, which means that either side may pass, to meet the total requirements.

Change line 4Ø to read, C=–121. In line 6Ø, change (C>B) to, (C<B) and (C=121) to (C=–121). Now the right half is 'true' and the left half is 'false,' but since either side (OR) may be 'true' to pass the test, it will still PRINT, PASSED.

Just for jollies, change line 4Ø to read, C=99. Now it will fail since neither side is 'true' and FAILED will be PRINTed.

AND, OR and NOT as Boolean Operators

There is another way to use AND, OR and NOT. When used in connection with Boolean logic, they become more like arithmetic operators. AND and OR work in much the same way that '+', '−', '*' and '/' do, in that they specify an operation that is to be performed on two numbers to produce a third.

Here, for instance, are some familiar arithmetic statements: 6 + 3 = 9. 6 − 3 = 3. 6 * 3 = 18. 6 / 3 = 2. Here are some similar statements using Boolean operators instead of the familiar arithmetic ones: (6 AND 3 = 2) (6 OR 3 = 7).

Don't worry about how these results were arrived at for the moment. The important thing is to see that you're dealing with arithmetic-like operators which, like '+', '−', '*' and '/' allow you to derive a number from two other numbers.

There is another kind of arithmetic operator that we're familiar with. I mean the kind that derives its result from (operates on) only one number or operand instead of two. The simplest example is the minus sign (−) which we put in front of a number to show that it's negative. Don't confuse this use of '−' with its use as a symbol of subtraction.

The '−' in '−1∅' is a minus sign which operates on one value. The '−' in '4−1' is a subtraction symbol which acts on two values. Note how the '−' in '−1∅' changes the 1∅ to a new number. Here's an example of '−' being used in both ways in the same expression: 1∅ − −1∅ = 2∅.

Arithmetic operators which, like the minus sign, operate on just one number at a time, are called *unary* operators. NOT is an example of a unary Boolean operator. Here are some examples of NOT being used in this manner. NOT 3 = −4. NOT 6 = −7.

Here, in case you are wondering, is how the AND, OR and NOT Boolean operators work. To begin with, they all work on the binary bit level.

In the PC-2, the AND, NOT and OR Boolean operators work on eight-bit binary operands. They each work bit by bit. Let's consider an example given earlier. 6 AND 3 = 2. How do you work this out? First let's write the two operands in binary: 6 = ∅∅∅∅∅11∅. Basically, the two one bits show that six is made out of a four and a two. 3 = ∅∅∅∅∅∅11. In this case, the two bits show that three is made from a two and a one.

Now, let's write the 6 AND 3 = 2 statement the way we wrote arithmetic examples in grade school:

```
        6
AND     3
        ?
```

Translating this into binary, we get:

```
        ∅∅∅∅∅11∅
AND     ∅∅∅∅∅∅11
        ????????
```

Remember the rule for AND is, both are true, and nothing else will do. Ah, but what is truth when we're dealing with ones and zeros? Zero is always considered false. Everything else is considered true. In this case, everything else is 'one,' so one is true.

Now all we have to do is a bit-by-bit evaluation of our problem. To make this simpler, I want to write out the problem once more, this time labeling each bit position:

```
    7 6 5 4 3 2 1 ∅   Bit Position
    ∅ ∅ ∅ ∅ ∅ 1 1 ∅   First Operand (6)
AND                   Operator
    ∅ ∅ ∅ ∅ ∅ ∅ 1 1   Second Operand (3)
    ? ? ? ? ? ? ? ?   Answer
```

We're going to start by ANDing the bit at position zero in the first operand with the bit in position zero in the second operand. We will write the result at position zero in the answer. The bit at position zero in the first operand is a zero. The bit in position zero of the second operand is a one. So we have Ø AND 1 or FALSE and TRUE. Remember, for AND, both are true, and nothing else will do. So the result of this AND operation is FALSE, or zero. We record this at position zero of the answer like this:

```
7 6 5 4 3 2 1 Ø    Bit Position
0 0 0 0 0 1 1 Ø    First Operand (six)

AND                Operator

0 0 0 0 0 0 1 1    Second Operand (three)
? ? ? ? ? ? ? Ø    Answer
```

Now we're going to repeat the process at position one. The bit at position one in the first operand is a one. The corresponding bit in the second operand is also a one. So we have 1 AND 1 or TRUE AND TRUE. Well, how about that — both are true, so the result is true! We record this in position one of the answer like so:

```
7 6 5 4 3 2 1 Ø    Bit Position
0 0 0 0 0 1 1 Ø    First Operand (six)

AND                Operator

0 0 0 0 0 0 1 1    Second Operand (three)
? ? ? ? ? ? 1 Ø    Answer
```

Now from position one to position two (below). The first operand contains a one in this position. The second operand contains a zero. So we have 1 AND Ø or TRUE AND FALSE. This evaluates as false and is recorded as shown below:

```
7 6 5 4 3 2 1 Ø    Bit Position
0 0 0 0 0 1 1 Ø    First Operand (six)

AND                Operator

0 0 0 0 0.1 1      Second Operand (three)
? ? ? ? ? 0 1 Ø    Answer
```

At position three, we find a zero in the first operand, and likewise, a zero in the second operand. This gives us Ø AND Ø or FALSE and FALSE. This yeilds a FALSE, or zero. After we record our result, the problem looks like this:

```
7 6 5 4 3 2 1 Ø    Bit Position
0 0 0 0 0 1 1 Ø    First Operand (six)

AND                Operator

0 0 0 0 0 0 1 1    Second Operand (three)
? ? ? ? 0 0 1 Ø    Answer
```

A quick examination of positions four through seven reveals that they're all just like position three, zero AND zero, which is FALSE AND FALSE. So positions four through seven all evaluate as FALSE, or zero. We may record our result as shown:

```
7 6 5 4 3 2 1 Ø    Bit Position
0 0 0 0 0 1 1 Ø    First Operand (six)

AND                Operator

0 0 0 0 0 0 1 1    Second Operand (three)
0 0 0 0 0 0 1 Ø    Answer
```

Since the binary number ØØØØØØ1Ø equals 2 in decimal, we have shown that 6 AND 3 = 2

— just what the PC-2 has been trying to tell us all along!

OR, of course, works just as AND does, except more ORly than ANDly. Let's calculate 6 OR 3 = 7. Translating this into binary, writing it in grade-school format and adding the bit-place header all in giant steps, we get:

```
        7 6 5 4 3 2 1 0    Bit Position
        0 0 0 0 0 1 1 0    First Operand (six)
OR                         Operator
        0 0 0 0 0 0 1 1    Second Operand (three)
        ? ? ? ? ? ? ? ?    Answer
```

In the zero column, we find a 0 in six and a one in three. Remember, with OR, if either of the two operands is true (i.e., a one), then the result is also true. So we enter a one in the zero column of the answer:

```
        7 6 5 4 3 2 1 0    Bit Position
        0 0 0 0 0 1 1 0    First Operand (six)
OR                         Operator
        0 0 0 0 0 0 1 1    Second Operand (three)
        ? ? ? ? ? ? ? 1    Answer
```

In the one position, we find a 1 in the six and a 1 in the three. 1 OR 1 yields a 1, so we enter a 1 in column one of the answer:

```
        7 6 5 4 3 2 1 0    Bit Position
        0 0 0 0 0 1 1 0    First Operand (six)
OR                         Operator
        0 0 0 0 0 0 1 1    Second Operand (three)
        ? ? ? ? ? ? 1 1    Answer
```

In position two, we find a 1 and a 0. By the Great Rule of OR, these bits yield a one, which we enter into the corresponding bit of the answer, like so:

```
        7 6 5 4 3 2 1 0    Bit Position
        0 0 0 0 0 1 1 0    First Operand (six)
OR                         Operator
        0 0 0 0 0 0 1 1    Second Operand (three)
        ? ? ? ? ? 1 1 1    Answer
```

Position four, and positions five, six and seven, for that matter, show a zero in each operand. Since zero OR zero is false (0), we complete our answer like this:

```
        7 6 5 4 3 2 1 0    Bit Position
        0 0 0 0 0 1 1 0    First Operand (six)
OR                         Operator
        0 0 0 0 0 0 1 1    Second Operand (three)
        0 0 0 0 0 1 1 1    Answer
```

00000111 is, let's see, uh, one plus two plus four equals, uh, oh my yes, seven! Just like the PC-2 predicted!

Finally, this brings us to NOT. NOT, remember, is a unary operator; it acts on only one operand at a time. NOT also works on the bit-level. However, in practical terms, it works at a higher level as well. First of all, I'd like you to visualize the number scale. We're concerned only with whole numbers. Counting up from left to right, you could represent the first few numbers like this:

```
Ø   1   2   3   4   5
```

Now let's add some negative numbers:

```
-6  -5  -4  -3  -2  -1   Ø   1   2   3   4   5
```

Now we have to do something special. We have to *think* of zero in a different way than we're accustomed to. Normally, we consider zero to be neither positive nor negative, just sort of neutral. However, for the purpose of *understanding* the PC-2's interpretation of NOT, we have to consider zero to be positive. I'll redraw our number scale now, with an arrow in the middle to represent an imaginary crossover-point from negative to positive:

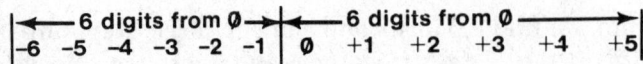

```
|◄—— 6 digits from Ø ——►|◄—— 6 digits from Ø ——►|
|-6  -5  -4  -3  -2  -1 | Ø  +1  +2  +3  +4  +5|
```

Ok, here's what 'NOT n' does. It figures out how far away from the arrow n is and picks a number the same distance away on the opposite side of the arrow. Thus NOT Ø = –1; NOT–1 = Ø; NOT 1 = –2; NOT –2 = 1; NOT 5 = –6, etc.

One last word while the operator's still on the line. The PC-2 performs Boolean operations only on whole numbers, not fractions. If you use a fraction or mixed number, such as 2.9, for one of the operands in a Boolean operation, the PC-2 will round the operand down to the nearest whole number that's lower for the purpose of completing the operation. For example, if you ask the PC-2 to display the result of 3.9 AND 5, the PC-2 will tell you the result of 3 AND 5. If you use a negative mixed number or fraction, the operand is rounded *up*, toward zero. For instance, -2.9 is rounded *up* to -2, not to -3.

AND

The AND operation looks at each bit position both in numbers and if the bit in the same position of both numbers is on (equal to 1), then the same bit position in the answer will be one. On the other hand, if one or the other of the two bits is off (equal to Ø), then the corresponding bit in the result will be off. Remember, AND means BOTH.

In a hotel, there is usually a connecting set of doors between rooms, so that the single rooms can be rented out as suites. In order to do this, both the door on your side AND the door on the other side must be opened.

The Primary Statement/Command
        variable = variable AND constant

Other Forms of the Statement/Command
        1Ø: A = variable AND variable
        1Ø: A = number AND number
        1Ø: A = (calculation) AND (calculation)
        1Ø: PRINT variable AND variable

Here's a sample program. Go to the PROgram MODE and type it in. . .

        1Ø: INPUT A,B
        2Ø: C = A AND B
        3Ø: PRINT C

Now change MODEs and RUN this sample.

1Ø: A = X AND Y
Here we have the results of the AND operation stored in the variable A. Let's say that X is

equal to 3Ø decimal, and Y is equal to 56 decimal. The AND operation would look like this:

```
         DECIMAL    BINARY
        X = 30 =  ØØØ1 111Ø
  AND   Y = 56 =  ØØ11 1ØØØ
        A = 24 =  ØØØ1 1ØØØ
```

As you can see, the resulting number in A, has only those bits on, which had a 1 in that position in each of the variables X and Y. There is no apparent correlation if you just look at the decimal values. You must get to the root of the matter by looking at it in binary.

1Ø: IF A AND B THEN LET X = 1

This illustrates that the AND logical operator can be used as part of another logical operation, such as the IF statement. In this example, BASIC performs the AND operation on variables A and B, and uses the result for the IF condition. This is a bit shakey, because any result other than zero will be seen as a true condition (which means that BOTH A and B had some value).

1Ø: IF A = 3 AND B = 1 THEN LET X = 1

Here, we are testing two conditions with the AND operation. Both conditions must be met, that is, A must be equal to 3, and B must be equal to 1 before the IF statement will be true.

AND is a method for testing values without changing the variables containing the targets. Using AND, you can test for specific conditions without being concerned with the values, only the result.

Some suggested uses – using AND, you can test for which names to use in a mailing list (if Aunt Alice sent you a present AND a card, then send her one of each). You could also test for which values to use in an accounting program, and so on.

Oops! What went wrong? Mis-typed it. Wrong variable type.

Also see: NOT – OR

OR

OR is the opposite of the AND statement we just discussed. Whereas AND means BOTH, OR means EITHER. In comparing the bits in two values, if one OR the other is on (equal to 1), then the corresponding bit in the result will also be on.

The Primary Statement/Command
          A = variable OR variable

Other Forms of the Statement/Command
          1Ø: A = variable OR variable
          1Ø: A = number OR number
          1Ø: A = (calculation) OR (calculation)
          1Ø: PRINT number OR number

Here's a sample program. Go to the PROgram MODE and type it in. . .

          1Ø: INPUT X,Y
          2Ø: Z = X OR Y
          3Ø: PRINT Z

Now change MODEs and RUN this sample.

1Ø: X = Y OR Z

In this example, X will contain the result of the value of Y ORed with the value of Z. Let's say that Y is equal to 3Ø decimal, and Z is equal to 56 decimal. The OR operation would be performed like this:

```
              DECIMAL    BINARY
         Y = 30 =  0001 1110
     OR  Z = 56 =  0011 1000
         X = 62 =  0011 1110
```

As you can see, the result of the operation (X) has those bits on which had a 1 in that position in either of the variables, Y or Z. As we mentioned earlier, there is no apparent correlation if you just look at the decimal values.

10: IF A=1 OR B=2 THEN GOSUB 100

Here, OR is used as a logical comparison between two values, rather than acting as an operator with two values. In this case, if A is equal to 1 OR B is equal to 2, then the rest of the statement will be executed. Only if both A and B failed the test will the program drop through this line to the next.

10: IF A OR B THEN GOSUB 100

In this form, if either A OR B has a value other than 0, then the test passes, and the GOSUB is executed. Only if neither had a value (positive or negative), would the test fail.

OR, like AND, is useful for testing conditions. If one variable OR the other meets the criteria for the test, then the test passes.

Some suggested uses – the OR comparison is handy for selecting non-exclusive data for charting, sorting, comparing lists, and so on.

Oops! What went wrong? Mis-typed it. Wrong variable types used in comparison.

Also see: AND – NOT

NOT

The NOT operator causes all of the bits to be flipped, or complemented in the binary representation of the number. This operation is a little more complicated than the AND and OR, in that it introduces the concept of negative and positive numbers in binary representation. What happens here is that bit number seven, the MSB (most significant bit), becomes a sign for the remaining number. That is, if the MSB is off (equal to 0), then the rest of the number is positive. If the MSB is on (equal to 1), the number is negative. This means that you are only using seven of the 8 bits (or 15 of the 16 bits in a two-byte word), so the values you have to work with (in a single byte) are –128 to +127. NOT, as well as many other operations in the PC-2, uses a 16-bit value (in the range of –32768 to +32767) for its operation. To use this function with a decimal number, 1 is added to the number, and then the sign is reversed.

The Primary Statement/Command
NOT number

Other Forms of the Statement/Command
```
10: A = NOT number
10: A = NOT variable
10: A = NOT (calculation)
10: PRINT NOT number
```

Here's a sample program. Go to the PROgram MODE and type it in. . .

```
10: INPUT X
20: PRINT NOT X
```

Now change MODEs and RUN this sample.

10: X = NOT Y

Let's say that Y is equal to Ø in this example. The binary operation would look like this:

$$ØØ = 0000\ 0000\ 0000\ 0000$$
$$NOT\ Ø = -1 = 1111\ 1111\ 1111\ 1111$$

As you can see, the high bit of this sixteen-bit number (the MSB) is on (equal to 1), which means it is a negative value. It is as though the operation added one and negated the result:

$$NOT\ Ø = -(Ø+1) = -1$$

The reverse condition (going from a negative number), works the same way:

$$-1 = 1111\ 1111\ \ 1111\ 1111$$
$$NOT\ -1 = Ø = 0000\ 0000\ \ 0000\ 0000$$

or, in decimal representation:

$$NOT\ -1 = (-1+1) = Ø$$

Here is another example, using the value of 3 for X:

$$3 = 0000\ 0000\ 0000\ 0011$$
$$NOT\ 3 = -4 = 1111\ 1111\ 1111\ 1100$$

Expressed in decimal, the formula looks like this:

$$NOT\ 3 = -(3+1) = -4$$

NOT has its main application in graphics programs, which we'll see in a later section.

Oops! What went wrong? Mis-typed it. Wrong variable type.

Also see: AND – OR

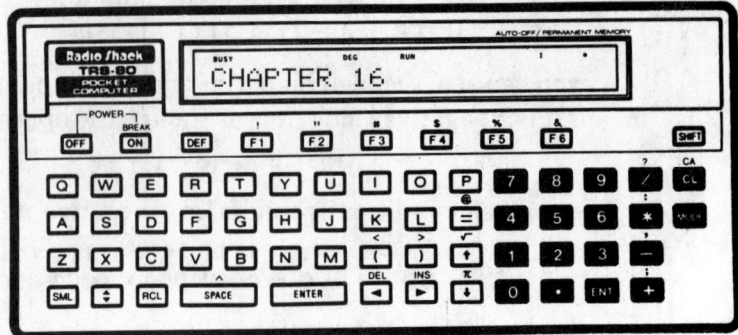

Numbers, Again . . . .

In this section, we will examine some more of the ways in which BASIC looks at numbers. As you will see, these statements are structured after the human way of understanding parts of those things we usually refer to as decimal numbers.

INT

INT returns the INTeger (or whole) part of a number. In the example, only the value to the left of a decimal point (that is, the integer value) is PRINTed, as any fractional number (the decimal portion) is ignored.

At last, your friend John is paying off some money he owes you, say $4.23, and you tell him to just give you the four dollars, and we can call it square. The $4 is the INTeger portion of the number. We cut off (or truncate) the cents because (in this instance) the rest is not important. Any time the numbers are smaller than one (which are the decimal fractions of numbers) and they are not important to the calculation, you could cut them off with INT. Now if you could just cut off that mooch, John!

The Primary Statement/Command
variable = INT number (or variable)

Other Forms of the Statement/Command
10: variable = INT number
10: variable = INT variable
10: variable = INT (calculation)
10: PRINT INT number

Here's a sample program. Go to the PROgram MODE and type it in. . .

10: INPUT"Enter a decimal number like 1.2";A
20: PRINT INT A

Now change MODEs and RUN this sample.

10: A = INT 1.2

After BASIC executes this line, the variable A will contain the INTeger value of the numeric constant 1.2 (A = 1).

1Ø: A = INT (1.2)

This produces the same result as that of the previous example, illustrating that parentheses may be used with this statement.

1Ø: PRINT INT 1.2

Here, the INTeger value of the numeric constant 1.2 (that is, 1) is PRINTed when this program line is executed.

1Ø: A = A/2 – INT(A/2)

This is a way in which a number may be tested to find out if it is odd or even. An even number will return a value of Ø and an odd number will always return a value of .5, or ½. Did you notice that the answer (A, in this case) will always equal the decimal fraction remainder? Subtracting the INT portion of half a number (the number divided by two) from the number with its decimal fraction remainder, leaves that remainder as the answer.

INT can be used in the RUN, PROgram and RESERVE mode.

With the INT statement, you only deal with the whole number portion of a calculation or number. This is useful in statements that need integer values, or to get rid of unneeded fractional numbers in calculations or displays.

Some suggested uses – rounding numbers to their whole number values. Calculated GOTOs, GOSUBs and ON ERROR GOTOs and FOR/NEXT loops.

Oops! What went wrong? Mis-typed it. Out of range. Not a number.

Also see: ABS

ABS

ABS returns the ABSolute value of a number. Essentially, it strips the sign from the number, so that a negative number becomes positive, while a positive number remains unchanged. When we use the ABS function, we look at the digits in the number, without considering whether it is negative or positive.

If you owe Fred $1Ø and John owes you $1Ø this time (he knows a soft touch), then if John pays you the $1Ø that's positive. Positive income, I mean. And, if Fred is standing behind you breathing fast, you give him the ten. That's negative. . . income, that is. But the point of all this (besides telling you to manage your money better) is that the $1Ø is still a ten, whether it is negative or positive, the absolute value (ABS) is ten with no sign. Easy come, easy go.

The Primary Statement/Command
> **ABS number (or variable)**

Other Forms of the Statement/Command
> **1Ø: A = ABS number (negative or positive)**
> **1Ø: A = ABS variable**
> **1Ø: A = ABS (calculation)**
> **1Ø: PRINT ABS number**

Here's a sample program. Go to the PROgram MODE and type it in. . .

> **1Ø: INPUT "Enter a + or – number ";A**
> **2Ø: PRINT ABS A**

Now change MODEs and RUN this sample.

1Ø: A = ABS A

Upon execution, the variable A will contain the same number as it did prior to this program line, but it will now be a positive number, regardless of whether it had been negative or positive. If A contained a value of –12 before this statement, it will be worth 12 after execution of this statement.

10: A = ABS (A)

This form is the same as in the previous example, but demonstrates that parentheses may be used with this function.

10: A = ABS –13

After execution of this program line, the variable A will contain the ABSolute value of the numeric constant –13. (A will equal 13.)

This function can be used in RUN, PROgram and RESERVE modes as well as in a program line.

Whenever a positive number is required and there is a possibility of a negative number being received, the ABS statement should be used.

Some suggested uses – in scientific calculations, some accounting applications and in any calculation in which the sign of the result *must* be positive.

Oops! What went wrong? Mis-typed. Not a number.

Also see: INT – SGN

SGN

SGN tells you the SiGN of a number. If the number is negative, SGN gives you –1; positive numbers return a 1, and zero returns a 0 (as 0 has no sign).

If you had written down your debts with Fred and John, you possibly would have put a negative sign in front of the ten that you owed Fred and a positive sign (or none, which assumes the same thing) in front of the $10 John owed you. If you applied the SGN test to your debt with Fred, it would return a –1 because it is negative. If it is applied to what's owed you from John, it would be +1 (or just 1) because it is positive. If you applied it to yourself, after the 10 passed too quickly through your hands, it would return a 0. That's what you got out of the deal. If only Fred wasn't there at the time. . . .

The Primary Statement/Command
> **SGN number**

Other Forms of the Statement/Command
> **10: A = SGN B**
> **10: A = SGN number**
> **10: A = SGN (calculation)**
> **10: PRINT SGN number**

Here's a sample program. Go to the PROgram MODE and type it in. . .

> **10: INPUT "Enter a + or – number ";A**
> **20: PRINT SGN A**

Now change MODEs and RUN this sample.

10: A = SGN B

After execution of this line, the numeric variable A will contain the value of the sign for the variable B, as described above.

10: A = SGN (B)

As with the previous statements, this function may use parentheses to contain the target value.

10: A = SGN –12

Here, the SiGN of the negative number will be in A after this line is executed. (A will equal –1)

10: A = SGN –12*15/23.7

It may also be used with a calculation, as in this example.

10: A = SGN B : IF A >0 THEN B=B * –1

This short routine tests a variable to determine its sign. If the sign is *positive*, it converts it to negative.

SGN can be used in RUN, PROgram and RESERVE modes as well as in a program line. It is primarily used to change the sign of a number from the program, or determine whether the value is plus or minus.

Some suggested uses – use this statement to test and create negative numbers.

Oops! What went wrong? Mis-typed. Not a number.

Also see: INT – ABS

The PI Key

It is time to explore the keyboard again. Perhaps you have noticed the *pi* symbol, just above the $<\pi>$ key. PI is pronounced 'pie' and it represents the ratio of a circle's diameter to its circumference. It is *extremely* useful for many problem solving applications.

The $<\pi>$, as a symbol, is a character borrowed from the Greek alphabet by mathematicians. Here it is used (as it is in most literature, with the possible exception of Greek) to represent a special number.

That number is a factor or a ratio (each number in a series of numbers multiplied together is a factor) of the circumference, (or distance around), of a circle to its diameter. It is also interesting to note that PI is simply a symbol that is a representation of that number, since the number is of infinite (endless) length.

Here, we use an approximate value which is ten (10) digits long. The $<\pi>$ symbol is displayed when the $<$SHIFT$>$, then the $<\pi>$ key is pressed. In a program, it remains as a symbol until used. In the RUN mode, it is converted to the value 3.141592654 and used or PRINTed as required. The word 'PI' is another way of writing $<\pi>$ in the PC-2.

PI (The Statement)

PI ($<\pi>$) supplies the pre-established value of PI to the program, which is the same as the $<\pi>$ key. It is a short-cut to typing in the entire value each time you need to use it in a calculation. In the sample program, we had the PC-2 PRINT the $<\pi>$ in line 40 to show you where to find it in the character set, in case you want to use it on the display as part of an output.

PI is a ratio of the circumference (distance around the circle) to the diameter, that is, PI = Circumference/Diameter. It is used in the calculation of virtually every problem in which a circle or sphere is an element of the area or volume, and believe me, there are a lot of them.

The PC-2 is unique . . . in that it uses both the statement PI, and the symbol π.

The Primary Statement/Command

PI or (π)

Other forms of the statement/command
```
10: A = PI
10: PRINT PI + calculation
10: A = PI + calculation
```

Here's a sample program. Go to the PROgram MODE and type it in . . . .

```
20: R = 5
30: PRINT PI
40: PRINT CHR$(93)
50: C = PI * R
60: PRINT C
```

Now change MODEs and RUN this sample.

10: A = PI

After execution of this line, the numeric variable A will contain the value of PI (A = 3.141592654).

10: A = π

This form uses the $<\pi>$, instead of the word 'PI', to assign the value to the variable A.

10: A = PI * RADIUS

Here, PI is used in a calculation, using a variable called RADIUS (which is recognized by the PC-2 as the variable RA, because only the first two letters are used). After execution of this line, A will contain the result of the operation.

PI (or $<\pi>$) can be used in RUN, PROgram and RESERVE modes as well as in a program line.

PI is used in calculations involving circular forms.

Some suggested uses – you will find this to be an invaluable aid for any calculation that involves a circular form. (For math types: add 'for polar coordinate functions and trig functions.')

Oops! What went wrong? Mis-typed.

Also see: The $<\pi>$

The $<\sqrt{\ }>$ key

The $<\sqrt{\ }>$ is a symbol representing a specific operation in mathematics (that phrase doesn't still scare you, does it?) The operation has always been complex and scary-looking to all but bespectacled, starry-eyed mathematicians, right? What it does is not as difficult to understand as it may seem, and certainly is less trouble than doing it.

If you take a number and multiply it times itself, you have squared it. Like 3 times 3 is 9, or the square of 3 is 9. On the other hand, the square root of 9 is 3. That is, the number which was multiplied by itself to get 9 as the result (or whatever number you want the square root of) is the square root of the number.

All we need to know to figure out a square root, is the form of the operation, or how to write it into the computer so it can do it for us, which is the real reason we have a computer anyway. In the RUN mode, type in $<\sqrt{\ }>$ 9 $<$ENTER$>$, and the computer will printout the square root of nine, which is 3. Now that is so easy, that you could do it in your head. Try this: $<\sqrt{\ }>$ 123.59 $<$ENTER$>$. The answer to this problem is 11.11710394 — this is sure a lot handier than having to figure it out each time, isn't it!

SQR

SQR performs the same function as the <√> key we discussed above. It returns the square root of the target number.

The Primary Statement/Command
>   SQR value (or variable)

Other Forms of the Statement/Command
>   10: A = SQR number
>   10: A = SQR variable
>   10: A = SQR (calculation)
>   10: PRINT SQR number

Here's a sample program. Go to the PROgram MODE and type it in . . . .

>   10: WAIT 100
>   20: A = SQR 9
>   30: PRINT "SQR OF 9 IS";A

Now change MODEs and RUN this sample.

10: A = SQR B

When this line executes, the numeric variable A will contain the square root (to 9 decimal places) of the value in B.

10: A = SQR (B)

Parentheses may be used to contain the target value. This is useful for performing other calculations on the value before returning the square root.

10: A = SQR 25

The target value may be in the form of a numeric constant, as well as contained in a variable.

SQR 25

SQR can be used in the RUN, PROgram and RESERVE modes as well as in a program line. You will find this handy to get the roots of numbers when needed.

Note: SQR can only be used with positive numbers. Negative numbers have 'imaginary' square roots. You can use the ABS (ABSolute) statement to obtain the 'imaginary' square root of a negative number.

Some suggested uses – used in the calculation of angles, area of triangles, volume of pyramid shapes and in trigonometric calculations.

Oops! What went wrong? Mis-typed. Not a number. Tried to take SQR of a negative number.

Also see: <√ > – ABS

17

CHAPTER 17

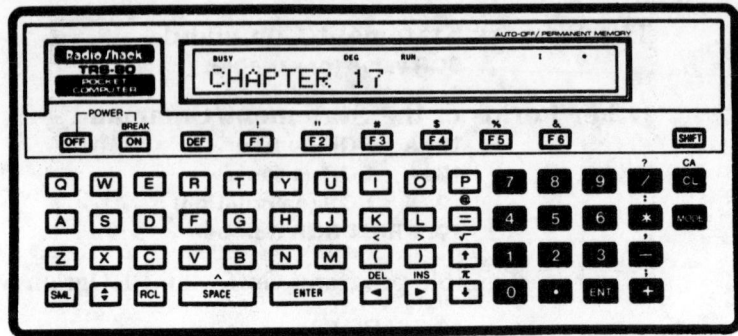

DEGREE — GRAD — RADIAN

There are an infinite number of ways to divide (cut) a circle (pie?). One method is to divide it into equal parts (slices). We can picture this with something that you likely have heard of, the 36Ø degrees of a circle, 9Ø degrees of a right angle, and so on. It is all just a way to 'cut the pie' into manageable pieces. In the PC-2, you have the further freedom of being able to convert from degrees in decimal parts or the more traditional minutes and seconds. (Also see DMS and DEG.)

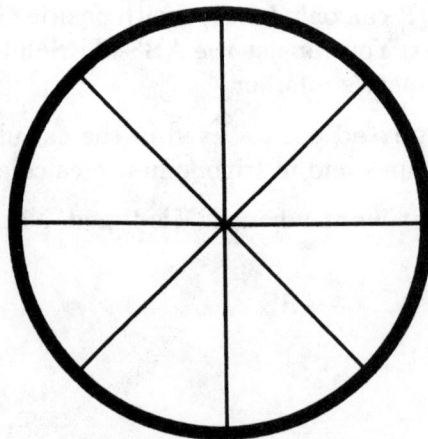

Figure 17.1 *Circle Cut into Sections*

The GRAD (short, but not very, for 'grade') is just another method of dividing a circle into 'slices' or parts. It was devised as a system that would be easier to use than degrees. It divides the circle into segments that are easier to work with, when using numbers of base ten. There are 4ØØ GRADes in a circle and 1ØØ in each right angle. That's easier for me, how about you?

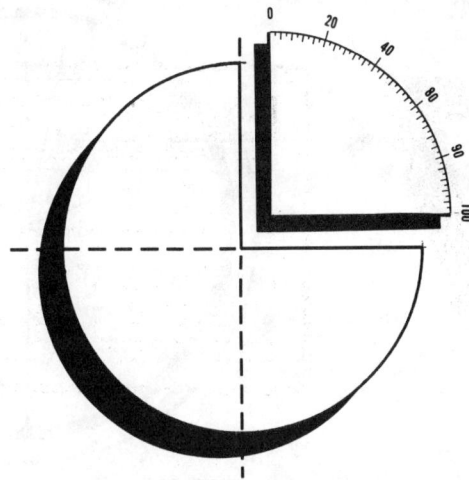

Figure 17.2 *Circle with 100 GRADS per Quarter*

The last one is radians (RAD). These are used, I think, mostly by scientists to help them write shorter equations. (I'll bet you thought they wanted to make them look longer, didn't you?) They can now write equations so long, even they have trouble with them. Now they are trying to find ways to make it easier for themselves (not necessarily for us).

The radian is an angle. It can best be visualized by a drawing. It's the angle made by the pie slice with its outer edge one radius long.

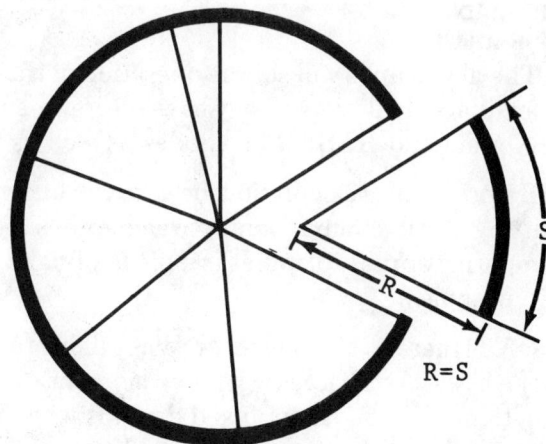

Figure 17.3 *Circle Segments of Unit Radius Length*

That's easy enough, I guess, but why pick such an odd number? It doesn't even divide into a circle evenly. Well, it allows us to use PI as the number of radians. There are 2PI radians in a circle, 1PI in a half circle (18Ø degrees), PI/6 in a 3Ø degree segment and PI/4 in 45 degrees.

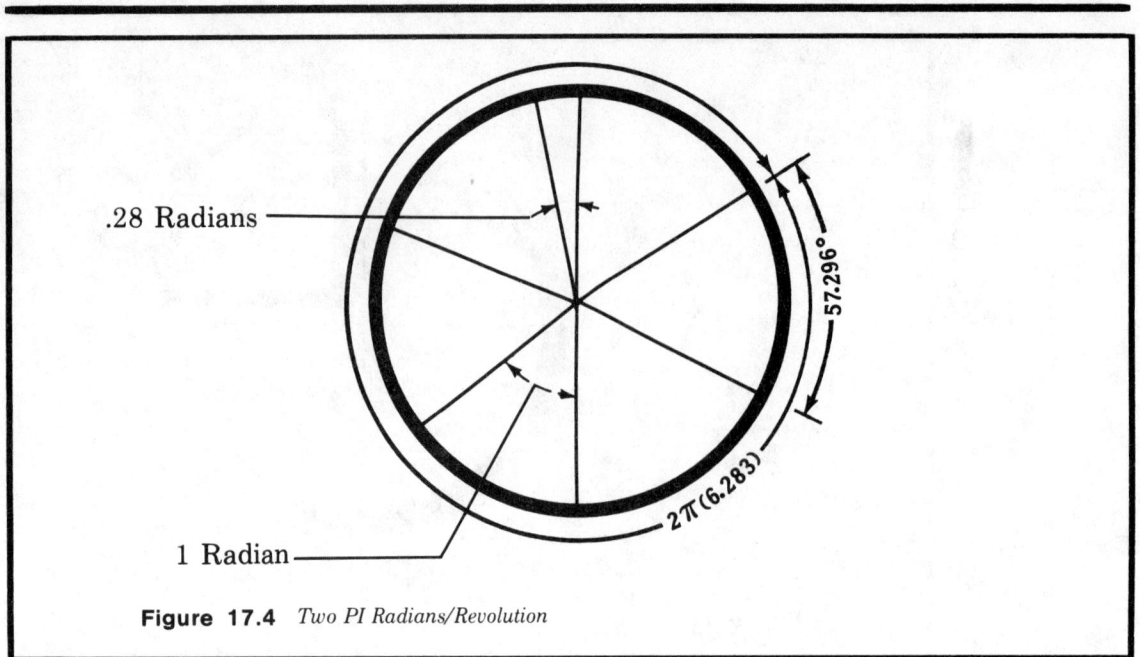

Figure 17.4   *Two PI Radians/Revolution*

For some reason PI/4 is more aesthetically pleasing and easier to use than 45 degrees or 5Ø grades to some scientists.

So you see, the PC-2 includes the capability to use degrees (DEG), grades (GRAD) or radians (RAD) — it's your choice.

The Primary Statement/Command
DEGREE <ENTER>
GRAD <ENTER>
RADIAN <ENTER>

1Ø: DEGREE
1Ø: GRAD
1Ø: RADIAN

The above lines will set the operation of the PC-2 to the respective form of measurement in angular calculations. They have no arguments or parameters. They may be used in RUN, PROgram and RESERVE modes as well as in program lines.

Before doing a calculation, be sure you know what kind of information you're dealing with. Getting a true comparison between apples and oranges takes lots of fancy foot-work, but comparing apples to apples is a piece-of-cake (or a piece of pie . . . ? PI??!? No. I was talking about apples).

Oh! hi there . . . I'm back now. Was talking to someone here about the strange ways you can plot a circle. To digress (just for a moment), I had a terrible time with this very subject ('trig functions'). My most confused day was when I tried to draw a circle with the SIN/COSign functions — at the time, I didn't realize how fussy computers could be, concerning the *form* of the data I gave them. So I told my friend (CPU) to plot the SIN and COSign (the percentage of rotation compared to one revolution) of a point on a circle. I wanted to rotate the whole circle, so I figured I'd just move one point at a time, until they had all been moved. Well, moving right along . . . I got *two* surprises. The darned thing worked! (I'm **always** amazed when math works for me.)

The second surprise was the *way* it worked. I set up a FOR . . . NEXT loop, from 1 to 360, figuring to rotate each point, one degree at a time, until it was back where it started . . . and here's the point of this whole digression (see? I remembered that we're wandering a bit). Anyway, back to the **point** of this. What I *said* was, "Comp, my friend, would you rotate this-here point for me?" Naturally, he was more than glad to do it, providing I told him 'how far.' So, (remember my FOR . . . NEXT loop) I told him to move it *ONE* position. Well . . . there's no doubt in my mind at all. He KNEW I meant degrees — but, he was thinkin' about RADIANS, and promptly moved my point One Radian. I *still* got my rotated circle, but every point LEAPED around the circle (one radian — plus one point, or 91 degrees . . . instead of the 'One Degree' I had in mind). I was talkin' apples, the computer was talkin' oranges . . . .

Before doing a calculation, enter the type of measurement mode you're going to work with — so the computer will know whether you want to talk about apples or oranges. If, for instance, you are using a formula to determine the area of a circular section of driveway (to find how much cement to order) you probably would use degrees. On the other hand, if you are dividing a right angle into even segments for a woodworking project, it might be a little easier in grades. Using radians is most likely to be for those doing homework or reading Martin Gardener books on mathematical puzzles (or perhaps you are a math whiz and are deep into transcendental relativistic semilogrithmic graphing).

Oops! What went wrong? Mis-typed it. Not the mode you really wanted.

Also see: DEG – DMS

DEG

DEG converts a number, which it assumes is in the form of dd.mmss (degrees(dd).minutes (mm)/seconds(ss) – two digits each) into the decimal form of degrees and a decimal fraction.

The Primary Statement/Command
> **DEG number**

Other Forms of the Statement/Command
> **10: A = DEG number**
> **10: A = DEG variable**
> **10: A = DEG (calculation)**
> **10: PRINT DEG number**

DEG 32.1425 <ENTER>
10: A = DEG 32.1425

After this line executes, the numeric variable 'A' will contain the normalized decimal equivalent of the constant 32.1425

10: A = DEG (B)

Here, the target value is contained in the variable B. The parentheses are optional in this statement.

Note: DEG can be used in the RUN, PROgram and RESERVE modes as well as in a program line.

Use DEG to convert from degrees with minutes and seconds to decimal divisions of a circle. Also use it for time calculations.

Some suggested uses – calculating pie chart graphs, or any other circular division that is easier to visualize in decimal parts rather than degrees. Converting the time to 'decimal' time.

Oops! What went wrong? Mis-typed it. Wrong number format. Numbers out of range or wrong variable type.

Also see: DEGREE – RADIAN – GRAD – DMS

DMS

DMS converts (translates) numbers to degrees, minutes and seconds format from decimal (including decimal fractions). The specific output is two digits of degrees, a decimal point, two digits of minutes and the last two digits (no space between any digits) for seconds, from a normalized decimal representation of the DMS number.

The Primary Statement/Command
DMS number

Other Forms of the Statement/Command
10: A = DMS variable
10: A = DMS number
10: A = DMS (calculation)
10: PRINT DMS number

Type in:

DMS 13.1234 <ENTER>

10: A = DMS B

After BASIC executes this statement, the decimal value in the variable B will be converted to the DMS representation, and stored in A.

10: A = DMS (B)

Here, the target value is contained in parentheses, which are optional and can contain of calculations, the results of which will be converted to DMS representation.

10: A = DMS 13.1425

This form uses a numeric constant to assign the value to A.

DMS 13.1425 <ENTER>

DMS can be used in the RUN, PROgram and RESERVE modes as well as in a program line.

Some suggested uses – DMS provides an easy way to convert the result of decimal operations, derived by using the DEG function described earlier, back to degrees, minutes and seconds. It is useful for charting programs, compass computations, surveying problems and problems involving the areas and volumes of any shape that is divided by angles. It can also be used to convert 'decimal time' to time in hours, minutes and seconds.

Oops! What went wrong? Mis-typed it. Wrong size or not a valid number format.

Also see: DEG – DEGREE – GRAD – RADIAN

The Trig Functions

Although this is definitely not going to be a substitute for a course in trigonometry, I can give you a little explanation to help your understanding of these mystical trig functions. . . .

First, let's draw a circle. Cut it in half, with a horizontal line through the center. Add a vertical line through the center. We now have a circle divided into quarters. Last, let's put a line from the center to the edge, in the upper right part or segment. We'll call this line (r) for radius.

An angle is made between the horizontal line and the new line, call it angle (A). While we are naming things, call the horizontal line the X axis and the vertical one the Y axis, so we can talk about X and Y coordinates.

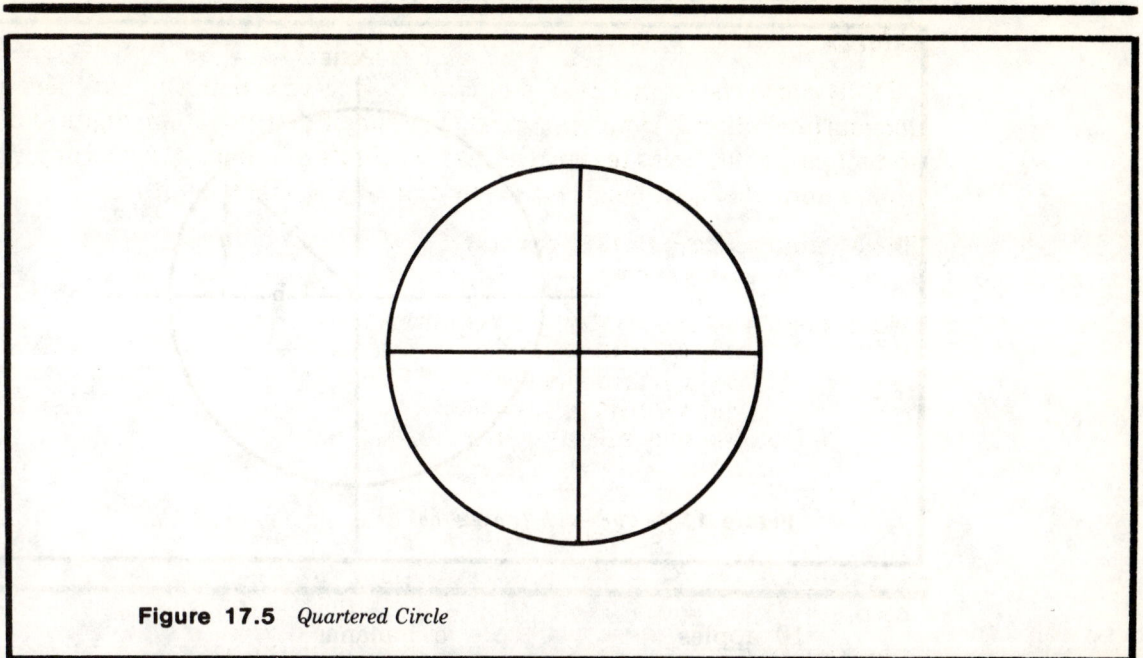

Figure 17.5 *Quartered Circle*

If we draw a vertical line from the point at which the (r) line intersects the circle down to the X axis, we form a right triangle. Since the line we just put in is opposite the (A) angle, let's call it (a), and the part of the horizontal line that goes from the center to the (a) line will be named (b), so we have the whole triangle named (rab).

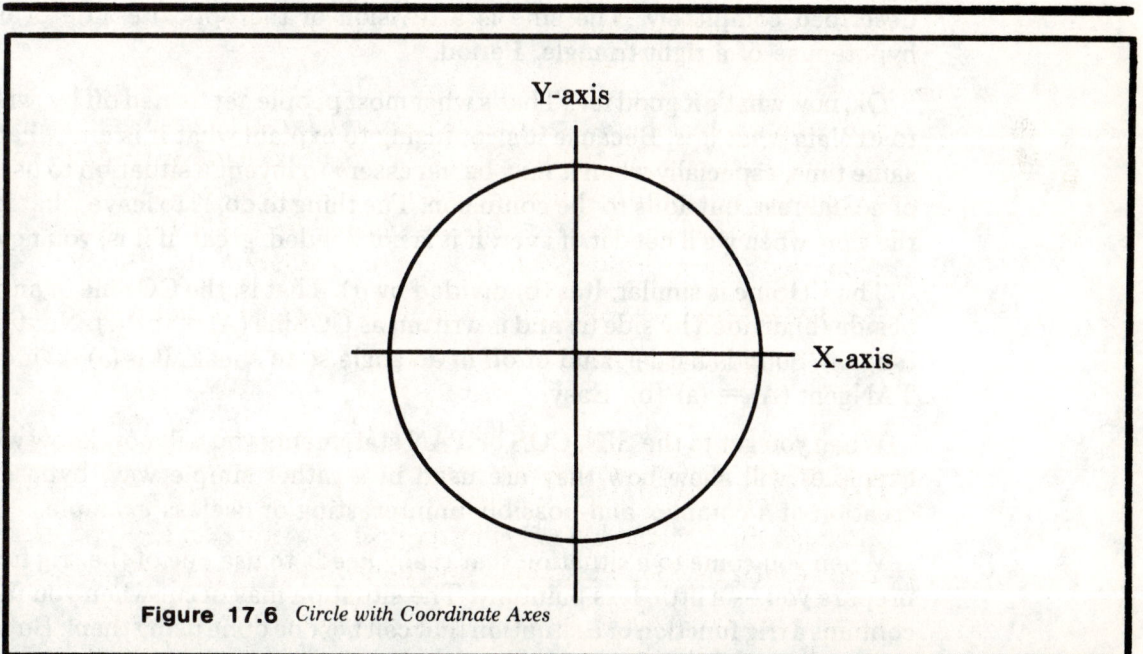

Figure 17.6 *Circle with Coordinate Axes*

If we divide (a) by (r), we get the sine of (a). Another way to look at it is that the sine of the angle (A) is just the *ratio* of (a) to (r).

A *ratio* is a comparison of one number divided into another. For instance suppose I had 1Ø apples and 5 bananas. The Ratio of apples to bananas is two to one (two apples for each banana) and the ratio of bananas to apples is .5 to 1 (one-half banana for each apple).

Chapter 17

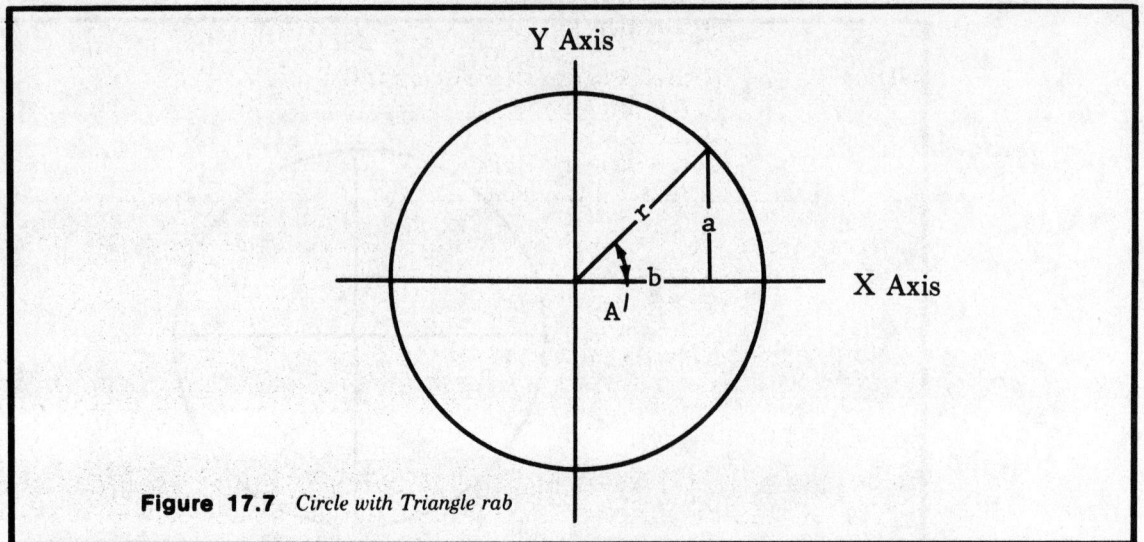

Figure 17.7 *Circle with Triangle rab*

$$\frac{1\emptyset \text{ apples}}{5 \text{ bananas}} = 2 \text{ (ratio)} \qquad \frac{5 \text{ bananas}}{1\emptyset \text{ apples}} = .5 \text{ (ratio)}$$

That's it. That's the explanation of SIN. Next question, please.

Kind of took you by surprise didn't I? After all, you thought that the trig functions like SIN would be some mysterious math hocus-pocus, not some simple thing like a few ratios. I can give you more information on what you can *do* with SIN, but *what it is* has just been described completely. The sine is a division of the opposite side of a triangle by the hypotenuse of a right triangle. Period.

Ok, now what's it good for? That's what most people get turned off by, when someone tries to explain what it *is*. Because it's confusing to explain what it is and what it can do, at the same time, especially when it may be necessary to invent a situation to use it in that may be of no interest, but adds to the confusion. The thing to do, is to leave what it is used for, until the time when we'll need it, if ever. If it is not needed, great. If it is, you now know what it is.

The COSine is similar. It is (b) divided by (r). That is, the COSine of angle (A) is the ratio of side (b) divided by side (r) and is written as COSine (A) = (b)/(r). Not too bad, eh? Go for tangent? Sounds harder, kind of off at an angle so to speak? It is (a) divided by (b). That is, TANgent (A) = (a)/(b). Easy.

When you get to the SIN, COS or TAN statements you will now know what they are. The examples will show how they are used in a rather simple way, bypassing the artificial creation of a complex and possibly uninteresting or useless example.

When you come to a situation that really needs to use one of the trig functions, this may prepare you — a little less painfully. The situation may occur when you find a formula that contains a trig function or a situation that can best be done using them. But, by then, much of the confusion will have vanished.

SIN

This BASIC statement word is pronounced 'sign' (rhymes with mine), — not 'sin' (rhymes with pen). . . and it is *not* a sin to use SIN. However it has nothing to do with the *sign of a number* (plus or minus), as the explanations of the trig functions above have already described.

The Primary Statement/Command
SIN number

Other Forms of the Statement/Command
10: A = SIN number
10: A = SIN variable
10: A = SIN (calculation)
10: PRINT SIN number

Here's a sample program. Go to the PROgram mode and type it in. . .
10: DEGREE
20: PRINT SIN 90

Now change MODEs and RUN this sample.

You might remember this if you ever had trig in school, it will PRINT a number 1, which is the sine of 90 degrees.

10: A = SIN B
The SINe of the value in B is returned in the variable A after this line is executed.

10: DEGREE
20: A = SIN 90
    or
10: GRAD
20: A = SIN 100
    or
10: RADIAN
20: A = SIN 2.33

Note that we must set the DEGREE, GRAD or RADIAN mode before using the program to be sure that it will give a result that is compatible with the result that we need. The argument can be a variable or number or a calculation in parentheses and can be used in a program line or directly in the RUN, PROgram or RESERVE modes.

Use these combinations for school work, trig formula solutions, and circle and triangle calculations.

Some suggested uses — in problems involving drafting or surveying. Plotting of nonlinear equations and drawing nonlinear graphs or plots.

Oops! What went wrong? Mis-typed it. Value out of range.

Also see: COS — TAN — ASN — ACS — ATN

COS

COSine is just the ratio of the sides of a triangle. See Trig Functions above.

The Primary Statement/Command
COS number

Other Forms of the Statement/Command
10: A = COS number
10: A = COS variable
10: A = COS (calculation)
10: PRINT COS number

Here's a sample program. Go to the PROgram mode and type it in. . .
10: DEGREE
20: PRINT COS 90
Now change MODEs and RUN this sample.

You will remember this if you've had trig in school. It will PRINT 0, which is the COSine of 90 degrees.

```
1Ø: A = COS B
```
or
```
1Ø: DEGREE
2Ø: A 5= COS 9Ø
```
or
```
1Ø: GRAD
2Ø: A = COS 1ØØ
```
or
```
1Ø: RADIAN
2Ø: A = COS 2.33
```

Note that we set the DEGREE, GRAD, or RADIAN mode before using COSine to be sure that it will give a result compatible with the result desired. The argument can be a variable, number or statement in parentheses. It can be used in the RUN, PROgram or RESERVE modes as a direct statement or program statement.

This is good for school work — trig, when applied to calculations involving circles and triangles (especially graphics). In engineering design projects, and similar functions, these functions are not only handy, but necessary.

Some suggested uses — in jobs involving scientific calculations, designing, drafting or surveying and calculating graphic plotting problems.

Oops! What went wrong? Mis-typed it. Values out of range.

Also see: SIN — TAN — ASN — ACS — ATN

TAN

TAN returns the TANgent of the target value. TAN is just the ratio of sides of a triangle. See Trig Functions, above.

The Primary Statement/Command
```
TAN number
```

Other Forms of the Statement/Command
```
1Ø: A = TAN number
1Ø: A = TAN variable
1Ø: A = TAN (calculation)
1Ø: PRINT TAN number
```

Here's a sample program. Go to the PROgram mode and type it in. . .
```
1Ø: DEGREE
2Ø: PRINT TAN 45
```
Now change MODEs and RUN this sample.

TAN 45 will PRINT 1, which is the TAN of 45 degrees.

```
1Ø: A = TAN B
```
The variable A will contain the TANgent of the contents of variable B after execution of this line.

```
1Ø: DEGREE
2Ø: A = TAN 9Ø
```
or
```
1Ø: GRAD
2Ø: A = TAN 1ØØ
```
or
```
1Ø: RADIAN
2Ø: A = TAN 2.33
```
Note that we must set the DEGREE, GRAD or RADIAN mode before using it to be sure that it will give a result compatible to the results we expect. The argument can be a variable or number or a calculation in parentheses and can be used in a program or immediately executed in the RUN, PROgram or RESERVE modes.

As we have seen, this is good for business or for school work requiring trig functions, and calculations involving circles, triangles and angles.

Some suggested uses — in jobs involving scientific calculations, designing, drafting or surveying and calculating graphic plotting problems.

Oops! What went wrong? Mis-typed it. Value out of range.

Also see: COS — SIN — ACS — ASN — ATN

An Insight

Let's stop a moment here and suggest that if SIN, COS and TAN are just ratios of numbers (which are just the lengths of the legs of a right triangle), then we might want to find the angle if we had the ratios. The ASN, ACS and ATN do this for us. They are the arcsine (ASN), arccosine (ACS) and arctangent (ATN). . . .

ASN

ASN returns the arcsine of the target value. ArcSiNe is just the opposite of the sine (the number of degrees it takes to get the ratio).

The Primary Statement/Command
    ASN number

Other Forms of the Statement/Command
    10: A = ASN number
    10: A = ASN variable
    10: A = ASN (calculation)
    10: PRINT ASN number

Here's a sample program. Go to the PROgram mode and type it in. . .
    10: DEGREE
    20: PRINT ASN 1
Now change MODEs and RUN this sample.

ASN 1 will PRINT 90 (DEGREEs), which is the ASN (arcsine) of 1.

10: A = ASN B
When this line executes, variable A will contain the arcsine of the contents of variable B.

10: DEGREE
20: A = ASN 1
    or
10: GRAD
20: A = ASN 1
    or
10: RADIAN
20: A = ASN 1

Note that we must set the DEGREE, GRAD or RADIAN mode before using the ASN function, to be sure that it will give a result that is compatible with our expectations. The argument can be a variable or number or a calculation in parentheses and can used be in a program line or immediately executed in RUN, PROgram or RESERVE modes.

Some suggested uses — in jobs involving scientific calculations, designing, drafting or surveying and calculating graphic plotting problems.

Oops! What went wrong? Mis-typed it. Value out of range.

Also see: SIN — COS — TAN — ACS — ATN

ACS

ACS returns the arccosine of the target value. ArcCoSine is the opposite of the cosine (the number of degees it takes to get the ratio).

The Primary Statement/Command
ACS number

Other Forms of the Statement/Command
10: A = ACS number
10: A = ACS variable
10: A = ACS (calculation)
10: PRINT ACS number

Here's a sample program. Go to the PROgram mode and type it in. . .
10: DEGREE
20: PRINT ACS 1
Now change MODEs and RUN this sample.

10: A = ACS B
When this line executes, A will contain the arccosine of the contents of B.

10: DEGREE
20: A = ACS 1
or
10: GRAD
20: A = ACS 1
or
10: RADIAN
20: A = ACS 1

Note that we set the DEGREE, GRAD or RADIAN mode before using the ACS function, to make sure that the results are compatible with the results we expect. The argument can be a variable or number or a calculation in parentheses and can used be in a program line or immediately executed in RUN, PROgram or RESERVE modes.

Some suggested uses — in jobs involving scientific calculations, designing, drafting or surveying and calculating graphic plotting problems.

Oops! What went wrong? Mis-typed it. Value out of range.

Also see: SIN — COS — TAN — ACS — ASN

ATN

ATN is the ArcTaNgent of an angle. It returns the arctangent of the target value. It is the opposite of the tangent (the number of degrees it takes to get the ratio).

The Primary Statement/Command
ATN number

Other Forms of the Statement/Command
10: A = ATN number
10: A = ATN variable
10: A = ATN (calculation)
10: PRINT ATN number

Here's a sample program. Go to the PROgram mode and type it in. . .
10: DEGREE
20: PRINT ATN 1
Now change MODEs and RUN this sample.

10: A = ATN B
When this line executes, A will contain the arctangent of the contents of B.

1Ø: DEGREE
2Ø: A = ATN 1
  or
1Ø: GRAD
2Ø: A = ATN 1
  or
1Ø: RADIAN
2Ø: A = ATN 1

Note that we set the DEGREE, GRAD or RADIAN mode before using the ATN function, to be sure that it will give a result that is compatible with our expectations. The argument can be a variable or number or a calculation in parentheses and can used be in a program line or immediately executed in RUN, PROgram and RESERVE modes.

Some suggested uses — in jobs involving scientific calculations, designing, drafting or surveying and calculating graphic plotting problems.

Oops! What went wrong? Mis-typed it. Value out of range.

Also see: SIN — COS — TAN — ACS — ASN

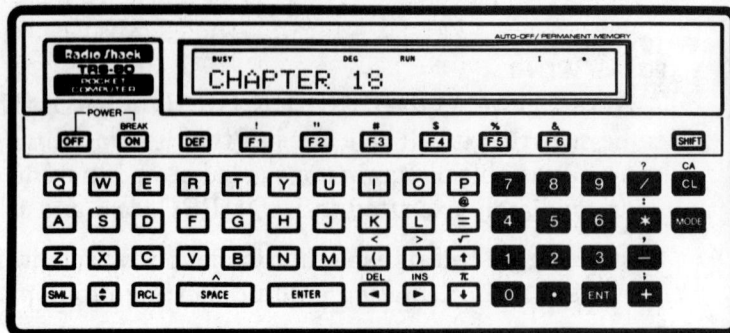

More Math

In this chapter, we will examine a few of the more powerful mathematical features which are built into the PC-2.

Logarithms

Common Logs — LOGS

Logarithms are almost the same as exponents. Let's review exponents. $2 \wedge 3$ means two multiplied by itself 3 times, which is $2 * 2 * 2$, or 8. Two is the base and three is the exponent. $2 \wedge 4$ is two multiplied by itself four times, or $2 * 2 * 2 * 2$, which is 16.

Well, just for the sake of argument, what would $2 \wedge 3$ times $2 \wedge 4$ be? Well, it would be (two multiplied by itself three times) times (two multiplied by itself four times), or $(2 * 2 * 2) * (2 * 2 * 2 * 2)$. Now, there's a fine old law in mathematics (which, if you must know, is called the *associative property of multiplication*) which allows us to remove all those parentheses. So what we end up with is $2 * 2 * 2 * 2 * 2 * 2 * 2$, or two multiplied by itself seven times. (That's 128, by the way, but who's counting?) Two multiplied by itself seven times can be written as $2 \wedge 7$.

Let's summarize what we've just demonstrated. $2 \wedge 3 * 2 \wedge 4 = 2 \wedge 7$. We could have taken a short cut in arriving at this answer. We could have said $2 \wedge 3 * 2 \wedge 4 = 2 \wedge (3+4)$ or $2 \wedge 7$. In fact, whenever numbers are written in exponential format, you can multiply them simply by adding their exponents and using the result as the new exponent, *provided all of the numbers being multiplied have the same base.*

When exponents are used in this manner, they are called logarithms. Since adding is usually easier than multiplying, logarithms can often be quite helpful. What makes them even better is that they work for division too. For instance, $2 \wedge 5$, which is 32, divided by $2 \wedge 3$, which is 8, equals $2 \wedge (5-3)$, or $2 \wedge 2$, which is 4.

The only hitch is that to make use of this simplified arithmetic, the numbers have to be in exponential form, all with the same base. To simplify things, tables of logarithms are available. They will tell you, for any number you're interested in, what that number would look like in exponential form.

There are two types of logarithms (or logs, as their buddies call them) commonly used in mathematics. The difference between the two is the base that is used. One, called *common* logs, uses a base of 1Ø. That is, given any number, a table of common logs would tell you what exponent you'd have to tack onto 1Ø in order to arrive at that number. For instance, if the number were 1ØØ, the logarithm would be 2, because $10 \wedge 2 = 100$. If the number were 1ØØØ, the log would be 3 because $10 \wedge 3 = 1000$. Ah, but what if the number were not a precise power of 1Ø?

The log of 5ØØ (to the base of 1Ø) is somewhere between the log of 1ØØ (2) and the log of 1ØØØ (3). If you had a log table handy, you could see that the log 5ØØ of (base 1Ø) is approximately 2.698970004.

You may not have a log table handy; I sure don't. The PC-2 will instantly calculate the base 1Ø log of any positive number. To find the common log of n, type: LOG n. (That lower-case 'n' represents any number — so when you see it, simply substitute any number in your head for the n. Your mental picture of LOG n could look like this:

Figure 18.1 *Mental Picture of LOG n*

For instance, go into the RUN mode and key in LOG 5ØØ<ENTER>. The PC-2 will display 2.698970004.

Natural Logs — LN

The other kind of logarithm frequently used by mathematicians uses a base of e instead of 1Ø. The base 'e' is a special mathematical constant approximately equal to 2.7. Logarithms using a base of e are called *natural* logarithms (as opposed to base 1Ø common logs).

The PC-2 also calculates natural logs. To find the natural log of a positive number, type LN n. For instance, to get the natural log of 7.3, go into the RUN mode and type: LN 7.3 <ENTER>. The computer will display 1.987874348.

So how can we actually use logs to simplify arithmetic? Let's review the problem of multiplying $2 \wedge 3$ by $2 \wedge 4$. A few paragraphs back, we discovered that since both expressions had the same base, namely two, we could add the exponents and say that $2 \wedge 3 * 2 \wedge 4 = 2 \wedge 7$. But that doesn't quite give us the solution. We have to know what number

$2 \wedge 7$ works out to be. In this case, it's easy to see that it's 128. We say that this makes 128 the *antilog* of 7 to the base of 2.

In general, if $X = Y \wedge n$, then X is the antilog, Y is the base and n is the exponent. If you're still not clear as to just what is meant by an antilog, think of it this way: the antilog is the number which answers the question, "What is this the logarithm of?"

Now we're really in a position to use logs to simplify arithmetic. Suppose we want to divide 108 by 36. We could work it out in the normal way, in which case we learn that the answer is 3. If you're not good at long division, you might not enjoy that.

Or, you could get the log of 108 and the log of 36, subtract the second from the first, and then look up the antilog of the result. Let's try this approach on the PC-2.

In the RUN mode, type A=LN 108 <ENTER>. 4.682131227 will appear on the screen. This is the natural log of 108, to 10 digits of accuracy. Now type B=LN 36 <ENTER>. You will see 3.583518938. This is the natural log of 36 to the same degree of accuracy. Now type C=A-B <ENTER>. The display will show 1.098612289. This is the log of 108 minus the log of 36. According to what we said before, the antilog of this number will be equivalent to 108/36.

Exponent — EXP

I bet you're wondering how we determine what that antilog is. Guess what? Right! The good ol' PC-2 will do it for us. When you type EXP followed by a number, the PC-2 will return the natural antilog of that number. When we left off, C was equal to the natural of log 108 minus the natural log of 36, or 1.098612289, which we agreed should be the antilog of 108/36. So just type EXP C <ENTER>. The PC-2 displays 3.0000000001.

Now you can see why I kept harping on the 10 digits of accuracy. The answer we got is off by one in the last decimal place, but it's still pretty darn close.

You may be wondering why we ever look up logs on the computer, since the computer handles all the math for us anyhow. The answer is that logs turn up in all kinds of formulas and equations. In fact, the PC-2 uses logs for a lot of its own internal calculations. Someday you will write a program which requires the use of logs. Maybe you think you won't, but you will, in time. You will then be very happy to have them preprogrammed into your PC-2.

By the way, do not confuse the EXP statement and the *exponent* function used in *scientific notation*, although both use exponent as their description.

EXP

EXP returns the natural antilog of the target number. This is a useful feature, especially in scientific calculations. EXP should not be confused with the exponent function $(\wedge)$ which is used in scientific notation to express large numbers.

If you have skipped the descriptions of LOG, LN and EXP above, go back and read them. They provide a lucid description of the functions of this and the following two statements.

The Primary Statement/Command
    EXP number

Other Forms of the Statement/Command
    10: A = EXP variable
    10: A = EXP number
    10: A = EXP (calculation)
    10: PRINT EXP number

Type this in: EXP 1 <ENTER> (This, by the way, is the value of 'e'.)

A = EXP B

The numeric variable A will contain the antilog of the variable B after this direct statement is executed.

1∅: A = EXP B

Here, the statement is used in a program line, with numeric variables.

1∅: A = EXP 9

In this example, the numeric variable A will contain the antilog of the constant 9 after execution of this line.

1∅: PRINT EXP B

The EXP function can be used in conjunction with other statements, such as this example, which PRINTs the result of the operation on the display.

1∅: A = EXP (8+1)

The target expression of the EXP function can be a calculation, as indicated in this example. In this case, the expression contained in parentheses is evaluated before the EXP function is performed. If stated in the form, 1∅: A=EXP 8+1, it will result in the EXP 8 portion being calculated first; then the value of 1 would be added to the result.

Oops! What went wrong? Mis-typed it. Value out of range.

Also see: LN – LOG

LN

LN returns the natural log (base e) of the target numeric value. See the description of 'logs' in *More Math* above.

The Primary Statement/Command
> **LN number**

Other Forms of the Statement/Command
> **1∅: A = LN number**
> **1∅: A = LN variable**
> **1∅: A = LN (calculation)**
> **1∅: PRINT LN number**

Type in the following example.

LN 2.7183 <ENTER>

The reason it is not exactly 1, is that 2.7183 is not exactly e, which cannot be written down. It is an endless number like PI. That is to say, no matter how many places it is written out to, it will never come out exactly right.

1∅: A = LN B
1∅: A = LN (29–2)
1∅: PRINT LN B
PRINT LN 1∅

LN is most useful to calculate obtuse physical constants.

Oops! What went wrong? Mis-typed it. Value out of range.

Also see: LOG

LOG

If 1∅ is chosen as a base number, and we raise it to a power (multiply it times itself so many times), then the power is the LOG. The LOG of 1∅∅ is 2. . .,in other words, 1∅ to the 2nd power.

You know about, or have seen, the numbers that scientists use to describe *big* things, right? 10^6 for example. Then they tell you that is a 1 with 6 zeros behind it (1,000,000). LOG is more or less the same type of thing.

The LOG of that number (1,000,000) is 6. Yet another way to explain it is that if you take ten and raise it to the second power (10 squared it's called), you get 100. The LOG (of 100) is the 2. If the power is 3, 10 to the third power, that's 1000, 3 being the log of 1000. LOG is the number of zeros behind the number (in base 10) or 'places' with decimal numbers.

If you want a number between 100 and 1000, it would be between 2 and 3, or 2 point something. That hurts my number-of-zeros description some. Anyway, the log of a number between 1000 and 10,000 would be between 3 and 4. For example, the LOG 1234 is, or gives 3.09131 . . . In any case, if you want the LOG of a number, let the PC-2 do it.

The Primary Statement/Command
LOG number

Other Forms of the Statement/Command
10: A = LOG number
10: A = LOG variable
10: A = LOG (calculation)
10: PRINT LOG number

Here's a sample program. Go to the PROgram mode and type it in. . . .

10: PRINT "If 10 to the power 2 is 100"
20: PRINT "what is the LOG of 100?"
30: PRINT LOG 100

Now change MODEs and RUN this sample.

10: A = LOG B
This form gets the LOG of the number in B and puts it in A, without changing B.

10: A = LOG (10 + 90)
The LOG can be taken of any real number and in this case the PC-2 adds 10 to 90 first. It always does the work inside parentheses first.

10: PRINT LOG 100
You can put the LOG function, like any other function, anywhere.

PRINT LOG 100
You can use LOG in the RUN, PROgram and RESERVE modes.

Oops! What went wrong? Mis-typed it. Value out of range.

Also see: LN – EXP

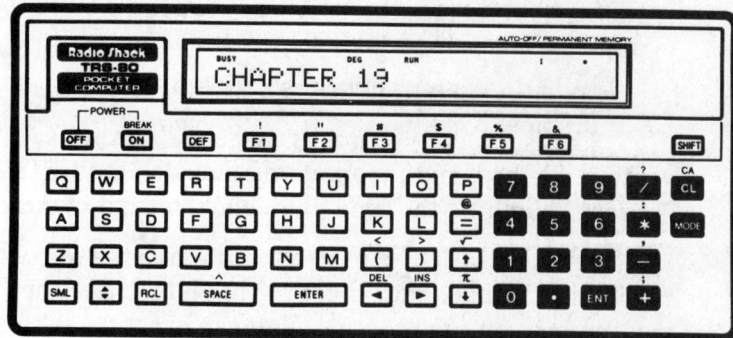

19

RESERVE Mode and Function Keys

There are some labor-saving devices built into the PC-2. The six keys marked <F1> to <F6> just under the display can be assigned to do almost any function that can be programmed into the PC-2. Further, there are three levels (called I, II, and III), which will allow a total of 18 different functions to be assigned to these keys.

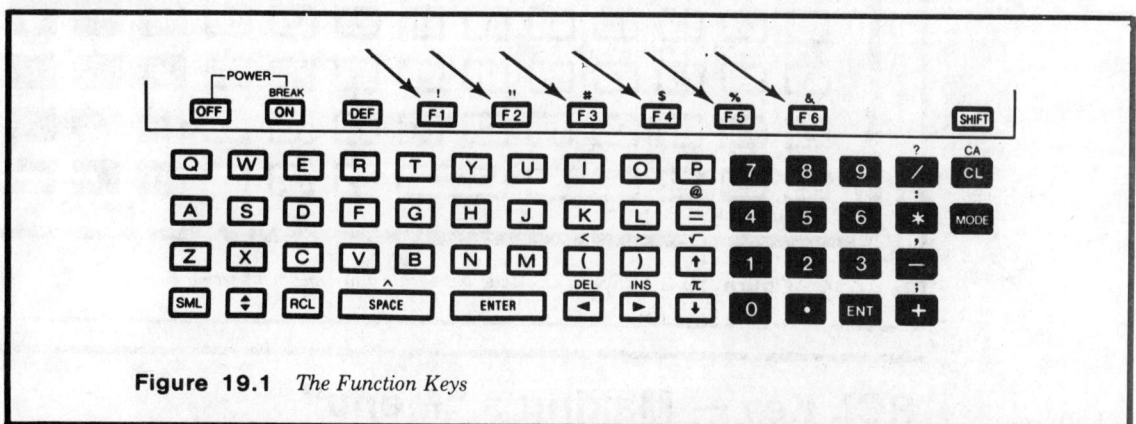

Figure 19.1 *The Function Keys*

The way to do this is to use RESERVE mode. Press <SHIFT> and then <MODE>. RESERVE will appear at the top of the display.

Now that the PC-2 is in RESERVE mode, press the <F1> key, near the left end of the display. The display will show F1: and maybe some other junk after the colon. The junk is really what the key is currently programmed to do, if anything. This is the way the PC-2 shows you what it is currently programmed to do.

You now have a choice; leave the function key programmed as it is or change its function. To leave it as is, press the <CL> key. To program the key for the first time, simply type in the function you desire. To reprogram a function key, press <SHIFT> then <MODE> to put the PC-2 into the RESERVE mode. Then press the <F1> key. The current function will be displayed. Press the ▶ key, and you will see the editing cursor. Now type in your new function, or simply edit the line, as you would a program line in PROgram mode. If there is any junk left to the right of your new function, simply space over it and press the <ENTER> key.

You are ready to program one of the function keys (F1). Make sure the PC-2 is in RESERVE I. Press the <F1> key to get the PC-2 ready to accept the function. Let's say we want the time displayed. Type in:

PRINT "TIME IS",TIME @ <ENTER>

"That's it folks, you done real good," as they say in parts of Texas and California. Touch the mode key, and the mode display will read RUN. Next hit the magical <F1> key, and presto-klunk . . . the time (in decimal format of mmddhh.mmss) will appear on the display.

Press that little [⇅] arrow and watch the top of the display (the main part of the display will also change, but I'll get to that later). See the I, II and III? This triples the number of functions you can program. You can program all the function keys in RESERVE mode I, II and III, giving you 18 functions at your finger tips.

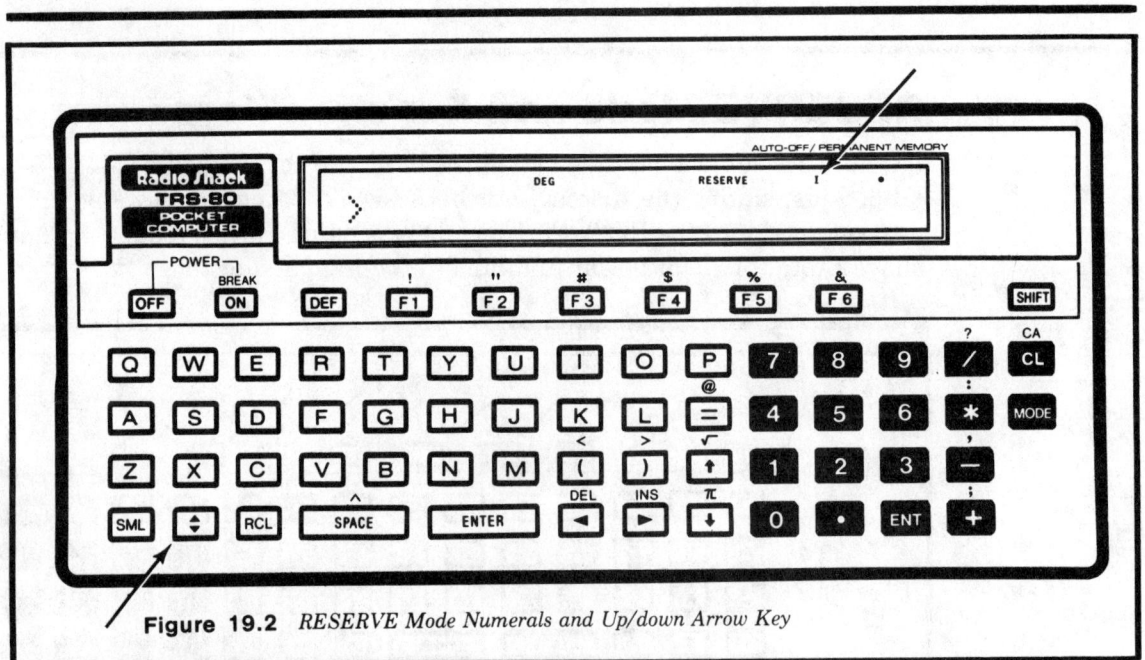

Figure 19.2 *RESERVE Mode Numerals and Up/down Arrow Key*

RCL Key — Making a "Menu"

Ok, now that you have the functions programmed, how can you remember them? We got you covered. Look next to the funny [⇅] key. There is a key named <RCL>. Short for ReCaLl.

We can leave messages to ourselves with it. To leave the message (program it, so to speak), you must have the PC-2 in RESERVE mode. That's press <SHIFT> and then <MODE>. Press <ENTER> for a prompt (>) and then put a quote mark, <SHIFT> <F2> (the <F2> key has the quote mark above it). The PC-2 is now ready for the message (which can only be 26 characters long).

You can put a different 26-character message on each of the three RESERVE levels. Usually the messages are 'menus' for the function keys at each of the three RESERVE levels. If you use the <RCL> for this purpose, you must make those 26 characters stretch for six functions at each RESERVE level. Kind of tight, so we normally abbreviate and use

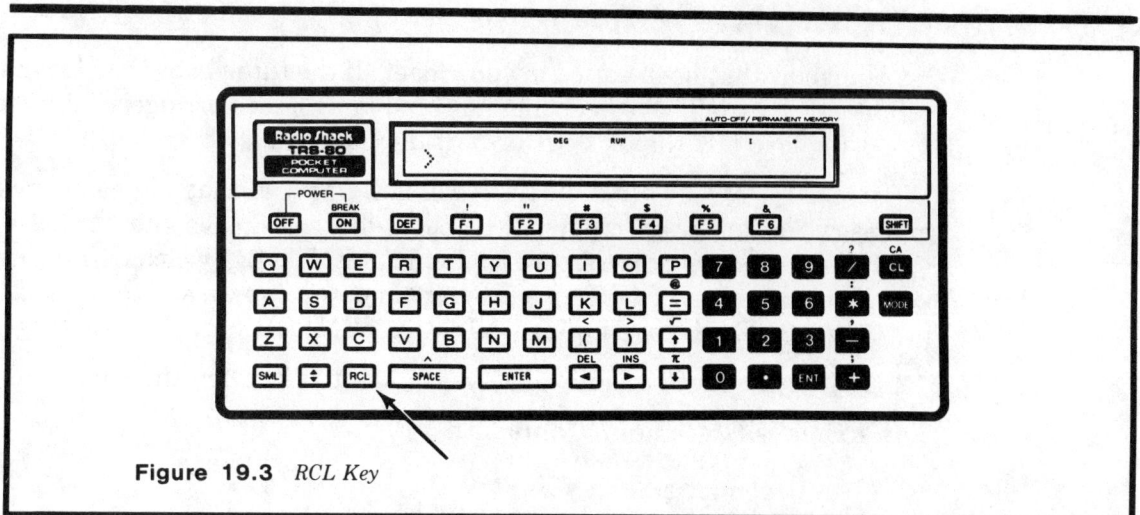

Figure 19.3 *RCL Key*

few spaces. Many times I don't program all the functions, and this gives me more freedom in making up a menu.

If a function is not programmed, say <F2>, when pressed it will PRINT the character above it as if you had previously pressed the <SHIFT> key. For <F2>, a quote mark will be displayed in the current cursor position. I use quotes so much that I try to leave it unprogrammed, so I only have to press that one key (<F2>) to get the quote marks.

Some suggested uses – use it reviewing your RESERVEd one-line programs. Store and ReCaLl reminder information on the programmed function keys.

Defined Functions and Defined Programs.

If 18 function keys are not enough for you (some people are power hungry), the PC-2 has a bunch more called <DEF> (DEFined) keys. They are divided into two groups and include all the alphabet keys plus the <=> and <SPACE> keys. These keys work differently from the function keys. The QWERTY line of your keyboard (second row from top — QWERTYUIOP) is pre-defined as shown below.

Q	INPUT		W	PRINT
E	USING		R	GOTO
T	GOSUB		Y	RETURN
U	CSAVE *		I	CLOAD *
O	MERGE *		P	LIST

* These functions require that the printer/cassette interface be attached or an error will be the result. However, an error message will *not* be displayed.

To use these keys, first press <DEF>, and then the key of your choice.

The rest of the keys (ASDFGHJKLZXCVBNM=<SPACE>) can be used to GOTO any line of a program. It is even easier to use these keys than the other function keys. Just make sure the key that you want to use is the first character in the program line that you want to GOTO. For example, if <DEF> A is to GOTO line 1Ø, then 1Ø should look like this:

     1Ø: "A"

When <DEF> key and then the <A> key are pressed, the program beginning on line 1Ø will be executed.

LOCK/UNLOCK

"Somebody has been eating my porridge!" If the three bears had locked up their house, Goldilocks wouldn't have been messing around with the porridge, chairs and beds. The PC-2 doesn't have any chairs, beds or porridge, but it *does* have a lock!

Essentially, LOCK turns off the <MODE> key, so that you can't accidentally change modes while doing something with the keyboard. To resume normal operation of the <MODE> selection process, type UNLOCK <ENTER>, which UNLOCKs the <MODE> key. If you have used LOCK in a program line, you can escape from the LOCKed state by pressing <BREAK> and typing UNLOCK <ENTER>, or have the program do it for you.

LOCK locks the PC-2 into whatever mode it is in when the command is entered.

The Primary Statement/Command
```
LOCK
UNLOCK
```

Other Forms of the Statement/Command
```
10: LOCK
10: UNLOCK
```

In the RUN mode, type LOCK <ENTER>. Now, press the <MODE> key, and see what happens. . . .

LOCK <ENTER>
LOCKs out the <MODE> key.

UNLOCK <ENTER>
UNLOCKs the <MODE> key for normal operation.

10: LOCK
In this example, the program will cause the PC-2 to LOCK into the RUN mode after this line executes.

10: UNLOCK
Here, the program UNLOCKs the <MODE> key when this line is executed.

Oops! What went wrong? Mis-typed it. Tried to change MODEs while LOCKed. Forgot to LOCK into current mode, and accidentally pressed the <MODE> key.

Also see: MODE

AREAD

As you know, you can label or <DEF>ine program lines in the PC-2 and then automatically execute them using the <DEF> key.

Suppose you have defined "Z" as a section of code that converts U.S. dollars to Japanese Yen. Here is what the code might look like:

```
100 "Z" INPUT "ENTER DOLLAR AMOUNT"; X
110 WAIT 300
120 PRINT X*240
```

You may have other programs which calculate the costs of various items in dollars. Every so often, when one of these programs gives you a result, you want to convert it into Yen.

For instance, suppose you've just calculated the cost of producing a component for a computer you are designing. The answer is in the display: $1.55. You want to convert this to Yen. However, If you now type <DEF> <Z> <ENTER>, you will be prompted to enter the amount. This seems like a waste of effort, since that amount was already on the display before you entered <DEF> <Z>.

To get around this problem, the PC-2 has a special input statement. AREAD. AREAD stands for 'Auto READ.' It works like an INPUT statement except that it *automatically reads* whatever is on the display when the AREAD is executed.

An INPUT statement, you will recall, has you enter information and inputs that information into the variable specified by the INPUT statement. For example, examine the INPUT statement in line 100 of the example above. Disregard the "Z" which is the DEFinable-key label, and not part of the INPUT statement. This INPUT statement transfers the dollar amount typed in by the user into the variable X.

An equivalent AREAD statement would look like this:

> **100 "Z" AREAD X**

Instead of having the person using your program (or even you, yourself) type in the dollar amount, this statement READs the display and transfers whatever it finds there into the variable X.

Note that in this example, the "Z" is again a <DEF>inable-key label, and not part of the AREAD statement. The reason it is present in the example is that an AREAD statement *must always* follow a label, just as is shown in the example. AREAD will work only in a <DEF>inable key sequence, and only if it immediately follows the label as shown.

Here is the entire dollars-to-yen program sequence using AREAD instead of INPUT.

> **100 "Z" AREAD X**
> **110 WAIT 300**
> **120 PRINT X*240**

To see how this works, type in the program from the PROgram mode and then go to the RUN mode. Type 3 so that it appears on the display. Then press the <DEF> key, and the <Z> key. You will see the 3 on the left side of the display immediately replaced by 720 on the right side of the display.

Here are a couple of other things to keep in mind about AREAD.

- 1. It only works from the RUN mode as a program line.
- 2. It doesn't matter how the information on the display got there, AREAD will transfer it to the variable in the AREAD statement.

In the example above, you typed the data in yourself. But it would work just as well if the data were left there by another program. This is what makes AREAD valuable. It allows the AREAD-containing program to process information left on the screen by another program, without your having to retype it.

Here is a summary of what we have just learned. AREAD will read the value on the display into a variable, so that you can do something with it. It only works with a line that is labeled, and RUN with the <DEF> key function.

The Primary Statement/Command
> AREAD variable

Other Forms of the Statement/Command
> 10: AREAD variable
> 10: AREAD string

Here's a sample program. Go to the PROgram mode and type it in. . .

> 10: "A"
> 20: AREAD A$
> 30: PRINT"Hi, ";A$

Now go to the RUN mode, type in your name at the prompt (>), press <DEF> then <A>

10: AREAD A

In this example, the numeric A will contain the value typed on the display prior to executing the program with the <DEF> key.

10: AREAD A$

This is the same as the previous example, but the PC-2 will treat anything on the display as a string, even if it is a number.

The AREAD statement can be very useful if you set up the PC-2 as a smart calculator, with a lot of programmed functions to be performed over and over again. You could have a program called "H," for example, which converts the number typed in, from decimal to hexadecimal. Also, a program called "D" which takes the hexadecimal number from the display, and returns the decimal value. AREAD can be used only in a program line in the PROgram mode.

Oops! What went wrong? Mis-typed it. Wrong mode. Used the wrong variable type.

Also see: INPUT – INKEY$ – ARUN

20

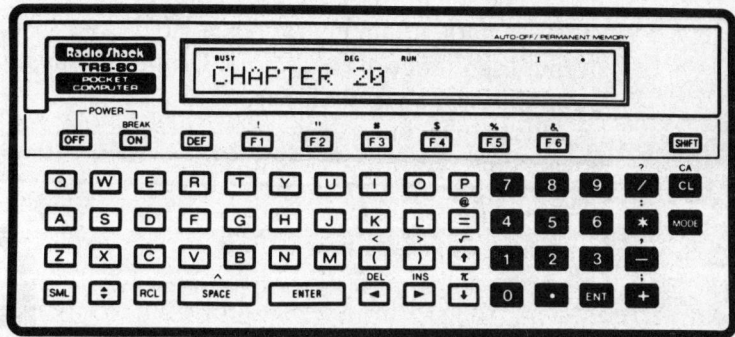

Graphics
How Graphics Differ from Text

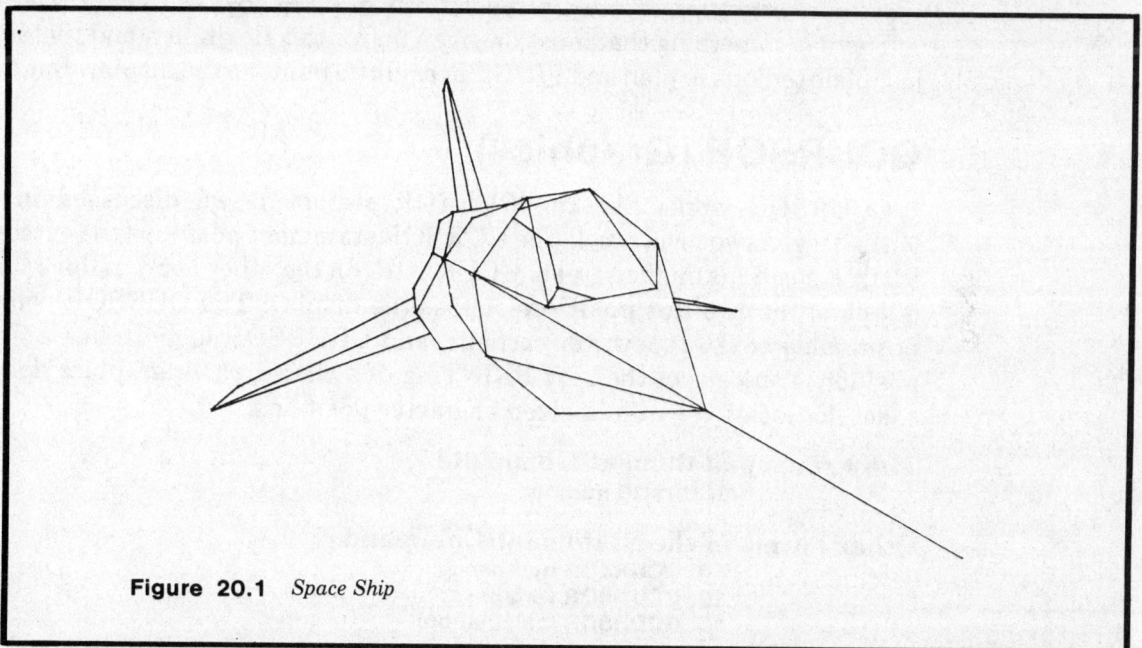

Figure 20.1 *Space Ship*

Graphics may be thought of as pictures, while text consists of letters and characters which are pre-defined shapes. You might think of the difference as a bit like that between a typewriter and a pencil. You 'write' words and sentences with a typewriter, using the 'characters' (letters, numbers and symbols, that is) which are available on the keyboard. But, with a pencil, you can write *and* draw.

With a pencil, you can write in an unlimited number of styles, such as block printing, script and handwriting, as well as draw anything that comes to mind. With the typewriter, you are limited to the characters on the keyboard.

It is the same with graphics and text on the PC-2. Graphics are nearly limitless, but text is confined to the character set available in the machine.

If you look closely at a character (such as the letter "A") on the liquid-crystal display of the PC-2, you will notice that it is composed of small dots. In fact, the entire screen is composed of these dots, and a character is PRINTed by *lighting up* (or darkening, if you will) a pre-defined sequence of these dots. Graphics may be drawn on the screen by lighting these dots individually, as we shall see.

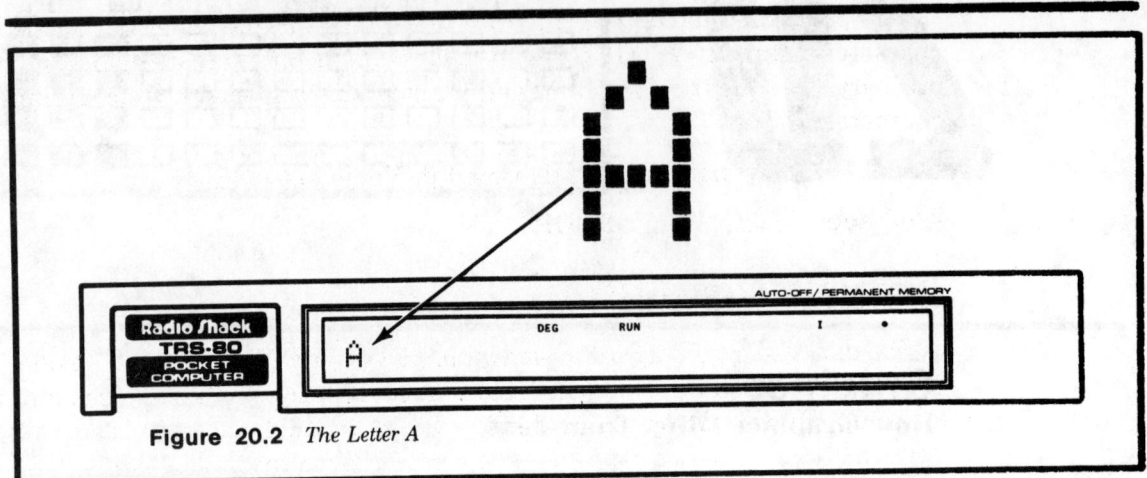

Figure 20.2   *The Letter A*

There is something that must be given up for this flexibility, and that is ease of use. It's just plain tedious to plan and PRINT every little point on the display. But there are ways....

GCURSOR (Graphics)

GCURSOR works like the CURSOR statement we discussed in the chapter on PRINTing. As you will recall, the CURSOR statement positions the cursor at one of the 26 PRINT positions on the screen. GCURSOR, on the other hand, refines the cursor position to one of the 156 **dot positions** across the display! The CURSOR command is like the positioning of the typewriter carriage, and GCURSOR is more like a fine tuning of that position. You can set the next PRINTing of a character (or graphics dot, of course) at an exact dot location within a given character position.

The Primary Statement/Command
          GCURSOR number

Other Forms of the Statement/Command
          10: GCURSOR number
          10: GCURSOR variable
          10: GCURSOR (calculation)

Here's a sample program. Go to the PROgram MODE and type it in . . . .

```
10: CLS
20: WAIT 5
30: FOR X=1 TO 155
40: GCURSOR X
50: PRINT "H";
60: NEXT X
70: GOTO 70
```

Now change MODEs and RUN this sample.

          10: GCURSOR 10

When BASIC executes this line, the cursor position will be set to the 10th dot from the left side of the screen. The next character PRINTed to the screen will have its left side on that dot position.

1Ø: GCURSOR X

Here, the cursor position is set by a variable, which can contain any value from Ø through 155.

Using GCURSOR with Text

The programs above demonstrate how you can 'fine tune' the PRINT position of a character on the screen: GCURSOR makes it possible to create displays that are out of the ordinary, by squeezing letters together, and, as we shall see, by combining graphics and characters.

Oops! What went wrong? Mis-typed it. Value out of range.

Also see: GPRINT – CURSOR

GPRINT (Graphics)

The demonstration program used with the GCURSOR statement, besides demonstrating the GCURSOR statement, also demonstrates how the small graphics blocks (called *pixels*) make up the text and graphic display. The GPRINT statement causes a single vertical pattern of dots to light up in one of the 156 columns specified by the GCURSOR statement.

Each vertical column consists of 7 dots, and any one or more of them can be turned on with the GPRINT statement. To demonstrate this, go to the PROgram mode and enter the following:

        1Ø: WAIT 5ØØ
        2Ø: GPRINT 127

This is what you will see:

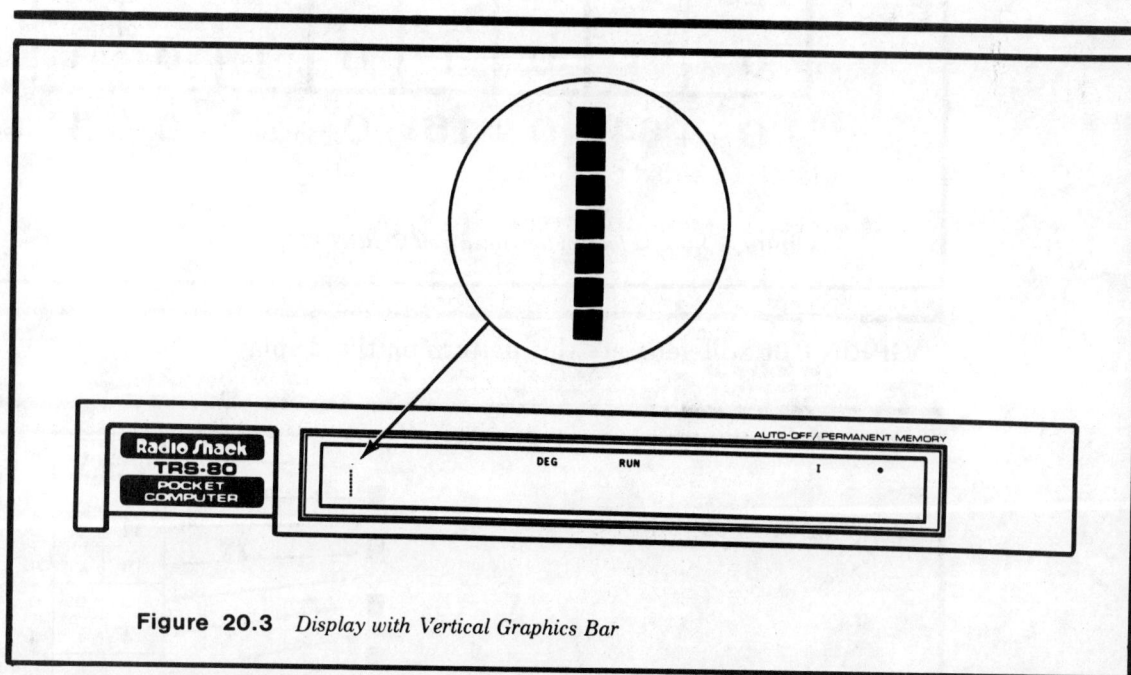

Figure 20.3 *Display with Vertical Graphics Bar*

Obviously, the next question is, "How did you arrive at the value of 127 to PRINT the seven pixels? Suppose I only want to PRINT the pixel on the bottom or the top?"

The dot pattern formed by the value given to GPRINT is based on binary code, which we discussed earlier. If you turn a byte on its side, so that the LSB (or least significant bit – the one on the right side) is at the top, then you can get a clear picture of the column structure. Each bit corresponds to one dot in the column, like this:

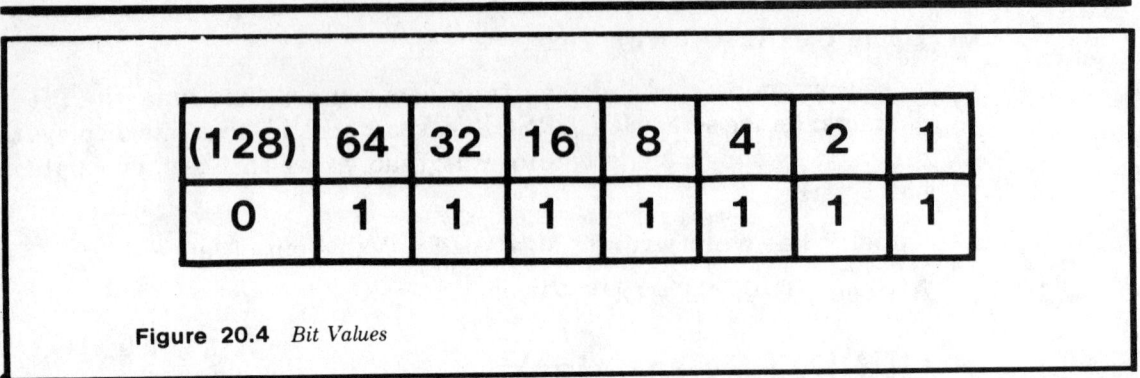

(128)	64	32	16	8	4	2	1
0	1	1	1	1	1	1	1

Figure 20.4 *Bit Values*

As you can see, only the first 7 bits are used to 'light up' or turn on the dots. You can enter any value up to 255 decimal. Any value over 127 (that is, with the MSB, Most Significant Bit or bit number 7 turned on) is treated as though 127 is subtracted from it, but the LCD display memory accepts the full value, as we shall see in a moment. To create a pattern, add together the value of the dots you want to light, and use the result to display the column. For example, if you want to create a pattern of every other dot, you do it like this:

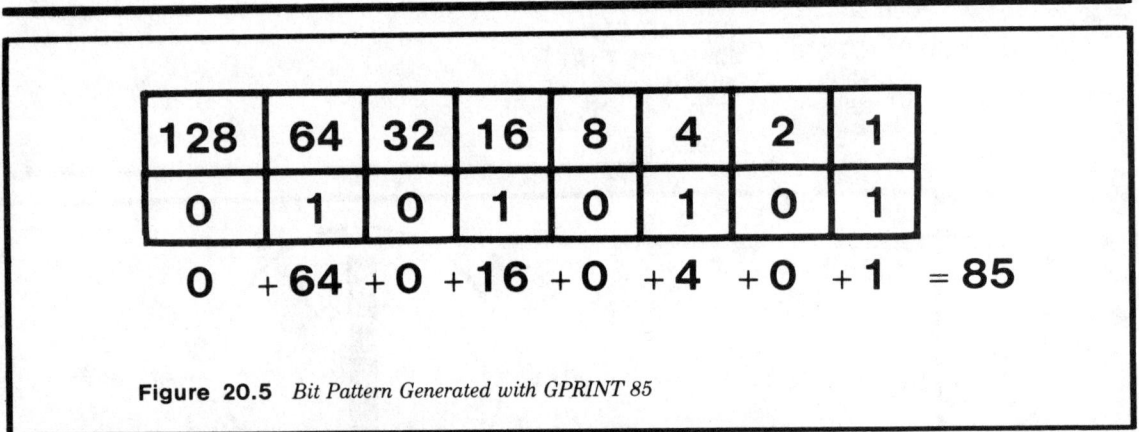

128	64	32	16	8	4	2	1
0	1	0	1	0	1	0	1

0 + 64 + 0 + 16 + 0 + 4 + 0 + 1 = 85

Figure 20.5 *Bit Pattern Generated with GPRINT 85*

GPRINT 85 will generate this pattern on the display:

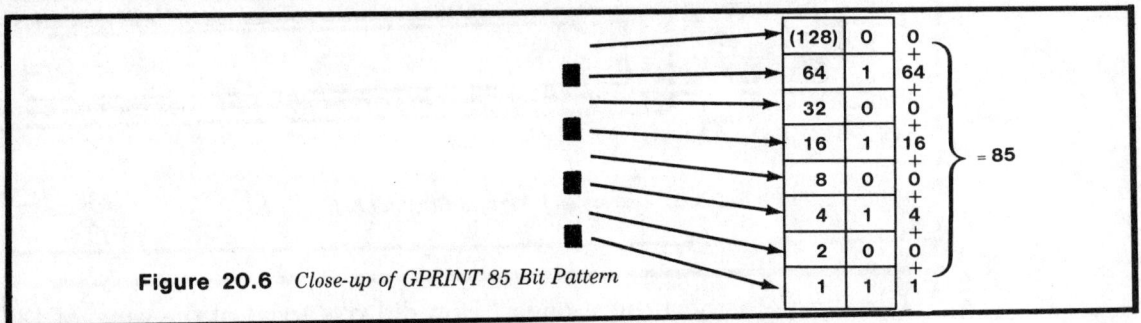

Figure 20.6 *Close-up of GPRINT 85 Bit Pattern*

Here is a demonstration that shows each pixil position lit in one of seven GCURSOR positions:

```
10: WAIT 0
20: G = 0
30: C = 0
40: FOR X = 0 TO 6
50: G = 2 ∧ X
60: GCURSOR C
70: C = C + 1
80: GPRINT G
90: NEXT X
100: GOTO 100
```

The result of RUNning this program will be a display that looks like this:

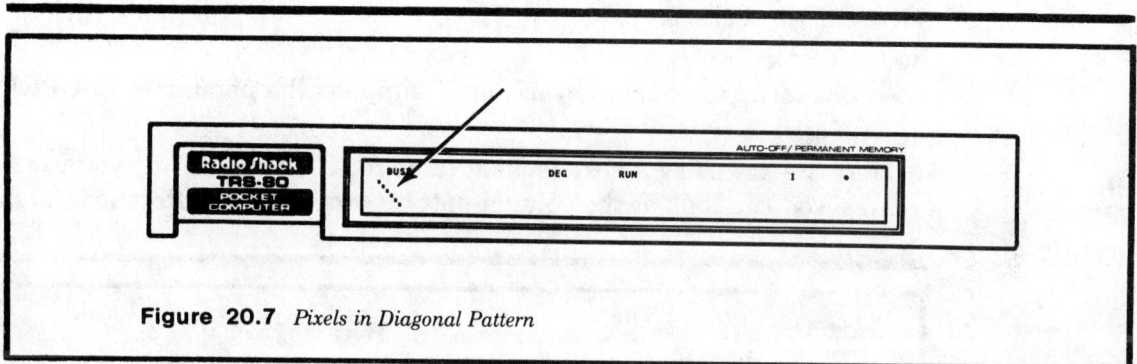

Figure 20.7 *Pixels in Diagonal Pattern*

Now change line 50 to look like this:

```
50: G = 2 ∧ X + 2 ∧ X - 1
```

and RUN it again. This time your display will look like this:

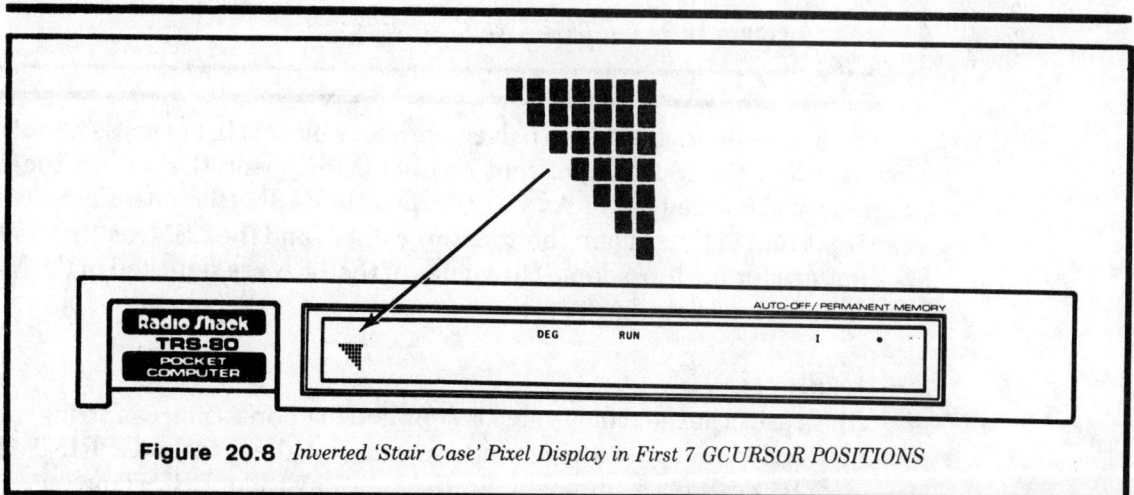

Figure 20.8 *Inverted 'Stair Case' Pixel Display in First 7 GCURSOR POSITIONS*

Just one more example and we'll move on. Add these two lines to the program and RUN it again.

```
35: FOR Y = 1 TO 22
95: NEXT Y
```

I'm not going to tell you what it does. You'll have to RUN it and see for yourself!

The Primary Statement/Command
GPRINT number

Other Forms of the Statement/Command
1Ø: GPRINT variable, variable, variable
1Ø: GPRINT number, number, number
1Ø: GPRINT (calculation), (calculation), (calculation)
1Ø: GPRINT variable, number, (calculation)

Here's an example. Go to the PROgram mode and type it in . . . .

1Ø: GPRINT 127

Now change MODEs and RUN this example.

1Ø: GPRINT value (Ø – 255)

As we have seen, the value supplied will PRINT the appropriate dot pattern at the current GCURSOR position.

1Ø: GPRINT X

In this form, the numeric variable X supplies the parameter to GPRINT.

1Ø: GPRINT &1E

Here, we are using a hexadecimal value for GPRINT. When you use hex to supply the values, you can look at the column pattern in a slightly different fashion:

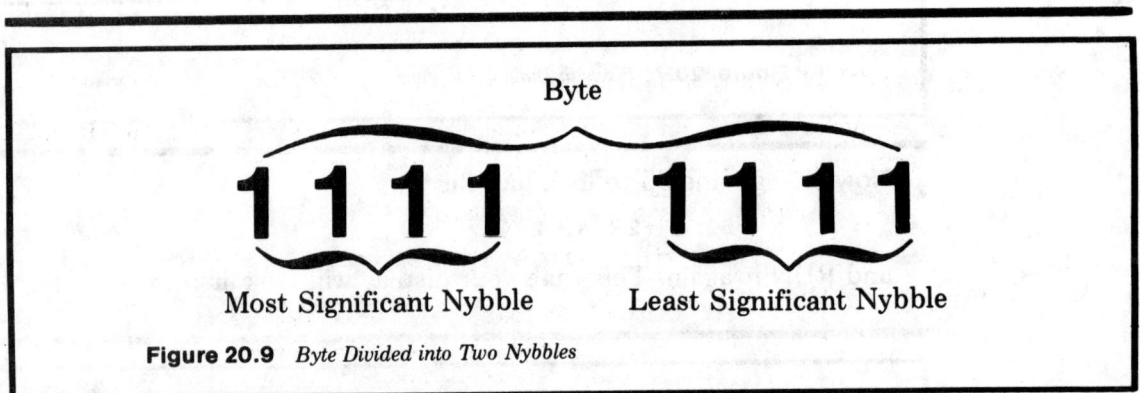

Byte

1 1 1 1   **1 1 1 1**

Most Significant Nybble   Least Significant Nybble

Figure 20.9 *Byte Divided into Two Nybbles*

The byte is divided into two halves, with four bits each, known as nybbles. The one on the left is called the Most Significant Nybble (MSN), and the one on the right is the Least Significant Nybble (LSN). As you can see, the MSN (the one on the left) represents the lower portion of the column (bottom three dots), and the LSN (on the right side of the byte) is a pattern for the top 4 dots. The values of the LSN are repeated in the MSN, which makes the hexadecimal calculation easier.

1Ø: GPRINT "1E"

In this case, a hexadecimal value is supplied in quotes. You can string together a bunch of hexadecimal values in a string and cause all of them to be GPRINTed, starting at the GCURSOR position, and moving to the right, just like PRINTing out a word.

1Ø: GPRINT A$

This is the same as the previous form, except a string variable is used (instead of a string constant) to contain the hexadecimal number string, such as A$ = "1E"

Here are a few approaches to using GPRINT. Each does the same thing, but use different methods:

```
100: WAIT Ø
110: CLS
```

```
120: FOR X = 1 TO 30
130: READ A
140: GCURSOR X
150: GPRINT A;
160: NEXT X
170: GOTO 170
180: DATA 127, 8, 8, 8, 127, 0, 127, 73, 73, 73, 65, 0
190: DATA 127, 64, 64, 64, 64, 0, 127, 64, 64, 64, 64, 0
200: DATA 62, 65, 65, 65, 62, 0
```

Now change MODEs and RUN this sample.

Another way of doing the same thing is to translate the data values into **hexadecimal** and put them in a string, like this:

In the PROgram mode, type in:

```
10: WAIT 0
20: CLS
```

(Don't type in the spaces inside the quotes — they are just to make it easier for you to read.)

```
30: GPRINT "7F 08 08 08 7F 00 7F 49 49 49 41 00";
40: GPRINT "7F 40 40 40 40 00 7F 40 40 40 40 00";
50: GPRINT "3E 41 41 41 41 3E 00"
60: GOTO 60
```

Now change MODEs and RUN this sample.

One more way to do the same thing using a string variable (If you typed in the last example, you can just edit the lines to do this one!):

Again, in the PROgram mode, type this in:

```
10: WAIT 0 : DIM A$(1)*26,B$(1)*26
20: CLS
30: A$(1) = "7F0808087F007F4949494100"
40: B$(1) = "7F404040400007F4040404000"
50: C$ = "3E414141413E00"
60: GPRINT A$(1);B$(1);C$
70: GOTO 70
```

Now RUN it again and see what happens.

I bet you can think of a better way to do what we just did, but wasn't it interesting to see it done with graphics?

GPRINT can be used to make special characters and shapes on the display to 'fancy up' the output of your programs.

Some suggested uses – In games, menus, and as program embellishments, this statement can give lots of variety to the output.

Oops! What went wrong? Mis-typed it. Forgot semicolon or overprinted it.

Also see: GCURSOR – POINT

POINT (Graphics)

We have told you how to 'light up' the pixels, but sometimes you need to know (within a program, and especially true for games) if one of the pixels is on or off. This statement will do the trick.

POINT looks at one of the 156 dot columns on the display (numbered Ø to 155) and returns the value stored at that location. Earlier, we mentioned that you can store a value of over 127 decimal on the display with the GPRINT statement, but only that portion of the value less than 128 (decimal) will be displayed. The fact is, the whole value you stored there is retained, and POINT will return the correct answer.

The Primary Statement/Command
POINT number

Other Forms of the Statement/Command
```
10: A = POINT number
10: A = POINT variable
10: A = POINT (calculation)
10: PRINT POINT number
```

Here's a sample program. Go to the PROgram mode and type it in. . .

```
10: GCURSOR 10
20: GPRINT 127
30: X = POINT 10
40: PRINT X
```

Now change MODEs and RUN this sample.

10: A = POINT 10

After this line executes, the numeric variable A will contain the value stored at column 1Ø on the display.

10: PRINT POINT 1ØØ

When this line executes, the value of whatever was stored at column number 1ØØ will be PRINTed on the display. Of course, the contents of point 1ØØ will be different after this PRINT statement executes, because it will erase whatever was on the screen.

10: A = POINT B

This illustrates that a numeric variable may be used to designate which point you wish to examine. After this line executes, the numeric variable A will contain the value that was in the column pointed to by the variable B.

10: IF POINT B THEN statement

In this case, the POINT statement is used to test whether a dot column contains any value other than Ø. IF POINT B contains a zero, the IF test will fail.

POINT can be used for a lot of different things, like testing the contents of a screen location during a game. For example, to see if a 'collision' between two graphics pixels has occurred.

Take a look at the "Rocket" program in the Appendix section. It uses the graphics statement to create a graphic image. In the sample programs for GPRINT, we had you create a word on the screen using graphics, rather than text. Now, we'll let you in on the secret for setting up a PRINTout like that. You can PRINT any character you like on the screen, then determine what it looks like graphically with POINT. Here is how we set up the data values for the sample program for GPRINT:

In the PROgram mode, type this program in.

```
10: CLS
20: DIM A(30)
30: PRINT"HELLO
40: FOR X = 0 TO 30
50: A(X) = POINT X
```

```
60: NEXT X
70: FOR X = 0 TO 30
80: PRINT A(X)
90: NEXT X
```

Now, go to the RUN mode and try it out.

What we have done is to PRINT the word "HELLO" on the display. Then, using POINT, we looked at the first 30 dot columns and stored the value in the A(X) array. This produced a *picture* of the letters, column by column, which we could then use in the GPRINT example. You could put the whole alphabet into an array, if you wished, and create new characters, or use the regular ones in graphics programs. Here is a program to store the upper-case alphabet in an array:

Again, in the PROgram MODE, type in . . .

```
110: DIM A(25,4)
120: WAIT0
130: FOR X = 0 TO 25
140: PRINT CHR$(65+X)
150: FOR Y = 0 TO 4
160: A(X,Y) = POINT Y
170: NEXT Y
180: NEXT X
190: REM printout the results
200: FOR X = 0 TO 25
210: CLS
220: FOR Y = 0 TO 4
230: GPRINT A(X,Y);
240: NEXT Y
250: IF INKEY$ = "" THEN 250
260: NEXT X
```

Now change MODEs and RUN it.

Using a few of the techniques we have learned along the way, this program sets up a doubly-dimensioned array to hold the 'characters' of the alphabet. There are 26 letters, so we have 'boxes' (array variables) 0 through 25 to contain the data for each one. Each 'character' is 5 dots wide, so there are slots 0 through 4 to put the dot columns into. Using CHR$ and an offset value to the first letter of the alphabet in ASCII (65), we PRINTed each letter, then saved each dot column with POINT for each letter of the alphabet. Finally, we GPRINTed the results for each letter.

Oops! What went wrong? Mis-typed it. Wrong MODE. Values out of range.

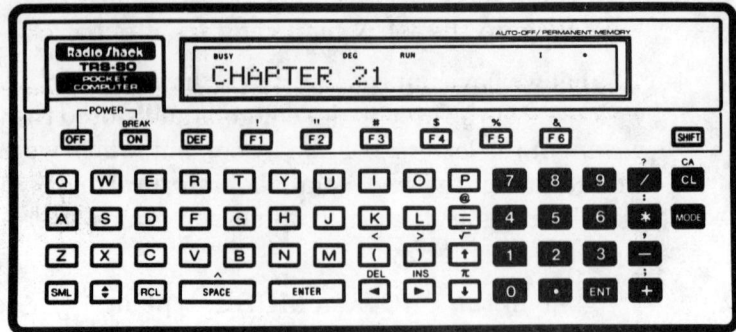

Looking into Things with PEEK and PEEK#

There are two BASIC statements that get pretty short shrift in almost every book on computers and computer programming. They are PEEK and POKE. We're going to explore PEEK first. We'll get to POKE next.

Most books tell you that these are *dangerous* statements, that they must be used carefully and that since they concern *machine-language* they are too hard to understand.

We have only one thing to say to that. Animal feathers!!! They are *not* hard; they are *not* machine-language and they are *not* dangerous. In fact, they are very powerful and have many uses, especially for the more creative programmer.

Now that I have gotten *that* off my chest, I'll climb down off my soap box and explain these incredibly powerful statements. . . .

Suppose you had some cardboard boxes. Suppose you had exactly 5Ø of those boxes (the exact number is unimportant), and each of those boxes has a separate number from 1 to 5Ø.

Figure 21.1 *Standing in Rows of Boxes*

Each box is sealed, but there is a small hole in the top of each one. Now, each one of those boxes has a slip of paper in it, and each slip of paper has a number written on it.

If you wanted to know what was in box number 2∅, you would pick up box number twenty and PEEK into the hole to read the number on the slip of paper.

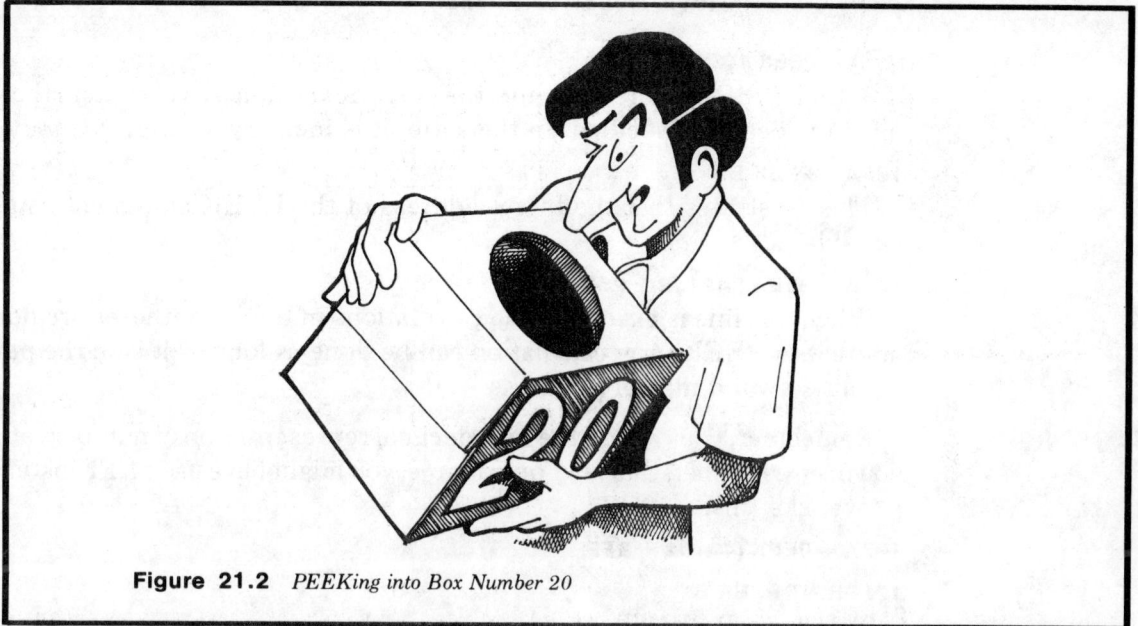

Figure 21.2 *PEEKing into Box Number 20*

What has that got to do with the PC-2? A lot! Each *box* represents a byte in memory. Each number on the outside of the box represents that byte's address. The slip of paper represents what is stored in each byte.

To demonstrate this, turn the computer on and in the RUN mode type: PEEK 2∅ <ENTER>. The answer you will get is 255. That is the value stored in memory location 2∅. This is the same as *PEEK*ing into box number 2∅. What could be simpler than that?

The next question you should have is, "So what! What good is it?" Not too tough a question. You see, everything that makes the computer run — its brains, so to speak — is stored in the computer's memory locations. The operating system; the BASIC language interpreter; the cassette, printer and RS232 I/O routines; your programs; the variables; the computer's 'scratch pad' or communications area; the display — *everything*. If we can *see* what a memory location contains, we can alter it, make other uses of it, manipulate it and generally do things that the designers of the PC-2 never thought of doing.

Now that we know what PEEK does and what it can be used for, let's talk about the so called *danger*. The PEEK statement won't ever disturb a thing. All it does is provide us with a window into the computer's memory—no more, no less. POKE, on the other hand, is the one that is regarded as the *really dangerous* one (it's not), and we'll deal with that a little later on.

There are two forms of PEEK. PEEK and PEEK#. They are used for looking into different parts of the PC-2's memory. Let's take a look at exactly how they are used and where. . . .

First, a short summary: PEEK *looks* into the computer's memory to see what is there. Each memory location (byte) can hold a value of ∅ thru 255 decimal, so the value returned will be in this range.

The Primary Statement/Statement
PEEK 10000

Other Forms of the Statement/Command
10: A = PEEK variable
10: A = PEEK number
10: A = PEEK calculation

10: A = PEEK 10000
After BASIC executes this line, the numeric variable A will contain the value stored in the memory location specified. In this case, it is memory location 10000.

10: A = PEEK B
This illustrates that the target address of the PEEK statement can be contained in a variable.

10: A = PEEK (49152 + 255)
When this line is executed, the calculations in the parentheses are done first to find the address to PEEK. Any calculation can be done as long as it is in the parentheses and the result is a valid memory address.

Remember, you can use the hexadecimal representation of numbers at any time (any time you need a number, that is). For example, you might have used &FF instead of 255 in the line above, like this:

10: A = PEEK (49152 + &FF)

10: PRINT PEEK B
This line will PRINT the value found in the main memory at the address specified by the variable B.

PEEK 10000 <ENTER>
Here we can see that the PEEK statement may be used in the RUN mode as well as in the PROgram mode.

Oops! What went wrong? Mis-typed it. Value out of range. Wrong memory address.

Also see: POKE — CALL

PEEK#

We told you earlier that there was another form of the PEEK statement. Here's why: There are two memory sets in the PC-2, each of which addresses up to 65,536 characters (bytes). The primary memory has the programs, ROM, and memory space for the expansion capabilities, such as the cassette/printer interface and the RS232 module. It is accessed with the PEEK statement (no abbreviations). The alternate memory could only be used for data storage if there was RAM there (none exists at this time). It is accessed with the PEEK# statement identically to PEEK, except it can be abbreviated to PE.

Getting into Things with POKE and POKE#

Aaaah! This is regarded, by those that don't know any better, as the most *dangerous* statement in BASIC. Actually it is a very friendly and useful statement.

First, let's find out how it works from a conceptual standpoint. Remember our fellow with the boxes — the one at the beginning of this chapter? Well, he's back! Here he is standing between his rows of boxes.

Figure 21.3 *Standing among Boxes*

Now imagine that he whips out a pad of paper from his pocket and writes a number on the top sheet.

Figure 21.4 *Writing 157 on Pad*

He tears off the sheet that he has written the number on, then picks up box number 2Ø and *POKE*s the paper into the hole on top.

Now, was that tough? A piece of cake, right? If we were writing that into a program it would look like this: POKE 2Ø,157 — that translates to: "POKE memory location 2Ø with the value of 157."

What about the danger? Well if you POKE around in the wrong places, you might cause your program to hang up, and you will not be able to BREAK the program. Or you might find

Figure 21.5 *POKEing Paper into Hole*

that it just won't respond to anything. What to do? Simple, — RESET the computer and try again. My advice is to experiment. The worst that can happen is that the computer will have to be RESET, and you will have to type in or reload your program from cassette. Now what is so *dangerous* about that?

For the life of me, I don't know why people make PEEK and POKE so hard to understand. Now let's look at the POKE statement in detail.

POKE and POKE#

POKE is the opposite of PEEK; it puts a value into a specified memory location.

The Primary Statement/Statement
        POKE memory location, value

Other Forms of the Statement/Statement
        10: POKE number, number
        10: POKE variable, variable
        10: POKE variable, number
        10: POKE number, variable
        10: POKE calculation, calculation
        10: POKE number, calculation
        10: POKE calculation, number
        10: POKE variable, calculation
        10: POKE number, calculation
        10: POKE address, data, data, data, data, data, ...

Here's a sample program. Go to the PROgram mode and type it in. . .

        10: POKE 30208, 3
        20: GOTO 20

Now change MODEs and RUN this sample.

How about a more elaborate example? Try typing in this program and RUNning it.

         5: WAIT 0
        10: I = 0 : A$ = ""
        20: A = PEEK (&C090 + I)
        30: A$ = A$ + CHR$ A

```
4Ø: PRINT A$
5Ø: IF I>15 LET A$ = RIGHT$ ( A$,15)
6Ø: I = I + 1 : GOTO 2Ø
```

The display will grow to 15 characters and then scroll to the left. What you see is the statement table that is stored in ROM. Don't ask me what it means, I'm not that advanced yet, but it has something to do with BASIC. You could change the starting address (&C9Ø9) and 'look' elsewhere if you like too.

1Ø: POKE 3Ø2Ø8, 5

When BASIC executes this line, the value 5 is put into location 3Ø2Ø8, which is the upper portion of the first dot column on the screen. Oddly, the screen is segmented in such a way that any value less than 16 which is POKEd into this location will light dots on the left side of the display, but values which are multiples of 16 will light the corresponding upper dots at the center of the display.

1Ø: POKE 1ØØØ, 1ØØ

This is how the POKE statement is most commonly used. It means POKE at address 1ØØØ the number 1ØØ. You need only be sure that the address 1ØØØ (or Ø to 65535) and the number 1ØØ (or Ø to 255) are within the range allowed.

1Ø: POKE A, B

When BASIC gets to this line, it simply looks up the variables A and B and uses them like the real numbers in the last example. If they are in the proper range, they are just like any number you might have put there directly. Either or both can be variables.

1Ø: POKE (1ØØØ + A, 1ØØ +B)

When BASIC gets to this line it does the calculation inside the parentheses first to get the numbers it needs for the address and POKE value. The restrictions are that no matter what the calculation is, it is evaluated and tested to see if it is in the allowed range for the address (Ø to 65535) or POKE value (Ø to 255).

Any calculation is allowed, as long as the maximum size of the numbers it uses to calculate with are within the range the computer can handle (-9.999999999 E-99 to 9.999999999 E99), but only addresses from Ø to 65535, and POKE values of Ø to 255 are legal.

The parentheses are needed so BASIC does not get confused about which to chose as the address value and the POKE value. A calculation can be used anywhere a number or variable can be used and can contain numbers, variables and other calculations like this:

1Ø: POKE (AD+2Ø*LOG 33–(3/1ØØ)+2*SIN2),(NU*2)

1Ø: POKE &FØØ, &FF

As BASIC sees this line; the &FF (hexadecimal representation of a number) is a 'legal' number if it's smaller than &FFFF for calculations. Don't forget the result must be reasonable and calculable, but other than that, anything goes. Again, you can mix and match this form of numbers with the others we have examined. That is, POKE &FØØ + 65, 3 is fine.

Don't you just hate trying to set up a loop to get the next address ready in a long series of POKE's? We saved the best for last — here's the trick:

1Ø: POKE 17ØØØ, Ø, 1, 2, 1ØØ, A, 255, &FF, 3+6, NU

This example will POKE all the data into consecutive memory addresses starting at location 17ØØØ. These data values are subject to the same restrictions that a single data item value has. All that has happened is that the computer has given you the option of incrementing the address location every time it 'sees' a comma (after the data items), it takes the next data item, and puts it in the next address location.

You can use hexadecimal numbers, such as &FF, or calculations like 3+6, or variable names like A or NU. Just follow the rules for POKE, as described in the previous examples that used only one data item.

In this example 17ØØØ is the memory address at which the first data item will be POKEd. The 'address' will be incremented once for each data item in the list. The data item list may be as long as you wish. Each data item must be preceeded by a comma, and the total length of the line may not exceed 8Ø characters (the limit of a line is usually 8Ø in either RUN or PROgram mode.)

The data may be a number, hexadecimal number, a named variable or calculation using any of these. If it is a calculation, parentheses may be used but are not necessary except for clarity.

POKE

There are two memory sets in the PC-2, each of which can address up to 65,536 characters (bytes). The primary memory has the programs, and ROM space for expansion. It is accessed with the POKE statement (no abbreviations). The alternate memory can only be used for data storage if there were RAM there (none exists at this time). It is accessed with the POKE# statement, identically to the POKE, except it can be abbreviated to PO.

Oops! What went wrong? Mis-typed it. Wrong memory address. Value out of range.

Also see: PEEK/PEEK#

Memory and the PEEK/POKE Functions

The PC-2 has 65,536 (64K) memory locations (numbered from Ø to 65535), or *addresses* in its *primary memory* and another 64K of addresses in the *alternate* memory, which can be accessed. Of course, there must be RAM or ROM present at those addresses to make them useful for our purposes, because the addresses exist even without memory actually being present.

PEEKing and POKEing are ways of getting directly into the memory cells of the computer from BASIC. Many computer 'hackers' feel this means more control and concurrently more responsibility. (You can alter the program in memory so that it will not RUN, or the PC-2 may 'hang' as a result of your POKEing around in RAM — simply use the SYSTEM RESET button and continue experimenting).

Using PEEK/POKE offers speed and versatility in execution time, program size, and especially for doing graphics, data storage, compression, sorts and a lot more. The compromise is that it is harder to write (and read) programs using data which is POKEd into memory, and they are far less portable to other BASICs.

PEEKing at Strings

In the PROgram MODE, type this in . . . .

```
10: A$ = "THIS IS A TEST"    set up variable A$
20: FOR A = Ø TO 13          set up a loop the length of A$
30: B = PEEK ( & 78CØ + A )  peek each location of A$
40: PRINT CHR$ B             PRINT the character found
50: NEXT A                   continue loop till done
60: END                      end of program
```

Remember to press <ENTER> after each character is displayed.

POKEing around in the LCD display.

In the PROgram mode, type in these lines. . .

```
10: FOR A = Ø TO 75          Setup loop – length of display
20: POKE &7600+A, RND 255    POKE left half with random number
30: POKE &7700+A, RND 255    POKE right half
40: NEXT A                   Loop until finished
50: GOTO 50                  Continue forever (or until BREAK)
```

Now change MODEs and RUN it.

Machine-language

The processes that go on inside the computer seem to be taking place invisibly. Actually, there is a lot going on in there, and it is taking place through the magic of machine-language. Machine-language is the language the Central Processing Unit (CPU) 'speaks.' It does not need to be interpreted, translated or otherwise decoded.

The main advantages of machine-language are its speed and compactness, but it is fairly complicated to write machine-language code, which is really beyond the scope of this book. BASIC itself, that part which interprets and executes the programs and statements that you type in, is a machine-language program. That does not mean that one language is better than the other, but it does mean that each has its uses. There are trade-offs that must be made when deciding which one to use.

Life is full of trade-offs. If you take your vacation in the summer, you can go to the beach, but you can't ski. If you buy a memory module for your PC-2, you won't be able to buy the RS-232 module as soon. You are faced with this type of trade-off when it comes to choosing between BASIC and machine-language or its close relative, assembly-language.

Machine-language is faster than BASIC, — typically hundreds of times faster. A machine-language program normally uses less memory than does a BASIC program; this leaves room for more or better programs.

Sound pretty good, huh? The catch is that machine-language is a *low level* language, as opposed to BASIC, which is a *high level language*. This means that machine-language is something a computer understands, but which is gibberish to a human. It's just a string of binary bits — ones and zeros — in memory. That's pretty hard for a human to make heads or tails of, though that's all it is, — heads and tails (ones and zeros). It's meaningful on a micro-electronic level.

A high level language (such as BASIC), on the other hand, makes sense to a human. Its statements relate to human *concepts*, such as PRINT or INPUT or GOTO. Unfortunately, these concepts are meaningless to the computer, which has to go through such contortions to interpret them that it slows the computer down to a relative crawl.

Assembly-language represents an intermediate step between high and low language-levels; but it is much closer to low. What it does, is take machine operations and let us name them with *mnemonics* instead of binary number sequences. The word 'mnemonic' means 'memory aid.' These memory aids attempt to conceptualize the machine-language instructions to make them more palatable to the human mind (or even mine). However, the events and operations being conceptualized are still machine events, not human ones.

For example, a high level program might deal with things like printing forms and calculating budgets. The program listing would clearly say INPUT this and PRINT that. Its math would consist of equation-like statements and variables, which would be familiar to many humans who had studied arithmetic and, possibly, algebra.

An assembly-language program which performed the same function as the program above would have statements telling the microprocessor to load various memory locations and registers with values to be found in other memory and registers. A computer register is like a special memory location contained right in the microprocessor itself. These registers can be accessed more quickly than other 'offboard' memory locations. Registers can also be used to perform a very limited number of arithmetic operations.

Talking about arithmetic, the preprogrammed functions you find in BASIC simply don't exist in assembly-language. There are a few commands that allow you to perform addition or subtraction of eight bit binary numbers. Anything beyond that (like larger numbers, fractions, or 'higher' operations like multiplication and division), you have to program yourself. Such a program actually has to 'manhandle' the numbers, byte by byte. The microprocessor hates long division more than you do!

Here are a few bytes of an assembly-language program:

```
LDI S, 784FH
SJP 0CFCCH
LDI A, 3EH
```

The machine-language, generated by this assembly code, would be even harder to understand. It would look like this:

```
10101010 01111000 01001111
10111110 11001111 11001100
10110101 00111110
```

This programming guide restricts itself to BASIC. We didn't go into assembly/machine-language for three reasons: 1. That would be a very advanced topic, well beyond the scope of this guide. 2. The PC-2 comes with a built-in BASIC interpreter. The purpose of this interpreter is to take English-like BASIC statements that *you* understand and translate them into the machine code that makes sense to the microprocessor. That's all you need to write and execute BASIC code. 3. The PC-2 does not have a built-in editor/assembler. You would need one of those to create assembly-language programs and convert them into the binary numbers the machine loves. Or, you could assemble the instruction by hand, a long and tedious process.

This is not to discourage your use of machine-language — indeed, we would like to see you 'jump in' and learn all you can.

CALL

Here is your chance to be adventurous. This example is not predictable — anything might happen. *Be sure the computer does not contain anything that you do not want lost*, but don't CLEAR or NEW it; that takes away some of the excitement. In the PROgram MODE, type in this program...

```
10: CALL &E8CA
20: GOTO 20
```

The CALL statement *CALLs* or transfers execution from BASIC to the computer's CPU (Central Processing Unit). The 'funny' number (& E8CA) is a hexadecimal number that is equal to 59594. At that address (59594), is the machine-language routine that displays the 'junk' you see after the machine-language routine RETURNs to BASIC.

What this does, is CALL a machine-language program, or subroutine, that the 'system' usually calls to display text and graphics. The unpredictability comes from the fact that we are not specifying what to PRINT or where it is found. The CALLed machine-language subroutine takes whatever was left over from who knows what and tries to do what it can. That is where the problems start; things could possibly get hung up. Not likely, but the display is usually interesting anyway, even if you don't crash the system.

It might be a good idea to press the 'all system reset' when you're through fooling around. By the way, none of this will hurt the PC-2, at worst, it just needs to be reset.

The CALL statement is a direct link to the microprocessor language that is in the PC-2. This statement, when used correctly, sends program execution to a specific machine-language subroutine. The address given is the first byte of the program (subroutine), and the variable is optional. If it is included, a register (the X register, if you must know) will be set to the address of the variable that is sent with the call. The called routine must do a machine-language RETURN to get back to BASIC. Be sure that the variable is defined and DIMmed first if it is not a single-letter variable. In this case, only a variable can be used, because it's the *address* of the variable that is being put in the X register, not the value.

By using the CALL statement, you can access machine-language routines from BASIC. This can be a very desirable feature when you need blinding speed to accomplish some programming task, — especially tasks that involve graphics programming or applications that require 'real time' handling of the display.

The Primary Statement/Command
CALL number

Other Forms of the Statement/Command
10: CALL number, variable
10: CALL variable, variable
10: CALL calculation, variable

CALL can be used in a program line or in RUN or PROgram modes.

10: CALL 32123, B

This form of this statement will send the execution to address 32123, and pass a value (in this case, B) to the machine-language routine at that memory location. The address must, as usual, be within the range allowed (Ø to 65535), and the maximum value that may be passed, is restricted to values from Ø to 255.

10: CALL A , B

Of course, you can use variables instead of the constant or 'hard coded' numbers, as in the previous example. By using A instead of the address 32123, we can set set A equal to 32123 or anything we want. This allows us to re-execute the line with A set to a different value. The same goes for B, the variable to be passed. Thus, you could change the address and the variable each time you executed this line, if you had several machine-language subroutines to execute.

10: CALL &ABCD, B

This is really the same as sending a decimal number, but it looks different. It is just the hexadecimal representation of a number, and if it is in the correct range (Ø to FFFF for address), all will be well.

10: CALL (2 + &FF * A), B

This example, with calculations, I'll admit, is a little far-fetched. The point is, any calculation or combination of calculations is fine, as long as the actual numbers can be handled and the final numbers, after the calculations are complete, are realistic and in the proper range.

You can mix and match real numbers such as 12345, the variables that are equal to 12345, the hexadecimal representations of the number 12345 (that's &3Ø39) or any calculation that will give the value 12345 when complete. All these can be used for the address requirement. The optional variable must be defined before the call is executed.

In the last case, the whole calculation must be put into parentheses to help the computer figure out what is to be done next. It is just the natural order of the computer to want things in a specific way.

Check the PC-2 Owner's Manual. There is a machine-language program ready for you to try. There is no explanation of the code or what is going on, but it does work, and it is a good demonstration of the the CALL statement.

Oops! What went wrong? Mis-typed it. Wrong mode. CALLed the wrong address. Literal (real number) used instead of the optional variable.

Also see: PEEK — POKE

22

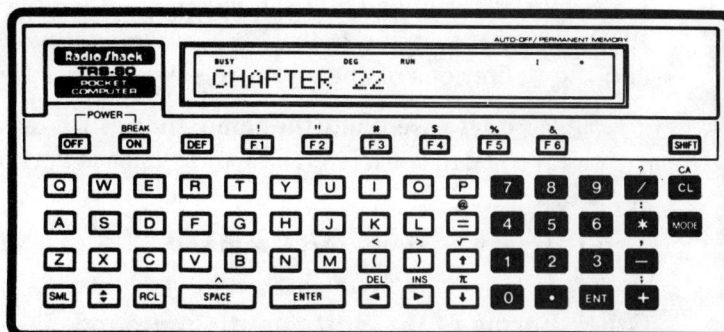

I/O and PERIPHERAL DEVICES

I/O or Input/Output are operations that move data into, and out of, the computer. The keyboard, screen, cassette recorder and printer/plotter are I/O devices. Each provides a way to put data in, or get data out (or both), of the computer.

The term *peripheral device* is used to refer to anything which attaches to the main body (or CPU, which means Central Processing Unit) of a computer. Because the configurations of computers are different in many ways, these *peripherals* can range from keyboards and video displays to internal memory and disk storage units, depending on the CPU.

The main body of the PC-2 has many built-in features such as the keyboard and display screen. 'Peripherals' are devices which attach to the PC-2, such as the printer/plotter and cassette interface. They connect to the side of the unit in a modular fashion. Other things may be attached to the *bus* (a fancy name for a plug), which is at the rear of the main body of the printer/plotter *interface* unit.

What's an *interface*? It is a device that allows the computer to communicate with another device. The cassette interface, which we will be dealing with shortly, is actually a machine that translates information from the CPU into electrical signals that can be stored on magnetic tape. You can use any type of tape recorder, but the cassette recorder is easier to work with than the 'open reel.'

Cassette Recorder (INPUT/OUTPUT)

The cassette recorder provides a means of storing programs and data for future use. The PC-2 provides a way for you to use two tape (cassette) recorders for your programs and data. In this section, we will discuss the commands and statements used with the cassette recorder. We'll begin with how to save and load programs.

Set up your interface and cassette recorder according to the instructions included with it and see your Owner's Manual before proceeding with this section.

CSAVE

CSAVE saves your programs to the cassette recorder. All program material from the first line to the last is saved. You cannot save just a portion of a program (unless you delete the lines you don't want to CSAVE before saving the program). If you have two recorders hooked up, you can use either of them to save your program.

CSAVE (as well as CLOAD, which we'll look at in a minute) can be used in RUN or PROgram mode. In the RESERVE mode, however, only the 'menu' for the function keys, and the definitions of the keys are saved — not the program.

CSAVE does essentially the same thing as when you copy a record album onto a cassette — it allows you to use it later. The difference is that you can 'play back' a CSAVEd tape into the PC-2.

The Primary Statement/Command
CSAVE

Other Forms of the Statement/Command
CSAVE "filename"
CSAVE –1, "filename"
10: CSAVE "filename"
10: CSAVE –1, "filename"
10: CSAVE string variable
10: CSAVE –1, string variable

To use CSAVE, you need to have a program in memory. Press the PLAY and RECORD buttons on the cassette recorder, then type CSAVE"TEST" <ENTER>. The prompt (>) will disappear from the display. You will then hear the beeping noise as the program code is spewing out to the cassette recorder — unless you have executed the BEEP OFF command. When the program has been saved, the prompt will return to the display. If you don't have a program in memory, type in this one-line program example and CSAVE it.

10: REM This is a test of the CSAVE statement <ENTER>

Now type in: CSAVE"TEST" <ENTER>. You now have a one-line program called "TEST" saved on the tape.

CSAVE"filename"

This form saves your program material to the main tape recorder. The file name can be up to 16 characters long.

CSAVE –1 "filename"

Appending the "–1" to the CSAVE command causes the program to be CSAVEd to the alternate cassette recorder, which is referred to as ReMoTe 2.

CSAVE

If you omit the *filename*, the program is CSAVEd with a blank filename, which makes it difficult to identify the program in future loading operations.

10: CSAVE"filename"

You can include the CSAVE command in a program line. When BASIC encounters the command, it will CSAVE the entire program to tape. The program will then go on to the next statement in the program list.

10: CSAVE A$

Here, the 'filename' is contained in a string variable (A$). As you can see, when the name is contained in a string variable, no quotes are used.

You will want to CSAVE your programs for future use, so that you don't have to type in old programs over and over. We will see other uses as we examine the loading operations.

Note: you can stop the CSAVE operation by pressing the <BREAK> key at any time during the program CSAVE.

Some suggested uses – saving programs for later use, saving subroutines and program segments for general use in many other programs. Transferring programs to other PC-2 users is also possible.

Oops! What went wrong? Mis-typed it. No tape in cassette recorder. Tape needs to be rewound. Cassette record button not pressed. Cables not properly attached or bad electrical connections. Cassette recorder battery weak or dead. Power cord not plugged in.

Also see: PRINT#, INPUT#, CLOAD

CLOAD

CLOAD is the opposite of CSAVE. It loads your programs from the cassette recorder or the 'menu,' and definitions for the function keys if used in the RESERVE mode.

Remember the example of the tape we made of the record album in the CSAVE section? CLOAD is like listening to the tape. Not as good as "Roll over Beethoven," but then, there is no accounting for taste.

The Primary Statement/Command
> **CLOAD**

Other Forms of the Statement/Command
> **CLOAD "filename"**
> **CLOAD –1, "filename"**
> **CLOAD string variable**
> **CLOAD –1, string variable**

Rewind the tape that has our "TEST" program on it; then press the PLAY button on the recorder. Now, press the <MODE> key for the PROgram mode. Type NEW <ENTER> to get rid of the program in memory. Finally, type CLOAD <ENTER>, and the tape recorder will begin to run. You will hear the same beeps you heard with CSAVE, but now it is loading the program back in.

The "filename" of the program CLOADing will be displayed after a moment, and the program will continue to CLOAD. When the prompt appears, you can use up and down arrows (in PROgram mode) to view the program that was CLOADed.

CLOAD and CLOAD –1

This form will CLOAD the first program it finds on the tape. If you include the (optional) device specifier (i.e., "–1"), then the alternate tape recorder is used.

CLOAD "filename"

Here, we are specifying a particular file to CLOAD. If there is more than one program on the tape, BASIC will search the tape until it finds the specified filename, then CLOAD that program. If it doesn't find the program, after you run to the end of the tape, either CLOAD a different cassette and continue searching or press the <BREAK> key.

CLOAD –1, "filename"

This form is essentially the same as the previous one, but in this case we have specified a filename to look for on the alternate cassette recorder.

CLOAD A$

Here, the "filename" is contained in a string variable (A$). As you can see, when the name is contained in a string variable, no quotes are used.

CLOAD re-loads programs or RESERVE mode data that has been CSAVEd on tape. Unlike CSAVE, CLOAD cannot be used in a program line, although it can be used in RUN, PROgram and RESERVE modes as a direct statement.

Some suggested uses – loading programs previously stored, or program tapes from other PC-2 users, including commercial programs bought for the PC-2.

Oops! What went wrong?. Mis-typed it. No tape in cassette recorder. Tape needs to be rewound. Cassette record button pressed (instead of 'CLOADing' something, whatever was on the tape will be **erased**). Cables not properly attached or bad electrical connections. Cassette recorder battery weak or dead. Power cord not plugged in. Playback volume set too high or low. Tone setting is too low (should be set high).

Also see: PRINT#, INPUT#, CSAVE

CLOAD?

The statement CLOAD? verifies that the program CSAVEd on tape is correct. It checks each byte, on the tape, against the corresponding byte in memory, to make sure they are the same. If there is a complete match, the prompt returns after the tape is checked. If there is not a match in any part of the program, an error message appears on the display.

CLOAD? is used immediately after CSAVEing a program. First the tape is rewound, then the *play* button is pressed.

The Primary Statement/Command
    CLOAD?

Other Forms of the Statement/Command
    CLOAD? "filename"
    CLOAD? –1, "filename"
    CLOAD? string variable
    CLOAD? –1, string variable

Rewind the tape again; press PLAY, and this time, type CLOAD? <ENTER>.

CLOAD?
This form of the command will check the first program it encounters on the tape against the program in memory.

CLOAD?"filename"
If you specify a filename, the PC-2 will search the tape until it finds the material CSAVEd under that name; then it will compare the data on tape to that in memory. If it doesn't find a file by that name, it will just let the tape run out. You will have to press the <BREAK> key to regain control.

CLOAD?–1"filename"
This statement will look for the file on the alternate recorder. Again, the filename is optional.

CLOAD? A$
Here, the "filename" is contained in a string variable (A$). As you can see, when the name is contained in a string variable, no quotes are used.

Sometimes things go awry when using the cassette recorder due to 'glitches' in the tape, or for other reasons. You will want to make sure that your program material is safely and correctly stored on tape before wiping out memory with the NEW statement or by CLOADing another program into memory.

CLOAD? cannot be used in a program line. It can be used in RUN, PROgram or RESERVE modes only as a direct statement.

Some suggested uses – testing all CSAVEd programs, to see if you got a 'good' CSAVE, is high on the list of 'very highly recommended' things to do. Folks with lots of spare time (for doing things twice) need not bother with this step.

Oops! What went wrong? Mis-typed it. No tape in cassette recorder. Tape needs to be rewound. Cassette record button pressed (in which case, the CLOAD? will never stop, and you will completely erase the tape). If you CLOAD? with the 'record button pressed, you *lost* any programs that were on the tape. The only one *not* lost is the program in memory, since you can now CSAVE it again on the nice clean tape you just made (all seriousness aside . . . **I've** done this! So be careful). Cables not properly attached or bad electrical connections. Cassette recorder battery weak or dead. Power cord not plugged in.

Also see: CLOAD – CSAVE

PRINT

No matter where you turn, there is the PRINT statement, in one form or another. We told you that this was a versatile statement.

PRINT # provides the means for saving *data* on the cassette recorder, as opposed to program or RESERVE data. This data may consist of the contents of whatever program variables you wish to CSAVE for later retrieval. An example of *data* would be tax tables, phone lists, payroll information, reminder lists scientific information and a thousand other things that you might have need of, or would like to store, for later retrieval. The data can be string or numeric or both.

You could almost think of this command as being like one of those pocket recorders people use for taking notes. It is the PC-2's 'note' taking recorder. Computers are getting so sharp, they are getting their own technological aids.

The Primary Statement/Command
> PRINT # variable

Other Forms of the Statement/Command
> 1Ø: PRINT # –1, variable list
> 1Ø: PRINT # –1, "filename"; variable list
> 1Ø: PRINT # –1, string; variable list.
> 1Ø: PRINT # number
> 1Ø: PRINT # number list
> 1Ø: PRINT # "literal"
> 1Ø: PRINT # "literal list"

First, set up the tape recorder as you did for CSAVE; then type in this program, and RUN it.

> 1Ø: A = 2Ø : B = 3Ø
> 2Ø: PRINT # A, B
> 3Ø: STOP

There are various ways to CSAVE your program data to tape, depending on the types of variables used . . . .

PRINT # A

When this line executes, the contents of the variable A will be saved to tape under a null (nonexistent) filename.

1Ø: PRINT # "TEST"; A

In this form, the variable A will be saved under the filename "TEST". Note that the filename must be enclosed in quotes and followed by a semicolon.

1Ø: PRINT # "filename"; A$

If the first variable is a string, the PRINT # must contain a name or at least a dummy name (two quotes back to back, that is, a null and the semicolon). The semicolon is required with all filenames.

1Ø: PRINT# –1, "TEST"; A

Here, the contents of the variable A will be saved under the filename "TEST", on the alternate cassette recorder (RMT 2).

1Ø: PRINT # A(*)

This is a special case of the PRINT# statement which is used to save the data stored in arrays. If you want to save the data in the fixed, @ (n) arrays, or any DIMensioned arrays, you must specify the asterisk (*) in parentheses. In this example, any data stored in the DIMensioned array named "A(n)", will be saved to tape. If you want to store @(), A() or A1( ), each must be saved separately.

1Ø: PRINT # A\$; A

Here, the "filename" is contained in a string variable (A\$). As you can see, when the name is contained in a string variable, no quotes are used.

1Ø: PRINT # –1, "filename"; A , B

This example addresses the second cassette recorder so the first one can be used to read data and the second can store it on another tape after processing. Note that –Ø instead of –1 gets the regular cassette recorder, it is the same as not specifying any (default, PRINT # "NAME"; A). When the –1 (or –Ø) are used, there must be a comma after it. Also never use –2 or any other device number, because the computer will very likely hang and ALL programs and data will be lost (not even the ON or OFF keys will work — you will have to press the SYSTEM RESET button, on the back of the PC-2).

Oftentimes it is necessary to save data separately from the program, especially in cases where new data is being entered into the variables each time you RUN the program. This is especially useful for maintaining mailing lists and similar programs.

PRINT# can be executed directly as a command from the keyboard, or may be included as a statement in a program line.

Some suggested uses – this statement is best suited for saving data and information for storage or later use or processing, such as in name/address lists, graphics data for printer or display, tables, lists and similar forms of information that is best stored and is possibly more data than can be in the computer at any one time.

Oops! What went wrong? Mis-typed. Wrong mode. No comma after –1 or –Ø. Used other than –1 or –Ø. No semicolon after filename. No filename when a string is the first variable. No tape in cassette recorder. Tape needs to be rewound. Cassette record button not pressed. Cables not properly attached or bad electrical connections. Cassette recorder battery weak or dead. Power cord not plugged in.

Also see: INPUT# – CSAVE

INPUT

INPUT # provides the means for your programs to retrieve the data previously saved to tape with the PRINT # statement.

If the PRINT # is the PC-2's note taking recorder, this statement plays them back.

The Primary Statement/Command
> **INPUT # variable list**

Other Forms of the Statement/Command
> **1Ø: INPUT # –1, variable list**
> **1Ø: INPUT # –1, "filename"; variable list**
> **1Ø: INPUT # –1, string; variable list.**
> **1Ø: INPUT # number**

```
10: INPUT # number list
10: INPUT # "literal"
10: INPUT # "literal list"
```

Rewind the tape we just made (under the PRINT # section); press PLAY, and RUN this program:

```
10: CLEAR
20: INPUT # A, B
30: PRINT A, B
```

INPUT # A

When this line executes, the contents of the variable A will be read from tape from the first data it finds, without consideration for any filename which may have been used to save (PRINT #) the data.

10: INPUT # "TEST"; A

In this form, the variable A will be loaded from the data saved (PRINT #) under the filename "TEST". Note that the filename must be enclosed in quotes and followed by a semicolon, as in PRINT #.

10: INPUT # –1, "TEST"; A

Here, the contents of the variable A will be loaded from the data saved under the filename "TEST" on the alternate cassette recorder (RMT 2).

10: INPUT # A(*)

This is a special case of the INPUT # statement which is used to read the stored data into arrays. If you want to load the data in the fixed @( ) arrays, or any DIMensioned arrays, you must specify the asterisk (*) in parentheses. In this example, DIMensioned arrays named "A( )", will be loaded from tape.

10: INPUT # A$; A

Here, the "filename" is contained in a string variable (A$). As you can see, when the name is contained in a string variable, no quotes are used.

The INPUT # statement is used to retrieve data stored to tape with the PRINT # statement. It is the only way to get this data back into a form useful to the program.

INPUT #, like PRINT #, can be used as an immediate command in RUN, PROgram and RESERVE modes or may be included in a program line.

Some suggested uses – to retrieve data saved with the PRINT # statement. It can be used as a means to quickly process data that was gathered over a period of time or to get it from other sources.

Oops! What went wrong? Mis-typed it. Wrong mode. No comma after –1 or –0. Used other than –1 or –0. No semicolon after filename. No filename when a string is the first variable. No tape in cassette recorder. Tape needs to be rewound. Cassette record button pressed (you **erased** instead of INPUTting). Cables not properly attached or bad electrical connections. Cassette recorder battery weak or dead. Power cord not plugged in.

Also see: PRINT# – CLOAD

CHAIN

There is an old computer saying that goes like this: Programs will expand until all available memory is used. I hate to tell you how true that is. You write a nice little program to do something useful. Then you decide that it needs some little tweek (adjustment) here and an improvement there. Next, you figure out a couple more neat things for it to do. You stroke it, refine it and add to it. Before you know it, you've used all the memory, and there are twenty other things you would like to add to the program.

This is as true of 'big' computers as it is of small computers like the PC-2. No matter how much memory you have, you wish you had more. CHAIN to the rescue!

You know what a chain looks like. It's a series of steel links. You can *chain* two cars together. You can *chain* yourself to the computer, and you can play a *chain* of tournament games. Chain, when it is used in the last sense, means to do a series of things one after another. (Ever see a chain smoker?) That is what the CHAIN statement means to the PC-2.

With CHAIN you can CLOAD and execute one program or program module after another and keep all of the program variables intact. No matter how big a program becomes, you can CHAIN the various parts of it together. Or, you can CHAIN individual programs, each of which is a separate application.

It is as though the CLOAD and GOTO commands were combined in one program statement. You can even specify a line number to RUN in the CHAINed program. When a program is CHAINed into the PC-2, the variables are preserved for use by that program, but the resident program (the one that CHAINed in the new one), is erased.

The CHAIN statement is a lot like cooking a meal with only one pan. You can only put so much in the pan and then cook it. When that is done, you can clean the pan and cook some more. The difference is that the PC-2 cleans itself and can even load the new 'food' to be 'cooked' (providing the cassette is ready to go!).

The Primary Statement/Command
```
10: CHAIN
```

Other Forms of the Statement/Command
```
10: CHAIN line number
10: CHAIN string,line number
10: CHAIN variable
10: CHAIN string, variable
10: CHAIN "filename", (calculation)
10: CHAIN string, (calculation)
```

Type in this program:
```
100: DIM A(10)
200: INPUT#"TEST";A(10)
300: FOR X = 0 TO 10
400: PRINT A(X)
500: NEXT X
```

Now, setup the cassette player to record, and CSAVE the program under the name "TEST". After the program is saved on tape, change it to read:
```
10: DIM A(10)
20: FOR X = 0 TO 10
30: A(X) = X*10
40: NEXT X
50: PRINT#"TEST";A(*)
```

RUN this program to save the data right after the program called "TEST". After this is done, rewind the tape, and press the PLAY button. Next, type in this program:
```
10: WAIT0
20: PRINT"Chaining"
30: CHAIN "TEST"
```

and RUN it.

```
10: CHAIN
```
When BASIC encounters this line, it will load the first program it finds on tape, and begin

execution at the first (or lowest numbered) line.

10: CHAIN"TEST"

If you specify a filename to load, the CHAIN command will search the tape and load the correct file if found.

10: CHAIN A$

Here, the filename of the program to load and execute is contained in a string variable.

10: CHAIN"TEST",100

When this line executes, the program called "TEST" is loaded into memory, and line 100 is executed.

10: CHAIN −1 "TEST",100

When this line executes, the program called "TEST" is loaded into memory from the alternate cassette recorder, and line 100 is executed.

CHAIN can only be used in a program line, unlike the other cassette I/O statements we have discussed. It cannot be used as a direct command.

Whenever there is more program than there is memory, CHAINing is a prime consideration. Also, consider that chaining several 'canned' programs together may be useful at times.

Some suggested uses – use it to do heavy processing of data, or when programs need to be broken into smaller 'pieces' or modules to fit into memory. Or, they can be chained together in different ways for differing effects. For instance, a name/address file could generate a Christmas list, address labels and even color graphics for individual cards on the printer.

Oops! What went wrong? Mis-typed it. Wrong mode. No tape in cassette recorder. Tape needs to be rewound. Cassette record button not pressed (**must** be pressed to CSAVE, **Must Not** be pressed to CHAIN). Cables not properly attached or bad electrical connections. Cassette recorder battery weak or dead. Power cord not plugged in.

Also see: MERGE

MERGE

A friend in need is a friend indeed. Meet your good friend, MERGE. It can save you *hours* and *hours* and *hours* of typing time. Conceptually, it is like a freeway or tollway on-ramp (depending upon which part of the country you live in) that MERGEs into the freeway. However, our MERGE statement only MERGEs one program onto the end of another.

In other words, MERGE causes a program stored on tape to be appended (that means 'added') to the *end* of the current program in memory. Once a program is MERGEd, it locks out editing of the program that was in memory before the MERGE, so be careful. That makes it akin to building a small house and then adding an upper story later on — it locks out any changes to the bottom floor.

The Primary Statement/Command

    MERGE "filename"

Other Forms of the Statement/Command

    MERGE −1 "filename"
    MERGE −1 string

Type in this program:

    10: "A"
    20: REM PROGRAM 2
    30: PRINT"PROGRAM 2"

CSAVE the above program to tape, then change it to read:

```
10: "B"
20: REM PROGRAM 1
30: PRINT"PROGRAM 1"
```

Rewind the tape, press the PLAY button and type MERGE <ENTER>. When the tape stops, LIST the program. You will see two programs in memory with the same line numbers. Go the RUN mode, and press <DEF> and <A>, then <DEF> and <B>.

The MERGE statement is useful for combining programs that are finished and debugged only! Each program *must* be labeled and can only be RUN using the <DEF> key and the appropriate label letter.

MERGE

This statement causes the first program encountered on the tape to be MERGEd onto the end of the resident program.

MERGE"filename"

This form will look for the program with the specified filename, and MERGE it to the resident program when found.

MERGE–1"filename"

This command will look for the specified filename on the alternate cassette recorder.

The MERGE function is a double-edged sword. On the one hand, it provides you with the ability to combine programs that exist separately into one 'master' program. On the other hand, any program that has had something MERGEd onto it is locked out from any editing, at any time, and can RUN only by using the <DEF> key.

Each program *must* be assigned a label before anything is MERGEd. This means that your programs must be perfect, because you can't change a thing after MERGEing. You may also have duplicate line numbers in memory, which will make the program listing look weird, but references in the program to duplicated line numbers will be alright — that is, a line in program "A", that says GOTO 10, will go to line 10 in program "A", even if program "B", which was MERGEd, has a line 10 as well.

If you try to edit something in program "A" (which has duplicate line numbers in program "B", which was MERGEd), the change will show up in the corresponding line number in program "B", and the line you thought you had changed in program "A" will not be altered in any way!

Some suggested uses – if you have working subroutines that you would like to use in new programs, this is the way to get them in without re-typing them. Be sure they work and load them in first; then write the rest of your new program.

Oops! What went wrong? Mis-typed it. Wrong mode. No tape in cassette recorder. Tape needs to be rewound. Cassette record button pressed (program you wanted to MERGE is now on a different plane of existence. Where *do* accidentally erased programs go?). Cables not properly attached or bad electrical connections. Cassette recorder battery weak or dead. Power cord not plugged in.

Also see: CLOAD – CHAIN

RMT ON and RMT OFF

Your television set is not broken . . . we have control. Remote control by computer is pretty spacey stuff. Nevertheless, the PC-2 does have the ability to *take control* . . . .

RMT ON and RMT OFF give you control over the cassette recorder. Plug in the cassette recorder as if you were going to save a program to tape, *except* you must plug the remote on/off jack into the REM 1 socket, instead of the REM Ø socket normally used. (See the PC-2's Operator's Manual on hooking up the recorder, if necessary.)

Press the play key on the recorder, then type: RMT ON <ENTER>. The cassette should not be running. Typing RMT OFF should start the cassette running. If this seems a little backwards, think of RMT ON as telling the PC-2, "your ReMoTe control *functions* are *ON*." RMT OFF tells the PC-2, "your ReMoTe control *functions* are *OFF*." Whenever the PC-2's remote control ability is on, it will keep the recorder shut-off unless an instruction is executed that needs to use the recorder. But when the computer's remote functions are *off*, then you have complete control of the recorder (as if the recorder were not plugged into the computer).

The remote control on a TV works about like that. If you have the remote on, it controls the TV; if it is off, only the channel selector will control it. This is not an exact analogy; the remote can't keep the kids from turning on Captain Kangaroo in the midst of the last crucial play of a tied World Series game!

The Primary Statement/Command
RMT option

Other Forms of the Statement/Command
10: RMT ON
10: RMT OFF

RMT ON
Lets the PC-2 control the relay that connects to the RMT 1 jack. Now recorder can be controlled by the PC-2 as needed.

RMT OFF
Closes the relay that connects to the RMT 1 jack. Now the recorder can be controlled by you.

10: RMT option
This is the form used from within a program.

RMTON or RMTOFF are ok, no space is needed.

Several uses are possible. Controlling two cassettes permits reading from one, and writing to another, for unattended processing. Also, other devices can be connected to the remote jack. Then they can be turned on or off by remote control, providing the current and voltage are low (not more than 12V at Ø.25 amps is safe).

Some suggested uses – when doing data-sorts that are on cassette — this allows the sorting of more data than can be in computer memory at one time, without needing supervision. Also, how about having a recorded message or messages played back under PC-2 control (leave the recorder in play and only the remote jack plugged in)? Remember that this could be exactly timed too, because of the PC-2's built-in clock. (Of course, you must write a program that tests the clock and turns on the recorder; we can't do everything for you!) RMT can be used to simply turn a cassette player on or off — you could coordinate voice playback with a PRINTout or other operation.

Oops! What went wrong? Mis-typed it. Recorder not ready. Cables not attached. No cassette in recorder. Batteries dead. Power not on.

Also see: CLOAD – CLOAD? – CSAVE – CHAIN – MERGE

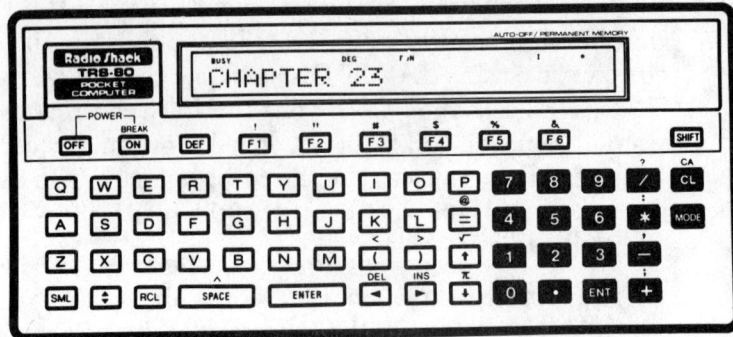

The Printer/plotter

Before trying out the various things we can do with the Printer/plotter, let's read the manual that came with it — at least that part that tells you how to hook it up properly; then we'll make sure it works. . . .

Here is a table of statements/commands, the modes that they work in and comments that may be helpful.

TEXT/GRAPH Table

COMMAND	TEXT	GRAPH	Comments
COLOR	Y	Y	
CSIZE	Y	Y	
GCURSOR	N	Y	
GRAPH	Y	Y	Sets CSIZE 2
LCURSOR	Y	N	
LF	Y	N	
LINE	N	Y	
LLIST	Y	Y	Sets Text Mode & CSIZE 2
LPRINT	Y	Y	
RLINE	N	Y	
ROTATE	N	Y	
SORGN	N	Y	
TAB	Y	N	
TEST	Y	Y	
TEXT	Y	Y	Sets CSIZE 2

GRAPH and TEXT mode can be likened to the 'mood' of the computer. When you feel like drawing pictures, you're in a drawing mood, and then if the mood hits you to write a letter, you just received a TEXT command (I wonder who sent it?).

The Primary Statement/Command
> **TEXT** <ENTER>

or

> **GRAPH** <ENTER>

Other Forms of the Statement/Command
> **10: TEXT**

or

> **10: GRAPH**

There are no parameters.

Type in TEXT <ENTER> and, most likely, nothing will appear to happen, but internally the PC-2 is now in the TEXT mode for the printer. The same is true for GRAPH, except, of course, it will be internally in GRAPHics mode.

TEXT

This can be used in any mode to set the PC-2 to the text state and reset the cursor and size.

GRAPH

Similarly, GRAPH sets the graphics state, including the defaults for cursor and origin.

You will want to use these commands to change to the state desired to accomplish a given task. Another reason might be a quick method of returning to the default cursor position or size.

Oops! What went wrong? Mis-typed it.

Also see: GCURSOR – GLCURSOR – SORGN – LINE

CSIZE

Products come in many sizes. There is the super-plus economy size, the super economy size, economy size, large, medium, small and personal size. Surprise! PRINTing on the PC-2 comes in different sizes too.

The PC-2 can PRINT in any one of 9 different sizes. Characters range from 1.2 mm tall to 10.8 mm. To tell the PC-2 what size you want it to PRINT, just use the CSIZE command with the size number after it. The table below shows the various sizes available, including the line spacing.

CSIZE	1	2	3	4	5	6	7	8	9
CHAR/LINE	36	18	12	9	7	6	5	4	4
HT (MM)	1.2	2.4	3.6	4.8	6	7.2	8.4	9.6	10.8
HT (IN)	.047	.094	.142	.189	.236	.283	.33	.377	.424
WD (MM)	.8	1.6	2.4	3.2	4	4.8	5.6	6.4	7.2
WD (IN)	.031	.063	.094	.126	.157	.189	.22	.251	.283
LF (MM)	2	4	6	8	10	12	14	16	18
LF (IN)	.070	.157	.236	.32	.394	.472	.551	6.29	.708

The PC-2 automatically starts in CSIZE 2. It also reverts to the CSIZE 2 when an LLIST is executed from the GRAPH mode (which reverts to the TEXT mode) or a TEXT or GRAPH statement is executed.

The Primary Statement/Command
> **CSIZE number**

Other Forms of the Statement/Command.
> **10: CSIZE number**
> **10: CSIZE variable**
> **10: CSIZE calculation**

In the PROgram mode, type in the following:

```
10: CSIZE 2
20: LPRINT "A"
30: CSIZE 1
40: LPRINT "A"
```

Now change MODEs and RUN it.

This short program will illustrate two of the sizes available in the PC-2 printout. First, it PRINTs the letter "A" in the default size (2), and then it changes to the smallest size and LPRINTs again. You could change the numbers to other values to see how they look, if you wish.

CSIZE number <ENTER>

If the size is in the range 1 to 9, the PC-2 will LPRINT characters (when commanded to LPRINT) in the height and width shown in the CSIZE TABLE. Of course, size can be a number, variable or calculation in parentheses. CSIZE can be executed from any mode

10: CSIZE number (or variable or calculation)

Can be used in a program line.

Some suggested uses — making labels and notes of various sizes, eye-catching printouts and headings.

Oops! What went wrong? Mis-typed it. Value out of range.

Also see: ROTATE — TEXT — GRAPH

Printer/plotter Keys

Paper Feed Symbol on Printer

The <LF> key feeds the paper from the paper storage, through the printer mechanism and out the top. It is at the top of the printer to the left of the display. Press the key, and the paper will feed till you let go (or it runs out of paper, or battery, or lightning strikes or...).

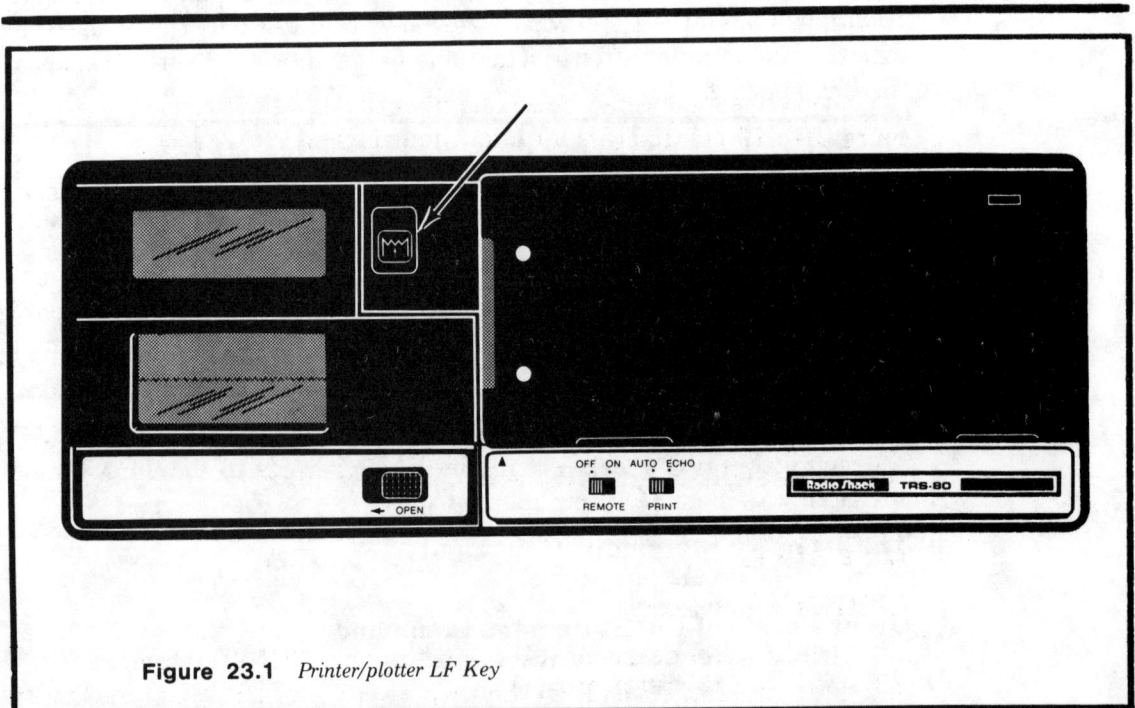

Figure 23.1 *Printer/plotter LF Key*

LF

The LF statement (Line Feed) is used for program control of the paper feed on the printer/plotter. It will feed both up and down (back into the paper storage well), which is what makes it a plotter *and* a printer. There is only one limitation of the negative feed (down or back into the paper storage well). That is, it can only roll back about 1Ø centimeters (4 inches or so) of paper. It could jam the mechanism if more paper than that were fed backwards through the printer mechanism.

Positive values, such as LF 1Ø, of the LF statement will feed paper out of the printer, and negative ones, such as LF -5, do the opposite. The LF statement is like a roller on a typewriter which feeds paper backward as well as forward.

The Primary Statement/Command
        LF number <ENTER>

Other Forms of the Statement/Command
        1Ø: LF number
        1Ø: LF variable
        1Ø: LF calculation

        1Ø: LF 5

This feeds 5 lines out of the printer without PRINTing on them. The length of the lines is dependent on the CSIZE that is currently set. Normally the CSIZE is set to 2 (the default value).

(See the the CSIZE table above for a complete description of the various CSIZES.)

Type LF 5 and see (press <ENTER> too). Magic. Well, if that was not good enough, try LF -5 <ENTER>. Put it right back. Not bad, having your own smart printer to impress your friends, entertain the kids and confuse the cat, eh?

1Ø: LF number

This is the main form. It will feed either into or out of the printer with a negative or positive number. LF 5 will issue five blank lines of paper, for instance. There is no alternate form of this command. Further, it can be used in any mode or program line.

The line feed value can be any number that does not cause the paper to feed backwards more than 1Ø centimeters, or about four inches.

You can use this statement any time you need paper to be fed out of the printer. Whenever there is too much paper, some can be called back; if the auto manufacturers can do it, so can the PC-2!

Some suggested uses — in a program that needs to feed some paper for tearing off after PRINTing, or perhaps, over-printing techniques may be tried. For plotting or making up tables and charts.

Oops! What went wrong? Mis-typed it. Value out of range. Dead or low batteries.

Also see: SORGN — LINE — RLINE (pen up)

LPRINT

LPRINTing Numbers

LPRINT is the same to the printer as the PRINT statement is to the LCD display. Anything you can PRINT on the display can be LPRINTed on the printer/plotter. The printer/plotter is, however, much more versatile when it comes to the LPRINTing of data in various formats, especially when used with the extension statements like TAB, LCURSOR, USING, LF, ROTATE and TEXT/GRAPH.

Numbers and characters can be LPRINTed as text, singly or in any combination. There are some important limitations. They are mostly related to the length of the material because the paper is only 2 1/4 inches wide.

You can LPRINT any number, the result of any calculation or numeric variable that the PC-2 can handle (and some it can't). The simplest form is, LPRINT number. A complication can arise if the PC-2 is not in CSIZE 1 or 2 and the number is bigger than the paper is wide — the result of a large character size. Since it is automatically in CSIZE 2, unless modified by a CSIZE statement, there is a safety factor built in.

When you change the CSIZE, you change the number of characters that can be put on a single line. (See the CSIZE table above for the different widths available. The PC-2 will take as many lines as necessary to LPRINT the number.)

Like all other commands, the LPRINT can take a numeric variable, a string variable, a literal, a calculation or a literal string, — for example, LPRINT A, where A has been previously defined. (A will be Ø if not defined). Further, like all other commands, a calculation can be substituted for a variable or number, such as LPRINT (2+COS.5). The parentheses are not necessary in cases where no confusion exists as to whether or not the second part of the calculation is part of a number, or part of a calculation (in this case 2). Unless you are short of memory, I recommend using the parentheses. They help make the program easier to read and understand, and there is no possibility of confusion.

All of the rules that apply to PRINT generally apply to LPRINT. Take for instance, the LPRINTing of multiple variables, strings, calculations and literals separated by a comma or a semicolon. The semicolon (;) puts the numbers up against one another (always leaving room for the negative sign, whether it is there or not), and the comma (,) causes each item to be LPRINTed in tabular form. For example:

1Ø: LPRINT 123456789; 987654321

will LPRINT the first number at the far left, leave a space (implied positive sign) and LPRINT the next number. If there is a third number (or more) each is LPRINTED with a space between, unless, of course, there is a negative number, — then the minus sign is before it.

CSIZE will also affect the number of characters that can be LPRINTed on a single line. If there is not enough room on a line, the characters are continued from line to line (this is called *wrap-around*) until the LPRINTing is complete.

The comma between two variables is a little more complex. It is a kind of crude TAB, but different for each CSIZE below 4. You can only use one comma in a single LPRINT statement. Any more will generate the infamous ERROR 1.

To get an idea of how the comma will modify the LPRINT output, divide the paper vertically down the middle, into two equal parts. CSIZE 1 puts the first number to the far right of the first half and the second number to the far right of the second half.

CSIZE 2 puts the first number in the right-most position of the line; then it LPRINTs the second number on the next line. Remember it can't LPRINT anymore lines when a comma is used in a single LPRINT statement.

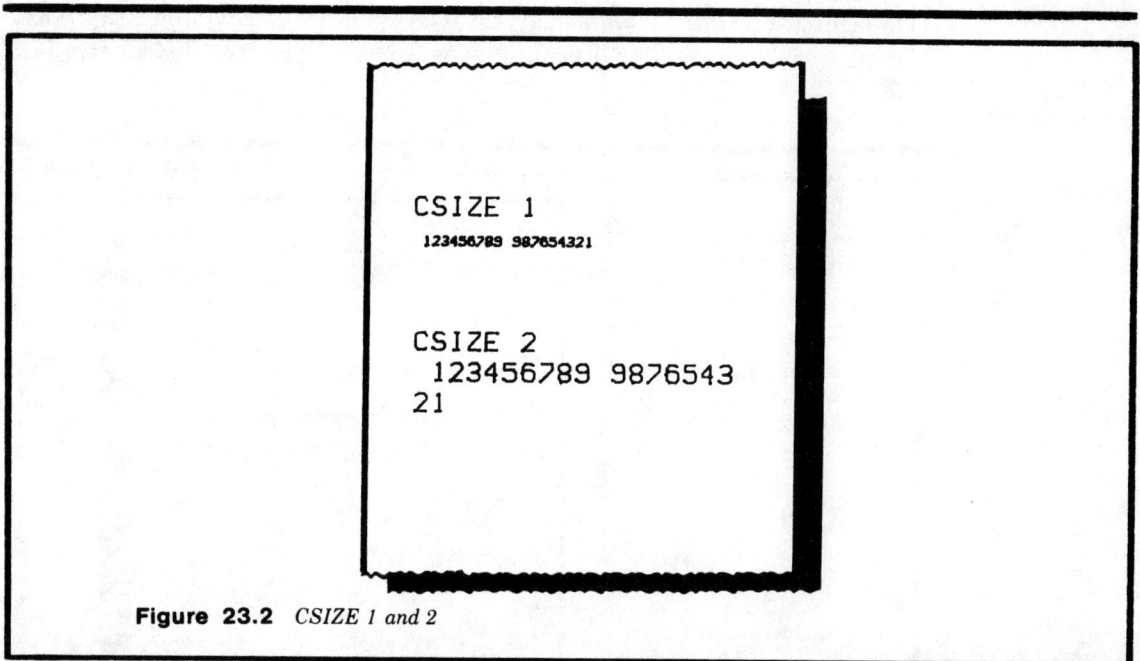

Figure 23.2 *CSIZE 1 and 2*

For CSIZE 3, the same is used as CSIZE 2, except that numbers in scientific notation (for example, 1.234567891 E17) that are too wide to fit on the line cannot be LPRINTed at all! An ERROR 76 will result. (There is a way to do this, however, and it is in the next section, — LPRINTing Text.)

Last, for CSIZE 4 and larger, the PC-2 cannot LPRINT any number that is too large for one line. That is only three digits in the 8 and 9 CSIZE (remember the sign position). Otherwise, CSIZE 4 to 9 follows the same rules as CSIZE 3.

LPRINTing Text

The above is for LPRINTing numbers only. Let's try LPRINTing characters (text) only.

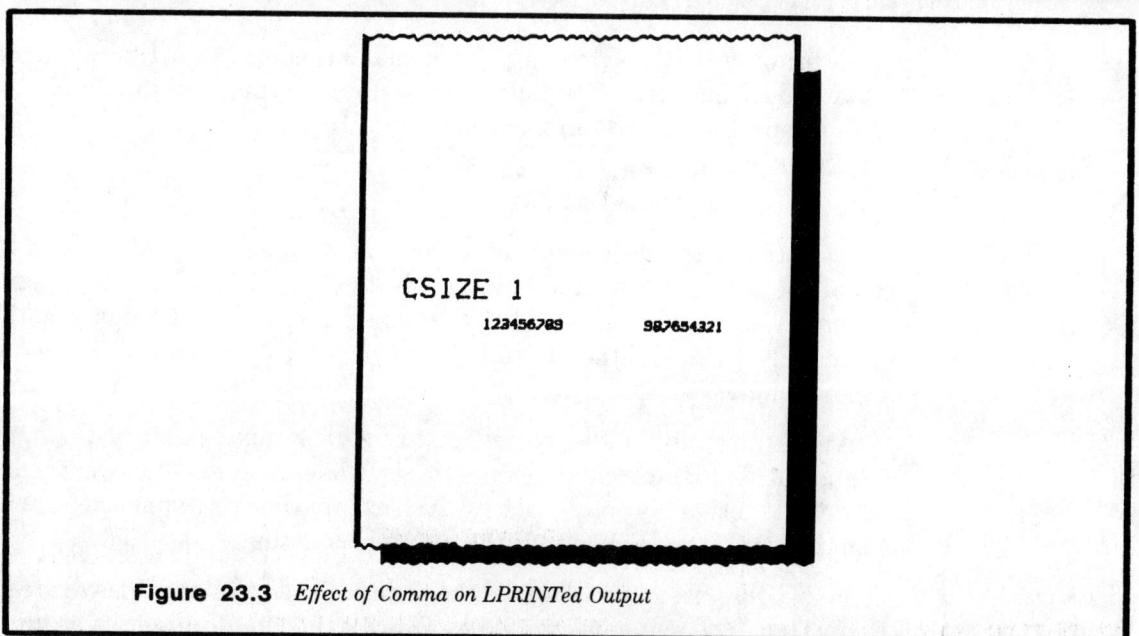

Figure 23.3 *Effect of Comma on LPRINTed Output*

One thing at a time. That is easy, LPRINT a literal string like "THIS IS A TEST", or set a string variable equal to a literal, such as A$ = "THIS IS A TEST" and LPRINT it like this: LPRINT A$. Easy.

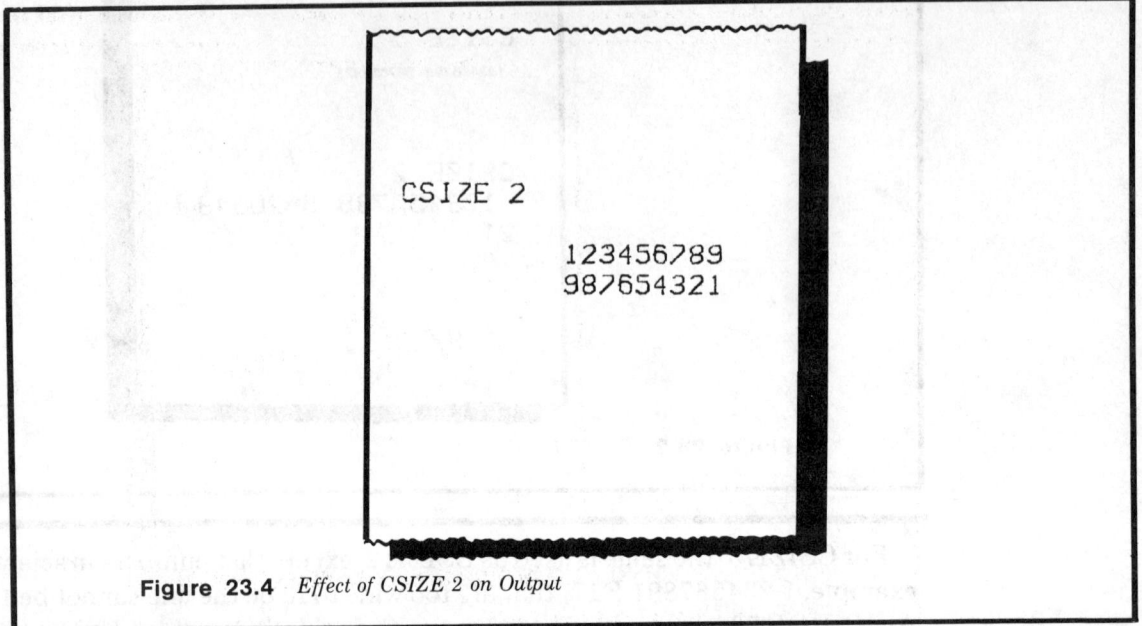

Figure 23.4 *Effect of CSIZE 2 on Output*

We can do the equivalent of calculations with text too. Look at this:

LPRINT A$ + " OF THE PRINTER" <ENTER>

If A$ were defined as shown earlier, the printer will printout "THIS IS A TEST OF THE PRINTER". When two or more strings are added together, it is called *concatenation*. The other logical string operations can be used with LPRINT as well. Take a few minutes to review them and the PRINT statement. While you're at it, you might also read the appropriate parts in the section on programming tips. The flexibility of the LPRINT statement is dramatic.

This brings us to the semicolon. It will act like a plus (+) in that it *concatenates* one string to the end of another. The following two statements accomplish the same thing using different operators between variables:

10: LPRINT A$ + A$
20: LPRINT A$; A$

These are the two different ways of joining strings for PRINTing and LPRINTing. They are not the same operations, however. Notice that in the above paragraph we said they *accomplish* the same thing. The + is used for adding strings together (and here we immediately LPRINT them), and the ; is a PRINT *formatting* statement made just to LPRINT things 'back to back'.

Let's get down to the tough stuff (not really) — mixing text and numeric printouts. The most useful way to mix text and numerics is to use the semicolon. Just remember that things are added together (as above with A$;A$), except there is a space in front of numbers for the imaginary sign (or a real sign if the number is actually negative).

The CSIZE statement will cause the printer to use as many lines as are necessary to finish LPRINTing. You can concatenate as many strings and numerics as you want, and in any order.

Originally, using the comma for tabular printouts was to take the easy way out (when BASIC was invented way back in the dark ages of the '5Ø's there was no TAB statement and commas were the only way to print tabular output.) Unfortunately, with the narrow paper and larger characters available, the comma is a bit of a pain when used for anything but CSIZE 1.

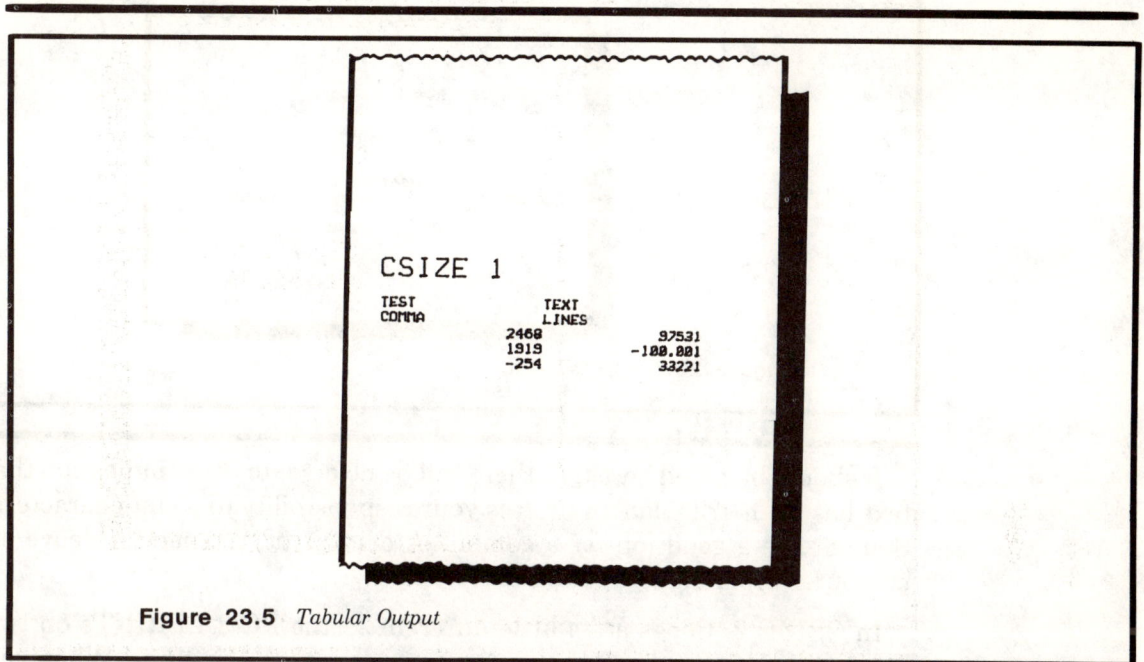

Figure 23.5 *Tabular Output*

Remember that you can not use a comma with a semicolon and you can only use one comma per LPRINT statement. When CSIZE 1 is used and you are LPRINTing numbers first and text second, the number will be LPRINTed on the right-most side of the first half, the text goes in the next half if there is room on that line for all of it. If not, then the rest is lost. The text is not continued on the next line.

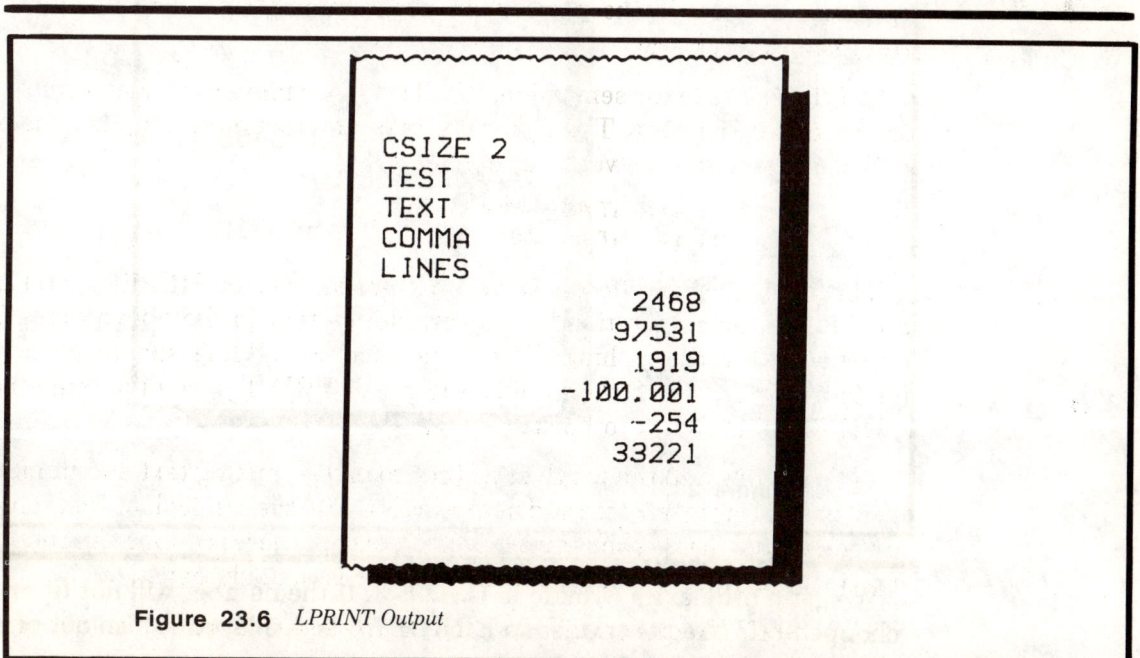

Figure 23.6 *LPRINT Output*

If the text is first, the text fills the first half of the line, and if there is more, it is also truncated ('chopped-off') and lost. This is identical to the way the PRINT statement works with commas. (See PRINT.)

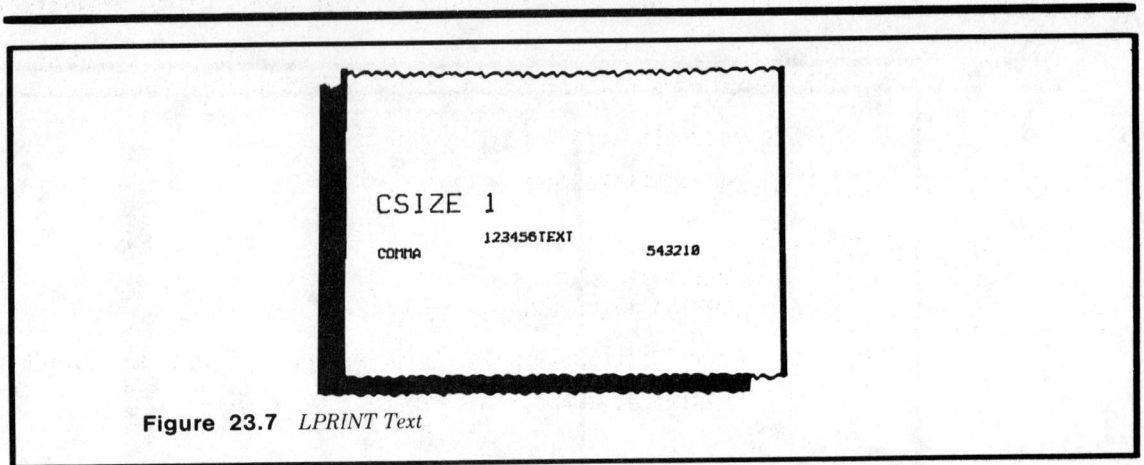

CSIZE 1

COMMA   123456TEXT   543210

Figure 23.7 *LPRINT Text*

It should be noted here that there will be no error or other indication that the LPRINTed text has been 'trimmed' to fit. It is your responsibility to count characters in this instance. Sounds like a good job for a computer, doesn't it? We need to leave something for the computer programmers to do, don't we?

In CSIZE 2, things are a little different — the PC-2 LPRINTs on two lines. If text or numbers are first (before the comma), they go on the first line. Whatever comes after the comma goes on the second line. For both text and numbers, the text is LPRINTed on the far left and numbers are LPRINTed on the far right.

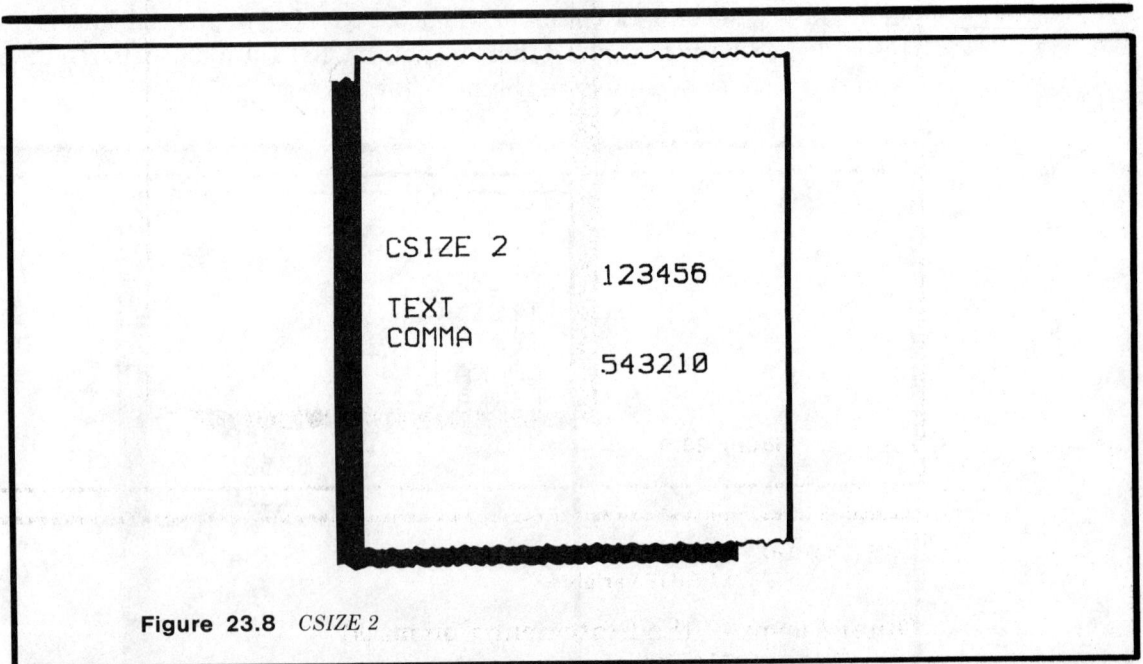

CSIZE 2

                        123456

TEXT
COMMA

                        543210

Figure 23.8 *CSIZE 2*

We get a little extra wrinkle in CSIZE 3. If the number will not fit on one line, it is not 'chopped-off,' like the text is; an ERROR 76 is displayed — "an out of room on one line" error.

For CSIZE of 4 or larger, the rules are about the same as CSIZE 3 except that it is easier to get the ERROR 76 or a chopped-off string. Two lines are used for LPRINTing.

There is a way, however, to LPRINT large numbers in any CSIZE, although not with the comma used to produce tabular outputs. Change all numeric representation to strings like this: A$ = STR$A.

Now the number is a string and will be handled as text would.

Prove it to yourself. In RUN mode type:

A=123456789000 <ENTER>

Now type:

CSIZE 9 <ENTER>
LPRINT A <ENTER>

The now famous "ERROR 76" will be displayed. Tough luck. Don't give up. Type:

LPRINT STR$ A <ENTER>

Now try this:

GRAPH <ENTER>
CSIZE 9 <ENTER>
LPRINT STR$ A <ENTER>

You see, there is almost always a way to do what seems almost impossible.

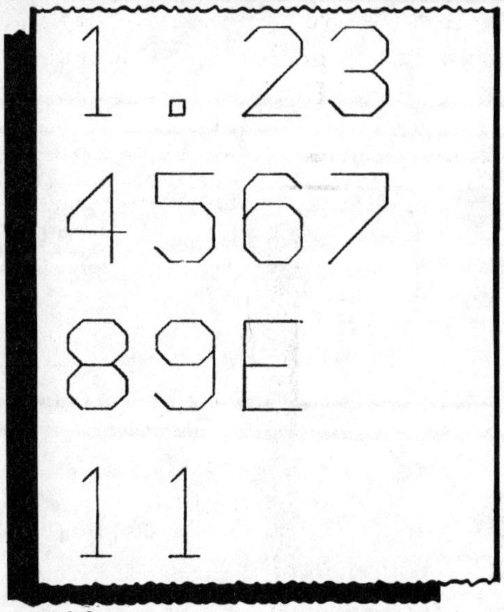

Figure 23.9 *Successful Output*

The Primary Statement/Command
LPRINT variable

Other Forms of the Statement/Command
10: LPRINT
10: LPRINT string
10: LPRINT "literal"
10: LPRINT (calculation)
10: LPRINT item, item
10: LPRINT number

Strings, "literals," calculations or item lists may be inter-mixed with commas, plus signs (+) or semicolons separating the items in the list, like this:

1Ø: LPRINT"Now is "+A$+" all good";A;B;QQ$;"get the lead out",B

With the printer hooked up, fresh batteries and paper loaded, set CSIZE to 2 and type in:

LPRINT "TEST ONE",1 <ENTER>

The text in quotes will now be LPRINTed on paper by the printer/plotter.

1Ø: LPRINT "ABCD"
2Ø: LPRINT 1234

Executing lines 1Ø and 2Ø will LPRINT the immediate numeric and text items on successive lines, unless they are too big for the line. In that case, they are carried over to the next until finished for text, — and display an ERROR 76 for numerics (can't LPRINT on one line).

Figure 23.10 *CSIZE 6 Output*

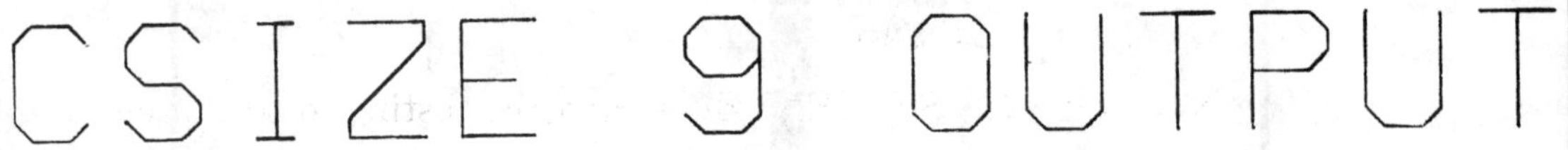

Figure 23.11 *CSIZE 9 Output*

Variables, and even calculations, can be put in the LPRINT statement, of course, just like in the PRINT command.

1Ø: LPRINT "ABCD",1234

This form of LPRINT, as described in detail above, is good for CSIZE 1 or 2, but care must be taken not to try to LPRINT anything that is too large for the line (or half line in CSIZE 1).

1Ø: LPRINT "ABCD";1234;A$

This is the most interesting form; it allows you to build up the printout as you would like it to be. Just keep in mind the number of characters you will use on each line (including the space before positive numbers). You can easily get nice-looking print-outs with a little care and planning.

Some suggested uses – LPRINTed output. Name and address lists or even address labels. The printing of the results of calculations.

Oops! What went wrong? Mis-typed it. Too long for line (numeric). No printer, paper, pens, or low battery. No ink in pen. Printer off.

Also see: LCURSOR – TAB – TEXT – GRAPH – USING – PRINT

LLIST

LLIST is a programming aid that LPRINTs an entire listing of the program lines that are in the computer, or any group of lines, if the starting number and ending number are given.

This statement, like all printer statements, will work in any PC-2 mode (PROgram, RUN OR RESERVE), and it will work in the printer's two modes (TEXT AND GRAPH). If the printer is in the GRAPH mode, the LLIST statement forces it to the TEXT mode. It also forces CSIZE to 2 at the same time.

The printer will LLIST in CSIZE 1 (which I like, but you need good vision — it's small), but the printer must first be set to CSIZE 1 by typing: TEXT : CSIZE 1 <ENTER> statement first. It is not possible to LLIST in any other CSIZE that is larger than size 2.

With LLIST, you can review your program on paper.

The Primary Statement/Command
LLIST options

Other Forms of the Statement/Command
LLIST line1 , line2 <ENTER>

where line1 is the starting line number, and line2 is the last line to be LLISTed. Neither line1 nor line2 are required. If no line number options are specified, the entire contents of program memory will be LLISTed.

In the PROgram mode, type in these lines:

```
10: REM TEST
20: REM LINE 2
30: END
```

Now, type LLIST <ENTER>, and the 'listing' of the program (as it is called) will magically appear on paper in just a few short seconds.

LLIST <ENTER>
This form LPRINTs out all BASIC program lines currently in the computer, in order, from lowest number to highest.

LLIST 100 <ENTER>
When a number is added to the LLIST command, the PC-2 LPRINTs that line only.

LLIST 10,1000 <ENTER>
Using the optional starting and ending line numbers lists those lines between the line numbers, as well as the specified line numbers themselves. The first number is the first line to be LPRINTed. The second number is the last line to be LPRINTed. The comma is necessary and tells the PC-2 to LPRINT all lines with numbers between the first and the last in their proper order.

LLIST ,1000 <ENTER>
A time-saving option is to leave off the first number, and the PC-2 LPRINTs the first line it comes to (the lowest numbered line) and continues to the ending line number.

LLIST 100, <ENTER>
similarly, leaves off the second number and sets the PC-2 to LPRINT all lines *after* (and including) 100.

An unusual feature of LLIST is that it can be used in a program line and works just the same as from the keyboard. All of the above options may be used also.

LLIST is an aid to programming, LPRINTing copy of a program to be kept, mailed, examined, notated or pasted on the back of the kitchen door. When programming, I find it much easier to follow the code when it is   LLISTed than when one line is displayed at a time on the display.

Some suggested uses – use it often for keeping records of your programs or subroutines. It's handy to send along with a program that you may be sending to someone on tape too, as a kind of back up, in case the cassette is damaged.

Oops! What went wrong? Mis-typed it. Low battery. Pens out of ink. No pens, or paper. Printer off.

Also see: LIST

Cartesian Coordinates for Graphics

There is an easy way to do almost everything. Graphics are *easy*, especially when you understand the concepts that are being used. The PC-2 uses a "Cartesian plotting system," and it is an easy concept in spite of its imposing name.

Once again we have encountered a strange term. Don't let it blow you in the weeds, because it is as easy as giving directions. I'll show you what I mean: You're walking home from the market and a kindly old gentleman stops you and says, "Say, young fella," (they always say that...) "can you tell me where the library is?" Of course, you say, "Sure. Go down this street 4 blocks, turn right and go over 2 more. You can't miss it."

You have just given directions using the Cartesian system, which amounts to counting down 4 blocks and over 2 to get to the point (4,2) on the plot, or in this case, the library.

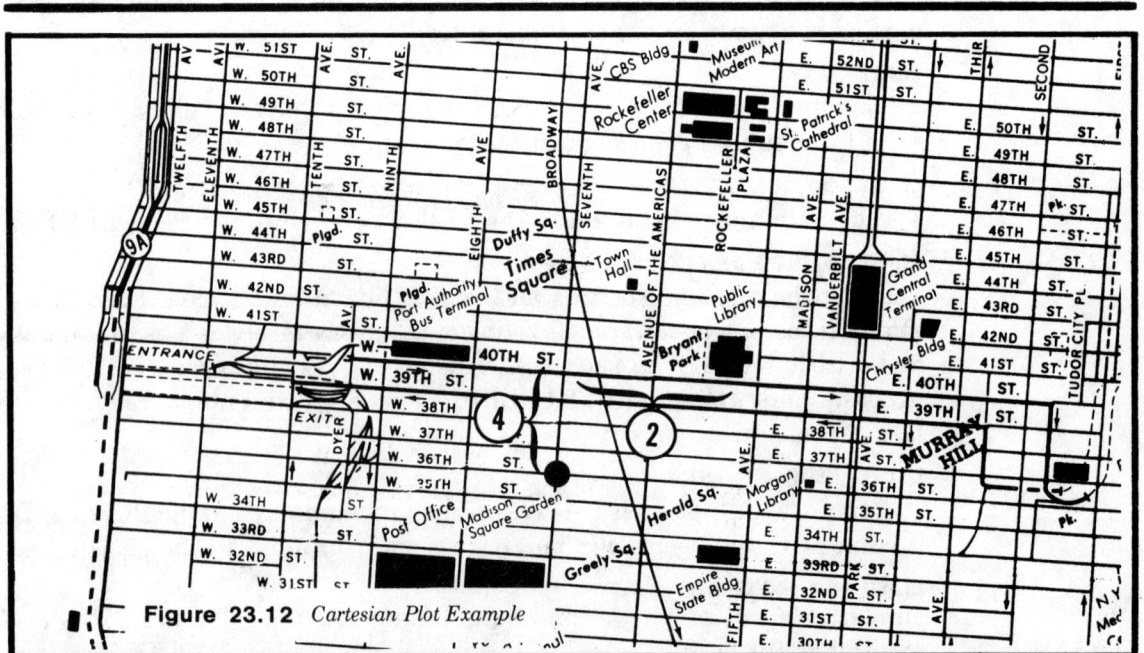

Figure 23.12 *Cartesian Plot Example*

The place you start counting *from* is called the *origin*. In our example above, the *origin* was at the point the old gentleman asked for directions. On the PC-2's printer/plotter, the default origin (the one that is set automatically) is at the far left of the line the pen is on when the GRAPHics mode is entered. If the pen moves (due to LPRINTing), the origin stays put unless commanded to move, and all moves are *relative* to that origin. There is a way to move the origin but we aren't ready for that yet.

A map of the PC-2's printer/plotter plotting area (see Figure 23.13 below) shows −2047 to +2047 for the horizontal movement (X axis). This is mis-leading in that you can only use a *segment* of this plotting area which is 216 plot positions wide. Normally that segment starts at 0, the X axis origin, and goes to +215 (zero counts as one position).

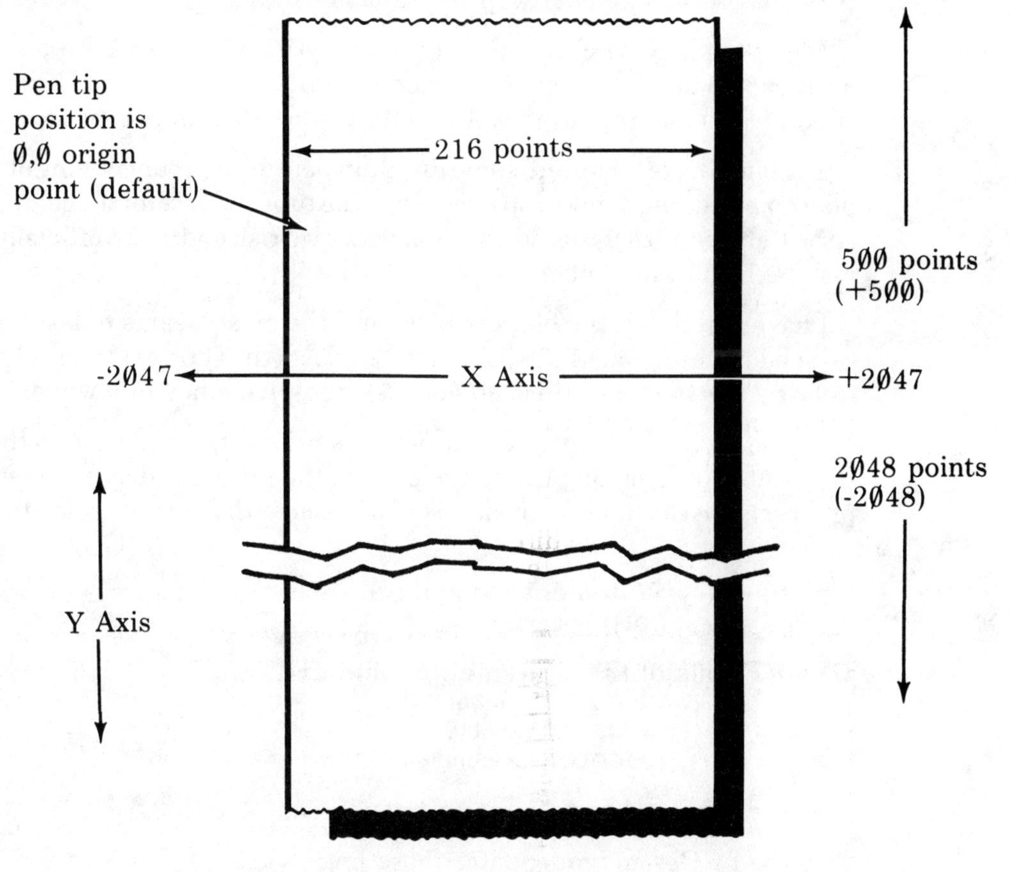

Figure 23.13 *Plotting Area with Plot Positions*

If you reset the origin with the SORGN statement (see below), then you could get to the other segments (still in the same plotting area, though).

There is another limitation to contend with. When plotting, it is sometimes necessary to use reverse paper feeds. The printer will only feed the paper in reverse for about 10 centimeters (4 inches); then it stops cold. No amount of coaxing and tricks will fool it. . . probably for a good reason. Have you ever cleared a miniature paper jam from a miniature printer? You need miniature fingers!

When the numbers are positive, the plot values move right and down for X and Y movements, respectively, somewhat like plotting on graph paper with a pencil and a ruler.

COLOR

COLOR sets the color (by changing the pens) which the PC-2 printer 'writes' (or 'draws') with. It will LPRINT in that color until commanded to change to another color. There are four colored pens, and they are numbered: black (Ø), blue (1), green (2) and red (3).

The pens are a lot like the ball point-pens we use every day but just a little shorter (a lot shorter, actually). They have a water-based ink in them, which means that they are bright, but they dry up pretty fast if you don't use them.

It is recommend that you take them out and replace the caps if you are not expecting to use them for a time. It will help you to keep them for long periods of time if you replace them in the packing tube and place a piece of wet tissue paper in the tube too. Don't forget to put the caps on each pen and cap the tube ends tightly.

New pens may be checked by trying to write with them on a piece of paper. It may be necessary to dip the tip into a drop of water to get the ink started flowing. It is probably not a good idea to lick the tip to wet it, and who needs a blue tongue, anyway?

In a jam, I have 'restored' some dried-up pens by carefuly pulling out the tips with a pair of pliers, and adding a tiny drop of water to the tube. Reassemble the tip, being careful to make it the right length. Of course, this is at your own risk and is not officially recommended, but it may be helpful in a pinch.

I have found that the black (which I use the most) seems to last the longest, and the red (which I use as much as the blue or green) lasts the shortest time. The green and blue seem to last a fair length of time, so consider their use once in a while.

The method of putting the pens into the printer can be found in the Owner's Manual for the printer/plotter. By putting the pens in the proper order, commercial or public domain programs that call out a given color, will cause the correct color to be printed.

The Primary Statement/Command
COLOR number

Other Forms of the Statement/Command
10: COLOR number
10: COLOR variable
10: COLOR (calculation)

where 'number,' variable or calculation can be Ø to 3.

In the PROgram mode, enter these lines:

```
10: COLOR 1
20: LLIST
30: END
```

RUN this program and see what your program looks like in blue.

10: COLOR A

If A is between Ø and 3, the pen holder will be rotated to the number (see above) corresponding to the pen color. If A is outside the range of Ø to 3, an error will result (Error 19). If A is not exactly Ø, 1, 2 or 3, the PC-2 takes the integer value, that is, COLOR 1, 1.2 and 1.9 will all select the same color (black).

COLOR can be executed in RUN, PROgram and RESERVE mode and used in the printer/plotter's TEXT or GRAPH modes, as well as in a program line. It can have a number, variable or calculation, in parentheses, for the color value.

This is good for livening up printouts with the bright colors, for allowing easy differentiation between graphed lines and enhanced or accented portions of printing and listings.

Some suggested uses — could be used to advantage in most charts and graphs, some games, plots and pictures. Color can make complex printouts easier to read.

Oops! What went wrong? Mis-typed it. Value out of range. Battery low or dead. Pens not installed or improperly installed. Pens dry or used up.

Also see: ROTATE — CSIZE

TAB

If you were to divide the paper on the printer into columns that are the same width as the characters that are printed, you could LPRINT tables of numbers and characters in nice, even columns. All that is needed is to get the pen to start LPRINTing in the column desired. TAB is the answer.

The TAB statement positions the pen over the location that you want to be LPRINTed. It can be used alone, as in TAB 5, or it can be used with LPRINT, as in LPRINT TAB 5 ; "TEST". The "TEST" can be replaced with a number, and, of course, either can be replaced with appropriate variables or calculations.

The semicolon is required to separate the tab position from the variable, literal, string, or calculation. Also the PC-2 must be in TEXT mode rather than GRAPH, or an error will result.

It is comparable to the CURSOR statement on the PC-2 display, except that TAB can be used with or without an LPRINT command. It takes its name from the tab function found on most typewriters, and you'll see why when it is demonstrated.

There can be only one variable LPRINTed with each TAB statement, so a different TAB must be used to LPRINT each variable.

The TAB range is proportional to the CSIZE in effect at the time of the TAB. See the TAB TABLE below.

CSIZE	Tab Width Millimeters	Tab width in Inches	Number of Tabs Possible
1	0.8	1/32	35
2	1.6	1/16	17
3	2.4	3/32	11
4	3.2	1/8	8
5	4.0	5/32	6
6	4.8	3/16	5
7	5.6	7/32	4
8	6.4	1/4	3
9	7.2	9/32	3

The Primary Statement/Command
    TAB position

Other Forms of the Statement/Command
    10: LPRINT TAB position ; "literal"
    10: LPRINT TAB position ; number
    10: LPRINT TAB position ; variable
    10: LPRINT TAB position ; string
    10: LPRINT TAB position ; (calculation)

A TAB *position* may be a number, variable or calculation. To test this statement, type in TAB 5 <ENTER>, and the PC-2 printer pen will move over 5 spaces from the left margin and stop. It is now ready to LPRINT at that position. If you now type LPRINT "TEST" <ENTER> the "TEST" will be written starting right where it is — at column 6 in this case.

TAB A <ENTER>

This will move the pen to the position where the next character will be LPRINTed. "A" can be a number, variable or a calculation to set the position.

10: TAB A

You can use the TAB without the LPRINT to just move the pen to a given position without LPRINTing.

10: LPRINT TAB A ; "TEST"

Of course, TAB can be used with the LPRINT statement too. It must contain the semicolon. If the variable to be LPRINTed is a *null*, that is, nothing, the pen will move to the tab position, then move back to the left margin, followed by a line feed ready for the next line. This will allow a calculated variable to be used as the message to be LPRINTed, and no error will result if that variable is empty (null).

The TAB statement allows a zero as a tab position, which means no movement of the pen. Again, this allows a calculated position with less chance of an error. Remember that the TAB also truncates the value to the next lowest integer number, so that a 2 or 2.3, or even a 2.9 will all tab over 2 spaces.

TAB can be used in any mode (RESERVE, RUN or PROgram) but the printer/plotter must be in TEXT mode rather than GRAPH mode.

Some suggested uses — TAB is specifically made for columnar or tabular output, such as tables — this might be useful for other things such as games, forms and pen alignment.

Oops! What went wrong? Mis-typed it. Value out of range.

Also see: GCURSOR — GLCURSOR — LPRINT

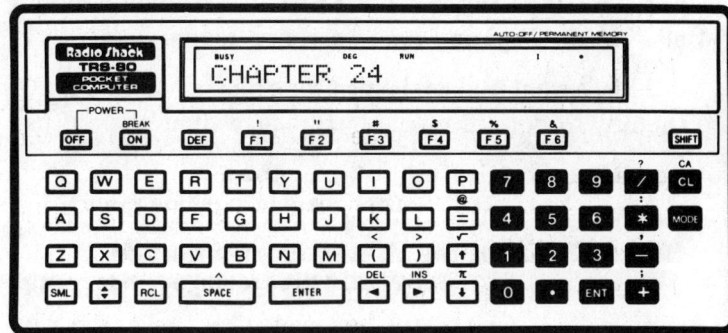

LCURSOR—The Plot thickens

LCURSOR is similar to the TAB statement, but it is even more similar to the CURSOR statement, in fact it is identical (in the manner in which it functions) to CURSOR as CURSOR is used alone — not with LPRINT. LCURSOR can only be used by itself, not with the LPRINT.

LCURSOR is a statement that will position the pen over the location which you want to be your next LPRINT vertical column position. The printer/plotter must be in TEXT mode rather than GRAPH mode, or an error will result.

It is comparable to the CURSOR statement, as used with the display. The LCURSOR range is proportional to the CSIZE in effect at the time the LCURSOR statement is executed. The LCURSOR spacing and character positioning are identical, so you can refer directly to the TAB TABLE, above.

The Primary Statement/Command
LCURSOR position

Other Forms of the Statement/Command
10: **LCURSOR variable**
10: **LCURSOR number**
10: **LCURSOR (calculation)**
10: **LCURSOR number   (0 – 35 max)**

Type in LCURSOR 5 <ENTER> and the PC-2 printer pen will move over 5 spaces from the far left and stop. It is ready to PRINT there. If you now type LPRINT "TEST" <ENTER>, "TEST" will be written, starting right where the pen is currently located, at column 5 in this case.

10: LCURSOR number

The primary (and only) use for this statement, is to place the cursor (pen) at a given location on the paper, ready for LPRINTing text (characters). It is identical to the stand-alone form of the TAB. You can use either one.

Some suggested uses: – LCURSOR is specifically made for columnar output (such as tables) – this might be useful for other things i.e. games, forms and pen alignment.

Oops! What went wrong? Mis-typed it. Value out of range.

Also see: TAB

GLCURSOR

GLCURSOR is a bit more than an extension of the CURSOR/TAB statement. It not only positions the printer/plotter pen over a given point on the line it is currently on, but it can also do forward and backward line feeds.

This is what makes the printer a plotter as well. It draws the characters, instead of forming them with dots or whole letters at-a-time as on other larger printers.

The Primary Statement/Command
> **GLCURSOR horizontal position value**

Other Forms of the Statement/Command
> **1Ø: GLCURSOR (Horizontal position, vertical position)**

Type in the following direct statements:

GRAPH : GLCURSOR (1Ø,15) <ENTER>

This will move the printer pen to a new location (coordinates 1Ø,15, as explained shortly). The GRAPH is not actually part of the GLCURSOR statement, but it is necessary to be assure that the PC-2 is in the right printer mode (GRAPH instead of TEXT).

1Ø: GLCURSOR (x , y)

PROgram or RESERVE mode. Must be used in printer's GRAPH mode, not TEXT mode.

The parentheses are mandatory, as is the comma. There are no default values, so the x-y point must be specified. Another limit is that the printer has an internal line count that won't permit it to reverse line feed (roll the paper back into the printer) more than 1Ø centimeters. (about 4 in.).

The mapping area that can be specified by the GLCURSOR is larger than the printer can actually LPRINT. (Whoa! Run that by again.) The paper is smaller than the plotting area. You see, the area which can actually be plotted at one time is 216 points wide and 5ØØ points high. The physical size of the paper is 216 points wide and as long as the roll of paper.

The plotting range that can be specified with the GLCURSOR statement is -2Ø48 to +2Ø47 points wide, -the X axis. That is a total of 4Ø96 points. (2Ø48 + 2Ø47 + 1 = 4Ø96 . . . remember the zero position counts as 1.) In the Y axis (vertical direction) the number of points is 2Ø48, as long as the value is *negative*! If the value is positive, the number of points is limited to 5ØØ, or about four inches (1Ø centimeters). Remember, there is a problem with feeding the paper backwards — that's why the positive values are limited to 5ØØ.

Of course, you are wondering, "If my plot can only be 216 points by 5ØØ points (maximum in the positive range), what good is a range of 4Ø96 points wide by 2Ø47 points high in the negative range?" The answer to such a question can only be, someone, somewhere, must have had plans for a wider plotter mechanism. At this time, such a plotter does not exist, and there is no information available that indicates that it will. However, someone *must* have had some expansion plans, or else it wouldn't have been implemented with such a wide range of permissible plotting values.

So, what seems to be a dumb oversight, may not be so dumb after all. Now we have to get on with our own problem, which is how do we use the 216 by +5ØØ or -2Ø48 points for plotting. Below is a picture of the plotter paper showing the plotting dimensions of the paper.

With the GLCURSOR statement, we can position the pen to any location on the paper. It requires two arguments, an X axis coordinate and a Y axis coordinate.

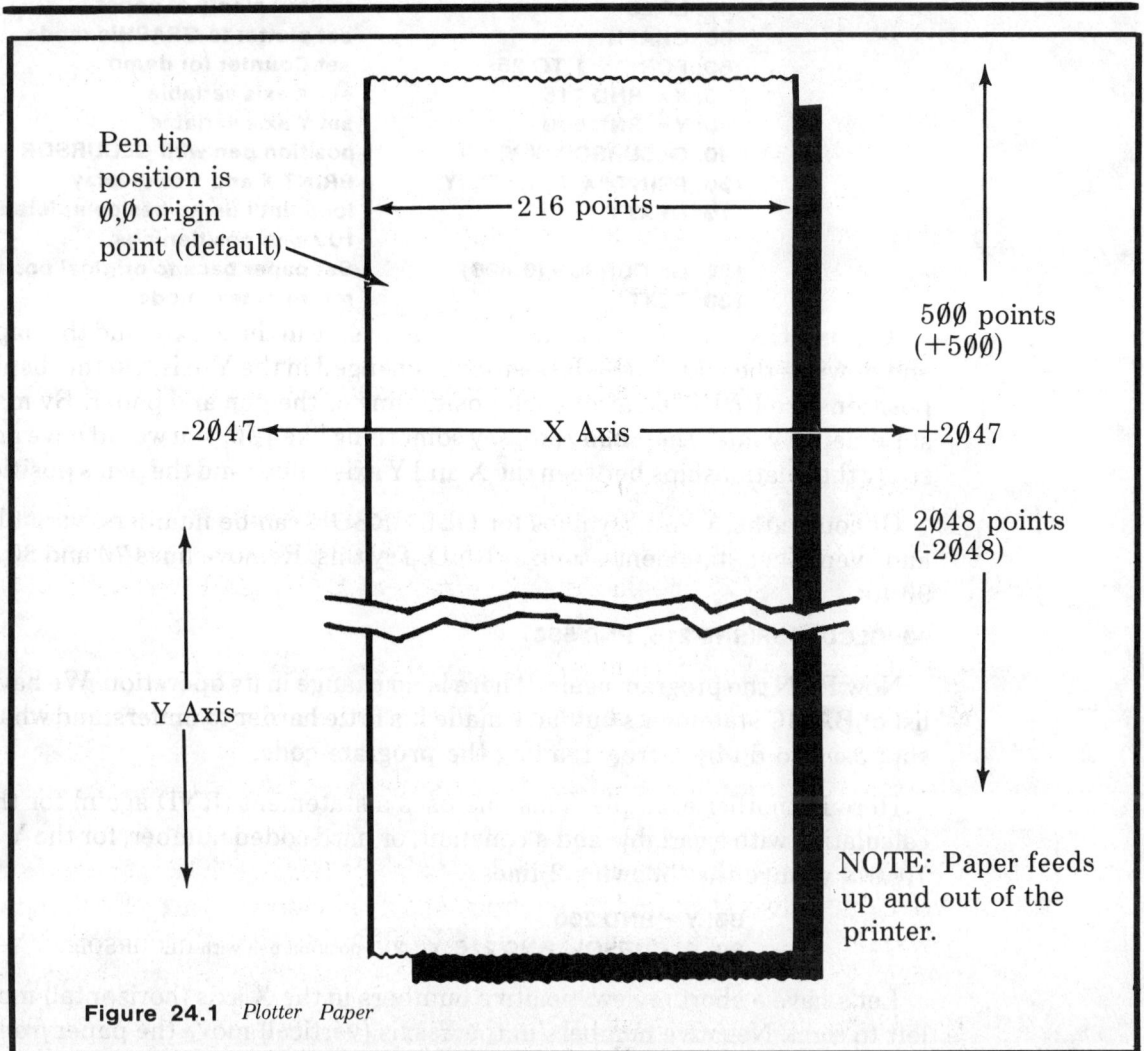

Pen tip position is Ø,Ø origin point (default)

216 points

5ØØ points (+5ØØ)

-2Ø47 ← X Axis → +2Ø47

2Ø48 points (-2Ø48)

X Axis

Y Axis

NOTE: Paper feeds up and out of the printer.

Figure 24.1 *Plotter Paper*

As you already know, the X-axis has only 216 *points* that we can use, but you can never have more than 500 points of reverse-feed stored in the machine at a time. Now we need an *origin* to plot from.

The plotter's starting point is called the *origin*. When we initialize the printer/plotter, issue the GRAPH statement or turn it on, so that we may plot on it, the X axis *origin* is set to the left-most side of the plotting area (in this case, the left hand edge of the paper) and the Y axis *origin* is set to whatever point the pen is currently at. That's not too tough.

The main difference between the GLCURSOR, TAB and GCURSOR statements is that GLCURSOR has a resolution of 216*points*, while the others have a maximum resolution of 1 character width for the CSIZE currently set. Another key difference is that TAB and GCURSOR are only effective from left to right, and they do not affect the vertical movement of the paper. GLCURSOR on the other hand, can move the pen *or* paper in either direction, within limits.

How about an example of the GLCURSOR statement? Ok, enter this example and RUN it. Make sure the printer/plotter is ready to go with pens, paper and power on.

```
1Ø: WAIT Ø          set PRINT waits to zero
2Ø: TEXT            set to text mode
3Ø: CSIZE 2         set line feed height
```

```
40: LF 25                       roll out plenty of paper
50: GRAPH                       set plotter to GRAPHic mode
60: FOR C = 1 TO 25             set Counter for demo
70: X = RND 215                 set X axis variable
80: Y = RND 500                 set Y axis variable
90: GLCURSOR (X,Y)              position pen with GLCURSOR
100: PRINT "X=";X;" ";"Y=";Y    PRINT X and Y to display
110: NEXT C                     loop until demo has completed
                                100 pen positionings.
120: GL CURSOR (0,400)          Set paper back to original position
130: TEXT                       return to text mode
```

As this RUNs, the pen will dart from side to side in the X axis, and the paper will shoot up and down as the GLCURSOR position is changed in the Y axis. On the display, the X and Y positions are PRINTed after each positioning of the pen and paper. By making the WAIT statement a value other than zero, say something like 100, you would have an opportunity to study the relationships between the X and Y axis values and the pen's position on the paper.

Of course, the X and Y values for GLCURSOR can be numbers, variables, calculations and even other statements, such as RND. Try this. Remove lines 70 and 80 and change line 90 to:

90: GLCURSOR(RND 215, RND 500)

Now RUN the program again. There is no change in its operation. We have simplified the list of BASIC statements but have made it a little harder to understand what the program is supposed to do by merely reading the program code.

Here is another example. This one uses a statement (RND again) for the X axis, and a calculation with a variable and a constant, or hard-coded number, for the Y axis. Delete line 70 and change the following 2 lines

80: Y = RND 200
90: GLCURSOR (RND 216,Y * 2)   position pen with GLCURSOR.

Let's have a short review: positive numbers in the X axis (horizontal) move the pen *from* left to right. Negative numbers in the Y axis (vertical) move the paper *from* the bottom up and out of the Printer/Plotter. Below is an X-Y plot showing the results of the paper movement for positive X and Y movements.

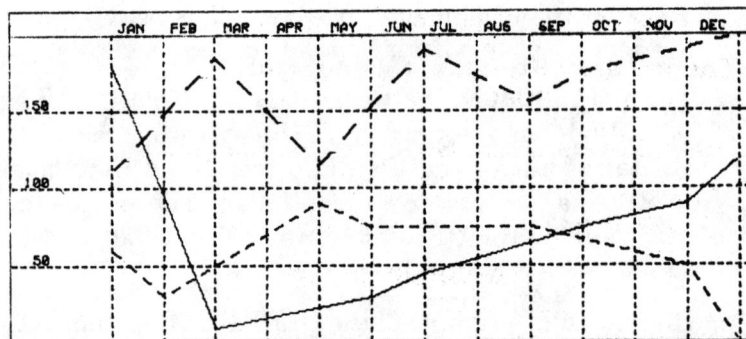

Figure 24.2   *X-Y Plot*

You would want to use the GLCURSOR statement for the same reasons you want to use CURSOR, TAB or GCURSOR, and then some. For instance, when plotting graphs, equations and pictures, you will need to move the pen to various positions before starting to plot the various parts of the picture or graph.

Some suggested uses — specific uses would be things such as moving the pen to specific (or random?) locations and then using RLINE to draw a repeating figure. Another might be to set up a new origin by first moving the pen with GLCURSOR and then SORGN it (see SORGN).

Oops! What went wrong? Mis-typed it. Value out of range. No printer, paper, or pens. Low battery, or low ink in pens. Wrong printer mode (GRAPH only).

Also see: GCURSOR — SORGN — LINE — RLINE

SORGN

Harking back to the example of the Cartesian coordinates (Hark, hark!) — the same old gentleman happens to cross our path again. He seems lost. "Say, aren't you the young fella' I met yesterday?" I answer in the affirmative, and he says, "I seem to be lost. Could you give me directions to the library again?" "Sure," I reply. "Go east six blocks, turn right and go south eight blocks. You can't miss it."

He seems to be confused and he says, "Didn't you give me different directions yesterday?" I answer, "Yes, I did. But we are in a different place. So from *here* it's east six blocks and right eight blocks." The point is, that we had changed our point of *origin* in giving the directions.

SORGN is a statement which also changes the point of *origin*, only it applies to the printer/plotter. Most graphics work is related to a specific location on the paper, and sometimes we want to change the location of the point where we want to start plotting *from*. To do that, we have the SORGN statement. It relocates the point we call the *origin*. When we execute the GRAPH statement, the *origin* is set to the far left side of the current line. With SORGN we can move it to any position on the paper — with the appropriate limitations.

There are no options or parameters used with the SORGN statement. It is used by first positioning the pen with the GLCURSOR statement and then by simply executing SORGN. To reset the origin to the left edge of the paper, simply execute the GRAPH statement again.

Note that the GRAPH statement, even when already in GRAPH mode, does a modified SORGN in that it moves the pen to the far left and then does a SORGN (of it's own) to put the origin at the beginning of the line.

The Primary Statement/Command
    SORGN

Other Forms of the Statement/Command
    1Ø: SORGN

In the PROgram mode, type in:

    1Ø: GLCUSOR (4Ø , 4Ø)
    2Ø: SORGN

If you RUN the two lines above, the pen will move about a quarter of an inch up and to the right. You can keep running it, and it will keep moving up and to the right (until it runs out of room, of course). The *origin* is being moved each time to the new end point of the last move. Then the GLCURSOR statement moves from the origin (the new one) up and right, as specified.

To run this more than a few times, it may be necessary to feed out some paper (use the paper feed key on the printer) and then do a GRAPH statement to be sure you're in the right mode (and at the left edge of the paper).

1Ø: SORGN

There are no options or parameters to set. The internal registers that keep track of the *origin* are changed to wherever the pen is when the statement is executed.

The SORGN statement can be in any mode (RUN, PROgram or RESERVE), but the printer/plotter must be in GRAPH mode, or an ERROR 73 will result.

Sections of a program can be written to draw pictures or graphs at a given origin and then, by just moving the origin, they can be used again to draw similar pictures or graphs at another site.

Some suggested uses — say you want to draw a forest. It is easier if you draw one tree, and then move the origin and draw another. By continuing this approach, you can quickly use up a lot of ink (and also draw the forest). Also see the RLINE statement. A more useful idea might be a form that you need drawn more than once, or results of a calculation might be plotted which may make the results more meaningful.

Oops! What went wrong? Mis-typed it. Wrong printer mode (GRAPH only). Value out of range. No paper, or pens. Low battery. No ink in pen.

Also see: GRAPH — LINE — RLINE

LINE

This is the line drawing statement you've been waiting for. It's the work-horse of the printer/plotter and the slave of your imagination. Given a large enough piece of paper, you can move the world (well, maybe draw it).

Did you ever do those connect-the-points drawings as a kid (I remember doing the Mona Lisa during English in 4th grade once). This statement is very similar. The points are made with two X-Y values and the printer does all the work of calculating how to get from one to the other (not that easy, let me tell you, my Mona Lisa had the funniest nose).

Figure 24.3 *Connect the Dots*

The LINE statement draws lines from one point to another, and it can have as many as 7 points. That's 6 lines (think about it) connected, one to the next. If that is not enough, you can change the color (any of the four: black, blue, green or red) or the line texture (solid, 7 varieties of dotted or not LPRINTed at all, which is just another form of GLCURSOR).

And that's not all, add a capital B to the end, and it draws a box using the first two points as the diagonal corners. Dots, lines, dashes, colors, boxes... what will they think of next? I'm waiting for them to come up with a CHANGTIRE statement for my Honda!

It works, like all printer statements, in any of the three modes of RUN, PROgram or RESERVE, but it is limited to the GRAPH mode of the printer.

We have an idea how the LINE statement works; now let's look at a drawn line — from a phlosophical standpoint. In geometry, a line is described as an infinite number of points between two points. An *infinite* amount of anything is a concept that is hard (if not impossible) to imagine. So, we won't try. Instead, we'll use a number that isn't so big — say, about 5∅. Here are 5∅ dots in a space of about five inches:

● ●

here is the same number of dots in 1 inch:

━━━━━━━━━━━

and the same number of dots in 1/4 inch:

━━

You'll notice that as we make the dots smaller and closer together they become a line — actually, they are still points, but our eye sees them as a line. Imagine now, if you will, that all lines are just a series of invisible points, but with a difference: there are only 216 points in the X axis and 5∅∅ in the Y axis when the PC-2 printer/plotter is used.

With the LINE statement, we can give it a starting point and an ending point, and it will automatically fill-in all of the points in between, and that is only for starters. We can give the LINE statement a *list* of up to seven points, and it will draw from one point to another until all seven points have lines between them.

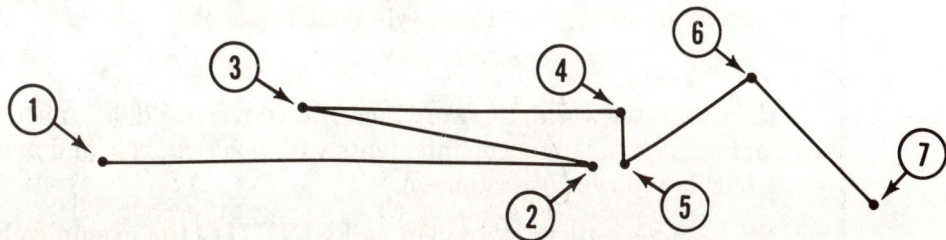

Next, we can give LINE a list of points and a number for a pen color, and it will not only draw our list of lines between points but also will make them a specific color.

We're not through. Next, we can tell LINE what *kind* of line we want drawn, everything from a solid line to seven styles of dashed lines (like this: -----), or even no line at all!

One more thing — when you specify only the two diagonal points of a box as LINE's list of points to draw to and make the last parameter of LINE's list of options a B, the LINE statement will draw a box. Show you what I mean. Suppose we want a box that looks like this to be drawn on the printer/plotter:

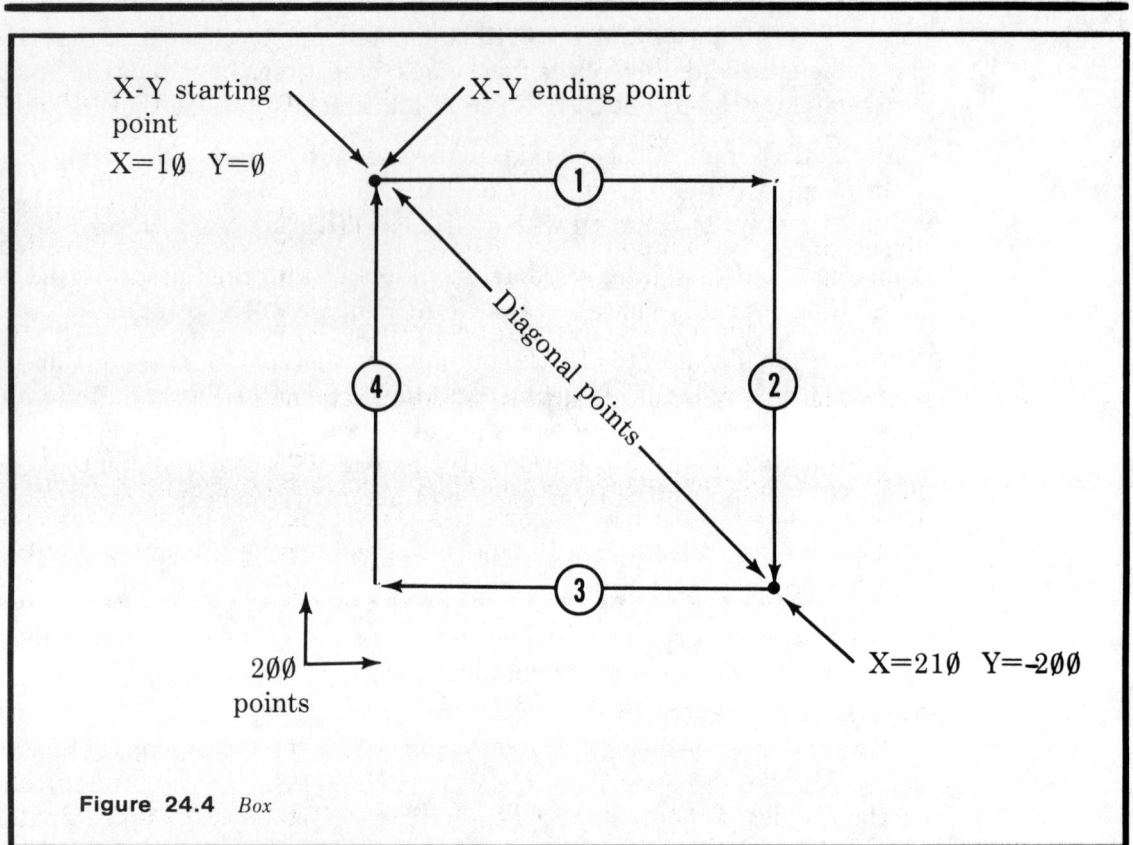

Figure 24.4 *Box*

We'll draw this with the red pen and use the finest dotted line. The LINE command is used like this:

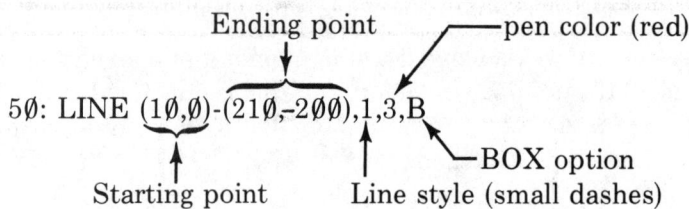

```
         Ending point        ┌─── pen color (red)
                    ╭───────╮
5Ø: LINE (1Ø,Ø)-(21Ø,-2ØØ),1,3,B
          │           │      └── BOX option
    Starting point  Line style (small dashes)
```

In the computer world, the word *powerful* is over-used. It is used to describe everything from paint color to language statements with *powerful* this and *powerful* that. Let me tell you, LINE *is* a powerful statement.

LINE is as versatile a statement as PRINT. Try the examples below and then see for yourself how many different ways you can use this statement. Remember, you can't hurt the hardware, and the worst that can happen with the software is that you'll have an error message on the display.

The Primary Statement/Command

LINE (X1, Y1) – (X2, Y2), line style number, color number, box option

Other Forms of the Statement/Command

1Ø: LINE (X1, Y1) – (X2, Y2) . . .(X7, Y7),s ,c ,B

1Ø: LINE (variable, variable). . .,variable,variable,B

1Ø: LINE (calculation, calculation). . ., calculation, calculation, B

In the PROgram mode, type in these lines without spaces, and RUN it.

```
10: GRAPH
20: LINE (0,0)-(40,40),2,1,B
```

RUNning this program will draw a small box on your printer, with a dotted blue line.

10: LINE (X1 , Y1) – (X2 , Y2) ... (X7 , Y7) , S , C

X and Y are the values of the horizontal and vertical coordinates for each point. The first one (X1) is the horizontal distance from the origin (see SORGN and the explanations of the origin) to the first point. Similarly, Y1 is for the vertical start of the point related to the origin. This is the place the pen moves to before it even starts to draw.

Next is X2 and Y2, which are mandatory, and are where the line draws to (from X1, Y1 to X2, Y2). The rest (X3,Y3 to X7,Y7) are optional and not needed. They allow making a somewhat more complex figure with one statement.

The "S" stands for style of printing (or drawing, actually). A number is expected if this optional parameter is used. 0 is for a solid line; 1 to 8 provide progressively larger dashes to draw the line, and 9 means don't draw anything, — just move the pen. 9 is like the GLCURSOR statement. If no number is found, the printer assumes 0 and draws with a solid line. The comma is mandatory, unless there are no parameters.

Last is the "C" parameter, which is the number of the colored pen. 0 is black, 1 blue, 2 green and 3 red. Again, the comma is mandatory if this option is used.

10: LINE (X1 , Y1) – (X2 , Y2) , S , C , B

Note that the B is the only thing here that's new. It is the parameter that makes the printer draw a Box. The other options can be used as before, but any points after X2,Y2 are ignored, so you may leave them off. The box that is drawn starts at the first point (X1,Y1) and draws over (horizontally) to X2, then up (vertically) to Y2. That's X1,Y1 to X2,Y1 to X2,Y2, so far. Then it goes to X1,Y2 and back to X1,Y1.

An easy way to think of all that X/Y stuff is to imagine a line drawn from the first to the second point. That is a slanted line, and it is the diagonal of the box, like this:

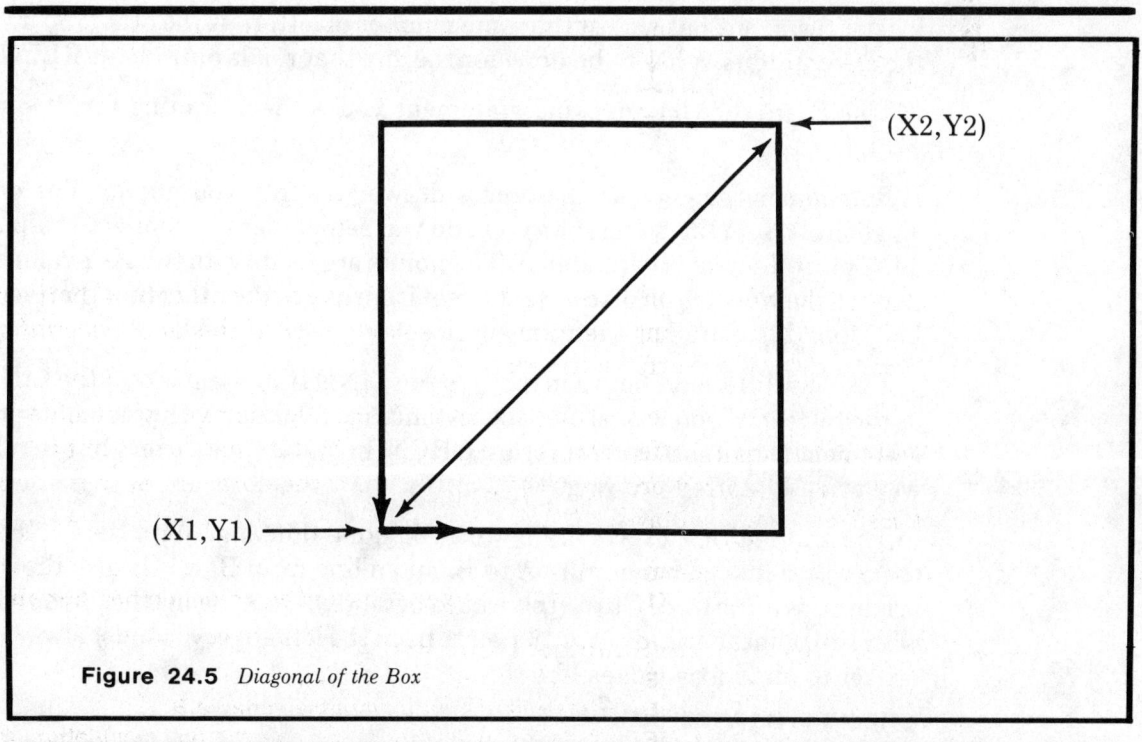

Figure 24.5 *Diagonal of the Box*

Chapter 24

You can leave off the first point (Xl,Y1) from the statement, but include the dash, and the printer assumes the first point is the pen's present location and starts drawing from there, like this:

1Ø: LINE – (X2 , Y2)

This will draw one line segment from wherever the pen is, to the new location X2,Y2 in the present color and style.

1Ø: LINE (X1 , Y1) – (X2 , Y2)

A line from X1,Y1 to X2,Y2 is drawn; color and style are as they were previously set or the defaults (black, Ø and solid lines) are used.

1Ø: LINE (X1 , Y1) – (X2 , Y2) , , C , B

Note that the style parameter is left out, but the comma must still be there to hold its place. The same can be done with the color (but not the Box), for instance:

LINE (X1 , Y1) – (X2 , Y2) , , ,B . . . is ok. . . .
LINE (X1 , Y1) – (X2 , Y2) , S , ,B . . . is ok but:
LINE (X1 , Y1) – (X2 , Y2) , S , c , . . . will cause an error.

This is handy for such things as drawing your own Mona Lisa, Snoopy or other work of art (such as Christmas or birthday cards). And as I said, it's good for forms, lines separating tables, graphs, bar charts and pie charts.

Some suggested uses – use LINE for shapes, graphs, drawings and patterns that are executed from a subroutine – this way they can be plotted from any starting point without recalculating the origin offset.

Oops! What went wrong? Mis-typed it. Wrong printer mode (GRAPH only). Value out of range. No printer, paper, or pens. Low battery. No ink in pen.

Also see: RLINE

RLINE

There are more similarities than you can shake a stick at between LINE and RLINE. Just look at them; one has almost the same number of letters as the other! So if I repeat myself in the descriptions, it has to be done for the guy that reads only about RLINE and not LINE.

This is another line drawing statement you've been waiting for. It's another graphics work-horse.

Remember the connect-the-points drawings I told you about? The ones I did during English class, in the 4th grade? Well, do you remember the connect-the-points drawings at all? This statement is very similar. The points are made with two X-Y values, and the printer does all the work of calculating how to get from one to the other (not that easy, let me tell you, my Mona Lisa still has the funniest nose).

The only difference between this and the LINE statement is that the LINE uses the *origin* as the reference point for all further distance calculations within the statement. The RLINE statement uses a sort of short term SORGN, in that it draws every line in relation to where it was when it started drawing.

Think about this a second. I'll wait. Ok, done thinking? With the LINE statement, from the *origin* a line is drawn from A to B, and a line from B to C is also drawn from the *same* origin, as is a line from C to A (this would be a box). That means that if you want to draw a box with 1ØØ points on a side, *and* 1Ø points from the left edge, you must always add the 1Ø point off-set to all X axis values, like this:

LINE (1Ø,Ø)-(11Ø,1ØØ),,,B

With the RLINE (Relative LINE), we always draw with the origin *relative* to the point where the pen is.

The only way to redraw an object at a new location with the LINE statement, is to move the origin with the SORGN statement. On the other hand, with the RLINE statement, a drawing can easily be redrawn from any point the pen is located.

RLINE, like LINE, draws lines from one point to.another. And it can have as many as 7 points. It also has the same options as LINE. A review of the LINE command will outline the options available for RLINE as well.

The Primary Statement/Command
        RLINE, (X1, Y1) – (X2, Y2), options

Other Forms of the Statement/Command
        10: RLINE (X1 , Y1) – (X2 , Y2) . . . (x7 , y7) , S , C , B
        10: RLINE (variable, variable). . .,variable,variable,B
        10: RLINE (calculation, calculation). . ., calculation, calculation, B

In the PROgram MODE, type this in (no spaces):

        10: GRAPH
        20: RLINE(0,0)-(40,40),1,3,B

Running this program will draw another box on your printer — in a bright red this time.

10: RLINE (1X , 1Y) – (X2 , Y2) . . . (x7 , y7) , S , C

In this example, X and Y are the values of the horizontal and vertical coordinates for each point. The first one, X1, is the horizontal distance from the temporary origin, that is where the pen was when this statement began, to the first point. Similarly Y1 is for the vertical start of the point relative to the same origin. This is the place the pen moves *to* before it starts to LPRINT.

Remember that this is not the real origin set by the SORGN or GRAPH statements, but is a temporary one that acts just like a real one for the duration of this one statement.

Next is X2 and Y2 (which are mandatory) and are where the line draws to (from X1, Y1 to X2, Y2). The rest, x3,y3 to x7,y7 are optional and not needed. They allow making a somewhat more complex figure in one statement.

The "S" stands for style of printing (or drawing actually). A number is expected if this optional parameter is used. 0 is for a solid line, 2 to 8 provide progressively larger dashes to draw the line, and 9 means don't draw anything, — just move the pen. 9 is like the GLCURSOR statement. If no number is found, the printer assumes 0 and draws with a solid line. The comma is mandatory unless no parameters are specified.

Last is the "C", which selects the colored pen. 0 is black, 1 blue, 2 green and 3 red. Again, the comma is mandatory if this option is used.

10: RLINE (X1 , Y1) – (X2 , Y2) , S , C , B

The "B" is the parameter that makes the printer/plotter draw a box. The other options can be used as before, but the points after X2-Y2 are ignored, so you may leave them off. The box that is drawn starts at the first point (X1,Y1) and draws (horizontally) to X2, — then up (vertically) to Y2. Thats X1,Y1 to X2,Y1 to X2,Y2 so far. Then it goes to X1,Y2 and back to X1,Y1. Remember that, the X and Y distances are from the temporary origin — the *first* point that was drawn *from*.

Imagine a line drawn from the first to the second point. That is a slanted line, and it is the diagonal of the box, like this:

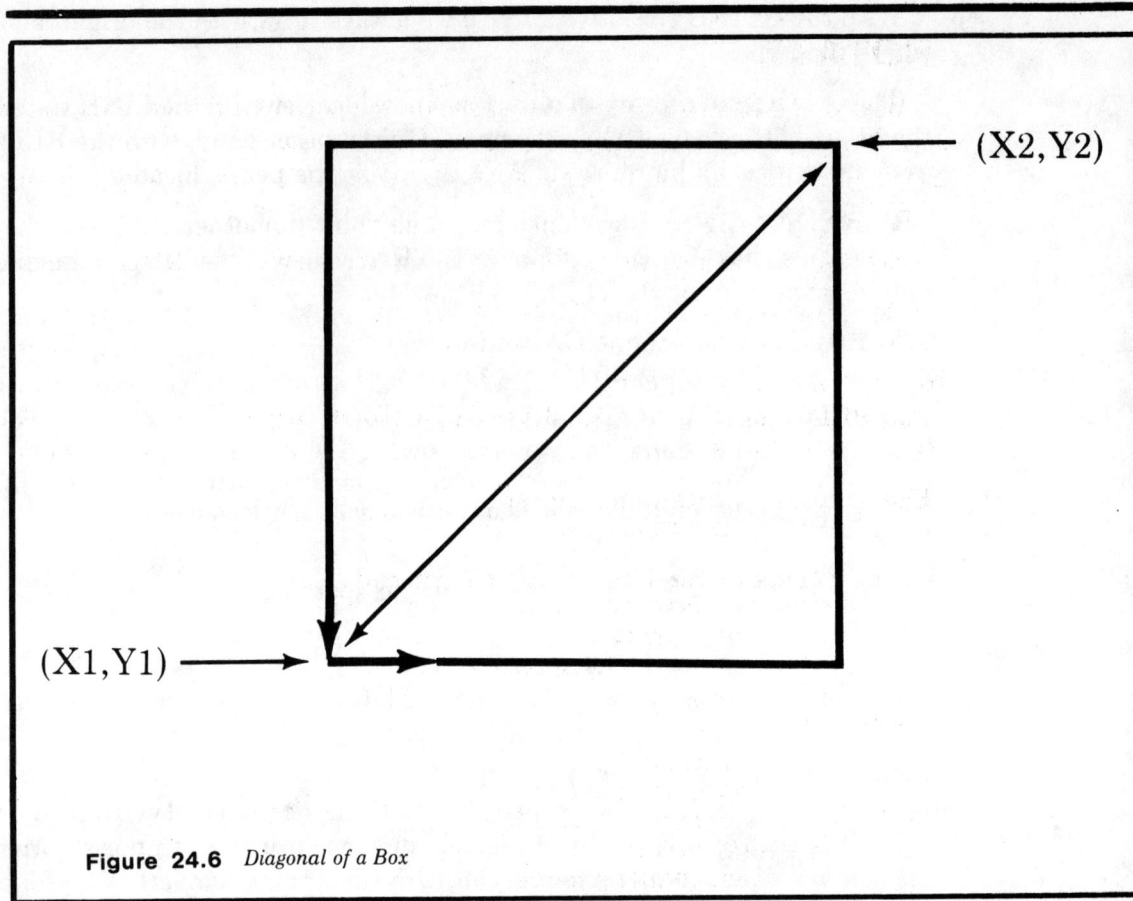

Figure 24.6 *Diagonal of a Box*

You can leave off the first point (X1,Y1), but include the dash, and the printer assumes the first point is the pen's present location and starts from there. Like this:

1∅: RLINE – (X2 , Y2)

This will draw one line segment, from wherever the pen is, to the new location, X2-Y2, in the present color and style.

1∅: RLINE (X1 , Y1) – (X2 , Y2)

A line from X1,Y1 to X2,Y2 is drawn; color and style are as they were previously set, or set to the defaults (black pen, and solid lines).

1∅: RLINE (X1 , Y1) – (X2 , Y2) , , C , B

Note that the style parameter is left out, but the comma must remain to indicate no value. The same can be done with the color (but not the box), for instance:

```
RLINE ( X1 , Y1 ) – ( X2 , Y2 ) , , ,B  . . . is ok. . . .
RLINE ( X1 , Y1 ) – ( X2 , Y2 ) , S , ,B  . . . is ok but:
RLINE ( X1 , Y1 ) – ( X2 , Y2 ) , S , C , . . . will give an error.
```

This particular statement is not only good for drawing, but since its origin is *relative* to the pen's present location, it is very convenient for placing figures or shapes in several locations.

Some suggested uses — use RLINE for shapes, graphs, drawings and patterns that are executed from a subroutine — this way they can be plotted from any starting point without recalculating the origin offset.

Oops! What went wrong? Mis-typed it. Wrong printer mode (GRAPH only). Value out of range. No printer, paper, or pens. Low battery. No ink in pen..

Also see: LINE

ROTATE

Would you like to printout messages on the paper vertically, upside-down or right side up? No problem. Use ROTATE. It rotates the normal text printout to any one of four directions: normal, top facing left, upside-down or top facing right. It can be used in any CSIZE from Ø to 9.

Sort of like turning the paper in the typewriter with a 6 letter statement!

Be aware that using the ROTATE statement means that you have to be careful about where the pen is located when you start PRINTing. If the pen is to the left, the ROTATE 2 or 3 will not print anything because the printer needs to move to the left from where it will start PRINTing. Use GCURSOR or GLCURSOR to move it to the right. The bottom line, as they say in the big time, is to be sure to leave room for the pen to work.

The Primary Statement/Command
> **ROTATE number**

Other Forms of the Statement/Command
> **1Ø: ROTATE number**
> **1Ø: ROTATE variable**
> **1Ø: ROTATE (calculation)**

Switch to the PROgram MODE and type in these lines:

> **1Ø: GRAPH**
> **2Ø: GLCURSOR (1ØØ , Ø)**
> **3Ø: FOR I = Ø TO 3**
> **4Ø: ROTATE I**
> **5Ø: LPRINT "ABCDE"**
> **6Ø: NEXT I**

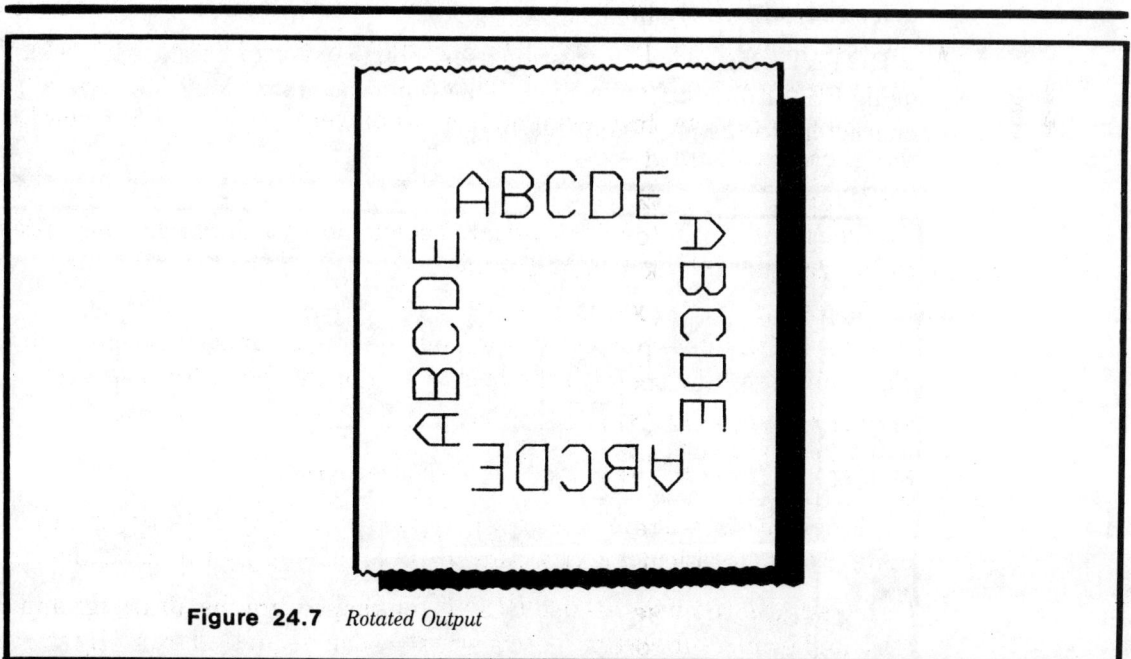

Figure 24.7 *Rotated Output*

It's pretty spiffy the way the printer can write upside-down.

1Ø: ROTATE 1

The above line will write any text down the side like this:

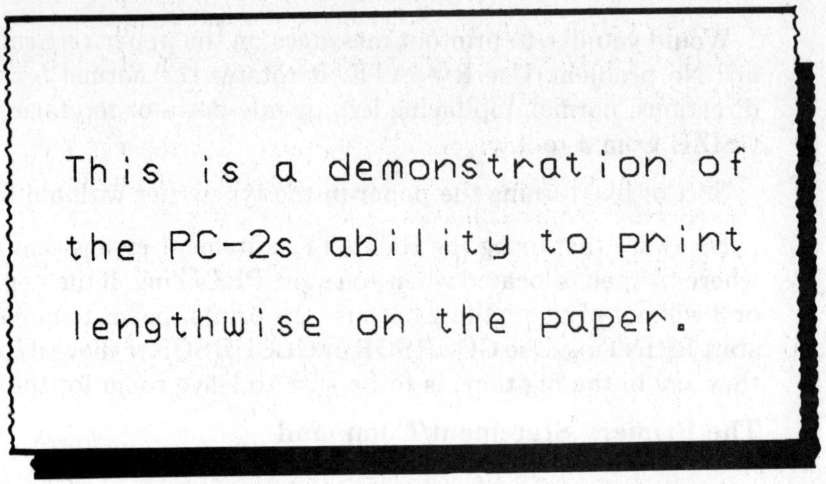

Figure 24.8 *Printer Output with Rotated Output*

After executing the ROTATE 1 statement, LPRINT a short message and see what it does.

Note that LLIST does an automatic TEXT statement if it is not in TEXT mode already, so it may *not* be used with the ROTATE statement. (I know what you were thinking!)

There are actually no other forms of this statement, except the usual freedom to use it in PROgram, RUN or RESERVE mode. It must be used with the printer/plotter in GRAPH, not TEXT mode. A numeric variable or calculation can be substituted for a hard-coded direction value (∅ to 3).

ROTATE has many interesting uses. You may want to make a larger and longer printout using CSIZE 9 and ROTATE 1. This would printout along the edge of the paper in large characters for as long as necessary.

Figure 24.9 *'Banner' Printed in Y-axis with CSIZE9*

If you want to PRINT upside-down — to read it from the other side of the computer — CSIZE 1 or 2 and ROTATE 2. This might be incorporated into a program that allows you to quickly change to upside-down PRINTing for receipts or point-of-sale messages (customers will be able to read them from the other side of the counter) or quotes and estimates provided to customers.

Oops! What went wrong? Mis-typed it. Value out of range. Wrong printer mode (GRAPH only). Power not on. Pens dry. Out of paper. Print area off paper due to GCURSOR or GLCURSOR miscalculation.

Also see: GRAPH — LPRINT — CSIZE — GCURSOR — GLCRUSOR

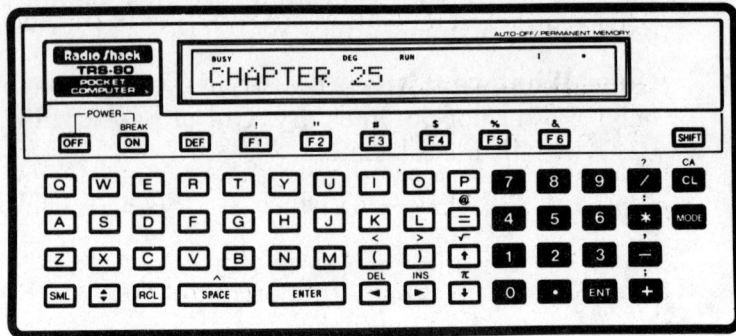

Keyboard Trickery

This chapter brings together many of the ideas that have already been presented, plus some others that are better presented separately. You will find some examples and techniques to improve your understanding and efficiency.

Some of this material may be repeated from other chapters, but it's important enough to be read twice. You'll also find that this material is in one continuous flow — this way, you'll find it easier to grasp the scope of the ideas presented.

We can break the programming process into three somewhat interrelated parts: entering programs, editing programs and trouble shooting (debugging) programs. A fourth part concerns the other three; programming techniques. With good techniques, you'll spend less time entering, editing and debugging.

Entering and Editing Program Lines

One form of *editing*, is entering the program initially. This can be to simply type in each line, or there are some tricks you can use that will speed things up.

For instance, if you are entering lines that are very similar to each other, type in the first one and press <ENTER>. Next, press the ◄ key until the blinking cursor is over the line number. Change the line number to the next line number to be entered, by typing over the old numbers. Now, move the cursor to the right to make any minor changes required for the new line. Press <ENTER> and smile. You have just saved yourself a bunch of typing.

Abbreviated Commands

All statements and commands in the PC-2 can be abbreviated to the shortest number of letters that distinctly identifies each statement followed by a period. For example, CU. is the minimum abbreviation of the CURSOR statement. There is only one command that starts with CU, but many that start with C, so CU is unique. Any series of letters longer than the minimum is allowed too, such as CUR., CURS. or CURSO.

One other keystroke savings is added. If there is more than one command that starts with the same letter, the more useful one is given the single first letter. Thus CONT (itself an abbreviation for CONTinue) is given exclusive use of C., as it is probably one of the most used statements that starts with a C. This does not change the rule given above, because CON. is still a unique abbreviation of CONT (although it takes four keystrokes).

Correcting and Editing Program Lines

Fixing errors in the program is usually done by editing the offending program line, or re-typing it. When an error is pinpointed in the RUN mode, go into the PROgram mode and press the [↑] key.

This will put the cursor on the exact spot where program execution was halted with the error. By using the <INS> (INSert) and <DEL> (DELete) keys, you can fix the error. Using the [◄] and [►] keys, the cursor can be moved over the line in both directions, and over the exact spot that needs your attention.

Now you can type in the correct form, or insert or delete letters by first pressing <SHIFT>, then the key marked <INS> or <DEL>. When INSerting, vertical bracket characters are displayed.

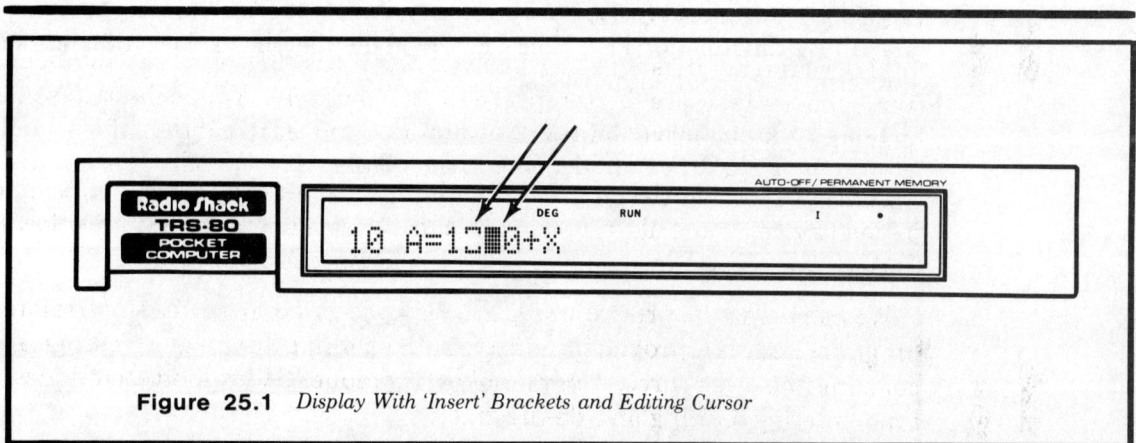

Figure 25.1 *Display With 'Insert' Brackets and Editing Cursor*

You can guess how many characters you will have to insert and put that many insert blanks in the line, before you type in the additions. If any insert blanks are left over, when you have completed your inserts, they will disappear (as will spaces that are not mandatory or that are in a REMark statement) after you press the <ENTER> key.

When you have fixed your problem, go back and RUN it again. See what new errors, if any, may crop up.

Function Keys

There are some labor-saving devices built into the PC-2. Six keys, under the display, may be assigned to do almost any function that can be programmed into the PC-2. Furthermore, there are three different function levels called: I, II and III. They allow up to 18 different functions to be assigned to these 6 keys (3 functions for each of the six keys).

The function keys are programmed in the RESERVE mode. Press <SHIFT> and then <MODE>, and the word RESERVE will appear at the top of the display. Now that it is in RESERVE mode, press the <F1> key. The display will now show "F1:" at the left side.

If the key was previously programmed, the current contents of that RESERVE key will

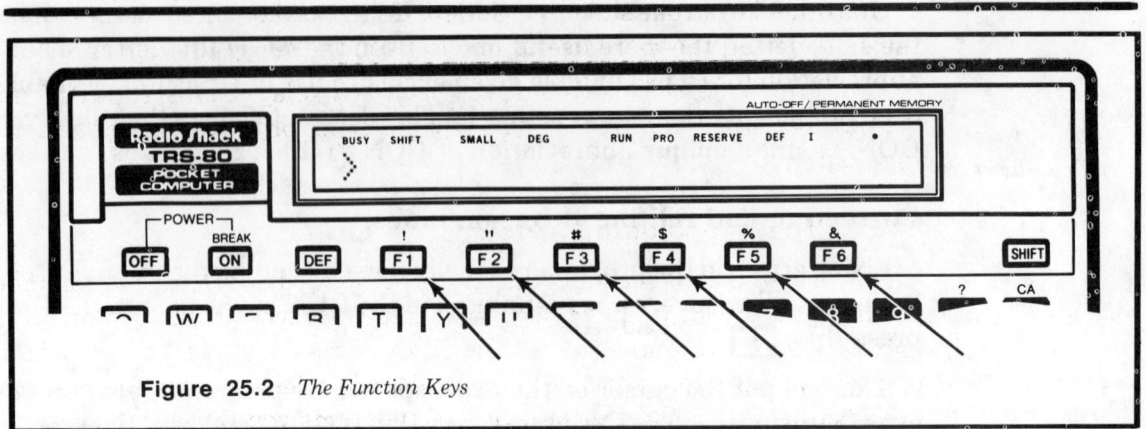

Figure 25.2 *The Function Keys*

appear after the colon. This way the PC-2 shows you what it is programmed to do. You may reprogram it by simply entering your new program for that key. You may leave it as is by pressing the <CL> key.

If there is any text that you wish to clear, press the left or right arrow key, and the editing cursor will begin blinking. Now press the space key until all is clear. Push <ENTER>, and the <F1> function key will now be empty. An empty function key will display the character just above the function key. The <F1> will display the exclamation mark (!), the <F2> the quote mark (") and so on.

Let's program the <F1> function key. Press <SHIFT> then the <MODE> key. We are now in the RESERVE mode. Check the display. If RESERVE is not displayed, try again.

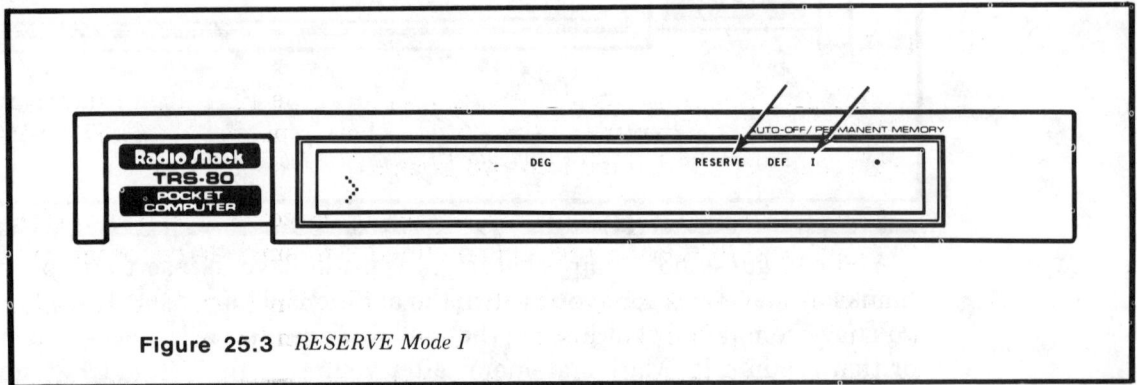

Figure 25.3 *RESERVE Mode I*

Now press the ⬍ key until a roman numeral I is displayed. The roman numerals indicate which function level will be displayed and/or executed. Press the <F1> key, and the display will look like this:

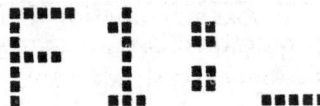

$$F1:\_$$

The <F1> key is now ready to be programmed Let's say we want the time displayed. Type in:

PRINT "TIME IS",TIME @ <ENTER>

When the "@" character (the 'at' sign) terminates the program you have entered into the function key, the command will *automatically* execute when the function key is pressed.

Touch the <MODE> key and note that the display should read RUN (mode). Next press the magical <F1> key, and the time (in decimal format of mmddhh.mmss) will appear on the display.

The RCL Key — Making a Menu

Now that you have the function keys programmed, how can you remember them? Next to the level selection [⏏] key, there is a key marked <RCL>, short for ReCaLl. We can leave messages to ourselves with it. This type of message, when it is used to select an operation from a list, is called a menu. Menus, like those used in restaurants, are usually designed to give a short description of the items you may select from.

To enter a message, "program" the menu, place the the PC-2 in RESERVE mode by pressing <SHIFT>, then <MODE>. Press <ENTER> for a > prompt and then put a quote mark, by pressing <SHIFT> and <F2>. It is now ready for a message of up to 26 characters.

This can serve as a reminder of what you have programmed into the function keys. You may enter a different message for each of the three RESERVE levels (I, II and III), and each message may be up to 26 characters long. Many times, you won't program all the function keys, and this gives you a little more freedom in writing your menus.

If a function, say <F2>, is not programmed, and is pressed, it will type the character above it as if you had previously pressed <SHIFT>. For <F2>, a quote sign will be displayed in the next cursor position. I use quotes so much that I try to leave it unprogrammed, so I need hit only that one key <F2>.

Defined Keys

If 18 function keys are not enough for you, the PC-2 has a bunch more called DEF (DEFined) keys. They are all the alphabet keys plus the <=> and <SPACE> keys. The DEFined keys are divided into two groups.

The first group is programmed with some of the common BASIC statements. The second group is used to execute programs defined with single letter program labels.

These keys work differently from the function keys. The so-called QWERTY line (QWERTYUIOP) of keys is pre-defined as shown below.

INPUT	PRINT	USING	GOTO	GOSUB	RETURN	CSAVE [note*]	CLOAD [note*]	MERGE [note*]	LIST
Q	W	E	R	T	Y	U	I	O	P

Note * *Indicates Keys that Require the Printer/Cassette Interface to be Attached*

To use these pre-defined keys, first press <DEF> and then the key of your choice, and the statement will appear on the display, saving you the necessity of having to type it in. The plastic keyboard overlay that came with your PC-2 has these keys labeled for you.

The rest of the keys (ASDFGHJKLZXCVBNM=<SPACE>) can be used to GOTO any labeled program in memory. Unlike the function keys, you don't actually program these keys. They are pre-defined to execute a GOTO to a program line which is labeled with the corresponding letter or symbol that is on that key.

To use the <DEF> key to execute a program line, just enclose a single character that you want to use in quotes as the first line of a program. For example, if <DEF> and <A> is pressed, a GOTO line A will be executed. The program label will look like this:

10: "A"

Additional statements may be placed on the same line like this:

10: "A" PRINT TIME

When <DEF> and <A> are pressed, the program beginning on line 10 will be executed.

A Stitch in Time. . . Using LOCK

LOCK locks the PC-2 into whatever mode it is in when the statement is executed. This is handy to prevent the accidental changing of modes while you are typing in a program, which has been known to happen when you have just finished entering a particularly long line, but haven't pressed <ENTER> yet!

To unlock the PC-2 simply type UNLOCK and press <ENTER>. Both of these commands work in all modes — RUN, PROgram and RESERVE.

A Quirk. . .

The <CL> key clears the display and shows the ">" (ready) prompt. You must press <CL> or <BREAK> key after an error message has been displayed.

Most keys will not function with the error message on the display. The exceptions are the ◄ , ► , ↕ , <RCL>, ↑ , <OFF>, <SHIFT> (which only works with <CL> and <CA>), and the <DEF> and <SML> keys, which won't do anything.

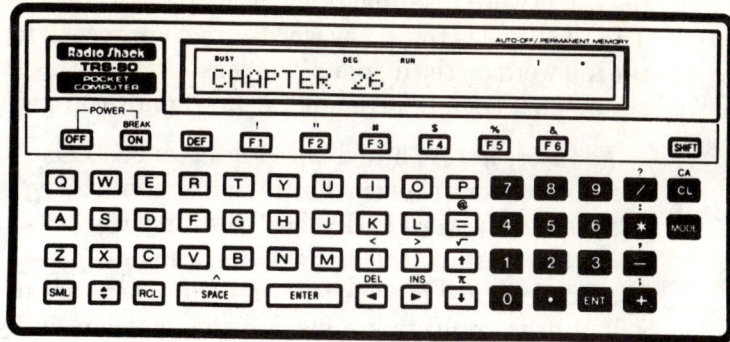

Debugging and Trouble Shooting

If a program fails to perform as you have expected it to after typing it in and RUNning it, it probably has an error somewhere. These ubiquitous little devils are known as bugs. Correcting them is what is known as debugging. Debugging, or the process of correcting a program, could easily take up a book by itself. However, we can give you a few tips to help you get started. We have a big advantage here, because the PC-2 has some powerful built-in features for debugging.

There are several types of bugs that can crop up, but the types most often found are those producing an 'ERROR 1', or syntax error, when RUNning the program. These are the easiest to fix, as well. It usually means you just have to fix a spelling error or have neglected to follow a statement with the proper parameter.

The more exotic types of bugs, such as incorrect results from numerical operations, may require a little more work to fix, as some of your program logic is probably not organized correctly. The PC-2 can pinpoint quite a few errors, and you can usually figure out what went wrong from the error message that is displayed.

The simplest technique is to RUN the program and see if it does what you want it to do (that is, what it is supposed to do). Remember that even if the program does not stop execution and give you an error message, it can still have a bug. It may not be doing what it should — it could be giving you erroneous results. Always check your results for accuracy. The easiest way to do this kind of testing is to enter data which will give you an answer that you already know.

If the program stops and displays an error message (such as 'ERROR 1 IN 2Ø'), then change to the PROgram mode and press the [↑] or [↓] keys, and the PC-2 will immediately display the line with the error (in this case line 2Ø), with the cursor blinking over the exact spot causing the error.

Examine the line for syntax errors ('ERROR 1' is a syntax error), such as mis-typed entries, arguments that have been left out, forgotten separators and so on. You can use the right and left arrows to move the cursor. Remember that the line can be up to 8Ø characters long, but the display can only show a window section which is 26 characters long. Be sure you don't miss part of it by not using the arrows.

When you find an error, move the cursor over the top of it (with the arrow keys) and type over the offending characters. Don't be alarmed if, as you try to change PRINT to LPRINT, the whole word disappears when you type the first letter! This will happen on *all* statements. The PC-2 saves these key words in a compressed format in its memory, and only prints out the full word on the display. The reason it does this is to save memory, but it makes changing statements seem a little odd at first, until you get used to it.

To insert letters into a line (for instance to insert LPRINT where PRINT was), position the cursor over the place the first letter would be typed (in this case, 'P'). When you press 'L,' the rest of the word PRINT will disappear because it is all part of one statement. Next, to insert the rest of the LPRINT statement, press <SHIFT> and then ▶ for each character to be added. Every time these keys are pressed, a top/bottom bracket character will appear, indicating a blank which you can fill by typing in the correct character.

Once a line has been tokenized, or compressed by BASIC (this occurs *after* you press <ENTER>) you can't change the nature of a statement. For instance, you cannot change PRINT to LPRINT by just inserting an 'L' in front of the word 'PRINT'. BASIC won't be able to re-interpret the statement correctly. You have to wipe out the old statement with the new one by typing over it.

Be sure to press <ENTER> when you have completed your editing. If <ENTER> is not pressed, no change will be made to the line! You have only modified the display until you press <ENTER>. This includes making my favorite mistake of fixing a line and then hitting ▼ to go to the next line or <MODE> to RUN it. In either case, the line will be as if I never touched it.

If you can't see an error in the line that has an 'ERROR 1,' then it is best to type the whole line over. There can be times when the error is somewhat invisible. It does not happen often, but sometimes Murphy gets creative.

For a syntax error, the line number PRINTed in the error message is always the line that the error occurred in, with one exception: if a data READ statement is told to look for string data and finds numeric data instead, (or vice versa) a syntax error will result, not in the line with the READ statement, but rather in the DATA line. This is where the error is, in the sense that it was told to find some data which was the wrong type. You will have to go back to the line that is doing the READing and check the variable type used, or change the DATA line to match the variable.

If the error is not a syntax error (the most popular), then be aware that the line number is where the PC-2 first detected something out of kilter, but is not necessarily the line where the error is. In fact, just as likely as not, it points to the result of the mistaken operation rather than at the operation itself. For example, if line 50 causes an 'ERROR 2' ('NEXT WITHOUT FOR'), the error occurred earlier in the program. Probably where the FOR should be, or the NEXT should have been preceded by a RETURN or an END because it must have been referred to as a GOTO line, rather than being in a logical place in the program flow. It's also possible that there's really no offending line. 'ARRAY NOT DIMENSIONED' or 'LINE NUMBER DOES NOT EXIST' would be examples of errors without line numbers. A few errors are not even in programs (ever see 'ERROR 26?'). Usually, the error itself will give the best clue to finding its source.

For example, 'NEXT WITHOUT FOR' can happen if the program tries to execute a NEXT before it was set up to handle it with a FOR statement. The best place to look (provided the NEXT truly belongs there and is not a typing mistake) is just before the NEXT, to see how it got there. Sometimes the FOR/NEXT loop has more than one NEXT at different lines, because of differing tests being carried out, or a nested loop has the

NEXT variables in the wrong order. A more careful analysis will turn up the error. By using better programming practices, this is less likely to happen.

Techniques of Program Problem Solving

There is a large class of bugs that do not PRINT error messages, or the errors are not related to the real problem which just confused the computer until it got so far off the track it gave up and finally PRINTed an error message.

We need a way to stop the computer at various places within the program to examine the variables, to see if everything is ok up to there. It just so happens that there are several ways to do this, the simplest of which is to press the <BREAK> key.

By pressing the <BREAK> key, you are telling the PC-2 that you want to stop the program (and, in fact, whatever else it may be doing) and do something else. The PC-2 saves the line number it was working on and keeps all the variables intact.

It also does some nice things for us to help trouble-shoot any problems that may have happened as a result of poor program or logic design. First, it sets the line number of the line it stopped at, into a *line pointer*. Now, when the [↑] key is pressed in the RUN mode, the last line executed will be displayed so you can examine it. If you go to PROgram mode and press an [↑] or [↓], that line will be displayed, ready for editing with the right or left arrow keys and <INS> or <DEL> keys.

If you go back to RUN, or you never left it, you can CONTinue the program in several ways. Typing CONT will let the program CONTinue on as if it never stopped. Pressing the [↓] key will execute the next instruction in the program and stop as if the <BREAK> key had been pressed, ready for you to examine it.

If you want to go to a different place in the program, but don't want to reset all the variables by using RUN, which erases the non-fixed variables, use GOTO *line-number*. This is especially handy for getting to the menu or display portion of programs without destroying all the variables entered up to that point.

The examination is not limited to the line displayed, or even program lines at all. You should, in fact, set up some special variables and look at them from time to time. See if they are what they should be at various points in the program. You can change the variables, from RUN or PROgram mode and still CONTinue. You may change certain types of program lines, as editing will *not* cause all the variables to be reset to zero or nulls.

For instance, you may change a 'GOTO line-number' to a different line number without resetting the simple one-letter variables. The requirement is that a line exists to GOTO! Thus, you can set things up to a known condition before RETURNing from a subroutine. Or you could add or modify lines to make quick checks, or even add lines that will PRINT important values to see how the variables change as the program progresses.

The CONT statement causes program execution to CONTinue after a STOP statement is encountered or the <BREAK> is pressed during the program's RUN. After testing the variables you are concerned with, CONTinue allows you to keep going to the next statement, as though nothing had happened.

You cannot CONTinue after the END of a program is reached, or after editing a line of the program. Programs that terminate in syntax errors or some other types of error conditions, cannot CONTinue either. However, you can use GOTO to get back to the program if you remembered the line number or know a good place to get back into the program. Don't try to GOTO the middle of a FOR/NEXT loop after <BREAK> or STOP, though, because the loop will not have been initialized, and the NEXT statement will not be able to figure out where it is supposed to get its FOR information — in any case, this will result in an error message.

Don't forget that you can place the STOP, TRON and TROFF statements in your program lines and remove them later on — after you are finished with the debugging process.

TRON and TROFF act as switches for a built-in debugging aid known as the TRace function. TRace ON and TRace OFF are used to turn this function on and off, as the statements suggest.

When the TRace is enabled (TRON), the line number currently being executed is shown on the display, prior to executing the instructions on that line. Pressing the ⬇ key causes the line to execute. The line to be executed next can be examined by pressing the ⬆ key. The TRace function can be shut off with the TROFF command, and you can CONTinue the program from that point, if you wish.

Single Stepping

There is another way to view the progress of a program without using the TRace function. In the RUN mode, you can stop the program by pressing the <BREAK> key, and then cause the program to execute one statement at a time by pressing the ⬇ key. This is called *single stepping*.

The line numbers will not be displayed, as in TRON, but you will be able to see the results of each program step each time you press the ⬇ key. You can test the variables at each stage, since control returns to you after each instruction is completed. You can view the line being executed by pressing the ⬆ key when in the RUN mode. As long as you hold this key down, the line will be displayed on the screen, with the cursor at the position in the line at which execution was halted.

You can see that putting a STOP or TRON in a line in which a bug occurs, or immediately *before* a suspected bug condition, is a good idea. But why a TROFF? Because you may want to single step (⬇ in RUN mode) up to a subroutine and then have the PC-2 turn trace off, buzz through the subroutine and then STOP or TRON again, so you can examine variables and single step again.

The best places to put STOP, TRON, TROFF and special PRINT statements (to see variables on the fly) are a matter of experience. Try to pick places that are likely to give valuable information, so as to refine your precision guesswork and zero-in on the problem.

If a value is different from what you expected it to be, PRINT it at various points in the program — to find out where it is incorrectly changed — and then, if necessary, TRON or single step as you zero-in on the problem. If there are problems in a loop, consider adding a PRINT of the variable within the loop, or maybe a test (IF/THEN) to STOP (IF A>100 THEN STOP).

If the program results in going to a wrong address or section of the program, examine the program for the only possible paths to get wherever it is going, and then put STOPs just before each branching point and single step past these points, to see if they go astray. If not, CONTinue and/or eliminate those points tested to narrow the possibilities.

Remember that there can be more than one STOP in a line (for those that use multiple statement lines to conserve memory). Don't be afraid to change the value of variables or the logic of the program line to help locate a problem. You can't hurt the machine from the keyboard! Be sure to have a copy of the correct (or best attempt) of the program saved on cassette and LLISTed on the printer/plotter, if you have one, or written out on paper if, not. You can't hurt the PC-2, but you can sure BOMB the program beyond belief. Protect yourself by saving your work!

Checking Things Out with the STATUS Statement

STATUS is a statement with which you can determine certain conditions that exist *within* the PC-2. There are actually 5 possible things you can check the STATUS of:

0 — Program steps used (that is, actual bytes used by the program, as each byte of program material is considered to be a step in the PC-2).
1 — Program steps available.
2 — The address of the end of your program.
3 — The address of the end of variable storage.
4 — The last line number executed when a program was halted.

Even though STATUS allows a parameter value of up to 255, only 0 through 4 are significant, as all values greater than 3 will return the last line number executed. It cannot be used for this purpose *after* editing, however, as the value of the last line number executed is reset to zero. This can be used as a way to find out what line was last executed if you forgot after checking variables or program lines.

It cannot be used *after* editing, however, as the value of STATUS is reset to zero.

Special Tips: Learn By Doing!

Here is an area of trouble-shooting that is almost never mentioned or discussed under trouble-shooting. When a person is learning the language and computer, he will make mistakes based on incomplete understanding, yet the literature on debugging usually assumes that he knows everything and just needs a little help with cleaning it up!

For those of us that learn by doing, this is not too helpful. So for those folks, we recommend you experiment with the various commands and statements until your understanding of each is sharpened to a fine edge. Many times it is not clear from the manual exactly what is happening with a given command, especially with complex commands, such as PRINT USING, or ON ERROR GOTO.

The best bet is to try it. *See* what it does and compare it to what you think it *should be* doing from your understanding of the manual. Don't shy away from experimenting, it will do more for you than all the books in the world — including this one!

Another thing is to read other peoples' commented programs (like those found in magazines or books). Study them until you understand them. Follow the program code as far as you can, especially the subroutines, which are usually somewhat self-contained and easier to understand. Use those pieces of code that you can, and start a library of program segments that do little tasks that are needed over and over (such as input and output tasks).

Try doing things in the RUN mode to see what happens. Go to the RUN mode and type in PRINT 5. The 5 appears, right? Now press the right arrow (or left) and the PRINT 5 re-appears. The PC-2 (usually) saves each immediate command in a *buffer*, and after execution you can edit that command just as if it were a program line. You could even make it a program line by inserting a line number in front of the statement, which is perfectly 'legal' if you are in the PROgram mode.

Now that the PRINT 5 is displayed, move the cursor over to the 5 and type "WHAT?". Press <ENTER>. Ok, press left arrow again — to get it back — and move the cursor to the very end (that displays an underline cursor instead of the flashing block). Type a comma and then the 5 (which we had earlier) and press <ENTER>. Note the placement on the screen. Now edit it again (using the arrow keys) and change the comma to a semicolon (just place the cursor over the comma and press <;>). Bump the <ENTER> key, and presto-gismo, a new display!

All right, edit again and (using the <SHIFT> and ▶) insert USING after PRINT and then move down the line and remove the ';5' that's at the end. Now, press <ENTER>.

Ahah, got you, didn't I!? Know why there was an error? Good, I knew I could trust my best student! Tell the rest of the class that we forgot to put in all the required arguments for the USING statement (that means edit again). Go into insert again and place the edit cursor just after the USING, and insert, "&&&" (including the quotes) and re-insert the value into the line. Dont forget the semicolon. Note that there are only three "&" characters after the PRINT USING statement. The 5 characters of the "WHAT?" (including the "?") are not accounted for in USING's PRINT format string of, "&&&". Press <ENTER> and, sure enough, "WHA" is all we get, but no error.

Thus, we learn what we can and cannot do, in a real sense, now that we have read and studied the manual for hours.

I might mention here that when debugging programs, it is often necessary to change the position of the lines (renumber them), and that can be done with the edit feature of insert (INS). Just insert the new line number if it is larger than the old one or write over the old number if it is smaller. Put spaces where you want, as they will be removed when the PC-2 packs the line to put it into memory.

To eliminate lines that you don't need, just type the line number and press <ENTER>. This is the only way to delete a line from the program. Don't forget that this will not work on programs that have been MERGEd, except on the *last* program MERGED.

The ON ERROR GOTO statement traps certain kinds of program errors so that you may correct a situation which may arise without the program stopping with an error message. This is a useful feature to include in programs which are already de-bugged, but it can cause maddening errors to occur if certain types of program errors have not been corrected, so I wouldn't consider it to be a useful de-bugging tool. It's more of a way to trap operator input errors in completed programs.

There are three rules to follow when learning to use a new computer and/or programming language:

Rule number 1: Experiment!

Rule number 2: Experiment!!

Rule number 3: Experiment!!!

appendix 1

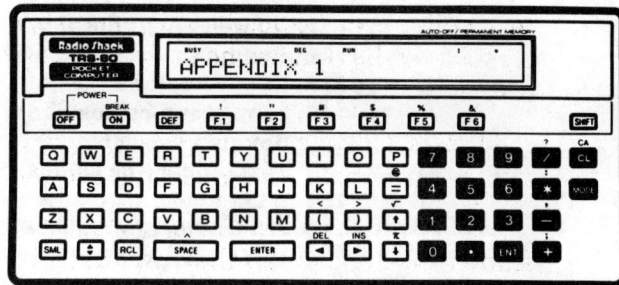

Your First Big Program
Ralph's Rocket — a Graphics Program

Here is a program you can type in that will give you an idea of what the future holds for learning BASIC on the PC-2. Press the <MODE> key until the word PRO appears on the upper portion of the display. You are now in the PROgramming mode. Copy the following lines exactly as they are shown below, and press the <ENTER> key at the end of each line. (Don't worry about what the statements mean right now. We will discuss that after you have seen the program work.) Be sure to include all the punctuation marks in each line. You will notice that a colon (:) will appear after the line number each time you press <ENTER> at the end of the line:

```
100  CLS <ENTER>
110  WAIT0 <ENTER>
120  GCURSOR RND 120+20 <ENTER>
130  GPRINT "7F" <ENTER>
140  FOR X = 0 TO 155 <ENTER>
160  GCURSOR X <ENTER>
170  Y = POINT (X+10) <ENTER>
180  IF Y <> 0 THEN 300 <ENTER>
190  GPRINT 4,0,17;17;27;14;14;4 <ENTER>
200  BEEP 1,1,RND 200 <ENTER>
210  NEXT X <ENTER>
220  END  <ENTER>
300  X=X/6 <ENTER>
310  CURSOR X <ENTER>
320  PRINT "*BOOM*"; <ENTER>
330  CURSOR 0 <ENTER>
340  FOR Y = 0 TO X <ENTER>
350  PRINT "*"; <ENTER>
360  BEEP 1,1,RND 200 <ENTER>
370  NEXT Y <ENTER>
380  GOTO 100 <ENTER>
```

Now that you have typed in the Rocket program, press the <MODE> key again, and the word RUN will replace the word PRO on the display. You are ready to see the results of your labor! Type RUN and press <ENTER>. You should see a little space ship move across the screen, accompanied by a beeping noise.

What the program does: Here is a list of comments that explain each line of the rocket program. This is just a brief description, so refer to the sections that cover each statement for additional information.

```
 1Ø: Clear screen
11Ø: No wait after print
12Ø: Graphics cursor 2Ø – 14Ø
13Ø: Print a bar (one way to do it)
14Ø: Loop graphics positions
16Ø: Set graphics cursor
17Ø: Test for bar (the ship is 1Ø dots wide)
18Ø: If bar found, exit loop
19Ø: Print picture (another way to print graphics)
2ØØ: Make a noise
21Ø: Loop until bar is found
22Ø: We'll never get here (END)
3ØØ: Text position = graphics divided by 6
31Ø: Text cursor
32Ø: Print message
33Ø: Start text at beginning
34Ø: Move text cursor
35Ø: Print a star
36Ø: Make a fast noise
37Ø: Finish loop
38Ø: Do it all again
```

Here are a few more programs you may find interesting. They are yours to play with and modify as you like, and are intended to give you an idea of some of the things you can do with your PC-2.

In the following program listings, many of the lines have multiple statements which are separated by a colon (:). To make it easier for you to follow as you type the lines in, each of the statements is listed on a separate line, preceded by a colon. You just type in the colon and the rest of the statements on the same line.

Holiday Tree Program

Here is a little program to draw up a holiday card (if you have the printer/plotter attached to the PC-2).

```
 4: TEXT                    initialize PC-2 printer mode
  :CSIZE 2                  set printout size
  :LF 2Ø                    advance paper by 2Ø lines
  :COLOR 2                  set pen color
 5: GRAPH                   select printer mode
  :GLCURSOR (16,Ø)          set location to start
1Ø: GOSUB 2Ø1Ø              tree draw subroutine
15: GRAPH                   restore printer mode
  :GLCURSOR (16,5)          offset cursor slightly
2Ø: GOSUB 2Ø1Ø              draw tree again
6Ø: LINE –(11Ø,9)           draw half bottom
7Ø: LINE –(16,Ø)            finish bottom
72: COLOR 3                 change color (red)
75: LPRINT "%  o  @  O"     print bottom decoration
8Ø: GLCURSOR (4Ø,35)        set printer for next position
85: COLOR Ø                 set color (black)
```

```
 90: LPRINT "*    ()"                              print decorations
100: GLCURSOR (25,60)                              set cursor again
105: COLOR 1                                       set color (blue)
110: LPRINT "<>   # ."                             decoration
120: GLCURSOR (39,99)                              set cursor
125: COLOR 3                                       set color (red)
130: LPRINT "PI  o  ";CHR$ (34)                    decoration
140: GLCURSOR (69,140)                             set cursor
145: COLOR 1                                       set color (blue)
150: LPRINT "Ø  :"                                 decoration
160: GLCURSOR (80,185)                             set cursor
165: COLOR Ø                                       set color (black)
170: LPRINT "+  o"                                 decoration
180: GLCURSOR (90,215)                             set cursor
185: COLOR 3                                       red
190: PRINT "& <>"                                  decoration
200: GLCURSOR (90,240)                             set cursor
205: COLOR 1                                       blue
210: LPRINT ", #"                                  decoration
214: GLCURSOR (99,265)                             set cursor
216: LPRINT "O"                                    last decoration
220: GLCURSOR (104,300)                            set cursor
225: COLOR Ø                                       black
230: LPRINT "!"                                    bottom of star at top
240: GLCURSOR (Ø92,318)                            set cursor
250: LPRINT "-*-"                                  print star
260: GLCURSOR (104,335)                            set cursor
270: LPRINT "i"                                    top of star
300: LINE (1Ø5,8)-(1Ø5,-4Ø)-(11Ø,-4Ø)-            draw base of tree
     (11Ø,8)-(1Ø5,8)                               (note, these are all on line 3ØØ as you type them in)
305: TEXT                                          restore mode for text
   :LF 5                                           feed 5 lines
   :COLOR 3                                        ready for text in red
31Ø: LPRINT "HAPPY HOLIDAYS"                        print message
999: END                                           end of program . . . subroutine follows
1000: RLINE -(ØØ,ØØ)-(-16,-1)-(39,Ø8Ø)             draw a segment of right side of tree
1010: RETURN                                       return to caller
1020: RLINE -(39,-8Ø)-(-16,+1)                     draw a segment of left side of tree
1030: RETURN                                       return to caller
2010: FOR I=ØTO 3                                  set up loop (4 count)
2020: GOSUB 1000                                   draw left segment of tree
2030: NEXT I                                       do it again
2040: FOR I=ØTO 3                                  set up loop (4 count)
2050: GOSUB 1020                                   draw right segment of tree
2060: NEXT I                                       do it again
2070: RETURN                                       done with tree
```

Notes Program

Here is a handy program for keeping notes to yourself:

```
10: CLEAR                                          clear variables
  :DIM N$(3Ø)*23                                   set up array
  :I=1                                             initialize index
18: WAIT Ø                                         no WAIT after PRINT
20: @$(2Ø)="1 ENTR 2LST 3FND                       menu part one
25: @$(21)="4TIME; PRESS A #                       menu part two
28: D=21                                           set pointer for which
  :E=2Ø                                             part of menu to PRINT
  :GOSUB 11ØØ                                      display menu & do input
```

```
 40: ON VAL A$ GOTO 100,200,300,500        execute command
 90: GOSUB 1020                            or display error message
    :GOTO 18                               repeat program
```

**START OF COMMANDS (SENT HERE FROM PARSER IN LINE 40 ABOVE)
ENTER THE DATA, NOTES, TIMES ETC. HERE**

```
100: PRINT I;                             print menu number
    :INPUT "=I TIME/NOTE,or END: ";N$(0)  menu for data entry
130: IF N$(0)="END"GOTO 18                return to main menu
140: N$(I)=N$(0)                           otherwise, take note
    :I=I+1                                point to next storage
    :CLS                                  clear display
    :GOTO 100                             process data, go again
```

DISPLAY ALL DATA

```
200: WAIT                                 set display delay
    :FOR A=1TO I-1                        loop through list
260: PRINT N$(A);A                        print note and number
    :NEXT A                               display whole list
    :GOTO 18                              then, repeat program
```

SEARCH FOR A STRING OF CHAR'S. IN ALL DATA

```
300: Y$=""                                initialize search string
    :INPUT "TYPE KEY TO FIND ";Y$         get string to search
310: FOR B=1TO I                           setup loop for search
320: GOSUB 2500                           execute search
330: IF X=0NEXT B                         not found,do again
340: IF X=0GOTO 18                        not found. restart
350: WAIT
    :PRINT N$(B);B                        print string found
360: WAIT 0
    :PRINT "1=DELETE,2=REDO,3=MENU        new choices menu
370: GOSUB 1000                           get command number
380: IF A$="1"LET N$(B)="X"               mark file if delete
    :GOTO 18  restart program
390: IF A$="2"INPUT N$(B)                 if redo, get new entry
    :GOTO 18                              and restart program
395: GOTO 18                              otherwise, repeat program
```

**COMPARE TIME TO "ALARM" SET ON EACH DATA
LINE (IF ANY)**

```
500: CLS
    :PRINT "MENU?"
    :GOSUB 1200                           return to menu test
510: FOR K=1TO I                           setup loop to check
520: T=TIME
    :T=T-INT (T/100)*100                  get time, process it
530: U=VAL (N$(K))                        get alarm into number
535: IF T>U AND T<(U+.01)THEN GOTO 600    compare, GOSUB if same
540: NEXT K                               loop through
    :GOTO 500                             keep trying
600: WAIT 0
    :PRINT N$(K)                          print alarm message
610: BEEP 2                               make a noise
620: GOSUB 1200
    :GOTO 610                             test for entry
```

Appendix 1

GET AN INPUT FROM THE KEYBOARD, KEEP TRYING

```
1000: IF INKEY$ <>""GOTO 1000              wait for input
1005: A$=INKEY$                            get input
    :IF A$=""GOTO 1005                     loop till got one
1010: FOR A=0TO 10                         loop for delay
    :NEXT A                                till delay over
    :RETURN                                return to caller
```

TRY IT AGAIN (ON ERROR) MESSAGE

```
1020: PRINT "TRY AGAIN"                     display error message
1030: PAUSE                                 wait a bit
    :RETURN                                 and return
```

ALTERNATING 2 MENU LINES (ON DISPLAY)

```
1100: B=E                                   set up which line
1110: PRINT @$(B)                           and print it
    :FOR A=0TO 20                            alternate lines
1140: A$=INKEY$                             while waiting for input
    :IF A$=""NEXT A
    :B=B+1
    :GOTO 1160
1150: RETURN                                return with input in A$
1160: IF B>DGOTO 1100                        change to other menu
1170: GOTO 1110                             an go again
```

ANY INPUT RETURNS TO MAIN MENU

```
1200: A$=INKEY$
    :IF A$=""RETURN                         look for input
1210: GOTO 18                               goto main menu
```

FIND IN DATA, N$(B), A STRING OF CHARACTERS FROM Y$

```
2500: IF LEN Y$>LEN N$(B)LET X=0            test for legal length
    :RETURN                                 if Y$ too big,return
2510: FOR X=1TO LEN (N$(B))−LEN (Y$)+1      setup loop of char's.
2520: IF Y$=MID$(N$(B),X,LEN(Y$))RETURN     if found,return
2530: NEXT X
    :X=0
    :RETURN                                 return, not found
```

Time Program

This program will display the time in the hours: minutes: seconds format in 12-hour mode. It converts the time from the standard 24-hour clock that the PC-2 uses. It also drops off the date that is included in the PC-2 format.

This is a sample program for using the PC-2 time, and would need some refinement if it were to be used in a real program environment, so look carefully if you need it.

```
1: WAIT 0                                   set no wait after PRINT
2: A=TIME                                    get the TIME into A
3: T$=STR$ A                                 make numbers a string
4: B$=MID$ (T$,4,7)                          take 7 characters,
                                             starting at 4th one
```

```
5: C$=LEFT$ (B$,2)                          get hours
  :IF C$>"12"LET C$=STR$ (VAL C$-12)        if past 12, sub 12
6: IF LEN C$=1THEN LET C$="0"+C$            if 1 digit long, add zero character to it
9: IF LEN B$=7THEN 13                       test for 7 digits (all ok)
                                            (SEC lost a zero)
10: IF LEN B$=6THEN12                        test for six digits
11: B$=B$+"00"                               add the zero seconds
   :BEEP 4,10,75                            signal minute
12: B$=B$+"0"                                beep hour
   :BEEP 1,10,75                            reset single minute and beep hour
13: LET B$=C$+                               get hour
   ":"+                                     put colon after it
   MID$(B$,4,2)+                            get minute
   ":"+                                     put colon after it
   MID$(B$,6,2)                             get second
   :PRINT B$                                print HR:MIN:SEC
14: GOTO 2                                   do it all again
```

Inverse Display Program

```
200: WAIT 0
no wait
210: CLS                                     clear display
230: GCURSOR 30                              set cursor
240: PRINT "** TRS-80 PC-2 **"              print sample display

LINES 250,260 ARE MACHINE CODE PROG

250: POKE 18409,72,118,74,0,5,189,255,65,
     78,78,153,8
260: POKE 18421,76,119,139,6,72,119,74,0,
     158,18,154
270: FOR I=1TO 11                           set number of reps
    :FOR J=1TO 50                           set time of
    :NEXT J                                 delay
280: CALL 18409                             go execute the machine code
290: NEXT I                                 loop through routine
300: GOTO 270                               repeat inverse till <BREAK> pressed.
```

appendix 2

```
Radio Shack
TRS-80
POCKET
COMPUTER

APPENDIX 2
```

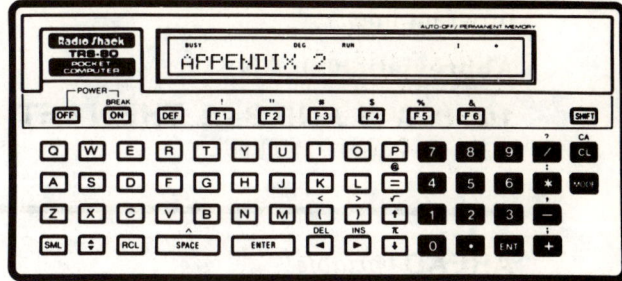

Command/Statement Summary and Index

Abbreviations or argument ranges are indicated below by special letters, unless otherwise indicated:

x: a numeric expression between +2047 and −2048
y: a numeric expression between +2047 and −2048
n: a number
c: a number from 0 to 255

ABS *n*

Computes the absolute value of 'n' where 'n' is any valid number between −9.999999999 E−99 and +9.999999999 E 99.

May be used in RUN, PROgram and RESERVE modes as a *direct statement* and in a program line.

Abbreviation(s): AB.

10: A = ABS n — A will contain the absolute value of the number 'n'
10: PRINT ABS n — The absolute value of the number 'n' will be PRINTed.

ACS *n*

Computes the arccosine (the reverse function of cosine) value of 'n' where 'n' is any cosine between 0 and 1. Arccosine means 'the angle whose cosine is…' For example, the cosine of 0 degrees is 1; therefore the arccosine (1) is 0 degrees.

May be used in RUN, PROgram and RESERVE modes as a *direct statement* and in a program line.

Abbreviation(s): AC.

10: A = ACS 0.50 — The variable A will contain the arccosine of the value 0.50 (60 degrees).

AND

Performs the *logical* AND fucntion between two numbers.

May be used in RUN, PROgram and RESERVE modes as a *direct statement* and in a program line.

Abbreviation(s): AN.

1Ø: IF A=1 AND B=2 THEN LET A\$ = "BOTH" — If both statements are *true*, A\$ will equal "BOTH".

AREAD *variable*

Assigns the display contents to the variable. Must be used with a DEF key label.

May be entered in PROgram mode as a program statement only.

Abbreviation(s): A. AR. ARE. AREA.

1Ø: "A" AREAD B — Any number, on the display at the time this statement is executed will be placed into the variable B when the program is RUN by using the <DEF> and <A> keys.

ARUN

Causes a program to automatically begin execution when the PC-2 is turned on.

May be entered in PROgram mode as a program statement only. Must be the first statement of the first program in memory.

Abbreviation(s): ARU.

1Ø: ARUN — This line will run upon power on if the PC-2 has been turned OFF. If the PC-2 turned itself off, this statement will not cause the PC-2 to begin RUNning automatically.

ASC *string*

Returns ASCII code of the first character in the string.

May be used in RUN, PROgram and RESERVE modes as a *direct statement* and in a program line.

Abbreviation(s): None.

1Ø: A = ASC "TEST" — A will contain the ASCII code of the first letter of the string.

ASN *n*

Computes the arcsine (the reverse function of sine) value of 'n' where 'n' is any sine between Ø and 1. Arcsine means 'the angle whose sine is . . .' For example, the sine of 9Ø degrees is 1; therefore, the arcsine (1) is 9Ø degrees.

May be used in RUN, PROgram and RESERVE modes as a *direct statement* and in a program line.

Abbreviation(s): AS.

1Ø: A = ASN 1 — The variable A will contain the arcsine of the value 1 (9Ø degrees).

ATN *n*

Computes the arctangent (the reverse function of tangent) value of 'n' where 'n' is any tangent between Ø and +9.999999999 E 99. Arctangent means 'the angle whose tangent is . . .' For example, the tangent of 45 degrees is 1; therefore, the arctangent (1) is 45 degrees.

May be used in RUN, PROgram and RESERVE modes as a *direct statement* and in a program line.

Abbreviation(s): **AT.**

1Ø: A = ATN 1 — A will contain the arctangent of the value 1 (45 degrees).

BEEP *options*

Turns the beeper capability on or off.

May be used in RUN, PROgram and RESERVE modes as a *direct statement* and in a program line.

Abbreviation(s): **B. BE. BEE.**

1Ø: BEEP ON — Turns the BEEP function on.
1Ø: BEEP OFF — Turns the BEEP function off. When BEEP is OFF, BEEP statements in programs will be ignored.

BEEP *n, frequency, duration*

Causes a beep to be sounded 'n' times where 'n' may be any number from Ø to 65535, of a frequency from Ø to 255 and a duration from Ø to 65279 time units. BEEP must be ON.

May be used in RUN, PROgram and RESERVE modes as a *direct statement* and in a program line.

Abbreviation(s): **B. BE. BEE.**

1Ø: BEEP 1Ø, 1ØØ, 1Ø — 1Ø beeps, frequency at 1ØØ, beep duration 1Ø units long. BEEP must be ON.

CALL *address, variable*

Calls machine-language routine stored at 'address' and passes a variable to the CALLed routine.

Abbreviation(s): **CA. CAL.**

1Ø: CALL &1234,A — Passes the value contained by variable A to a machine language program at address 1234 (hexidecimal).

CHAIN *–1, "filename", line*

Execution of program loaded from tape, –1, for second recorder. Program only. No variables changed.

May be entered in PROgram mode as a program statement only.

Abbreviation(s): CHA. CHAI.

10: CHAIN –1 "TEST",100 — LOADS and RUNs a program named "TEST", starting at line 100.

CHR$ *c*

Converts ASCII decimal code to the equivalent character, where c is any number from 0 to 255.

May be used in RUN, PROgram and RESERVE modes as a *direct statement* and in a program line.

Abbreviation(s): CH. CHR.

10: CHR$ c — PRINTs a character whose ASCII code is 'c', where 'c' is any number from 0 to 255.

CLEAR

Clears all data, resets all variables, DIMensioned arrays, to 0 or null.

May be used in RUN, PROgram and RESERVE modes as a *direct statement*. program line.

Abbreviation(s): CL. CLE. CLEA.

10: CLEAR — Clears variables.

CLOAD –1, *"filename"*

Loads program from tape, erasing all previous programs in memory.

May be used in RUN, PROgram and RESERVE modes as a *direct statement* and in a

Abbreviation(s): CLO. CLOA.

10: CLOAD –1 "TEST" — Loads TEST from second recorder.

CLOAD? –1, *"filename"*

Used immediatly after CSAVE to verify that program in memory is identical to program CSAVED that on the tape. CLOAD? does not alter memory.

May be entered in PROgram mode as a direct statement only.

Abbreviation(s): CLO.? CLOA.?

10: CLOAD?–1 "TEST" — Compares resident program to program "TEST" on second recorder.

CLS

Erases display.

May be used in RUN, PROgram and RESERVE modes as a *direct statement* and in a program line.

Abbreviation(s): None.

1Ø: CLS — Clears the display.

COLOR *n*

Rotates pen holder to specified pen location 'n', which may be any number between Ø and three.

May be used in RUN, PROgram and RESERVE modes as a *direct statement* and in a program line.

Abbreviation(s): COL. COLO.

1Ø: COLOR 3 — Rotates the penholder to position 3.

CONT

Continues execution of program from point of where BREAK or STOP halted it. Cannot be used within program.

May be used in RUN mode as a *direct statement* only.

Abbreviation(s): C. CO. CON.

CONT <ENTER> — Causes a program that was STOPped to CONTine execution.

COS *n*

Computes the cosine value of 'n' where 'n' is any angle.

May be used in RUN, PROgram and RESERVE modes as a *direct statement* and in a program line.

Abbreviation(s): None

1Ø: A = COS Ø — The variable A will contain the cosine of the value Ø (1).

CSAVE *–1, "filename"*

Saves program on second recorder as named filename.

Abbreviation(s): CS. CSA. CSAV.

1Ø: CSAVE –1, "TEST" — Save current program to second recorder as "TEST".

CSIZE *n*

Sets printing size on the printer/plotter, where 'n' is any number from Ø to 9.

May be used in RUN, PROgram and RESERVE modes as a *direct statement* and in a program line.

Abbreviation(s): CSI. CSIZ.

1Ø: CSIZE 9 — Sets printer/plotter to LPRINT in largest print size.

CURSOR *n*

Display printing will start at position 'n', where 'n' is any number from Ø to 25.

May be used in RUN, PROgram and RESERVE modes as a *direct statement* and in a program line.

Abbreviation(s): CU. CUR. CURS. CURSO.

1Ø: CURSOR 5 — Will start printing at position 5 (from left) at next PRINT statement.

DATA *items*

Stores data to be accessed by READ statement.

May be entered in PROgram mode as a program statement only.

Abbreviation(s): DA. DAT.

1Ø: DATA 1Ø,3Ø,56.8,"FRED" — 5 data items stored with DATA statement.

DEG *n*

Converts given number 'n' from 'degrees.minutes seconds' format to degrees in decimal fractions — the opposite of the DMS statement.

May be used in RUN, PROgram and RESERVE modes as a *direct statement* and in a program line.

Abbreviation(s): None

1Ø:A = DEG 3Ø.3ØØØ — A will contain 3Ø.5.

DEGREE

Sets the PC-2 to display calculations of angles in 'degrees.minutes seconds'.

May be used in RUN, PROgram and RESERVE modes as a *direct statement* and in a program line.

Abbreviation(s): DE. DEG. DEGR. DEGRE.

1Ø: DEGREE — Sets PC-2 to calculate in angles in degrees.

DIM *arrays*

Dimension one or more arrays (except '@' type).

May be entered in PROgram mode as a program statement only.

Abbreviation(s): D. DI.

1Ø: DIM A(1Ø) — Dimension variable A( ) to have 11 array elements (Ø – 1Ø)

DMS *n*

Converts decimal degrees to degrees, minutes and seconds – the opposite of the DEG statement.

GOSUB *line number*

Transfers program control to the specified line and returns to the next line, after GOSUB, on execution of the RETURN statement at the end of the subroutine. Note: Requires that a RETURN statement be the last statement of the subroutine.

May be entered in PROgram mode as a program statement only.

Abbreviation(s): GOS. GOSU.

10: GOSUB 20 — Transfers program execution.

GOTO *line number*

Transfers program control to the specified line.

May be used in RUN mode as a *direct statement* and in PROgram mode as a program line.

Abbreviation(s): G. GO. GOT.

10: GOTO 100 — Transfers progam execution to line number 100.

GPRINT *options*

Prints individual graphics dots, by column, on the display. Options are one or more columns of dots, (0 to 127) or hex., in a string or with the &, separated by a comma (skips a column) or semicolon (columns back to back).

May be used in RUN, PROgram and RESERVE modes as a *direct statement* and in a program line.

Abbreviation(s): GP. GPR. GPRI. GPRIN.

10: GPRINT 10,127 — Displays two columns of dots
10: GPRINT &0A,"7F" — Separated by a blank column.
10: GPRINT "0A007F" — All three lines are identical.

GRAD

Sets the PC-2 to display calculations of angles in grades.

May be used in RUN, PROgram and RESERVE modes as a *direct statement* and in a program line.

Abbreviation(s): GR. GRA.

10: GRAD — Calculate all angles in grades.

GRAPH

Puts the printer in its graphics mode.

May be used in RUN, PROgram and RESERVE modes as a *direct statement* and in a program line.

Abbreviation(s): GRAP.

10: GRAPH — Sets printer/plotter to GRAPhics mode.

IF. . .THEN
Tests conditional expression.

Abbreviation(s): T. TH. THE. (There is no abbreviation for IF.)

May be entered in PROgram mode as a program statement only.

1Ø: IF A = Ø THEN PRINT "ZERO" — Tests variable A for 'truth' (A equal Ø?) – if true, then will PRINT "ZERO"

INKEY$
Gets a single character from keyboard, if available.

May be entered in PROgram mode as a program statement only.

Abbreviation(s): INK. INKE. INKEY.

**1Ø: A$ = INKEY$** — Puts character from keyboard in A$ as INKEY$ is executed.

INPUT *options*
Waits for input from the keyboard, ends on <ENTER>. Optional printed comment (prompt) in quotes.

May be entered in PROgram mode as a program statement only.

Abbreviation(s): I. IN. INP. INPU.

**1Ø: INPUT "NAME?"; A$** — Puts keyboard input into A$
1Ø: INPUT A$

INPUT # *–1, "filename"; variable,. . .*
Transfers data from cassette to memory.

Abbreviation(s): IN.# INP.# INPU.#

1Ø: INPUT # –Ø, "DATANAME"; A$, A(*) — Loads from tape recorder Ø (normal), searches for the specified file and gets one string variable and A( ) array.

INT *n*
Returns the largest whole number not greater than n.

May be used in RUN, PROgram and RESERVE modes as a *direct statement* and in a program line.

Abbreviation(s): None.

1Ø: Y = INT 11.234 — Y will contain the integer portion of the number (11).

LCURSOR *position*
Positions, the pen, (TEXT mode only).

May be used in RUN, PROgram and RESERVE modes as a *direct statement* and in a program line.

Abbreviation(s): LC. LCU. LCUR. LCURS. LCURSO.

1Ø: LCURSOR 12 — Positions pen to 12th position.

LEFT$(*string, c*)
Returns c characters from left side of string, where 'c' can be any number from Ø to 255.

May be used in RUN, PROgram and RESERVE modes as a *direct statement* and in a program line.

Abbreviation(s): LEF. LEFT.

1Ø: A$ = LEFT$ "THREE", 2 — A$ will contain the left most two characters ("TH") of the string ("THREE").

LEN *string*
Returns the number of characters in string.

May be used in RUN, PROgram and RESERVE modes as a *direct statement* and in a program line.

Abbreviation(s): None.

1Ø: A = LEN "TEST" — A will contain the length of the specified string or literal.

LET *variable*
Optional statement that assigns a value to a variable except when preceded by an IF... THEN statement.

May be used in RUN, PROgram and RESERVE modes as a *direct statement* and in a program line.

Abbreviation(s): LE.

1Ø: LET A = 1Ø — Optional form. Assigns the variable A the value of 1Ø.

1Ø: IF A < C THEN LET C = 5Ø — Mandatory form. LET must be used to assign a variable (string and numeric) when an assignment is made in the IF...THEN statement.

LF *lines*
Cause the given number of line feeds (positive or negative) to be done. Negative line feeds must be less than 1Ø cm.

May be used in RUN, PROgram and RESERVE modes as a *direct statement* and in a program line.

Abbreviation(s): None

1Ø: LF 6 — Causes the printer/plotter to issue six line feeds.

LINE (*x1,y1*)–...(*x7,y7*), *line style, color, B*

Draws a line (or lines) from point to point relative to origin. (x1,y1) is optional, current position used if left out.

May be used in RUN, PROgram and RESERVE modes as a *direct statement* and in a program line.

Abbreviation(s): LIN.

10: LINE (10,10)–(20,20),0,1,B — Draws a box from starting position to 10,10 in solid blue line.

LIST *line*

Lists the program line to the display; if line number is not given, first line is assumed.

May be used in PROgram as a *direct statement* only.

Abbreviation(s): L. LI. LIS.

LIST 10 — Will cause line number 10 to be displayed.

LLIST *startline, endline*

Lists program lines to printer, inclusively. If startline or endline are not given, the first and last line are assumed.

May be used in RUN, PROgram and RESERVE modes as a *direct statement* and in a program line.

Abbreviation(s): LL. LLI. LLIS.

LLIST — Will cause the program to listed on the printer/plotter.

LN *n*

Computes the natural log of 'n' to the base e.

May be used in RUN, PROgram and RESERVE modes as a *direct statement* and in a program line.

Abbreviation(s): None

10: A = LN 10 — A will be the natural log of 10.

LOCK

Locks the PC-2 into the current mode.

May be used in RUN, PROgram and RESERVE modes as a *direct statement* only.

Abbreviation(s): LOC.

LOCK — If in RUN, PC-2 will stay there.

LOG *n*

Computes logarithm (to base 10) of the value of 'n', where 'n' is any number greater than zero.

May be used in RUN, PROgram and RESERVE modes as a *direct statement* and in a program line.

Abbreviation(s): LO.

1Ø: A = LOG 1Ø — A will be 1, the LOG of 1Ø.

LPRINT *item; item; item . . .*
Prints numbers or strings seperated by a comma or semicolons on paper.

May be used in RUN, PROgram and RESERVE modes as a *direct statement* and in a program line.

Abbreviation(s): LP. LPR. LPRI. LPRIN.

1Ø: LPRINT "TEST"; 1Ø; A$ — Prints items on the printer/plotter.

MEM
Get free memory.

May be used in RUN, PROgram and RESERVE modes as a *direct statement* and in a program line.

Abbreviation(s): M. ME.

1Ø: A = MEM — Puts unused memory size in A.

MERGE *–1 "filename"*
Appends cassette program to resident program (restricts editing) for use now.

May be used in RUN, PROgram and RESERVE modes as a *direct statement* only.

Abbreviation(s): MER. MERG.

MERGE "A" — Appends program "A" to current program in memory.

MID$ *(string, position, n)*
Takes 'n' character(s) beginning at position in the string.

May be used in RUN, PROgram and RESERVE modes as a *direct statement* and in a program line.

Abbreviation(s): MI. MID.

1Ø: A$ = MID$ ("TEST", 2, 2) — Puts "ES" in A$.

NEW
Erases *all* programs in memory and clears variables.

May be used in PROgram mode as a *direct statement* only.

Abbreviation(s): None

NEW <ENTER> — Will erase all programs in memory and clear all variables.

NEWØ

Resets PC-2 and erases *all* programs in memory and clears variables

May used in PROgram mode as a *direct statement* only.

Abbreviation(s): None

NEWØ <ENTER> — Will cause PC-2 to re-initialize and clears all programs and variables.

NEXT *variable*

Used with FOR statement only.

May be entered in PROgram mode as a program statement only.
Requires a previous FOR — TO statement.

Abbreviation(s): N. NE. NEX.

1Ø NEXT X — Causes the FOR loop, associated with the variable X, to be closed.

NOT

Logical inversion (on binary level).

May be used in RUN, PROgram and RESERVE modes as a *direct statement* and in a program line.

Abbreviation(s): NO.

1Ø: A = NOT 1 — Puts –2 in variable A.

ON ERROR GOTO *n*

Sends execution to line 'n' on any error except ERROR 1.

May be entered in PROgram mode as a program statement only.

Abbreviation(s): O. ER. ERR. ERRO. G. GO. GOT.

1Ø: ON ERROR GOTO 1ØØ — jumps to line 1ØØ on error.

ON. . .GOSUB. . .

Multi-path branch to numbered subroutine, 1 to first, etc. If not specified, next line after ON. . .GOSUB is executed. Must be a program line.

May be entered in PROgram mode as a program statement only.

Abbreviation(s): O. GOS. GOSU.

1Ø: ON A GOSUB 1ØØ,2ØØ,3ØØ — Transfers program execution to line number 2ØØ if A is equal to 2, line number 1ØØ if A is equal to 1 and line number 3ØØ if A is equal to 3.

ON. . .GOTO *line number*

Multi-path branch to specified lines, 1 to first, etc. If not specified, next line after ON. .

.GOTO is executed. Program only.

May be entered in PROgram mode as a program statement only.

Abbreviation(s): O. G. GO. GOT.

10: ON A GOTO 100,200,300 — Transfers program execution to line number 200 if A is equal to 2, line number 100 if A is equal to 1 and line number 300 if A is equal to 3.

OR
Logical comparison, on a binary level.

May be used in RUN, PROgram and RESERVE modes as a *direct statement* and in a program line.

Abbreviation(s): None

10: IF A = 1 OR B = 2 THEN LET A\$ = "EITHER" — If either A or B is true, then A\$ will equal "EITHER".

PAUSE *item, item, item*
Prints numbers or strings to LCD display, separated by commas or semicolons. One second built-in delay.

May be used in RUN, PROgram and RESERVE modes as a *direct statement* and in a program line.

Abbreviation(s): PA. PAU. PAUS.

10: PAUSE "TEST"; A\$ — PRINTs, waits one second and then continues program execution.

PEEK *address*
Gets value at address (0 – 65535) in primary memory.

May be used in RUN, PROgram and RESERVE modes as a *direct statement* and in a program line.

Abbreviation(s): None

10: PRINT PEEK 12345 — PRINTs value found at address 12345.

PEEK # *address*
Gets value at address (0 – 65535) in secondary memory.

May be used in RUN, PROgram and RESERVE modes as a *direct statement* and in a program line.

Abbreviation(s): P. PE. PEE. PEEK.

10: PRINT PEEK # 12345 — PRINTs value found at address 12345.

PI
Returns approximate value of PI (3.141592654).

May be used in RUN, PROgram and RESERVE modes as a *direct statement* and in a program line.

Abbreviation(s): None

10: A = PI + 5   A will be sum of 5 and PI

POINT *position*
   Gets dot pattern, column at position (∅ − 155).

May be used in RUN, PROgram and RESERVE modes as a *direct statement* and in a program line.

Abbreviation(s): None

10: PRINT POINT 10 — PRINTs dot value at column 1∅.

POKE *address, variable*
   Puts value (∅ − 255) into primary memory address (∅ − 65535).

May be used in RUN, PROgram and RESERVE modes as a *direct statement* and in a program line.

Abbreviation(s): None

10: POKE 1,∅ — Puts ∅ in address 1.

POKE # *address, variable*
   Puts value (∅ to 255) into secondary memory address (∅ to 65535).

May be used in RUN, PROgram and RESERVE modes as a *direct statement* and in a program line.

Abbreviation(s): PO. POK. POKE.

10: POKE # 1,1 — Puts 1 in address 1.

PRINT # *−1, "filename"; variable, . . .*
   Transfers data from memory to cassette.

May be used in RUN, PROgram and RESERVE modes as a *direct statement* and in a program line.

Abbreviation(s): P.# PR.# PRI.# PRIN.#

10: PRINT # −∅, "DATANAME"; A$, A(*) — Saves to tape recorder ∅ (normal), in file named, one string variable and A( ) array.

PRINT *item, item*
   Prints numbers or strings to LCD display, separated by commas or semicolons.

May be used in RUN, PROgram and RESERVE modes as a *direct statement* and in a program line.

Abbreviation(s): **P. PR. PRI. PRIN.**

1Ø: PRINT "TEST"; A$ — Prints two items.

PRINT USING *item(s)*
Formats strings and numbers for printing to LCD or printer (LPRINT). Width of numeric field must be one more than width of data.

Abbreviation(s): **P.U. PR.US. PRI.USI. PRIN.USIN.**

Specifies how many positions to use for the number.
1Ø: PRINT USING "####";1Ø — PRINTs 1Ø

* Specifies '*' fill of positions with no numbers.
1Ø: PRINT USING "**###";1Ø** — PRINTs * * *1Ø

. Decimal point placement.
1Ø: PRINT USING "##.##";1.1 — PRINTs 1.1Ø

, Displays comma to left of each third digit from decimal.
1Ø: PRINT USING "###,###,###,";234567 — PRINTs 234,567

∧ Exponential format (scientific notation).
1Ø: PRINT USING "###.#∧";12.2 — PRINTs 1.2E Ø1

+ Puts + in front if number is positive, – if negative.
1Ø: PRINT USING "+###";1Ø — PRINTs +1Ø

& Specifies the number of characters to be printed.
1Ø: PRINT USING "&&&&";"TESTING" — PRINTs "TEST"

RADIAN
Sets angle calculation to radians.

May be used in RUN, PROgram and RESERVE modes as a *direct statement* and in a program line.

Abbreviation(s): **RAD. RADI. RADIA.**

1Ø: RADIAN — Causes the PC-2 to be set to RADIAN mode.

RANDOM
Reseeds random number generator.

May be used in RUN, PROgram and RESERVE modes as a *direct statement* and in a program line.

Abbreviation(s): **RA. RAN. RAND. RANDO.**

1Ø: RANDOM — Causes the random number to the seeded.

READ *variable*
Reads item(s) from DATA statement.

May be entered in PROgram mode as a program statement only.

Abbreviation(s): REA.

10: READ A, A$ — READs two items contained in a DATA statement.

REM

Remark, PC-2 ignores everything on present line from REM.

May be entered in PROgram mode as a program statement only.

Abbreviation(s): None

10: REM EVERYTHING FOLLOWING 'REM' WILL BE IGNORED — Used to make notations within a program.

RESTORE *n*

Resets pointer to first item in DATA line n, or first DATA line if 'n' is not given.

May be entered in PROgram mode as a program statement only.

Abbreviation(s): RES. REST. RESTO. RESTOR.

10: RESTORE 100 — RESTOREs READ data pointer to line number 100.

RETURN

Used at end of subroutine to RETURN program execution to program line following associated GOSUB statement.

May be entered in PROgram mode as a program statement only.

Abbreviation(s): RE. RET. RETU. RETUR.

500: RETURN — Causes program execution to RETURN to statement following associated GOSUB statement.

RIGHT$ *(string, n)*

Gets right most 'n' characters from string.

May be used in RUN, PROgram and RESERVE modes as a *direct statement* and in a program line.

Abbreviation(s): RI. RIG. RIGH. RIGHT.

10: A$ = RIGHT$ ("TESTING",3) — Return right most three characters of "TESTING" (A$ will be "ING").

RLINE *(x1,y1)–. . .(x7,y7),line style,color, B*

Draws a line (or lines) from point to point relative to present position of pen. (x1,y1) is optional, current position used if left out.

May be used in RUN, PROgram and RESERVE modes as a *direct statement* and in a program line.

Abbreviation(s): RL. RLI. RLIN.

10: RLINE –(10,10)–(20,20),0,1,B — Draws a box from starting position to 10,10 in solid blue line ignoring 20,20.

RMT *switch*
Disables (OFF), enables (ON) remote switch, second recorder only (REM1).

May be used in RUN, PROgram and RESERVE modes as a *direct statement* and in a program line.

Abbreviation(s): RM. OF.(OFF) O.(ON) RMTOF. (OFF) RMTO (ON)

10: RMT OFF — Turns REMote 1 off.

RND *n*
Generates pseudo-random number between 1 and 'n' if n>1, or between 0 and 1 if n=0.

May be used in RUN, PROgram and RESERVE modes as a *direct statement* and in a program line.

Abbreviation(s): RN.

10: A = RND 10 — Variable A will contain a random number between 1 and 10.

ROTATE *direction*
Rotates printing direction (0 – 3) on printer/plotter.

May be used in RUN, PROgram and RESERVE modes as a *direct statement* and in a program line.

Abbreviation(s): RO. ROT. ROTA. ROTAT.

10: ROTATE 0 — Causes the printer/plotter to revert to normal printing.

RUN *n*
Executes program from line n, or beginning if 'n' not present. Or 'n' could be a quoted character or string variable.

May be used in RUN mode only.

Abbreviation(s): R. RU.

RUN <ENTER> — Causes the first program in memory to begin execution.

SGN *n*
Returns –1 if sign of 'n' is negative; 1 if sign of 'n' is positive or 0 if the value of 'n' is zero. The value of 'n' may be a number between -9.999999999 E-99 to +9.999999999 E 99.

May be used in RUN, PROgram and RESERVE modes as a *direct statement* and in a program line.

Abbreviation(s): SG.

10: A = SGN –20 — The variable A will contain the sign (positive or negative) of the value –20 (–1).

SIN *n*

Computes sine of 'n', where 'n' is any angle.

May be used in RUN, PROgram and RESERVE modes as a *direct statement* and in a program line.

Abbreviation(s): SI.

1Ø: A = SIN 3Ø — The variable A will contain the sine of the value 3Ø (Ø.5).

SORGN

Sets the origin to the plotter pen's current position

May be used in RUN, PROgram and RESERVE modes as a *direct statement* and in a program line.

Abbreviation(s): SO. SOR. SORG.

1Ø: SORGN — Causes the current position to the printer/plotter to become the 'origin' for all subsequent plotting operations.

SQR *n*

Computes the square root value of 'n' where 'n' is any positive number.

May be used in RUN, PROgram and RESERVE modes as a *direct statement* and in a program line.

Abbreviation(s): SQ.

1Ø: A = SQR 4 — The variable A will contain the square root of the value 4 (2).

STATUS *n*

Checks current memory status. If 'n' = Ø, returns availible program memory; if 1, memory used in program steps; if 2, address + 1 of end of program; if 3, address of end of variable storage area; if > 3, last line executing.

May be used in RUN, PROgram and RESERVE modes as a *direct statement* and in a program line.

Abbreviation(s): STA. STAT. STATU.

1Ø: PRINT STATUS Ø — PRINTs the current memory size.

STOP

Halts a program that is executing.

May be entered in PROgram mode as a program statement only.

Abbreviation(s): S. ST. STO.

1ØØ: STOP — Will cause program execution to halt. Execution may be continued with the CONT statement.

STR$ *n*

Converts a number 'n' to a string of ASCII characters where 'n' is any number between −9.999999999 E−99 and +9.999999999 E 99.

May be used in RUN, PROgram and RESERVE modes as a *direct statement* and in a program line.

Abbreviation(s): STR.

1Ø: A$ = STR$ 123 — Converts numeric values to a string representation. A$ will be "123".

TAB *n*

Positions pen over character position n.

May be used in RUN, PROgram and RESERVE modes as a *direct statement* and in a program line.

Abbreviation(s): None

1Ø: TAB 2Ø — Moves pen to position 2Ø.

TAN *n*

Computes tangent of 'n', where 'n' is any angle.

May be used in RUN, PROgram and RESERVE modes as a *direct statement* and in a program line.

Abbreviation(s): TA.

1Ø: A = TAN 45 — The variable A will contain the tangent of the value 45 (1).

TEST

Printer self test, in color.

May be used in RUN mode as a *direct statement* only.

Abbreviation(s): TE. TES.

TEST <ENTER> — Runs printer test.

TEXT

Puts printer/plotter in TEXT mode.

May be used in RUN, PROgram and RESERVE modes as a *direct statement* and in a program line.

Abbreviation(s): TEX.

1Ø: TEXT — Sets printer/plotter to TEXT mode.

TIME *month day hour. minutes seconds*

Sets time in 24 hr. format or returns time.

May be used in RUN, PROgram and RESERVE modes as a *direct statement* and in a program line.

Abbreviation(s): TI. TIM.

1Ø: TIME = 12314.5432 — Sets date and time to January 23, 2:54:32 P.M.
1Ø: A = TIME — Puts current time in variable A.

TROFF
Sets program trace function off.

May be used in RUN and PROgram modes as a *direct statement* and in a program line.

Abbreviation(s): TROF.

1Ø: TROFF — Causes trace function to be turned off.

TRON
Sets program trace function on.

May be used in RUN and PROgram modes as a *direct statement* and in a program line.

Abbreviation(s): TR. TRO.

1Ø: TRON — Causes trace function to be turned on.

UNLOCK
Cancels LOCK command

May be used in RUN, PROgram and RESERVE modes as a *direct statement* and in a program line.
Abbreviation(s): UN. UNL. UNLO. UNLOC.

UNLOCK <ENTER> — Causes LOCK statement to be cancelled.

USING
Used exclusively with PRINT and LPRINT (see PRINT USING above).

May be used in RUN, PROgram and RESERVE modes as a *direct statement* and in a program line.

Abbreviation(s): U. US. USI. USIN.

VAL *string*
Converts a value contained in a string to numeric representation.

May be used in RUN, PROgram and RESERVE modes as a *direct statement* and in a program line.

Abbreviation(s): V. Va.

1Ø: A = VAL "1234" — The numeric variable A will contain the value 1234.

WAIT *n*

Delay after each PRINT. If 'n' = Ø, no waiting, if no n, wait for <ENTER>. Otherwise,'n' = Ø to 65535.

May be used in RUN, PROgram and RESERVE modes as a *direct statement* and in a program line.

Abbreviation(s): W. WA. WAI.

1Ø: WAIT 1ØØ — Will cause the PRINT statement to WAIT for 1ØØ time units.

appendix 3

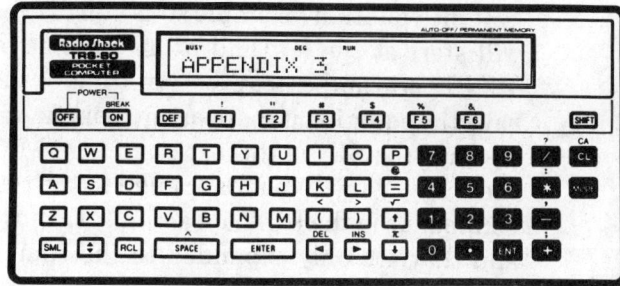

Using Your Computer as a Super Calculator

One of the neat things about the PC-2 is that it is a super calculator, in addition to all its other attributes. Now, I will grant you that there are other calculators that have more built-in functions, but this slight restriction goes away by programming any and all of their functions in BASIC. Yet the functions can still be used as though they were calculator functions! Also, there are programmable calculators that could do this too, but they are much harder to program than the PC-2. Programable calculators are not as versatile, nor do they have expandable memory, printers, cassette I/O, RS232 or permanent memories, as does the PC-2.

Ok, for starters, to do a simple calculation, just enter a calculation in the normal calculator style, with the exception that you press <ENTER> instead of "=" to tell the PC-2 to do its thing. In fact, using the equal sign will cause an error to be displayed instead of an answer.

For example, 2 times 3 equals on a common calculator would be 2 * 3 <ENTER> on the PC-2, which will print the answer 6 on the display.

If you want the result (6) to be added to 25, just press + 25 (unless you cleared the 6 with the <CL> key or did another operation, — as long as it's showing, you can use it). If you want a trigonometric function like sine of 3Ø degrees, try SIN 3Ø <ENTER> to get Ø.5 at the right side of the display (all answers will be to the right, normally).

All very mundane, right? Now here is a trick few other computers can match, no matter what the cost. You can edit or save the equation or answer even after you get the answer, and all in immediate execute mode. Let me explain.

Enter an equation, such as:

2 * 3 + 6 – SIN 3Ø <ENTER>

Here is a good place to mention that the variables in the computer are all available for use in calculations. For instance if A = 3Ø, the example could be 2*3+6-SIN A too. If you are using multiply or divide with a trig function, such as SIN 3/4, you must use parentheses: SIN (3/4).

After the <ENTER> has been pressed, 11.5 should be displayed to the right, just like a calculator. Now the trick stuff. Press the ◄ or ► key and note that the original equation is back. If you entered it wrong, you can change it, just like editing a BASIC line (see editing). More important, if you want to calculate a similar (but not identical) function, just change it, or change the values entered, or make it bigger, or change variables.

If the equation (example A) is still displayed, press the ◄ key, and the blinking cursor will start at the left end of all the line you have just entered. Now do four <SHIFT> <INS>erts and enter A$=" in front of the equation. This is normally all that is needed to save the equation if there are no commands in it, only numbers and numeric operators. But we have the SIN in there, remember? Move the blinking cursor over the S, and then press the S key. Wow! What happened to the rest of the SIN word? You might remember that the commands in the PC-2 are actually saved and used in the computer in a more compact form, and they are only expanded to the command words we see displayed for readability.

So, that means it is not the set of letters it looks like. In order to save it, you must be sure it is a string of characters. Insert the letters IN now, and all will be well. In fact, if anything but variables (and numbers, of course) are in the equation, you had better test them by moving the cursor over the first letter and then pressing that letter. If the word shrinks, it needs inserting; if not, then go to the next word until all have been checked. By the way, if we had saved this equation before executing it, the PC-2 would not have compacted the commands, and we could save it more simply.

Ok, press <ENTER> and get (on the left side this time, because it's a string), the equation, without the A$=". It is saved. Now press the editing arrow and delete the A$="; press <ENTER>, and there is the result on the right. If you want to save it too, there are several ways.

First, you can always write the answer down. That is not very elegant, but it's simple and easy. Or you could insert a numeric variable similar to the way the equation was saved. For our example, instead of deleting A$=", just delete the $ and the ", so it looks like this:

A = 2 * 3 + 6 − SIN 30 <ENTER>

The answer will be saved in variable A, as well as being displayed.

Another way to save it is a hard copy of the result (or the equation) by inserting an LPRINT" in front of the calculation you want to save. The only problem is that you can't get it back with the edit arrow now. Any line printing destroys the line used to out-put it. It had better be the last thing you want to do with the equation or answer, or you will have to re-enter it.

While we are on the subject of limitations, remember that the largest line that the PC-2 can process is 80 characters (79 plus 1 for the <ENTER>). If you want to save equations longer than 16 characters, you have to do some preparation. Fixed strings, like A$, are only good for 16 characters. (I know you remember that, but I just wanted to show you I remembered too.) So, you must write and execute a little program like this:

10:DIM AA$(10)*80

You can use any 2-character variable, and this will give you 10 (actually 11, including AA$(0)) variables to store equations in for printout later, or to save on tape. Don't forget, it must be a 2-character string, and *80 makes each able to hold 80 characters, which could be less if your equations are usually shorter. Also remember that you can't execute these equations once they are in a variable except just after storing them and using the arrow keys as described above. The DIMensioned variables will remain intact as long as another program is not RUN, which will reset the DIM to null.

A little should be said about what is available as far as functions on the PC-2. Table X-1 gives the basic commands that are readily accessible in the *calculator* or *immediate execution* mode of operation. Also usable are things like hexadecimal/decimal conversions (&), the DEGREE, GRAD and RAD for angles, and some *TIME* manipulation with DEGREE.

PC-2 MATHEMATICAL FUNCTIONS

TABLE X-1

			ABS
+			ABS
−			ACS
*			ASN
/			ATN
∧ (POWER)			COS
( )			DEG
< (LOGIC)			DMS
> (LOGIC)			EXP
>= (LOGIC)			INT
<= (LOGIC)			LN
= (LOGIC)			LOG
AND (LOGIC)			SGN
OR (LOGIC)			SIN
NOT (LOGIC)			SQR
√			TAN
π			PI
			E

The order of operations in an equation is given in the PC-2 manual, and you should refer to it every now and then to be sure you have some of the less-used operations brought to mind. It can sometimes be very important, for instance (as mentioned above) SIN 3/4 is different from SIN (3/4). Try it and see.

If you want to get more complicated, try using program lines accessed with <DEF> keys and inputs from AREAD, or even normal INPUT statements. Remember that you can inter-mix programs and immediate operations as much as you like. The restriction being, that you may not RUN programs, except to set up the DIM statement; just use GOTO or <DEF> key. You can use the function keys, too, and even have them GOTO program lines. When the program line has finished execution, the variables can PRINTed or used in immediate equations.

Here is a simple example (simple in the respect that the numbers and functions are simple). First define a few program lines for later use:

```
10 WAIT 0                    set no wait after PRINT
20 DIM ZZ(5)*50              set up 6 variables to hold 50 CHAR. each
30 "A" A=256 * 9 + C : PRINT A   do equation then PRINT the result
40 END                       separate program segments
50 "B" AREAD B               get the number on the display (DEF B)
60 LPRINT 3 * B + SIN A      do calculation and PRINT result to printer
70 END
```

Now define <F1> to PRINT the A and B. Press <SHIFT>, then <MODE> to get to the RESERVE mode, then enter:
F1:PRINT A + B @ <ENTER>

Now try some experiments. Be sure to RUN once to set up the DIM statement. Then only use GOTO or the <DEF> key or the function keys to go to a program line. Try 3 * 66 and then <DEF> <B>, which takes the 198 (3*66), then goes to line 5∅. That puts the 198 into B and line 6∅ processes it and PRINTs the result to the printer (change all LPRINTs to PRINTs if you have no printer).

How about C=2+2+2 and then <DEF> <A> which sends execution to line 3∅? Now execute function <F1>, since the A and B variables contain results now. Experiment with it some. It will sure take some getting used to, but I think you can see that there is a lot of power here.

appendix 4

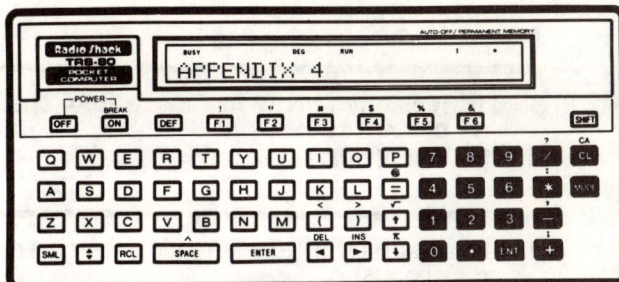

ERROR Codes

This is a complete list of the errors found in the PC-2 with examples, where possible, that allow you to do it right and wrong.

| **ERROR CODE** | **EXPLANATION** |

---

1 Syntax Error. Incorrectly typed or *nonexistent* command. This is the most common error you will find. It usually means you misspelled or forgot something in a line.

    10: GOT 50 — *wrong*
    10: GOTO 50 — *right*

---

2 NEXT statement without a FOR.

    10: NEXT A — *wrong*
    10: FOR A = 1 TO 2 : NEXT A — *right*

---

4 READ statement without a DATA statement, or not enough data in the DATA statement to fill the READ.

    10: READ A , B — *wrong*

    5: DATA 22 — *wrong*
    10: READ A , B

    5: DATA 22 , 33 — *right*
    10: READ A , B

---

5 Array variable already exists; you tried to DIM it twice.

    10: DIM A(5)
    20: DIM A(5,5) — *wrong*

    10: DIM A(5,5) — *right*

---

6 Array specified without DIMensioning it.

    10: A(1) = 1 — *wrong*

    5: DIM A(1) — *right*
    10: A(1) = 1

---

7 Inappropriate variable name.
   10: A$ = 22 — *wrong*
   10: AS = "22" — *right*

   20: A = "XY" — *wrong*
   20: A = XY — *right*

---

8 DIMensioned array has more than the allowed 2 levels.
   10: DIM A(1,2,3) — *wrong*
   10: DIM A(1,2) — *right*

---

9 Array subscript exceeds size specified in DIM statement.
   10: DIM A(5) — *wrong*
   20: A(6) = 1

   10: DIM A(6) — *right*
   20: A(6) = 1

---

10 Out of memory relating to the space necessary for new variables.
   If MEM <ENTER> displays a 7 (PC is very full)
   10: LET AA = 22 <ENTER> — *ERROR 10 will be displayed.*

   The only thing to do is:
   1. Add memory module.
   2. Reprogram the PC-2 more efficiently.
   3. Use CHAINing if you have a cassette adapter.
   4. Give up some program features.

---

11 Referenced program line does not exist.
   10: GOTO 20 — *wrong*
   30: END

   10: GOTO 20 — *right*
   20: END

---

12 Incorrect format for PRINT USING statement used.
   10: PRINT USING "A##"; 22 — *wrong*
   10: PRINT USING "###"; 22 — *right*

---

13 Program exceeds program-memory capacity, or Function Key specification exceeds Function Key memory capacity.

If MEM <ENTER> displays a 7 (PC is very full), trying to add 10: PRINT "TEST" <ENTER> will cause ERROR 13 to be displayed because there is not enough room in the PC-2 to add a line.

   The only thing to do is:
   1. Add memory module.
   2. Reprogram the PC-2 more efficiently.
   3. Use CHAINing if you have a cassette adapter.
   4. Give up some program features.

14 Buffer space exceeded, or FOR statement nested too deeply (too many nested FOR/NEXT loops or GOSUBs), and stack capacity has been exceeded.

```
10: DIM I(100)
20: FOR I(A) = 0 TO 2 : A = A + 1
30: GOTO 20
```

ERROR 14 will be displayed because the stack that holds the different FOR/NEXT indexes are filled up. I get A = 15 on my plain Jane PC-2 with the standard 1800 byte memory. That is 15 levels of FOR/NEXT statements, one inside the next, before you get an error. If the FOR/NEXTs are not nested (inside each other), then many more can be used.

15 GOSUB statement nested too deeply (too many GOSUBs inside each other), and stack capacity has been exceeded, or string buffer space has been exceeded by the character strings while parsing an expression.

(Parsing is figuring out where in the computer's internal operating program to send the next command to get it executed.)

```
10: DIM A$(2)*80
20: INPUT A$(1),A$(2)
30: A$(0)=A$(1)+A$(2)
```

This short program will demonstrate ERROR 15 if (when run) the sum of A$(1) and A$(2) is larger than 80 characters. Don't worry about the fact that the size of A$(0) is exceeded; the excess is just dropped into the bit bucket and lost with no error. The error is caused in line 3 because the PC tries to put A$(1) and A$(2) into its buffer and runs out of room.

16 Number is too large (or small). Specified value is equal to or greater than 1E100, or equal to or less than 1E100 (the range allowed for numbers in the PC-2). Note that this applies to negative numbers as well.

```
10:A = 11 E 99  — wrong
10:A = 9.999999999 E 99  — right
```

Perhaps the hex value is larger than FFFF hex (65535 decimal), its allowed range.

```
10: A = &1FFFF  — wrong
10: A = &FFFF  — right
```

17 Data type is not appropriate for calculation expression. Numeric or character used when the other type was expected. Did you try to multiply your name?

```
10: A = 1 + "X"  — wrong
10: A = 1 + X  — right
```

18 Number of arguments is wrong for expression, too many or too few for that command.

```
10: RIGHT$ (A$)  — wrong
10: RIGHT$ (A$ , 2)  — right
```

19 Specified value is outside permitted range.

```
10: COLOR 22  — wrong
10: COLOR 3  — right
```

20 No parentheses after @ or @$ when used as a fixed variable.

```
10: LET @ = 3  — wrong
10: LET @(1) = 3  — right
```

or
20: LET @$ = "C" — *wrong*
20: LET @$(J) = "C" — *right*

---

21 Required variable is not in the expression.
10: NEXT — *wrong*
10: NEXT I — *right*

---

22 Not enough memory available to load the program that is loading.

---

23 TIME is incorrectly typed in.
10: TIME = 130000.01 — *wrong*
10: TIME = 120000.01 — *right*
This example tried to put month 13 into TIME.

---

25 The NEW argument is other than zero.
NEW 1 <ENTER> — *wrong*
NEW 0 <ENTER> — *right*

---

26 Wrong mode for execution of command.
RUN <ENTER> — *when in PRO mode is wrong*
RUN <ENTER> — *when in RUN mode is right*

---

27 Printer/cassette adapter is not connected and a command is issued to it with the DEF key.
<DEF> I <ENTER> — *wrong when printer/cassette interface is not attached.*
<DEF> I <ENTER> — *right when printer/cassette interface is attached.*

---

28 Command is inside quotes, usually because you are editing a line that has commands in it and trying to put quotes around them.
10: PRINT <ENTER>
10: "PRINT" <ENTER> — *wrong*
The above line will display ERROR 28 if the quotes were inserted with the INS and arrow keys into the original line ten. No error will result if the quoted PRINT is typed completely over.

Also, ERROR 28 comes from trying to put a command as the input to an INPUT or AREAD command.
10: INPUT A$ <ENTER> <RUN>
<DEF> R <ENTER> — *wrong*
(DEF R is GOTO single key.)

10: INPUT A$ <ENTER> <RUN>
GOTO <ENTER> — *right*

---

30 Line number out of range (larger than 65535).
65540: PRINT — *wrong*
65279: PRINT — *right*
Note that a line number between 65280 and 65535 will cause a syntax error (ERROR 1) because these numbers are reserved for the end-of-program RAM indicator.

32 Graphics cursor is too close to the end of the display (152 to 155) for an input command. There is no room for the prompt left on the LCD display if the cursor is higher than 152.

1Ø: GCURSOR 152
2Ø: INPUT A — *wrong*

1Ø: GCURSOR 151 — *right*
2Ø: INPUT A

---

34 Specified optional device is not attached.

---

35 The optional device specified in the PRINT # or INPUT # expression is not consistant, or the specified optional device cannot handle input/output commands according to the given syntax. Also the PRINT # AND INPUT # will not work without a printer/cassette adapter.

1Ø: INPUT # — *wrong when printer/cassette interface is not attached.*
1Ø: INPUT # — *right when printer/cassette interface is attached.*

---

36 Inappropriate PRINT USING format, see PRINT USING.

1Ø: USING "####.##"
2Ø: PRINT 12345 — *wrong*

1Ø: USING "####.##"
2Ø: PRINT 123 — *right*

Note that the number 12345 is larger than the allocated 4 spaces. Do not forget the sign takes one space too.

---

37 The results of a calculation have exceeded the capacity of the PC-2, 9.999999999 E99

1Ø: PRINT 9.999999998 E99 + .ØØØØØØØØ2 — *wrong*
1Ø: print 9.999999998 E99 + .ØØØØØØØØ1 — *right*

---

38 Division by zero in a calculation.

1Ø: PRINT 9/Ø — *wrong*
1Ø: PRINT 9/1 — *right*

---

39 An illogical calculation has been attempted.

1Ø: SQR(–1) — *square root of minus number is wrong*
1Ø: SQR(1) — *right*

Cassette Related Commands

4Ø Inappropriate specification for expression.

---

41 SAVE or LOAD has been specified for ROM area.

---

42 The cassette file data is too large for available memory.

43 Data which is being verified with "CLOAD?" does not match file format. This error can be caused by a bad save, usually due to poor-quality tape. Try to change the playback volume to different settings if this is an only copy. Always save things twice on good tape, and preferably on two different tapes. It is too easy to damage tape with heat or magnetic fields to trust one copy of important data.

I forced this error by saving a short file and verifying it with INPUT#, and then erasing the very end of it. When an INPUT# of a similar format is tried, the check sum will be wrong and this error will display.

44 Checksum error, data or program incorrectly read. This error can be caused by a bad save, usually due to poor-quality tape. Try changing the play back volume to other settings if this is an only copy. Always save data twice on on high quality tape, and preferably on separate tapes. It is too easy to damage tape with heat or magnetic fields to trust one copy of important programs.

This error can be forced by saving a short file and verifying it with CLOAD? and then erasing the very end of it. When a CLOAD is attempted, the checksum will be wrong and this error will display.

Printer Related Commands

70 The pen has exceeded or reached the limit of the coordinate range allowed (-2048 to +2047 for either x or y)
```
10: GRAPH
20: GLCURSOR (2050 , 2050)  — wrong

10: GRAPH
20: GLCURSOR (2040 , 2040)  — right
```
Note that the pen will move to the extreme right and then will do nothing for several seconds (BUSY will be on); then it will retract about 4 inches of paper and stop again for several seconds before the BUSY goes off and ready appears again. The reason is that the points it moved to are legal, but off the paper and can not be reached, but no error will result.

71 The paper has exceeded or reached the limit of the range allowed for reverse line feed (10 centimeters, or 4 in.)
```
10: TEXT
20: LF -51  — wrong

10: TEXT
20: LF -4  — right
```
The example will work in any CSIZE, and each CSIZE will have a different effect on how many reverse line feeds can be done.

72 The value given is inappropriate for the value of TAB or LCURSOR.

73 Wrong printer mode (GRAPH or TEXT) for command issued.
```
10: GRAPH : LF 10  — wrong
10: TEXT : LF 10  — right
```

74 Too many line segments in the RLINE or LINE command, the maximum is 6. The commas referred to in the PC-2 manual are the commas separating the x and y end points of the lines.

```
10: GRAPH
20: LINE (0,0)-(10,10)-(20,20)-(30,30)-(40,40)-(50,50)-(60,60)-(70,70),0,0  — wrong

10: GRAPH
20: LINE (1,1)-(10,10)-(21,21)-(30,30)-(40,40)-(50,50)-(60,60),0,0  — right
```

76 This error is for LPRINT, in TEXT mode, a number that cannot be printed on one line (it will not print on the next line like normal text will).

```
10: TEXT : CSIZE 3
20: LPRINT 1.111111111 E 11  — wrong

10: TEXT : CSIZE 2
20: LPRINT 1.111111111 E 11  — right
```

78 The pens are not able to move or print because of a low battery, or the printer is in a pen change condition. If the printer has a low battery, it must be turned off and recharged before it can work. If the pens are being changed, press and hold the <CL> key and then the paper feed at the same time when the pens are loaded and ready.

Press the <0> key and hold it while pressing the paper feed key. The printer is in the pen change condition now.

```
LPRINT "TEST"  — wrong
```

Press the <CL> key and hold while pressing the paper feed key. The printer will be in the normal operating state now.

```
LPRINT "TEST"  — right
```

79 The printer could not get a color signal from the pen carrier. The most likely cause of this error is something keeping the printer from moving the pen carrier to the left to check the pen position. The pen carrier contains a small metal rod (in the COLOR 1 position) which is sensed at the left side of the printer. Check for an obstruction to the free movement of the carrier.

One way to get this error is to run the PC-2 connected to the printer while printing until it gives an ERROR 79.

80 Low battery. After re-charging the printer, you can press <ON> and continue as before.

One way to get this error is to run the PC-2 connected to the printer, but without printing (so you don't get an ERROR 79), until it gives an ERROR 80. This will take a long time.

177–181 Program has over-written the data area. This comes about when adding to a large program/data combination that just fits in memory. Then, when you stop the program (it must have RUN to set the DIM) and try to add a line, that line over-writes the area in memory reserved by the DIM (and any data there too).

```
10: DIM A$(181)*10  — RUN this, then add
20: PRINT "THIS IS A TEST"  — this will error
20: PRINT "THIS"  — this will not error
```

270

Appendix 4

appendix 5

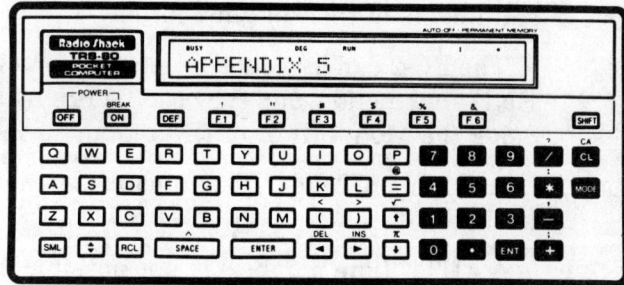

Programming Similarities . . . PC-2 and the Model III

This appendix is for the more advanced beginning programmer who feels he has mastered the basics of the PC-2. There might be too much confusion for someone who knows nothing about BASIC programming to try to learn the PC-2 syntax at the same time as on the Model III or similar computer. Get a little experience on one or the other first; then you will find this appendix to be a great help to furthering your programming education.

There are more similarities than differences between BASIC programs in the PC-2 and the TRS80 Model III (if you eliminate differences in hardware, such as video display or disk drives available for the Model III). Restricting ourselves to those things that both can do, shows us that there is a lot of overlap. Many programs written and used on one can be translated to the other very easily. The speed of the two is comparable. In many bench tests, the PC-2 seems to be about 50% as fast as the Model III. That's not bad, considering the PC-2 is perhaps one fiftieth the size and uses one hundredth the power.

The following discusses some of the more important similarities to and differences from the Model III, for those of you who might like to write programs that will work on both. Note that since both have the RS232 adapter, they can be connected together, and programs and data can be transferred back and forth. I have done this, and it has a number of advantages. For instance, use the Model III to enter and develop larger programs; load them to the PC-2, and then transfer the results to the Model III at the end of a day or week. The portability of the PC-2 makes it ideal for collecting data right on the spot when it is needed (on a sales route, inspection tour, in the warehouse to be inventoried, etc.). There is tremendous potential here for the innovative PC-2 owner.

Below are some things to keep in mind about the Model III (or the Model I, for the most part) and the PC-2.

The PC-2 allows command abbreviations not normally found in the larger TRS-80's. This allows a compensating speed increase that may equal or exceed the speed lost due to the small key board.

The use of spaces in the PC-2 is very much different. The PC-2 generally packs commands by removing the spaces, except when displaying the line. Spaces cannot be added or removed for clarity or size due to the automatic compaction feature, unless they are enclosed in quotes for use in strings. Sometimes spaces are needed where they otherwise weren't needed in the Model III. The best thing to do when writing or translating programs is to use the most standard BASIC form. That is, use LET, THEN and other such statements in their original form.

The PC-2 can have, and use more than one program in memory (optionally separated by END statements), and they can be run by a variety of methods. Care must be taken when using the Model III or other computers in this way.

A number of Model III commands are not present or are handled by different commands in the PC-2.

- AUTO (line number) is not possible in PC BASIC.
- There is an ARUN that is similar to AUTO in DOS.
- EDIT is not supported; it is done with the arrow keys.
- DELETE is not possible except by typing in the line number in PRO mode.
- ERR, ERL, and ERROR are not supported (ERROR is only used in ON ERROR GOTO in the PC).
- The apostrophe is not used for the abbreviation for REM.
- INSTRING is not supported.
- ARRAYS — the PC-2 cannot have two different arrays with the same letter name, even if different DIMensions.

On the other hand, the PC-2 can single step programs for debugging. It can GOTO and GOSUB named lines (structured programming). Also, it is a more powerful calculator when that function is needed.

In addition, it has some commands that the Model III lacks, which means that these will need to be avoided when writing programs to be used on both. Examples are: AREAD, BEEP, CALL, LOCK, PAUSE, STATUS or WAIT.

There is also an obvious incompatibility of graphics use and disk storage.

A number of commands are handled differently in the PC-2:

- NEXT must have the variable after it (NEXT A).
- PRINT uses WAIT to set a delay before going on to the next printed line.
- LIST lists only one line (of course) and the UP/DOWN arrows do the rest.
- In an IF/THEN, a LET is needed for assigning a variable.
- MID$ can only be on the right side of the "=."
- POKE can be followed by a list of numbers to poke in.
- PEEK/POKE addresses two 64K memories (POKE and POKE#).
- RESTORE can refer to a line number or program.
- GOTO/GOSUB can goto a named line.
- CSAVE can have up to 16 characters in the name.
- CSAVE #-1 on the PC-2 saves to the second cassette, but on the Model III it saves to the first (main) one.

● ON ERROR GOTO may not be used the same way as on the Model III.

PC-2 has modes RUN/PRO/RESERVE, where the Model III does not. This might cause a few problems, so keep it in mind.

Index